国家精品课程系列教材
GUOJIA JINGPIN KECHENG XILIE JIAOCAI

英美诗歌欣赏教程

李正栓　申玉革◎主　编

北京师范大学出版集团
BEIJING NORMAL UNIVERSITY PUBLISHING GROUP
北京师范大学出版社

图书在版编目（CIP）数据

英美诗歌欣赏教程/李正栓，申玉革编著．—北京：北京师范大学出版社，2014.1（2022.7 重印）

（国家精品课程系列教材）

ISBN 978-7-303-17181-1

Ⅰ．英…　Ⅱ．①李…　②申…　Ⅲ．①英语—高等学校—教材　②诗歌欣赏—英国　③诗歌欣赏—美国　Ⅳ．①H319.4：I

中国版本图书馆 CIP 数据核字(2013) 第 246536 号

营销中心电话　010-58807651
北师大出版社高等教育分社微信公众号　新外大街拾玖号

YINGMEI SHIGE XINSHANG JIAOCHENG

出版发行：北京师范大学出版社　www.bnupg.com
北京市西城区新街口外大街 12-3 号
邮政编码：100088

印　　刷：北京虎彩文化传播有限公司
经　　销：全国新华书店
开　　本：170 mm×230 mm
印　　张：32.25
字　　数：590 千字
版　　次：2014 年 1 月第 1 版
印　　次：2022 年 7 月第 5 次印刷
定　　价：50.00 元

策划编辑：王　强　　责任编辑：王　强　于　乐
封面设计：毛　佳　　装帧设计：毛　佳
责任校对：李　菡　　责任印制：马　洁

作者简历

李正栓

文学博士、教授，河北师范大学外国语学院院长，河北省高校教学名师，河北省有突出贡献的中青年专家，河北省中青年社科专家五十人工程人员，国家精品课程《英美诗歌欣赏》和国家精品资源共享平台《英美诗歌欣赏》课程主持人和主讲教师。自1992年以来为本科生开设"英美诗歌欣赏"课程20余年，该课程先后获得学校、省和国家精品课程名称。为研究生开设英国文艺复兴时期诗歌。

科研领域主要为英国文艺复兴时期文学和英汉诗歌互译。主要研究英国玄学派诗人约翰·邓恩，出版邓恩研究专著3部，分别是《邓恩诗歌研究》(商务印书馆)、《邓恩诗歌思想与艺术研究》(外研社)及《陌生化：约翰·邓恩的诗歌艺术》(北京大学出版社)，发表邓恩诗歌研究文章若干篇。典籍英译作品主要有《汉英对照乐府诗选》、《藏族格言诗英译》、《毛泽东诗词精选汉英对照读本》。

主要社会兼职：教育部外语教学指导委员会英语分委员会委员、教育部高校翻译专业教学协作组成员、中华文化典籍翻译研究会常务副会长、河北省高校教学指导委员会主任委员、河北省高等学校外语教学研究会会长。

申玉革

女，河北内丘人，硕士，在读博士，邢台学院外语系讲师，河北省莎士比亚学会会员、邢台市莎士比亚学会副秘书长。研究方向为英美文学，主要承担英国文学史及选读和英美诗歌教学工作。先后荣获2007和2012年度校级优秀教学奖、2011年度校级说课比赛优胜奖、第三届"外教社杯"河北赛区青年教师讲课比赛二等奖和邢台市百名魅力教师称号并两度荣获邢台市政府嘉奖。主持或参与省市级课题20余项，发表论文20余篇，曾获得河北省和邢台市优秀社会科学成果奖，参编《英语语音简明教程》等教材，出版学术著作4部。

《英美诗歌欣赏教程》精品课程网站网址：

http：//course.jingpinke.com/details？uuid＝49300ada－1292－1000－9b95－b7b5f3b2d8d7&courseID＝K100124

前 言

诗歌以其抒情和言志、无与伦比的修辞和比喻、令人愉悦的功能、令人感动的意象和意境吸引读者诵读，激励着人们学习、工作和诗意地生活。

学习诗歌一定要学会欣赏，不会欣赏就不能吸收，就难以成为滋养人们的养料。为此，我们决定编写这本《英美诗歌欣赏教程》，旨在帮助读者高效地学习和吸收语言，帮助读者诗意地沟通，丰富读者的生活，提高读者的生活质量。

全书分为英诗入门、英国诗歌和美国诗歌三部分。英诗入门包含诗歌定义、诗歌功用、诗歌类型和诗歌要素，内容简洁但比较全面，旨在为广大读者提供学习和欣赏英诗的入门知识，使大家能够徜徉于诗歌艺术的海洋；英国诗歌包含从中世纪到现代的32位诗人的63首经典诗歌；美国诗歌涉及20位诗人的36首经典诗歌，所选诗歌尽量兼顾典型性和全面性，充分反映出各个诗歌流派的特点。

本书的体例是：诗人生平简介，按出生年代排序；诗歌选文；题解；注释；诗歌赏析(每个诗人选其一或二)；思考题；参考译文。

生平尽量简洁，为读者简要介绍所选诗人的基本情况和创作生涯的主要内容，有时还对部分作品进行简要的评论。

选文力求精当，入选诗作大多是所选诗人的代表性作品或抒情力作，篇幅以短诗为主。为了便于读者更好地理解和欣赏诗歌，诗人和诗歌的选择非常具有代表性，诗人尽量选择不同时期、不同流派的代表作家，每位诗人的诗歌尽量选用诗人不同类型的代表作。

所选诗作标题下有题解，用英文写成，概括所选诗作的主旨。

注释不厌其烦，对一些难词、偏词和词义已经发生变化的词、意象、意义等内容进行注释。

思考题旨在帮助读者深刻理解所学诗歌，巩固所学，启发思维。有时还涉及比较研究，与中国诗歌进行比较。

参考译文选用忠实对等、传神达意之作。

诗歌赏析部分起到示范作用，用汉语行文，具体分析所选诗歌的形式、主题、音韵、修辞等诗艺技巧。

本书还对主要的诗歌术语进行了解析，有很强的参考性，翔实地介绍了抑扬格、十四行诗、自由体、无韵体、格律分析等诗歌常识以及湖畔诗人、玄学派、意象派等诗歌流派的特点。

在选材原则上，基本按照历史发展的脉络，注重代表性和艺术性，尽量兼顾不同时期不同诗人不同风格的作品。

本书旨在通过对英美诗歌的具体文本的阅读，让读者比较系统地了解并掌握英美诗歌的发展，了解英诗在各个历史时期的形式、风格、技巧和与之相关的时代背景、文学思潮等，掌握诗歌分析和欣赏的基本方法。分析各个时期英美诗歌的经典佳作，阐述这些诗作的格式、韵律、风格和诗歌创作理论，重点在于对具体诗歌的赏析。通过比较详尽的分析，让读者掌握英诗的特点，提高欣赏英语的能力和分析水平，熟悉英美诗歌的创作理论。

本书的编写宗旨是力求中英文结合，从对比的角度欣赏英语诗歌，即运用中英、英美、翻译、对比手法来分析诗歌，做到简明易懂，有独到视角，不求面面俱到。围绕每首诗歌中包含的相关知识点进行详细解析，既方便教师进行教学，也有利于学生自学。

特别需要指出的是，我们学习和研究英美诗歌的基础，是对中国文学与文化自身价值的充分认识与肯定。党的十八大以来，习近平总书记曾在多个场合提到文化自信，并在庆祝中国共产党成立95周年大会的讲话上，特别对文化自信加以阐释，观点鲜明、态度坚决地传递出了新时代中国特色社会主义文化建设的理念和指导思想。文化自信，既包含着文化主体的自我认同，又体现为文化主体从文化角度拓展自我的心理诉求。中华民族是一个兼容并蓄、海纳百川的民族，在漫长的历史进程中，不断学习他人好的东西，把他人的好东西转化成自己的东西，这才形成我们的民族特色。我们寄望于阅读和学习本书的读者，尤其是广大青年学子能立足中国文化的根基，广泛吸取其他民族的优秀文化经验，在不断吸收各种文明养分中丰富和发展中华文化。

本书适用于本科院校的英语专业的诗歌教学，也适合作为非英语专业学生的选修课教材。对于报考英语专业研究生而言，本书是一本极有参考价值的辅导书。

本书在编写过程中，参考了很多学者的教材和著作，使用和借鉴了很多名家译作，在此一并表示感谢。

李正栓　申玉革

目 录

Part One Entrée to English Poetry

Ⅰ. What is poetry?

What is poetry? It is not easy to know what poetry is, but it is not difficult to know what is not poetry. It depends on what a poet writes and how he writes. It also depends on how a reader understands a poetic writing. So the level and the taste of the reader also determine what poetry is and what good poetry is. Thus the knowledge of poetry and approaches to appreciating poetry become important and basic elements. There have been many attempts to define what poetry is. Any of them is useful, but none is absolute.

Plato thus defines a poet: The poet is a light and winged holy thing, and there is no invention in him until he has been inspired and is out of his senses, and then the mind is no longer in him.

One can see that Plato thought that poetry comes out inspiration and ecstasy.

According to Aristotle, poetry is a more philosophical and higher thing than history, for poetry tends to express the universe, history and the particular. Poetry is a species of imitation or mimesis.

In other words, Aristotle stresses that poetry imitates the world, to be more exact, reflects man's action.

Sir Philip Sidney affirmed the theory of imitation: "Poesy therefore is an art of imitation, for as Aristotle termeth it in the word mimesis—that is to say, a representing, counterfeiting, or figuring forth. Poetry, above all the other arts and sciences, embodies truth."

By saying that poetry embodies truth, Sidney is repeating that poetry imitates or reflects the world (truth or reality).

William Wordsworth said that "All good poetry is the spontaneous overflow of powerful feelings: it takes its origin from emotion recollected in tranquility."

What Wordsworth stressed is that poetry should first of all express feeling. It is more subjective. It is the display of the poet's inner mind.

Samuel Taylor Coleridge said, "The proper and immediate object of Poetry is the communication of pleasure. Poetry is the best words in the best order."

Coleridge meant that the purpose of poetry is the exchange of delight, or the poet tells the reader about his happiness. Coleridge also displayed his view on diction. Poetry should use defined words.

Percy Bysshe Shelley said that "Poetry is the record of the best and happiest moments of the happiest and best minds. Poets are the unacknowledged legislators of the world."

Shelley's theory of poetry as record is an echo of Aristotle's theory of imitation. It memorizes the people's feeling and action. What is more, Shelley held that poets are legislators or makers.

Raymond MacDonald Alden said, "Poetry is imaginative metrical discourse… Poetry is the art of representing human experiences, in so far as they are of lasting or universal interest, in metrical language, usually with chief reference to the emotions and by means of the imagination."

Alden thought of poetry as imagination and representation of experience full of feeling. He also touched upon the basic element of poetry, that is, meter.

Carl Sandburg said, "Poetry is the synthesis of hyacinths and biscuits… a series of explanations of life, fading off into horizons too swift for explanation."

Sandburg was talking about the importance of images in poetry, especially the synthesis of different images.

Thomas Sterns Eliot was against the Romantic poets' idea of poetry as the overflow of feeling by saying that Poetry is "not the assertion of truth, but the making of that truth more fully real to us."

Robert Frost said that "A poem begins with a lump in the throat, a home-sickness or a love-sickness. It is a reaching-out toward expression; an effort to find fulfillment. A complete poem is one where the emotion has found its thought and the thought has found the words."

One can see that Frost laid stress on feeling and expression of the feeling in suitable words.

Louis Untermeyer said, "Poetry is the power of defining the indefinable in terms of the unforgettable." He is talking about abstractness of poetry.

One can never finish a summary of people's definitions of poetry.

Each definition given above can only reveal one part of its features. However, one can make an attempt to describe its properties, function, and characteristics as clearly as possible. It is a method to express one's emotion and make his reader feel it by means of the best language. Through poetry, one can acquire knowledge how to do with the change, how to come to terms with joy and grief, and how to celebrate the wonder still to be found in the extraordinary energy of daily life. Due to this perspective by itself, poetry can not be limited by definitions. It can not be communicated or fathomed other than by the use of poetry itself.

Generally speaking, poetry has the following major characteristics:

1. Poetry is divided by lines.
2. Poetry is lyrical, even the epics.
3. Poetry is metaphorical. No metaphor or rhetoric device in general, no poetry.
4. Poetry is built of images, no matter in which country and what time.
5. Poetry is mostly personal.
6. Poetry is brief. It can describe things in the fewest words.
7. Poetry is music composed with words.
8. Emotion and imagination play an important role in poetry.

Ⅱ. The Function of Poetry

No matter in Chinese or western culture, generally speaking, poetry has two functions. One is to delight; the other is to instruct.

Since ancient times, the Chinese agreed to the function of poetry as expressing the poet's will. Some even said that poetry should teach how to become good husband and wife, how one should be filial, how one should abide by ethics, how one should act on moralization, and how one should improve the customs.

Plato thought that poetry can not only bring pleasure to people but also should be useful to the state. He attached importance to the function of instruction and thought that too much delight harms the function of instruction or education.

Horace defined the function of poetry as giving the reader benefit and pleasure, to give the reader joy and teach the reader how to live. He advocated the function of giving amusement and teaching, that is, to delight and instruct.

Sir Philip Sidney repeated this theory by saying that poesy's chief end is "to teach and delight."

This is also repeated by Samuel Johnson who insisted that "The end of writing is to instruct; the end of poetry is to instruct by pleasing."

Ⅲ. Major Types of Poetry

According to the French critic Gérard Genette, poetry can be classified into three major types: narrative poetry, lyric poetry and dramatic poetry. Some of these types have several subdivisions and each adheres to different conventions.

1. Narrative poetry

A narrative poem tells a story. It is always told by a narrator. Narrative poetry is written with the poet standing outside his material, representing human experiences by what is often called the "objective" method. It aims primarily at telling a story in a sequence of events. Epic, ballad and metrical romance are three main categories of narrative poetry.

(1) The Epic

The Epic is a long narrative poem of great scale and grand style, typically a recounting of history or legend or of the deeds of a national hero. It deals with noble characters and heroic deeds. Many nations have their own epics. For example, *Iliad*, *Odyssey*, *Aeneid*, *Beowulf*, *Song of Rolland*, *The Divine Comedy*, and *Paradise Lost*, etc.

(2) Metrical Romance

Romance is the prevailing literary form of literature in the Middle Ages. It was a long composition, mostly in verse, describing the life and adventures of a noble hero. *Sir Gawain and the Green Knight* is a famous metrical romance.

(3) Ballad

A ballad is a story told in song, usually in 4-line stanzas, with the second and fourth lines rhymed.

(4) Dramatic Monologue

Dramatic monologue is a kind of narrative poem in which one character speaks to one or more listeners whose replies are not given in the poem. The occasion is usually a crucial one in the speaker's life, and the dramatic monologue reveals the speaker's personality as well as the incident that is the subject of the poem. The main user of dramatic monologue was Robert Browning whose principal achievement lies in his introduction of dramatic monologue into English poetry. His *My Last Duchess* is one of its examples.

2. Lyric poetry

Lyric poetry is the type in which the poet speaks for himself, setting forth inner experiences by subjective method. It has many forms of expression, such as song, ode, elegy, sonnet, pastoral, etc.

(1) Song

A Song is a short lyric poem with distinct musical qualities, normally written to be set to music. It expresses a simple but intense emotion. George Gordon Byron's "She Walks in Beauty" is a song. There are many poems entitled "song".

(2) Ode

Ode is a complex lyric poem of some length, dealing with a noble theme in a dignified manner and originally intended to be sung. Odes are often written for a special occasion, to honor a person or a season or to commemorate an event. John Keats is famous for his odes such as "Ode to the Nightingale" and "Ode on a Grecian Urn".

(3) Elegy

Elegy is a poem of mourning, usually over the passing of life and beauty or a meditation on the nature of death. An elegy is a type of lyric poem, usually formal in language and structure, and solemn or even melancholy in tone. Among the best are Thomas Gray's "*Elegy written in the Country Churchyard*" and John Milton's "*Lycidas*".

(4) Sonnet

Sonnet is a lyric poem consisting of a single stanza of fourteen iambic pentameter lines linked by an intricate rhyme scheme. There are mainly two major patterns of rhyme scheme in sonnets written in English. The Italian or Petrarchan sonnet comprises an octave (eight lines) rhyming abbaabba and a sestet (six lines) rhyming cdecde or cdccdc. The transition from octave to sestet usually coincides with a "turn" in the argument or mood of the poem, ususlly in Line 9. The English or Shakespearean sonnet comprises three quatrains and a final couplet, rhyming abab cdcd efef gg. The "turn" comes with the final couplet, which may sometimes achieve an epigram. Yet, one can still the influence of the Italian form, that is, in some sonnets one can still find the turn in Line 9. There was one notable variant, the Spenserian sonnet, in which Spenser linked each quatrain to the next by a continuing rhyme: abab bcbc cdcd ee. There are three famous sonnet sequences in the Elizabethan Age: Spenser's Amoretti, Shakespeare's sonnets and Sidney's Astrophel and Stella.

(5) Pastoral

Pastoral is a highly conventional mode of writing that celebrates the innocent life of shepherds and shepherdesses in poems, plays and prose romances. Pastoral literature describes the loves and sorrows of shepherds, usually in an idealized Golden Age of rustic innocence and idleness; paradoxically, it is an elaborately artificial cult of simplicity and virtuous frugality.

3. Dramatic poetry

Dramatic poetry is the type intended for the stage. It presents human life in conflict, mainly including comedy, tragedy and the historical drama.

(1) Comedy

A comedy typically deals with common people and is dominated by a light tone that encourages laughter (or at least amusement or entertainment) and ends happily, often with the uniting of a pair of young lovers. Shakespeare wrote many comedies, such as *Twelfth Night*, *The Merchant of Venice* and *As You Like It*, etc.

(2) Tragedy

Traditionally, a tragedy is dominated by a serious tone, concerns characters of noble birth, perhaps a king like Oedipus or a prince like Hamlet, deals with profound issues, and usually concludes with the death of the leading character. Shakespeare is famous for his four great tragedies *Hamlet*, *Othello*, *King Lear* and *Macbeth*.

(3) Historical Drama

The historical drama deals with some historic events or personages. For example, Shakespeare's *Henry* Ⅳ, *Richard* Ⅲ, etc.

Ⅳ. Elements of Poetry

1. Rhyme (韵)

Rhyme refers to the repetition of certain sound in words, usually at the end of poetic lines.

A. Types of rhyme according to its place

(1) End rhyme (尾韵)

End rhyme is the repetition of the last stressed vowel in a line and all the following syllables. End rhyme is the commonest type of rhyme in English poetry after the medieval period.

(2) Internal rhyme (行内韵)

Internal rhyme is also called crossed rhyme. An internal rhyme occurs when the word in the middle rhymes with the one at the end of a line. For example, "The guests are *met*, the feast is *set*" and "Spring, the sweet spring, ..."

B. Types of rhyme according to its structure

(1) Masculine rhyme (阳韵)

Masculine rhyme is the repetition of one syllable at the end of respective lines. For example,

Under the green wood tr*ee*,
Who loves to lie with m*e*.

(2) Feminine rhyme (阴韵)

A feminine rhyme is a rhyme that matches two or more syllables, usually at the end of respective lines, in which the final syllable or syllables are unstressed. Feminine rhyme is relatively rare in English poetry and usually appears as a special effect. William Shakespeare's Sonnet number 20 makes use of feminine rhymes:

	Rhyming Syllables	Rhyme Pattern
"A woman's face with nature's own hand **painted**,	pain-ted	A—B
Hast thou, the master mistress of my **passion**;	pass-ion	C—D
A woman's gentle heart, but not ac**quainted**,	quain-ted	A—B
With shifting change, as is false women's **fashion** …	fash-ion	C—D
But since she prick'd thee out for women's **pleasure**,	plea-sure	E—F
Mine be thy love and thy love's use their **treasure**".	trea-sure	E—F

C. Other types of rhyme

Besides the above rhymes, there are other types of rhyme frequently used in English poetry as follows.

(1) Alliteration (also called Head rhyme or Initial rhyme, 头韵)

Alliteration is the repetition of the same sounds—usually initial consonants of words or of stressed syllables—in any sequence of neighboring words. For example, "O *w*ild *W*est *W*ind, thou *b*reath of Autumn's *b*eing."

(2) Assonance (腹韵，亦称元音韵)

Assonance is the repetition of vowel sounds within a noticeable range. Assonance occurs in words as: fight / bike; fat / map; morning / falling. In poetry, it goes as follows.

She walks in beauty, l*i*ke the n*i*ght
Of cloudless cl*i*mes and starry sk*i*es.

(3) Consonance (辅音韵)

Consonance is the repetition of consonant sounds before and after different vowels. Consonance occurs in words as *bl*ock / *bl*ack; *cr*eak / *cr*oak.

(4) Eye rhyme or sight rhyme (眼韵)

Eye rhyme occurs when the spelling of the rhyming element match, but the sound does not. For example,

Come live with me and be my L*ove*,
And we will all the pleasures pr*ove*.

D. Rhyme scheme (押韵格式，亦称韵式)

English poetry has various rhyme schemes. Here we take the 4-line stanza as an example to illustrate its diverse patterns.

(1) crossed rhyme / alternating rhyme: abab (隔行押韵，交叉韵). For example,

Gather ye rosebuds while ye may,
Old time is still a-flying;
And this same flower that smiles today,
Tomorrow will be dying.

(2) aabb (双偶四行). For example,

Come live with me and be my Love,
And we will all the pleasures prove,
That valleys, groves, hills and fields,
Woods, or steepy mountain yields.

(3) aaaa (通韵，一韵到底). For example,

The woods are lovely, dark, and deep,
But I have promises to keep,
And miles to go before I sleep.
And miles to go before I sleep.

(4) enclosed rhyme: abba (抱韵). For example,

I envy not in any moods,
The captive void of noble rage,
The linnet born within the cage,
That never knew the summer woods.

2. Metre（格律）

Metre is rhythm in poetry. It is the essential feature of poetry. It refers to a generally regular pattern of stressed and unstressed syllables in poetry. There are various types of metre. The four popular types in English poetry are illustrated as follows.

(1) Iamb（iambic, adj.，抑扬格）: ˇˊ

ˇ ˊ ˇˊ ˇˇˇ ˊ

She walks in beauty, like the night.

(2) Trochee（trochaic, adj.，扬抑格）: ˊˇ

ˊ ˇ ˊ ˇ ˊ ˇ ˊ ˇ

Tell me not, in mournful numbers,

(3) Anapest（anapestic, adj.，抑抑扬格）: ˇˇˊ

ˇˇ ˊ ˇˇ ˊ ˇˇˊ

And a sound of a voice that is still!

(4) Dactyl（dactylic, adj.，扬抑抑格）: ˊˇˇ

ˊ ˇˇ ˊ ˇˇ

Gently and Humanly,

Except the four major types of metre, there are also other variations, like spondee（spondaic, adj.，扬扬格）, for example,

ˊ ˊ

Rough winds do shake the daling buds of May,

and the pyrrhic（抑抑格）. For example,

ˇˇ

Thou art more lovely and more temperate.

3. Foot（音步）

Foot is the unit of measurement in metre. A line consisting of one metrical foot is monometer, and so on.

monometer（one foot，单音步）

dimeter（two feet，双音步）

trimester（three feet，三音步）

tetrameter（four feet，四音步）

pentameter (five feet，五音步)

hexameter (six feet，六音步)

4. Metrical pattern (音律)

Foot and metre can form many patterns of combination in a poetic line, that is, the metrical pattern. The most popular metrical pattern in English poetry is iambic feet. Let us take iambic pentameter as an example to illustrate.

˘ ˊ ˘ ˊ ˘ ˊ ˘ˊ ˘ ˊ

The cur | few tolls | the knell | of part | ing day,

˘ ˊ ˘ ˊ ˘ ˊ ˘ ˊ ˘ˊ

The low | ing herd | wind slow | ly o'er | the lea…

In each line, there are five feet in iambic meter, each foot beginning with an unstressed syllable and ending with a stressed syllable.

5. Stanza (诗节)

Stanza refers to a group of poetic lines forming a unit. The common stanzaic forms include couplet, triplet, quatrain, etc.

(1) Couplet

Couplet refers to the rhymed pair of lines. The most commonly-used form is Heroic Couplet, a rhymed pair of iambic pentameter lines. It was established by Chaucer as a major English verse form for narrative and other kinds of non-dramatic poetry; it dominated English poetry of the 18th century notably in the poetry of Pope, before declining in importance in the early 19th century. For example,

Vice is a monster of so frightful mien,
As, to be hated, needs but to be seen.

(2) Triplet

Triplet refers to the stanza with three lines rhyming the same. For example,

He claps the crag with crooked hands; [a]
Close to the sun in lonely lands, [a]
Ring'd with the azure world, he stands. [a]

(3) Quatrain

Quatrain is commonly used in English poetry. It refers to the 4-line stanza of different forms, among which ballad stanza or Ballad meter is the most popular. Ballad stanza, the usual form of the folk ballad and its literary imitations, consists of a quatrain in which the first and third lines have four stresses while the second and fourth have three stresses. Usually only the second and fourth lines rhyme. The rhythm is basically iambic. For example,

O my Luve's like a red, red rose,
That's newly sprung in June;
O my Luve's like the melodie,
That's sweetly played in tune.

Apart from the above stanzaic forms, there are also other forms, such as the 5-line stanza, the six-line stanza, the 7-line stanza named rime royal rhymed ababbcc, Ottava rima, containing eight iambic pentameter lines rhymed abababcc, the nine-line stanza, sonnet, a lyric poem of a single stanza in fourteen iambic pentameter lines linked by an intricate rhyme scheme.

6. Image (意象)

An image mainly refers to a mental picture, something seen in the mind's eye. Images are primarily visual. They are used to convey intangible states of mind or feeling through sense impressions. If we say words are the body of poetry, image is the soul of poetry. Images are verbal concretions, words that call up sensations. Images can be divided into many types.

Visual images (of sight) 视觉意象

Auditory images (of sound) 听觉意象

Olfactory images (of smell) 嗅觉意象

Gustatory images (of taste) 味觉意象

Tactile images (of touch) 触觉意象

Kinesthetic images (of muscle movement) 动觉意象

Organic (of internal sensation) 有机意象，如饥饿、渴等

7. Symbol (象征)

A symbol is an image that means not only what it is, but something else as well. A symbol can be universal or unique. For example, as is known to all, a dove suggests peace and a rose signifies love. But in Donne's poetry, a flea, which is a common, ugly insect to others, can be the symbol of love.

8. Figures of speech (修辞手法)

Poetry is generally indirect. The poets often put forward their ideas or meanings through figures of speech. The following ones are commonly used in poetry:

(1) Allusion (用典)

The figure of speech that is commonly used in poetry is allusion, the reference to some event, person, place or artistic work. The classical myths and works provide the major sources for allusions. In "To Helen", Edgar Allan Poe uses an allusion to the divine figures in Greek myth to show his admiration for the lady he truly cares about:

Helen, thy beauty is to me
Like those Nicean barks of yore,
That gently, o'er a perfumed sea,
The weary, way-worn wanderer bore
To his own native shore.

Helen is a beautiful woman in Greek mythology, whose abduction by Paris is the cause of the Trojan War. Odysseus is a prominent Greek leader, who ended the ten years' Trojan War and spent another ten years getting back home. The meaning of the allusion is not explained by the poet but relies on the reader's familiarity with what is thus mentioned.

(2) Simile and metaphor (明喻和暗喻)

Poets rarely call a rose a rose. When Robert Burns wrote: "O my Luve's like a red, red rose, / That's newly sprung in June," he wanted to show us how youthful, how beautiful his beloved is. Here he uses a simile, that is, to compare two similar things with "like", "as", "than", etc. Sometimes poets will make a comparison between two seemingly dissimilar things with no signals. It is the metaphor, which is less obvious than a simile. In John Keats' "On First Looking into Chapman's Homer", he compares the classic literature to "the realms of gold": "Much have I travell'd in the realms of gold, / And many goodly states and kingdoms seen". Here he means he has read many classic works which he treasured very much.

(3) Personification (拟人化)

Personification, another common figure of speech, is used when we want to give an object or idea human features. Percy Bysshe Shelley, in his "Ode to the West Wind", says that "O wild West Wind, thou breath of Autumn's being", as if Autumn were a human that had breath. In this famous ode, he further compares the west wind to both destroyer and preserver, as if the west wind were a powerful man that could destroy all the old and decayed, and preserve the new and fresh. The west wind represents the great power of the revolutionary people. The comparison makes this concept vivid and alive.

(4) Metonymy (借代)

Metonymy is used when one word or phrase is substituted for another to which it is closely related. In Shelley's "A Song: Men of England", he uses "cradle" and "grave" to signify a man in his early age and the old age.

(5) Paradox (似非而是)

Paradox is an argument that produces an inconsistency in common sense, yet contains a truth. Paradox in poetry is usually meaningful and thought-provoking. One of the best examples appears in John Milton's "On His Deceased Wife".

But O, as to embrace me she inclined,
I waked, she fled, and day brought back my night.

By the famous paradox in the last line, Milton shows his great happiness in seeing his wife in his dream and his deep sorrow when he has lost her in reality.

(6) Irony (反讽)

Henry Watson Fowler, in *The King's English*, says "any definition of irony—though hundreds might be given, and very few of them would be accepted—must include this, that the surface meaning and the underlying meaning of what is said are not the same." There are three types of irony: verbal irony, situational irony and dramatic irony. Verbal irony occurs when the given words imply a meaning in opposition to their literal meaning. A situation is often considered to be ironic if there is discordance between the actual result and the expected. Verbal irony and situational irony are often used to emphasize a truth. Dramatic irony is created when a character speaks or acts blindly out of ignorance of some truth of which the audience is aware. In William Blake's "The Chimney Sweeper" (from *Songs of Innocence*), the tragic fate are highlighted by the description of the happy scenes in the innocent chimney sweepers' life.

(7) Understatement (低调陈述)

Understatement refers to the statement that expresses an idea, etc., too weakly. No strong feeling is shown in words when William Wordsworth says in his "She Dwelt Among the Untrodden Ways": "But she is in her grave, and, oh, /The difference to me!" But everyone knows how mournful the speaker is and what great changes has happened after the death of Lucy.

(8) Hyperbole (夸张)

Hyperbole, also called overstatement or exaggeration, occurs when a poet describes something in order to make it sound bigger, smaller, better, worse, etc., than it really is. Shakespeare does this in the famous soliloquy in *Hamlet* to suggest the endless troubles that Hamlet went through: "Whether'tis nobler in the mind to suffer / The slings and arrows of outrageous Fortune, / Or to take arms against a sea of troubles…" In Robert Burns' "A Red, Red Rose", the speaker expresses his constant love for his beloved girl:

Till a' the seas gang dry, my Dear,
And the rocks melt wi'the sun:
O I will love thee still, my Dear,
While the sands o' life shall run.

Surely the exaggerated statement is not meant to be taken literally, but we are deeply moved by the passion between the lines.

9. Speaker and tone (说话者和语气)

Speaker and tone are also two important factors that need to be heeded to understand poetry.

When reading a poem, one needs to know who is talking and to whom he or she is talking. T. S. Eliot says in his *The Three Voices of Poetry*:

"The first voice is the voice of the poet talking to himself or to nobody.

The second is the voice of the poet addressing an audience, whether large or small. The third is the voice of the poet when he attempts to create a dramatic character speaking in verse; when he is saying, not what he would say in his own person, but only what he can say within the limits of one imaginary character addressing another imaginary character.

The speaker's voice conveys the tone of the poem. Tone refers to the poet or the imaginary speaker's attitude toward his subject, his reader or himself. It could be happy or sad, gloomy or light, serious or satiric, calm or excited, etc. The tone of the poem is not never-changing. To know clearly the tone of the poem, the reader needs to read the poem carefully. Tone can be revealed through many elements of poetry, like meter.

10. Diction (措辞)

Readers of poetry need to pay attention to the diction and syntax employed by the poet. Diction is the choice of words. Samuel Taylor Coleridge says poetry is the best words in the best order. Normally the diction will be adapted to the subject, unless the poet wants to display a sharp contrast or satire through their language. George Gordon Byron describes a graceful lady with harmonious beauty in "She Walks in Beauty", the diction of which is also elegant and exquisite. When reading a poem, one should pay attention to the connotations of words as well as denotations. The multiple meanings of words function well in poetry.

11. Subject matter and theme (题材和主题)

Subject matter refers to what is directly treated in poetry, while theme means the central idea conveyed between lines. For example, the subject matter of Shelley's "Ode to the West Wind" is the west wind in nature while the theme is about politics. The common themes of poetry include love, friendship, death, religion, society and nature. A poem may have one theme or more.

Rhyme, metrical pattern, image, symbol, figures of speech, speaker and tone, and poetic theme cannot cover all the elements of poetry. But to know about them will help you understand and appreciate it more fully and insightfully. This book will discuss 52 English and American poets and their representative poems. The poems are always indirect or even ambiguous. This book is not designed to provide you an authoritative interpretation of each work, but to lead you into the gold realms of poetry. The process of your individual exploration is sure to be pleasant and enjoyable!

V. How to Read a Poem?

In his book *Sound and Sense: an Introduction to Poetry*, Laurence Perrine provides wonderful suggestions on reading poetry. Here are some of the main ideas:

1. Read a poem more than once

The full meaning of a good poem cannot be understood on a single reading. Two readings or more readings are necessary. Any poem needs repeated and prolonged examination. A poem is not like a newspaper, to be hastily read and cast away. It is to be hung on the wall of one's mind.

2. Keep a dictionary nearby and use it

If you want to understand poetry, you have to learn the meanings of the words of which poetry is composed. You should build a good and large vocabulary through different means. It is advisable for you to keep a good dictionary or a few other reference books. You should also particularly keep a good dictionary on mythology and the Bible.

3. Read so as to hear the sounds of the words in your mind

Poetry is written to be heard. Its meanings are conveyed through sound as well as through print. Every word is therefore important. You should read a poem as slowly as possible at first. Either read it aloud or lip-read it. With ordinary reading material, lip-reading is a bad habit; with poetry it is a good habit.

4. Pay full attention to what the poem is saying

You should be conscious of the sounds of the poem, but you should pay equal attention to what the poem means. Make your utmost effort to follow the thought continuously and to grasp the full implications and suggestions.

Because a poem says so much, several readings may be necessary, but on the very first reading you should use your grammar knowledge to help you understand the meaning.

5. Practice reading poems aloud

Read the poems you like to other people and make them like the poems through your reading.

Read it affectionately, but not affectedly. Do not read a poem as if you were reading a railroad timetable, unexpressively, in a monotone. Neither read a poem with artificial flourishes and vocal histrionics. It is not necessary to put emotion into reading a poem. The emotion is already there. It only wants a fair chance to get out. It will express itself if the poem is read naturally and sensitively.

Do not read too fast. Reading too fast offers greater danger than reading too slow. Read slowly enough that each word is clear and distinct and that the meaning has time to be guessed and got by the hearer.

Read the poem so that the rhythmical pattern is felt but not exaggerated. Poetry is written in sentences, just as prose is. Punctuation is a signal as to how it should be read. Give all grammatical pauses their full due. Do not distort the natural pronunciation of words or a normal accentuation of the sentence to fit into what you have decided is its metrical pattern. One of the worst ways to read a poem is to read it with an exaggerated emphasis on every other syllable. On the other hand, it should not be read as if it were prose. An important test of your reading will be how you handle the end of a line when there is no punctuation there. A frequent mistake of the beginning reader is to treat each line as if it were a complete thought, whether grammatically complete or not, and to drop his voice at the end of it. A frequent mistake of the sophisticated reader is to take a running start upon approaching the end of a line and fly over it as if it were not there. The line is a rhythmical unit, and its end should be observed whether there is punctuation or not. If there is no punctuation, one observes it ordinarily by the slightest of pauses or by holding onto the last word in the line just a little longer than usual. One should not drop his voice.

Part Two British Poetry

1. Edmund Spenser

Edmund Spenser (埃德蒙·斯宾塞, 1552—1599), the greatest nondramatic poet of the English Renaissance, is regarded as "the poet's poet" because of his great influence on later poets.

Spenser was born and educated in London. Then he studied at Cambridge, where he read the classics and Italian poets and wrote poems. After he left Cambridge in 1576, he took a series of positions in the service of prominent English noblemen, including Dr. John Young, Bishop of Rochester, the Earl of Leicester, the Queen's favourite, and finally, Lord Gray of Wilton, Lord Deputy of Ireland. While he was in the service of Earl of Leicester, he made friends with Sir Philip Sidney, with whom he often discussed literature and exchanged poems, to whom he dedicated *The Shepherd's Calendar* in 1579.

The Shepherd's Calendar, a series of pastoral poems arranged according to the months of the year, was Spenser's first major work. The traditional pastoral was adapted to diverse satirical and allegorical uses. *The Shepherd's Calendar*, which popularized the mode in English poetry, included most of the varieties of pastoral poems current in that period.

Spenser's masterpiece *The Faerie Queene* was published in 1590. It consists of six books.

Amoretti, one of his major works, is a sonnet sequence of 89 sonnets published in 1595. It is a record of his courtship of Elizabeth Boyle. He also wrote two marriage poems *Prothalamion* and *Epithalamion* (1591—1595).

Spenser's contribution to English literature lies not only in what he wrote, but also in how he wrote it. He created many new poetic forms. The 9-line stanza form, called Spenserian stanza, with the rhyme scheme of ababbcbcc is one of his inventions, of which the first eight are iambic pentameter lines, and the last line is an iambic hexameter line. The sonnet form he invented is called Spenserian sonnet, which comprises three quatrains and a final couplet as others', containing such an intricate pattern of interlocking rhymes as abab bcbc cdcd ee. He tried his hand on different forms and meters.

Spenser holds a very high position in English literature. First, the publication of *The Shepherd's Calendar* marked the budding of the Renaissance flower in England. Second, Spenser was the first master to make English (Modern English) the natural music of his poetic creation. Third, his sonnets in *Amoretti* , together with Shakespeare's sonnets and Sidney's *Astrophel and Stella* were, and still are, regarded as the most famous sonnet sequences of the Elizabethan Age. Fourth, he influenced many later poets. In the 19th century alone his influence may be seen in Shelley's *Revolt of Islam*, Byron's *Childe Harold's Pilgrimage*, Keats' *Eve of St. Agnes*, and Tennyson's *The Lotos Eaters*. Spenser's last few years were darkened by the Irish uprisings. In an uprising in 1599, his house at Kilcoman was burned down. He had to return to London, where he died on January 13, 1599. He was buried beside Chaucer, his great medieval forerunner, in the poets' corner of Westminster Abbey.

Sonnet 34[1]

This sonnet is chosen from *Amoretti* (an Italian word meaning little love poems). It shows the author's deep love for his beloved and the importance of his beloved to him. The poet compares his love journey to the journey of a ship by using three images: ocean, ship and bright star. Though a representative of the Renaissance, Spenser frequently uses alliteration in his poems, especially in this poem. Various sound effects, comparisons and vivid images make the poem both readable and enjoyable.

Lyke as[2] a ship that through the Ocean wyde[3],
By conduct of[4] some star[5] doth make her way,
Whenas a storme hath dimd[6] her trusty[7] guyde,
Out of her course doth wander far astray[8]:
So I whose star, that wont with her bright ray

Me to direct[9], with cloudes is overcast,
Doe wander now in darkenesse and dismay,
Through hidden perils round about me plast[10].
Yet hope I well, that when this storme is past
My Helice[11] the lodestar[12] of my lyfe
Will shine again, and looke on me at last,
With lovely light to cleare my cloudy grief.
Till then I wander careful comfortlesse[13],
In secret sorow[14] and sad pensivenesse.

Notes

1. It is written in Spenserian sonnet, a notable variant of English sonnet, in which Spenser linked each quatrain to the next by a continuing rhyme: abab bcbc cdcd ee.
2. lyke as: like as, like. lyke: (archaic) like. Other archaic words in this poem: wyde-wide, doth-does, whenas-when, guyde-guide, cloudes-clouds, doe-do, darknesse-darkness, storme-storm, lyfe-life, looke-look, cleare-clear, comfortlesse-comfortless, pensivenesse-pensiveness.
3. Ocean wyde: wide ocean.
4. by conduct of: under the guidance of; guided by.
5. some star: referring to the North star. His lady is important to him as a North star to a wandering ship. Cf. Shakespeare's Sonnet 116: "It is the star to every wandering bark."
6. dimd: dimmed, darkened.
7. trusty: faithful.
8. far astray: in a wrong course.
9. that wont with her bright ray/Me to direct: that wont to direct me with her bright ray. wont: was used.
10. round about me plast: placed round about me. plast: placed.
11. Helice: the Big Dipper.
12. lodestar: North Star.
13. careful comfortlesse: full of care and discomforts.
14. sorow: sorrow.

诗歌赏析

斯宾塞的十四行诗集《爱情小唱》由89首十四行诗组成。这首诗是其中的一首，歌颂了他与未婚妻伊丽莎白·鲍伊尔的真挚感情，用英国十四行诗的一种变体“斯宾塞体十四行诗”（Spenserian sonnet）写成。同样由三个四行诗节和一个双偶句组成，斯宾塞体十四行诗前三个诗节的韵脚采用连环抱韵的形式，即abab bcbc cdcd，环环相扣，极其复杂。这一创新为英国十四行诗体的丰富和发展做出了卓越的贡献。斯宾塞的很多十四行诗至今为人称颂。

在这首诗里，诗人将爱的历程比作船只的航行，把意中人比作北斗星，时时指引他的航向。虽然暂时的阴霾遮住了星的光辉，但诗人希望意中人能重新照亮爱情的天空。这一比喻在莎士比亚的第116首十四行诗中也出现过：“爱是一颗星，它引导迷途的船只。”这首诗结构谨严，韵律优美，展示了诗人高超的诗歌技艺。

在第一组四行诗中，诗人把自己比作在大海中航行的船只，把所爱之人比作给船只领航的星斗。他把生活中因误解或某种原因而造成的短暂的冷漠关系比作星斗被暴风雨遮暗，此时，船在大海中丧失了航向，盲目漂荡。女人作为指路明星，作用多么伟大！第二个四行诗组继续这一比喻，乌云遮挡了指路的星，所以诗人只能在黑暗和暗礁中徘徊，忧郁满怀。黑暗和暗礁既指自然环境，也暗示诗人阴郁的心情。转折发生在第三个四行诗组——然而，诗人希望这一切都是暂时的，他希望风雨过后，北斗星会依然闪亮，用温柔的光芒涤清他心中的阴霾。在这里，诗人直接把意中人喻为生命的北斗星，表达了意中人在诗人生活中的重要性以及诗人对爱情的天空重获风清日朗的企盼。最后，诗人指出，不到那个时候，他依然会默默悲伤，忧思忡忡。这是该诗的基调。这首诗结构谨严，三个四行诗和一个双偶句起到起承转合的作用，诗歌主题在诗行间步步展开、层层递进。

斯宾塞不愧为“诗人中的诗人”，除了严谨的结构和形象的比喻外，这首诗还使用了丰富的音韵手段，头韵几乎行行有，腹韵此起彼伏，加上环环相扣的韵脚，使整首诗节奏感强，充满了音乐美。

当然，爱情的主题只是这首诗的一种阐释。北斗星的比喻可以指爱人，也可以指生命中重要的人物，比如伊丽莎白女王，也可以指诗人的创作灵感。

For Study and Discussion

1. What did the poet compare his love to? How important was her love to him?

2. Identify the three images in the poem. What's their function?
3. Study the structure of this sonnet. Discuss how the poem develops with the help of its structure.
4. Compare the Spenserian sonnet with that of Shakespeare. Identify the similarities and differences of them.

参考译文

第 34 首十四行诗

如同一条船驶在茫茫的海面，
凭靠某一颗星辰来为它导航，
一旦风暴把可靠的向导遮暗，
它就会远离自己的航道漂荡。
我的星辰也常常用它的亮光，
为我指路，现已被乌云笼罩，
我在深深的黑暗和苦闷中彷徨，
穿行于周围重重的险滩暗礁。
但是我希望，经过这一场风暴，
我的北斗呵，我那生命的北极星，
将重放光芒，最终把我来照耀，
用明丽的光辉驱除我忧郁的阴云。
在这以前，我忧心忡忡地徘徊，
独自暗暗地悲伤，愁思满怀。

（胡家峦　译）

Sonnet 75[1]

In this sonnet, addressing to his love, the speaker claims to give her immortality in his verse, in which their love as well as his fame shall live forever. It follows the traditional poetic theme in the Elizabethan period, that is, poetry can bring eternity to the one he loves (Cf. Shakespeare's Sonnet 18: "So long as men can breathe, or eyes can see, / So long lives this, and this gives life to thee" and Sonnet 55: "Not marble, nor the guilded monument, / Of Princes shall outlive this powerful rhyme, / But you shall shine more bright in these contents/Than unswept stone, besmeared with sluttish time."). Spenser starts from an ordinary incident that may occur any day in summer by the seaside. But he makes it intimately personal by developing it through the conversation between his lady and himself. The innocent, young love is put against the background of sea, art and time, thus immortal. This sonnet is of dramatic quality with lively dialogue full of nobility. It is also like telling a story.

One day I wrote her name upon the strand[2],
But came the waves[3] and washed it away:
Agayne[4] I wrote it with a second hand[5],
But came the tyde, and made my paynes his pray[6].
"Vayne man," said she, "that doest in vaine assay[7],
A mortal thing so to immortalize[8],
For I myselve shall lyke to this decay[9],
And eek[10] my name bee wyped out lykewize.
"Not so," quod[11] I, "let baser[12] things devize[13]
To dy in dust[14], but you shall live by fame:
My verse your virtues rare shall eternize[15],
And in the heavens wryte your glorious name[16].
Where whenas[17] death shall all the world subdew,
Out love shall live, and later life renew[18]."

Notes

1. This poem is also a Spenserian sonnet.
2. strand: seashore, beach.
3. came the waves: the waves came.
4. agayne: (archaic) again. Other archaic words in this poem: tyde-tide, pray-prey, paynes-pains, vayne-vain, sayd-said, doest-does, vaine-vain, mortall-mortal, my selve-myself, lyke-like, bee-be, wyped-wiped, lykewize-likewise, quod-quoth, dy-die, vertues-virtues, wryte-write, subdew-subdue.
5. with a second hand: for the second time, again.

6. made my paynes his pray: made my pains his prey. The tide washed her name away and made it a waste of effort for him to write her name on the beach.
7. that doest in vaine assay: that does try in vain. assay: try, attempt.
8. A mortal thing so to immortalize: so to immortalize a mortal thing.
9. lyke to this decay: to decay like this. decay: decline.
10. eek: also.
11. quod: quoth, said.
12. baser: lower.
13. devize: contrive.
14. To dy in dust: to die in dust. Cf. Genesis 3: 19 in Old Testament: "you are dust, and to dust you shall return."
15. My verse your virtues rare shall eternize: My verse shall eternize your rare virtues. eternize: make immortal. rare: unusual.
16. And in the heavens wryte your glorious name: and write your glorious name in the heavens. To write your name in heaven means: you will become one of the saints in heaven and hence immortal.
17. whenas: whereas.
18. life renew: renew life.

诗歌赏析

文艺复兴时期的人们相信文学作品具有战胜时空、使人不朽的伟大力量。这首十四行诗和莎士比亚的第18首、第55首十四行诗表达了同样的主题。诗人坚信自己的作品会不朽，而爱人的美德与圣名也会随之流传于世。同时诗人相信被不朽诗行见证的爱情也将永存。诗人采用对话体的形式，将这一严肃的主题在恋人的对话间逐步展开。

For Study and Discussion

1. Identify the metrical pattern and rhyme scheme of this poem.
2. After a brief narration for one quatrain, the poem goes on in dialogue. What do you think of this writing style?
3. What's the central image of the sonnet? How is it personified?
4. Is there a pun on "second hand" in Line 3?

5. Explain the structure of this sonnet. How does the theme develop with its structure?

参考译文

第 75 首十四行诗

有一天，我把她的名字写在沙滩，
但海浪来了，把那个名字冲跑；
我用手再一次把它写了一遍，
但潮水来了，把我的辛苦又吞掉。
“自负的人啊，”她说，“你这是徒劳，
妄想使世间凡俗的事物不朽；
我本身就会像这样云散烟消，
我的名字也同样会化为乌有。”
“不，”我说，“让低贱的东西去筹谋
死亡之路，但你将靠美名而永活：
我的诗将使你罕见的美德长留，
并把你光辉的名字写在天国。
死亡可以征服整个的世界，
我们的爱将永存，生命永不绝。”

（胡家峦 译）

2. Christopher Marlowe

Christopher Marlowe（克里斯托弗·马洛，1564—1593）was born in 1564，two months before William Shakespeare. His father was a shoemaker. In 1580，he went to Corpus Christi College，Cambridge. There he studied for six years and took his Master of Arts degree.

Marlowe is chiefly remembered for his plays such as *Tamburlaine* （1587），*The Jew of Malta* （1592）and

Doctor Faustus (1588). He is regarded as the greatest of the pioneers in English drama, first making blank verse the principal instrument of English drama. Marlowe's works, especially his use of blank verse, paved the way for plays of the greatest English dramatist Shakespeare.

In 1591, he was living in London with another playwright called Thomas Kyd, who later accused Marlowe of atheism and treason. On May 30, 1593, at the inn of the Widow Bill, in an argument over the bill he was killed. Modern scholars have pointed out that he was murdered deliberately because the Privy Council had already released a warrant to arrest Marlowe. It's a great pity that he died too young at the age of only 29. With all he had written, when he died in 1593, he had established an immortal place for himself in English drama and poetry. If Shakespeare also had died at the same age, he would scarcely be known today.

Apart from his plays, Marlowe also wrote some lyrics. Among them the pastoral "The Passionate Shepherd to His Love" is the most quoted one. Pastoral is a highly conventional mode of writing that celebrates the innocent life of shepherds and shepherdesses in poems, plays, and prose romances. Pastoral literature describes the love and sorrow of musical shepherds, usually in an idealized Golden Age of rustic innocence and idleness; paradoxically, it is an elaborately artificial cult of simplicity and virtuous frugality. English pastorals were written in several forms, from the prose romance of Sir Philip Sidney's *Arcadia* (1590), the eclogues of Edmund Spenser's *The Shepherd's Calendar* and the comedy of Shakespeare's *As You Like It* (1599) to lyrics like Marlowe's "The Passionate Shepherd to His Love".

The Passionate Shepherd to His Love[1]

This lyric is one of the best pastorals in English literature and a few lines from it are sung in Shakespeare's *Merry Wives of Windsor* (1598). It describes a shepherd's invitation to a girl by promising to give her all the pleasures nature can give. With simple language and rich images, the poet shows us the innocent happiness of the pastoral life, romantic and moving, though not quite believable.

Come live with me and be my love,
And we will all the pleasures prove[2]
That valleys, groves[3], hills, and fields,
Woods, or steepy mountain yields[4].

And we will sit upon the rocks,
Seeing the shepherds[5] feed their flocks[6]
By shallow rivers[7] to whose falls[8]
Melodious[9] birds sing madrigals[10].

And I will make thee beds of roses
And a thousand fragrant posies[11],
A cap of flowers, and a kirtle[12]
Embroidered[13] all with leaves of myrtle[14];

A gown[15] made of the finest wool
Which from our pretty lambs we pull;
Fair lined slippers for the cold[16],
With buckles of the purest gold;

A belt of straw and ivy[17] buds,
With coral clasps[18] and amber studs:
And if these pleasures may thee move,
Come live with me, and be my love.

The shepherd swains[19] shall dance and sing
For thy delight each May morning:
If these delights thy mind may move,
Then live with me and be my love.

1599, 1600

Notes

1. This short lyric was first published in the miscellany "England's Helicon"

(1600). Many poets have written replies to it. The finest reply is "The Nymph's Reply to the Shepherd" by Sir Walter Raleigh. Another of the many replies was Donne's "The Bait". The poem consists of six quatrains of iambic tetrameter rhyming aabb.

2. prove: test, experience. The first two lines form an eye rhyme with "love" and "prove." Cf. Shakespeare's Sonnet 117: "Since my appeal says I did strive to prove / The constancy and virtue of your love."
3. groves: grassland.
4. yields: gives.
5. shepherds: (other) shepherds.
6. flocks: flocks of sheep.
7. shallow rivers: small rivers.
8. falls: flowing water.
9. Melodious: sweet-throated.
10. madrigals: love songs sung by the townspeople.
11. posies: bouquets, small bunch of flowers.
12. kirtle: skirt, dress.
13. Embroidered: decorated.
14. myrtle: a kind of evergreen plant, the sacred tree of Venus, the goddess of love in Roman mythology.
15. gown: long dress.
16. for the cold: for (you to wear) in the cold weather.
17. ivy: the sacred thing of Bacchus, the god of wine in Roman mythology. Here "myrtle" and "ivy" are both symbols of worldly pleasures.
18. clasps: shoe buckles, buttons.
19. swains: lovers.

诗歌赏析

克里斯托弗·马洛，诗人和剧作家，是文艺复兴时期有名的“大学才子派”(University Wits) 作家之一。1593 年，马洛被人刺死于一个小酒馆，年仅 29 岁。如果他不是这样过早离世，英国戏剧的辉煌可能轮不上莎士比亚来照耀。马洛主要以剧作家著称，被认为是英国戏剧的先驱，首次将无韵诗树立为英国戏剧的主要写作工具。他的剧作为最伟大的戏剧家莎士比亚开辟了道路。除了戏剧以外，马洛还写了一些抒情诗。其中最著名的就是这首《痴情的牧羊人致意中人》，很多诗人为它写了和诗，最有名的要数罗利爵士的《美女答牧羊人》和邓恩的《诱饵》。

《痴情的牧羊人致意中人》以牧歌的形式写成，既是田园诗，也是引诱诗，有及时行乐倾向。全诗包括六个四行诗节，每行有八个音节，韵脚为aabb。该诗开篇直抒胸臆，“来，和我住在一起，做我的爱人”，表达了牧羊人急于赢得爱情的迫切心情，并做出承诺——只要和他在一起，就可以遍享山谷、田野带来的一切乐趣，也就是大自然的一切乐趣；接着，诗人用五节诗历数了各种欢欣。

在第二节中，诗人描绘出一幅美丽的田园风光和浪漫的爱情画卷：牧羊人和他的恋人坐在岩石上，看其他牧羊人放牧着群羊，旁边有着婉转歌喉的鸟儿对着潺潺的溪水唱着爱情小曲儿，并且是城市人唱的爱情小曲儿，很时髦，很惬意。好一幅动静结合、有声有色的田园图画！

除了给予恋人这怡人的田园风光和浪漫的闲暇时刻，牧羊人还在接下来的三节诗给恋人展现了一幅怡然自得、丰衣足食的生活画面：牧羊人会给恋人制作玫瑰花床，还有成百上千的芳香的花环、艳丽的花冠和装饰着爱情木叶子的长裙；还会用最漂亮的小羊羔身上的羊毛为她做长袍，用纯金鞋扣装饰的精美拖鞋为她御寒；一条草和常春藤叶子编织的腰带，上面装饰着珊瑚纽扣和琥珀饰钉。爱情木和常春藤分别是爱神和酒神的圣物，象征着俗世的快乐。牧羊人想用各种各样现世的快乐来打动女子的心。在这些承诺之后，诗人说道：“如果这些欢欣能打动你，/ 来，和我住在一起，做我的爱人。”

最后一节，牧羊人又把恋人推为英国乡村庆丰收的五朔节的王后，牧羊青年们在五月的早晨载歌载舞都是为了赢得恋人的欢心，“如果这些欢乐能打动你的心，/ 那么，和我住在一起，做我的爱人。”

他的诗平铺直叙，以“来，与我同住，做我的爱人”开始，毫不绕弯，接下来是各式田园的欢欣——山野的俏丽、小鸟的欢歌、鲜花的芬芳、华丽的衣裳，展现了牧羊人理想化的生活场景，这里无忧无虑、华服美食，怎不让人动心！另外，诗人还使用了反复和排比的手法，使牧羊人的爱情诉求步步推进，逐渐升华。“Live with me and be my Love”在全诗出现三次，但各有不同。第一次出现在全诗第一行，直抒胸臆，表达了牧羊人急于赢得爱情的迫不及待的心情；第二次出现在第五节的行尾，但是多了说理，“如果这些快乐能打动你的心，/ 来，和我住在一起，做我的恋人”；整首诗的最后一行又落在这一句上：“如果这些快乐能打动你的心，/ 那么，和我住在一起，做我的爱人。”

"来"和"那么"，一个主观的呼吁，一个是理性的诉求，从激情到理性，牧羊人完成了他田园牧歌式的爱情诉求，他的承诺或许不能实现，但他的允诺说不定会赢得恋人的心！

For Study and Discussion

1. What kind of life is idealized in this poem?
2. How does the shepherd pay court to the girl in the poem?
3. Do you think the shepherd could succeed in courtship by the way described in the poem?
4. Lines 19 and 20 almost repeat the poem's opening lines. What effect is created by this near repetition? Instead of ending with this refrain like repetition, the shepherd goes on for another stanza. Does the promise of the final stanza add anything new to the promises made earlier? If so, what does it add?
5. Sir Walter Raleigh's "The Nymph's Reply to the Shepherd" and Donne's "The Bait" are both famous replies to this poem. Make a comparative study of these three poems and offer your comments.

参考译文

痴情的牧羊人致意中人

来，和我住在一起，做我的爱人，
我们会把各样的乐趣来尝品；
品尝所有巅连高山的俏丽，
还有山谷田野带来的乐趣。

在那里，我们将坐在山石上，
看牧羊人放牧他们的群羊。
在浅唱的小溪边，悦耳动听的
小鸟欢唱着恋人们爱唱的情歌。

在那里，我将用玫瑰给你铺床，
还伴有千朵花儿吐芬芳；
为你编做一顶花冠，还有一条长裙，
上面桃金娘绿叶散发香馨。

从美丽羔羊身上揪采最好的羊毛
为你做一件长袍；
用纯金为你制作鞋扣，
为御寒把鞋子也要精美地刺绣；

为你做一条腰带，用草和藤编织，
上边点缀着珊瑚扣和琥珀的纽饰：
如果这各样的乐趣能让你动心，
来，和我住在一起，做我的爱人。

牧羊少年群歌舞，
领略五月早晨的幸福。
如果这各种欣喜能让你动心，
那么，和我住在一起，做我的爱人。

（李正栓　译）

3. William Shakespeare

William Shakespeare（威廉·莎士比亚，1564—1616）was one of the greatest figures in English literature. In his lifetime, he wrote 37 plays, two long narrative poems *Venus and Adonis*（1593）and *The Rape of Lucrece*（1594）and 154 sonnets. Ben Jonson thus comments on Shakespeare: "He was not of an age, but for all time."

Shakespeare was born into a merchant's family in Stratford-Upon-Avon. He received little formal education. Ben Jonson said he knew little Latin and few Greek. He married Anne Hathaway, a girl 8 years older than him in 1582. In 1585 or 1586 he left for London. There he first took some odd jobs, from taking care of gentlemen's horses to minor roles on the stage, then he began to rewrite old plays and write new plays. By the end of the 16th century, he had become popular as a famous playwright. One of the University Wits Robert Green called him "the upstart crow with our feathers". And later he became a shareholder in the playhouses. He went back to his hometown in 1612 and died there on the very day of his birth in 1616.

Though he was always taken as the greatest dramatist of his day, his genius for poetic creation also shone bright in his sonnets, which formed the peak of English sonnets in the Elizabethan period. There are three famous sonnet sequences in the Elizabethan Age — Spenser's *Amoretti*, Sidney's *Astrophel and Stella*, and Shakespeare's sonnets. Because of his great contribution, the English sonnet was also called Shakespearean sonnet.

Shakespeare's sonnets (1609) were mainly dedicated to "W. H.", a handsome young man, maybe his friend and patron. Sonnets 1-126 mainly discuss his friendship with him. In Sonnets 1-17, the poet advises the young man to get married and preserve his beauty by having children. In Sonnets 18-126, the poet gives up the attempts to persuade the young man to marry and tries to keep the beauty of the young man in his everlasting poetry. Sonnets 127-152 are about a mysterious "dark lady", who is thought to be the poet's ideal woman. The last two sonnets have no relationship with the others. The main theme of his sonnets is love and friendship. Not a few of the sonnets describe the destructive power of time and human's struggle against it by offspring, art and love.

Sonnet 29[1]

The poet sings praise of the power of friendship and shows his admiration for the young man in the poem. At the beginning of the poem, the poet feels dejected by his ignored condition and complains of his bad fate and the indifference of God. Then he becomes joyful when thinking of his friend. The poet uses many a poetic device to show the theme of his poem, such as rhymes, pun, repetition, contrast , etc.

When, in disgrace with[2] Fortune and men' eyes,
I all alone beweep[3] my outcast state[4],
And trouble deaf heaven[5] with my bootless[6] cries,
And look upon myself, and curse[7] my fate,
Wishing me like to[8] one more rich in hope[9],
Featured like him[10], like him with friends possessed[11],

Desiring this man's art[12] and that man's scope[13],
With what I most enjoy contented least[14];
Yet in these thoughts myself almost despising[15],
Haply I think on thee[16], and then my state[17]
(Like to the lark at break of day arising[18]
From sullen[19] earth) sings hymns at heaven' gate;
For thy sweet love remembered such wealth brings[20]
That then I scorn[21] to change my state[22] with kings.

Notes

1. This is an English or Shakespearean sonnet, which has a typical structure of Shakespeare's sonnets. The turn happens in the first line of the third quatrain.
2. in disgrace with: out of favour with.
3. beweep: weep over.
4. my outcast state: my rejected condition. outcast: rejected, being ignored. state: condition.
5. deaf heaven: deaf God. Heaven is used as a synecdoche for God, which is compared to a deaf person who gives no ear to his complaint.
6. bootless: useless, futile.
7. curse: complain of.
8. like to: like.
9. one more rich in hope: someone with great expectations.
10. Featured like him: with physical appearance like him.
11. like him with friends possessed: like him possessed with friends, like him who has lots of friends.
12. art: skill, ability.
13. scope: range of knowledge.
14. With what I most enjoy contented least: least satisfied with what I most enjoy. contented: satisfied.
15. myself almost despising: i. e. almost despising myself, when I am almost looking down upon myself. despising: looking down upon.

16. haply I think on thee: by chance I think of you. Haply: fortunately, by chance. think on: think of. thee: the accusative form of "you". Cf. Sonnet 30: "But if the while I think on thee, dear friend, / All losses are restored, and sorrows end." In the 17th century, the forms of "you" are as follows:

	主格	宾格	所有格
单数	thou	thee	thy, thine
复数	you, ye	you	your, yours

17. state: mental mood, state of mind.
18. Like to the lark at break of day arising: like the lark arising at break of day. like to: like. at break of day: at dawn. The lark is often taken as a joyful spirit in English poetry. The higher it flies, the louder it sings. Cf. *Cymbeline* 2.3: "Hark, hark! The lark at heaven's gate sings."
19. sullen: gloomy, unhappy.
20. For thy sweet love remembered such wealth brings: i. e. for thy sweet love rememb'red brings such wealth. rememb'red: remembered. wealth: great value, benefits.
21. scorn: refuse, disdain.
22. state: a pun, condition and chair of state, throne.

诗歌赏析

莎士比亚一生生活在盛名和冷遇叠加之下。第 29 首十四行诗或许反映了他当时的心情。这首诗和第 18 首一样是莎士比亚十四行诗的经典之作，诗人使用了丰富的音韵手段和诗歌技巧来表达对生活现状的不满和友谊的重要性。

第 29 首延续了典型的莎士比亚十四行诗的形式，由三个四行诗组和一个双偶句组成，呈现出十四行诗常见的起承转合的逻辑关系。全诗逻辑严密，结构紧凑，展示了诗人对十四行诗这一诗歌形式非凡的驾驭能力。第一个四行组表达了诗人既得不到命运的眷顾又见弃于世人，郁郁寡欢的落寞心情。诗人忍不住内心的愤懑，仰头向苍天哭喊，可是老天爷充耳不闻，低头想想自己的境遇，不禁落落寡欢，悲叹命运的不公。第二个四行组承接了以上话题，说明诗人叫天天不应，叫地地不灵，开始羡慕别人拥有的东西，对自己拥有的却毫不在意。诗人陷入自卑的情绪中不能自拔。正在这时，他想到了他的朋友！于是，他的心情豁然开朗，像破晓高飞的云雀，在天堂的门口唱起了赞美诗。这种情绪上的转折，发生在以 Yet 为首的第三个四行组，预示着诗人心境的转移。最后一个双偶句道出了诗人的心迹——只要有朋友相伴，即使国王拿王位也甭想换！友人在诗人心目中的重要性可见一斑。诗歌结构的变化和诗人心情的转变交相呼应，使这首诗堪称形式表达内容的典范。

莎士比亚的十四行诗几乎每首都是华美的乐章。第 29 首就是这样的范例。诗人思绪的变化内嵌在诗歌音乐的变化中，流畅自然，丰富的音韵手段展现了诗人绝佳的诗艺技巧。首先，这首诗基本遵循传统十四行诗抑扬格的格律，但关键的地方诗人看似随意的浓墨一点，形成了抑扬顿挫又富有变化的音律空间。诗歌的第三行突然出现两个重读音节 deaf heaven（聋耳的苍天），即“重——重”的扬扬格形式，偏离了和谐的一轻一重的十四行诗的普遍节奏，而且重复使用短音［e］，构成一个鲜明紧凑的腹韵，突出这组词的重要性，充分表达了诗人对上天的愤懑。另外，诗人在关键的几行诗的行首使用了扬抑格的音步，比如 When in，Wishing，Featured，Yet in，Haply 等，以突出这首诗的逻辑性和诗人情感的变化。而最后一行诗，随着诗人心态的平和，又回归到工整的抑扬格五音步诗行。其次，这首诗和莎士比亚的其他十四行诗一样，押 abab cdcd efef gg 韵，但是看似工整划一的韵式中有着新奇的变化。全诗其他行都押铿锵有力的阳韵，只有第 9 行和第 11 行的 despising 和 arising 押的是阴韵。仔细读来，despising 出现在诗人情绪最低落的时候，拖沓的阴韵巧妙地烘托了诗人沉郁的心情，到了 arising 节奏再一次舒缓下来，表现了诗人安逸纯美的心境。阳韵和阴韵的恰当使用，既不呆板，又颇有表意功能，再一次阐释了这首诗音、形、意的完美结合。节奏的变化也是这首诗的特征。在前两个四行组，诗人连续使用长元音和双元音，形成呜咽悲切的氛围，很多双音节词也产生迟滞的效果。诗人想起了朋友，心情一下子变得欢快起来，诗歌的节奏也随之变得轻快：Haply I think on thee，and then my state / Like to the lark at break of day arising。这两行诗，除了首尾两个单词，几乎都是单音节词，读起来清脆上口，而 arising 之前自然的停顿，更加突出了“升腾”的意象，烘托出诗人想起朋友快乐满怀的心境。最后几行，则连续使用了 z，v 等舒缓的辅音，产生和谐愉快的声音效果。

丰富的修辞手段是第 29 首的亮点。诗人在这首诗中反复使用了重复的手法，其中鲜明的例子就是三个 state 的重复。它分别出现在第一个四行组、第三个四行组和最后的双偶句中，产生强烈的结构效应和意义效能。State 虽然在诗中反复出现，但它不是简单的重复：它在诗中分别代表了诗人不同的境遇和心情。第一个 state 指诗人郁郁不得志的人生遭遇；第二个 state 指诗人想到朋友后，像云雀般欢快的心情；最后一个 state 更是双关的用法，既可以指有朋友相伴的境遇，即便是国王也不予交换，同时还有“王位、江山”的意思。而且，这首诗几乎每行都使用了头韵和腹韵，呈现出很强的音乐性。除了诗行内的音韵手法外，when，Yet 和 then 三个词遥相呼应，既反映了诗人心境的发展、变化，又构成短音 e 的腹韵，使全诗首尾相连，成为紧密结合的整体。在腹韵和头韵的配合下，诗人的声音在诗行里不断加强和回响，诗歌的主题和意义得以不断呈现。另外，诗人把想起朋友的心情比喻成破晓飞天的“云雀”。这个明喻的使用是这首诗的点睛之笔。云雀展翅飞翔的意象，一方面预示着朋友在诗人心中的作用。一想到朋友，诗人的心情就像展翅高飞的云雀一样，轻盈、欢快。在英诗中云雀历来被视为欢乐的精灵。19 世纪浪漫主义诗人雪莱就写过著名的《致云雀》。另一方面，代表着朋友在诗人心目中至高无上的地位，就像虔诚的信徒仰望主一样。因为《圣经》上说，“通过痛苦，心灵将‘仰望主’，并因‘重新得力’而‘展翅上腾’”。17 世纪著名的宗教诗人赫伯特也曾经在《复活节翅膀中》第一节中使用这一意象：“让我像 / 宛转的云雀 / 和你呀同上天堂。”（黄杲炘译）从阴郁的大地升腾而起，向着天堂飞翔的云雀象征着诗人通过云雀的意象，实现了天——地——人的完美结合。只要有朋友陪伴，诗人的世界就是天堂，世间的一切烦扰不再重要。

诗人通过音、形、意的完美结合，辅以丰富的修辞手段，成就了这首十四行诗的经典之作。

For Study and Discussion

1. Explain the meaning of the word “state” in Lines 2，10 and 14.
2. There are two moods contrasted in this sonnet. What are they?
3. What causes his change of mood in the last few lines of the poem?
4. How do you understand the image of a lark in the sonnet?

参考译文

第 29 首十四行诗

我一旦失去了幸福，又遭人白眼，
就独自哭泣，叹人家把我抛弃，
白白地用哭喊来麻烦聋耳的苍天，

又看看自己，只痛恨时运不济，
愿自己像人家那样：或前途远大，
或一表人才，或胜友如云广交谊，
想有这人的见识，那人的才华，
于自己平素最得意的，倒最不满意；
但在这几乎是自轻自贱的思绪里，
我偶尔想到了你呵，——我的心怀
顿时像破晓的云雀从阴郁的大地
冲上了天门，歌唱起赞美诗来；
我怀着你的厚爱，如获至宝，
教我不屑把处境跟帝王对调。

（屠　岸　译）

Sonnet 18[1]

This poem is Shakespeare's most frequently quoted sonnet. In the first 17 sonnets, the poet mainly persuades the young man to get married and preserve his beauty by offspring. But in Sonnet 18, the poet gives up his previous persuasion and hopes the young man to live in his poems for ever, another way of preserving the beauty of his friend. The sonnet starts with a question "Shall I compare thee to a summer's day", develops the argument in three quatrains, and concludes with a final couplet that art, in the form of this sonnet, will bring eternity to his friend. It is a typical structure of Shakespeare's sonnets. The first quatrain raises a question or an argument; the second develops it; the third has a change in argument or mood; while the final couplet gives a solution, thus settles the argument.

Shall I compare thee to a summer's day[2]?
Thou art more lovely and more temperate[3]:
Rough winds[4] do shake the darling[5] buds of May,
And summer's lease hath all too short a date[6];
Sometime[7] too hot the eye of heaven[8] shines,
And often is his gold complexion[9] dimmed[10];
And every fair from fair sometime declines[11],

By chance[12], or nature's changing course[13] untrimmed[14].
But thy eternal summer shall not fade[15],
Nor lose possession of that fair thou ow'st[16];
Nor shall death brag thou wander'st in his shade[17],
When in eternal lines to time thou grow'st[18]:
So long as men can breathe or eyes can see,
So long lives this, and this gives life to thee[19].

Notes

1. It is written in Shakespearean sonnet form rhyming abab cdcd efef gg.
2. Shall I compare thee to a summer's day: It is a rhetorical question which can be explained as "how could I compare you to a summer's day?" The poet gives the answer in the second line. a summer's day: a happy, joyful, beautiful day. He compares his friend to a summer's day to show his admiration for his friend. This comparison may show the good character or the beauty and youth of his friend since summer is the most beautiful season in England and the second season of the four in a year. There are four stages in human life (childhood, youth, adulthood and old age) and four seasons in a year. The counterpart of summer in life is youth. Shakespeare often compares different stages of life with different seasons. Cf. Sonnet 73: autumn vs. the old age.
3. Thou art more lovely and more temperate: you are more attractive and moderate than a summer's day. Thou art: you are. lovely: attractive. temperate: moderate. It's a pun which can refer to the gentle character of a person or the mild weather. Here Shakespeare uses two trochaic feet other than the typical iambic ones to show emphasis on the loveliness of his friend. In the following lines, the poet lists several reasons to support his idea.
4. Rough winds: it's a spondee to stress the rough weather in summer. In this spondee, sound and sense match perfectly.
5. darling: lovely.
6. And summer's lease hath all too short a date: and summer lasts for only a short period of time. Here Shakespeare uses two legal terms ("lease" and

"period") to describe the length of summer. lease: period. hath: has. date: a limited period of time.

7. Sometime: sometimes.

8. the eye of heaven: the sun. It's a metaphor. The normal order of this line is "Sometime the eye of heaven shines too hot".

9. his gold complexion: the sun's gold facial expression.

10. dimmed: not clear, covered by clouds.

11. every fair from fair sometimes declines: every beautiful thing or person may sometimes lose its, his or her beauty. The normal order of this line is "every fair sometimes declines from fair". every fair: every beautiful thing or person. from fair: from beauty. declines: withers.

12. By chance: unexpectedly, accidentally.

13. nature's changing course: natural law.

14. untrimmed: stripped of beauty. The normal order of this line is "untrimmed by chance or nature's changing course".

15. But thy eternal summer shall not fade: but your eternal summer shall never disappear. You shall have your own beauty and energy for ever. "But" marks a turn in this sonnet. The turns in Shakespearean sonnets always appear in the ninth line. Here "thy" can be stressed.

16. ow'st: ownest, own. 与 thou 连用的动词，后面接 -est, -st, -t, 如 wander'st＝wanderest.

17. Nor shall death brag thou wander'st in his shade: Nor shall death boast you roam about in his realm. "death" here is personified. brag: boast. wander'st: wander. in his shade: in his shadow, in the kingdom of death.

18. When in eternal lines to time thou grow'st: When thou grow'st to time in eternal lines. eternal lines: the immortal lines of this sonnet. The poet has confidence that his poetry will be everlasting in the world. thou: you. grow'st: grow, are grafted.

19. So long as men can breathe or eyes can see, / So long lives this, and this gives life to thee: As long as there are people in this world and people have eyes to see this poem, as long as this poem exists in this world, you'll exist in this poem for ever. The last two lines have become a famous epigram. this: this poem. It is a traditional theme for poetry in the Elizabethan

period, that is, poetry can bring eternity to the one he loves and eulogizes. Sonnet 55, Sonnet 60 and Spenser's Sonnet 75 all reflect the same theme. Cf. Sonnet 55: "So, till the judgment that yourself arise, / You live in this, and dwell in lovers' eyes." Sonnet 60: "And yet to times in hope my verse shall stand, / Praising thy worth, despite his cruel hand." Spenser's sonnet 75: "My verse your vertues rare shall eternize, / And in the heavens wryte your glorious name. / Where whenas death shall all the world subdew, / Our love shall live, and later life renew."

诗歌赏析

第 18 首十四行诗采用文艺复兴时期诗歌惯用的主题，即文学具有战胜时间、使人不朽的神奇力量。该诗歌颂了诗人所歌颂的男子的骄人风姿，堪与夏日同辉，但比夏日更辉煌，夏季有诸多不便，并且时日不长，而诗人所歌咏的友人却能因其创作在诗行中获得永生。这首诗是莎士比亚十四行诗中被引用最多的一首。

For Study and Discussion

1. Explain the function of variation in metrical pattern of this poem, such as the trochee "Shall I" or the spondee "Rough wind" for stress.
2. Analyze the development of thought in this sonnet.
3. Taking this poem as a sample, explain carefully the structure, turning point, conclusion and rhyme scheme of Shakespearean sonnet.
4. Why does the poet compare his love to a summer's day?

参考译文

第 18 首十四行诗

我能否把你比做夏季的一天？
你可是更加可爱，更加温婉；
狂风会吹落五月的娇花嫩瓣，
夏季租出的日子又未免太短：
有时候苍天的巨眼照得太灼热，
他金光闪耀的圣颜也会被遮暗；

每一样美呀，总会失去美而凋落，
被时机或者自然的代谢所摧残；
但是你永久的夏天决不会凋枯，
你永远不会丧失你美的形象：
死神夸不着你在他影子里踯躅，
你将在不朽的诗中与时间同长；
只要人类在呼吸，眼睛看得见，
我这诗就活着，使你的生命绵延。

（屠 岸 译）

Sonnet 73[1]

This poem is famous for the effectiveness of its images, in which the poet looks ahead at his old age. He describes his old age by three images: autumn, twilight and dying fire, one in each quatrain. He hopes his beloved could love him more since he is approaching death.

That time of year thou mayst in me behold[2]
When yellow leaves[3], or none, or few, do hang
Upon those boughs which shake against the cold[4],
Bare ruined choirs[5], where late[6] the sweet birds sang.
In me thou seest the twilight of such day[7]
As after sunset fadeth[8] in the west,
Which by and by black night doth take away,
Death's second self[9], that seals up[10] all in rest[11].
In me thou seest the glowing of such fire[12]
That on the ashes of his youth doth lie[13],
As the deathbed whereon it must expire[14],
Consumed with that which it was nourished by[15].
This thou perceiv'st[16], which makes thy love more strong,
To love that well, which thou must leave ere long[17].

Notes

1. It is written in Shakespearean sonnet form rhyming abab cdcd efef gg.

2. That time of year thou mayst in me behold: thou mayst behold that time of year in me. thou mayst: you may. behold: see. That time of year: referring to autumn which is approaching winter. In the first quatrain, the poet uses autumn to describe the old age of the poet. In Sonnet 18, the poet compares his young friend to summer.
3. yellow leaves: leaves in autumn, here referring to the grey hair of an old man.
4. against the cold: in the cold wind or in the cold weather.
5. Bare ruined choirs: bare deserted choirs. choirs: the part of a church where services are held. In the reign of Henry Ⅷ, many churches were deserted or destroyed. The ruined choirs without choristers are compared to the bare boughs of an autumn tree, which both refer to the bare head of an old man.
6. late: lately, not long ago, recently.
7. twilight of such day: the dusk of a day. In the second quatrain, the old age is compared to the dusk of a day.
8. fadeth: fades.
9. Death's second self: the close friend of Death, referring to "black night" in Line 7.
10. seals up: encloses, covers.
11. rest: sleep.
12. the glowing of such fire: the faint light of the dying fire, another image to describe the old age.
13. That on the ashes of his youth doth lie: that does lie on the ashes of his youth.
14. As the deathbed whereon it must expire: as the deathbed on which it must die. whereon: on which. expire: die, extinguish. Here the poet takes the ashes as the deathbed of the fire.
15. Consumed with that which it was nourished by: destroyed by the fuel that the fire was nourished by. Consumed with: destroyed by. that: the fuel. It is a paradox. The fuel that gave life to the fire now took away its life because the fuel was used up. Cf. Sonnet 1: "Feed'st thy light's flame with self-substantial feul".
16. This thou perceiv'st: you understand this. perceiv'st: understand, recog-

nize. This: this situation that I'm old and approaching death.

17. To love that well, which thou must leave ere long: To love that person whom you must leave before long deeply and faithfully. that: that person. ere long: before long, soon. ere: before.

诗歌赏析

希腊诗人西摩尼得斯（Simonides）说过："诗为有声之画，画为无声之诗。"（朱光潜著：《诗论》，安徽教育出版社，2003）在十四行诗第73首中，莎士比亚用生动的意象为我们勾勒出一幅秋日黄昏的画面：几片黄叶孤零零地在枝头打战，落日在西边苟延残喘，炉内的火焰一息奄奄。晚秋枝头的几片黄叶形容老人疏离的白发；落日的黄昏形容暗夜将至，老人已去日无多；即将燃尽的火焰形容老人渐渐退去的活力。诗人在前三个四行诗节中用三个意象出神入化地描写了一位将近迟暮之年的老人的形象，即诗人想象中老年的摹拟自画像。最后的双偶句提醒友人，既然我们都会老去，就好好珍惜我们的友情吧！

For Study and Discussion

1. What's the theme of this poem?
2. What are the three metaphors in the poem?
3. How do the three principal images in the three quatrains relate to the mood and theme of the poem?
4. Compare different Chinese versions of this sonnet. Point out the strong points and weak points of each version.

参考译文

第73首十四行诗

你从我身上能看到这个时令：
黄叶落光了，或者还剩下几片
没脱离那乱打冷战的一簇簇枝梗——
不再有好鸟歌唱的荒凉唱诗坛。
你从我身上能看到这样的黄昏：
夕阳的回光沉入了西方的天际，
死神的化身——黑夜，慢慢地临近，

挤走黄昏，把一切封进了安息。
你从我身上能看到这种火焰：
它躺在自己青春的余烬上缭绕，
像躺在临终的床上，一息奄奄，
跟供它养料的燃料一同毁灭掉。
看出了这个，你的爱会更加坚贞，
好好地爱着你快要失去的爱人。

（屠　岸　译）

To Be, or Not to Be, —That Is the Question[1]

It is a famous soliloquy by Hamlet. It reflects the inner conflict of Hamlet, a hero of the Renaissance and a representative of humanism. It also reflects the contradictions between thoughts and action, the ideal of a humanist and the sordid reality at that time.

To be, or not to be[2], —that is the question:
Whether 'tis nobler in the mind to suffer[3]
The slings and arrows[4] of outrageous Fortune[5],
Or to take arms against[6] a sea of troubles[7],
And by opposing end them[8]? To die, —to sleep, —
No more[9]; and, by a sleep, to say[10] we end
The heart-ache[11], and the thousand natural shocks[12]
That flesh is heir to[13], —'Tis a consummation[14]
Devoutly to be wish'd[15]. To die, —to sleep; —
To sleep! perchance[16] to dream: —ay[17], there's the rub[18];
For in that sleep of death what dreams may come,
When we have shuffled off this mortal coil[19],
Must give us pause[20]. There's the respect[21]
That makes calamity of so long life[22];
For who would bear[23] the whips and scorns of time[24],
The oppressor's wrong[25], the proud man's contumely[26],
The pangs of dispriz'd love[27], the law's delay,
The insolence of office, and the spurns[28]

That patient merit of th' unworthy takes[29],
When he himself might his quietus make[30]
With a bare bodkin[31]? Who would fardels[32] bear,
To grunt[33] and sweat under a weary life,
But that[34] the dread[35] of something after death,
The undiscover'd country[36], from whose bourn[37]
No traveller returns, puzzles the will[38],
And makes us rather bear those ills[39] we have
Than fly to others that we know not of[40]?
Thus conscience[41] does make cowards of us all;
And thus the native hue of resolution[42]
Is sicklied o'er[43] with the pale cast of thought[44];
And enterprises of great pith and moment[45],
With this regard[46], their currents turn awry[47],
And lose the name of action[48].

Notes

1. It is written in blank verse. *Hamlet* is one of Shakespeare's great tragedies. The excerpt is chosen from Act Ⅲ, Scene Ⅰ, Lines 55-86.
2. To be, or not to be: whether to live or to die. To be: to live, to exist. The first line has become a famous saying in English. It has many explanations. Different readers have different understanding.
3. 'tis nobler in the mind to suffer: it is nobler to suffer in the mind, that is, it is nobler to endure passively. 'tis: it is. suffer: endure.
4. slings and arrows: they are both war images. slings: a weapon consisting of a looped strap in which a stone is whirled and then let fly.
5. outrageous Fortune: cruel fate.
6. take arms against: fight against with arms. It's an active attitude toward life contrasted to "to suffer in the mind".
7. a sea of troubles: lots of troubles. It's a hyperbole.
8. by opposing end them: end them by opposing.
9. To die, —to sleep, —/No more: to die is to sleep; to die is to be no more.
10. to say: it is to say.

11. heart-ache: mental sorrow.
12. natural shocks: attacks by nature, here referring to physical pains.
13. That flesh is heir to: that the human body is an heir to. flesh: the human body.
14. 'Tis a consummation: it is a final settlement of everything.
15. Devoutly to be wish'd: to be wished passionately. Devoutly: passionately. wish'd: wished.
16. perchance: perhaps.
17. ay: yes.
18. rub: obstacles.
19. shuffled off this mortal coil: ended life. shuffled off: thrown off. mortal coil: trouble in this world. coil: trouble.
20. Must give us pause: must make us hesitate. The subject of this line is what dreams may come.
21. respect: consideration.
22. makes calamity of so long life: makes the disaster last so long. calamity: disaster.
23. bear: endure.
24. the whips and scorns of time: the hardships of life at that time. From here on, Shakespeare makes a list of misfortunes people may suffer at that time.
25. wrong: wrong deeds.
26. contumely: arrogant behaviors.
27. pangs of dispriz'd love: pains of rejected love. pangs: pains. dispriz'd: rejected.
28. spurns: contempt.
29. That patient merit of th' unworthy takes: that man of virtue takes from the unworthy patiently. merit: man with virtue. th': the.
30. might his quietus make: might pay all his debts, might die. his quietus make: make his quietus, pay off debts. Cf. The saying: "He that dies pays all debts."
31. With a bare bodkin: with a mere dagger (to end life).
32. fardels: burdens. The normal order of this sentence is who would bear

fardels.

33. grunt：groan.
34. But that：unless.
35. dread：fear.
36. The undiscover'd country：death，the life after death.
37. bourn：boundary.
38. puzzles the will：puzzles our will，make us hesitate to take action. will：will (to commit suicide).
39. ills：evils.
40. others that we know not of：other ills that we don't know of. know not of：don't know of.
41. conscience：consideration.
42. native hue of resolution：natural color of determination.
43. Is sicklied o'er：is covered with a pale color.
44. pale cast of thought：a sick colour of meditation. cast：colour. thought：meditation.
45. enterprises of great pitch and moment：great and important plans. enterprises：plans. pitch：height. moment：importance.
46. With this regard：on this account.
47. their currents turn awry：turn their course aside. currents：course. awry：aside.
48. lose the name of action：fail to put it into action.

诗歌赏析

《To Be，or Not to Be》是莎士比亚戏剧的经典独白，用无韵诗的形式写成。它选自莎士比亚四大悲剧之一的《哈姆雷特》(*Hamlet*)，是剧中哈姆雷特王子的独白，探讨了生与死、思考与行动之间的关系问题，反映了一个年轻的人文主义者矛盾的心理探索过程。他敏锐地意识到丹麦王朝的腐败和现实的黑暗。他的性格中既有强烈的进取精神，又有无法摆脱的犹豫和疑虑。面对国仇家恨，是勇敢地挑起重担，还是简单地一死了之？经过反复的思索，哈姆雷特终于找出了彷徨的原因。内心的尖锐矛盾在这段著名的独白中表现无遗。

For Study and Discussion

1. According to Hamlet, why would people rather bear all the sufferings of the world instead of choosing death to get rid of them?

2. What, after all, makes people lose their determination to take action? Please explain it in relation to the so-called hesitation of Hamlet.

参考译文

活下去还是不活：这是个问题

活下去还是不活，这是个问题：
要做到高贵，究竟该忍气吞声
来容忍狂暴的命运矢石交攻呢，
还是该挺身反抗无边的苦恼，
扫它个干净？死，就是睡眠——
就这样；而如果睡眠就等于了结了
心痛以及千百种身体要担受的
皮痛肉痛，那该是天大的好事，
正求之不得啊！死，就是睡眠；
睡眠也许要做梦，这就麻烦了！
我们一旦摆脱了尘世的牵缠
在死的睡眠里还会做些什么梦，
一想到就不能不踌躇。这一点顾虑
正好使灾难变成了长期的折磨。
谁甘心忍受人世的鞭挞和嘲弄，
忍受压迫者虐待、傲慢者凌辱，
忍受失恋的痛苦、法庭的拖延、
衙门的横暴、做埋头苦干的大才
受作威作福的小人一脚踢出去，
如果他只消自己来使一下尖刀
就可以得到解脱？谁甘心挑担子，
拖着疲累的生命，呻吟，流汗，
要不是怕一死就去了没有人回来的

那个从未发现的国土，怕那边
还不知会怎样，因此意志动摇了，
因此就宁愿忍受目前的灾殃，
而不愿投奔另一些未知的苦难？
这样子，顾虑使我们都成了懦夫，
也就这样了，决断决行的本色
蒙上了惨白的一层思虑的病容；
本可以轰轰烈烈的大作大为，
由于这一点想不通，就出了别扭，
失去了行动的名分。

（卞之琳　译）

All the World is a Stage[1]

It is one of the most frequently cited quotations in English literature, chosen from *As You Like It*, Act Ⅱ, Scene Ⅶ, Lines 139-166. By comparing the world to a stage, Shakespeare displays the essence of the world. Cf. Spenser's Sonnet 54: "Of this worlds theatre in which we stay, / My love like the spectator ydly sits / Beholding me that all pageants play, / Disguysing diversly my troubled wits." And Cf. *Macbeth*, V. v. 24-26: "Life's but a walking shadow, a poor player / That struts and frets his hour on the stage, / And then is heard no more."

All the world's a stage,
And all the men and women merely players:
They have their exits and their entrances;
And one man in his time plays many parts,
His acts being seven ages. At first, the infant,
Mewling and puking[2] in the nurse's arms.
Then the whining[3] school-boy, with his satchel[4]
And shining morning face, creeping like snail
Unwillingly to school. And then the lover,
Sighing like furnace, with a woeful ballad
Made to his mistress' eyebrow. Then a soldier,

Full of strange oaths and bearded like the pard[5],
Jealous in honour, sudden and quick in quarrel,
Seeking the bubble reputation[6]
Even in the cannon's mouth. And then the justice,
In fair round belly with good capon[7] lined,
With eyes severe and beard of formal cut,
Full of wise saws[8] and modern instances;
And so he plays his part. The sixth age shifts
Into the lean and slipper'd pantaloon[9],
With spectacles on nose and pouch on side;
His youthful hose, well saved, a world too wide
For his shrunk shank[10]; and his big manly voice,
Turning again toward childish treble, pipes
And whistles in his sound. Last scene of all,
That ends this strange eventful history,
Is second childishness and mere oblivion,
Sans[11] teeth, sans eyes, sans taste, sans everything.

Notes

1. It is written in blank verse. In *As You Like It*, the "melancholy" Jacques speaks these lines just before Orlando brings the good old man Adam onto stage.
2. Mewling and puking: crying and vomiting.
3. whining: complaining.
4. satchel: school bag.
5. bearded like the pard: having beards like a leopard. pard: leopard.
6. bubble reputation: reputation here is compared to a bubble.
7. capon: castrated rooster.
8. saws: proverbs.
9. pantaloon: a traditional image of the old man in the Italian comedies, here referring to the old age in its general sense.
10. shrunk shank: shrunk or thin leg.
11. Sans: without.

For Study and Discussion

1. Shakespeare divides human life into seven stages. What are they? Do you agree with his division?
2. Shakespeare compares the world to a stage, men and women mere players. Do you agree with his comparision? What attitude toward life is reflected in his comparison?
3. Find similar comparisons in Chinese poetry and compare them.

参考译文

全世界是一个舞台

全世界是一个舞台，
所有的男男女女不过是一些演员；
他们都有上场的时候，也都有下场的时候。
一个人的一生中扮演着好几个角色，
他的表演可以分为七个时期。最初是婴孩，
在保姆的怀中啼哭呕吐。
然后是背着书包、满脸红光的学童，像蜗牛一样
慢腾腾地拖着脚步，不情愿地呜咽着上学堂。然后是情人，
像炉灶一样叹着气，写了一首悲哀的诗
歌咏着他恋人的眉毛。然后是一个军人，
满口发着古怪的誓，胡须长得像豹子一样，
爱惜着名誉，动不动就要打架，
在炮口上寻求着
泡沫一样的荣名。然后是法官，
胖胖圆圆的肚子塞满了阉鸡，
凛然的眼光，整洁的胡须，
满嘴都是格言和老生常谈；
他这样扮了他的一个角色。第六个时期变成了
精瘦的趿着拖鞋的龙钟老叟，
鼻子上架着眼镜，腰边悬着钱袋；
他那年轻时候节省下来的长袜子套在他

皱瘪的小腿上显得宽大异常；他那朗朗的男子的口音
又变成了孩子似的尖声，像是吹着风笛和哨子。
终结着这段古怪的多事的历史的最后一场，
是孩提时代的再现，全然的遗忘，
没有牙齿，没有眼睛，没有口味，没有一切。

（朱生豪　译）

4. Ben Jonson

Ben Jonson（本·琼生，1572—1637）was one of the most outstanding figures in the literary world of the early 17th century. He was a man of versatility, a soldier, actor, playwright, poet and poet laureate, scholar, critic, translator, man of letter, and head of a literary "school", the so-called "sons of Ben"（the later Cavalier school of English poets like Robert Herrick, Thomas Carew, Sir John Suckling called themselves "sons of Ben" or the "Tribe of Ben" to show their worship toward Ben Jonson). In short, he was a giant.

His father died before he was born. He was brought up by a bricklayer and educated by the great classical scholar William Camden. After he returned from Flanders where he as a soldier fought against the Spaniards, he became an actor and playwright in 1595. His learning helped him to be pardoned after he killed a fellow actor. He had other troubles but rode them out. He grew mellower as he grew older and became in fact the unofficial literary dictator of London, the King's pensioned poet, a favorite around the court, and a good friend of men like Shakespeare, Donne, Francis Beaumont, John Selden, Francis Bacon, dukes, diplomats and distinguished folk generally.

Jonson's main dramatic works include *Every Man in His Humor*（1598）, a comedy of humors, *Sejanus*（1603）, a classical tragedy, *Volpone*（1606）and *The Alchemist*（1610）, two supreme satiric comedies of the English stage.

Besides being a dramatist, Ben Jonson was also a poet, though his poetry was certainly not his chief contribution to literature as his drama is. His poetry can be divided into five groups: poems of festive ceremony, poems in imitation of Horace with English tonality, elegies and epitaphs, compliments and tributes, and epigrams. Three books of his non-dramatic poetry were published. Among them, *The Epigrams* (1616) and *The Forest* (1616) were published in his lifetime, while the third one *The Underwood* (1640) was collected and published posthumously.

Ben Jonson was also very important as a critic. He advocated classicism, modeling on the old Greek and Roman masters, taking a firm stand for the three unities in play writing.

Song: To Celia[1]

This poem, which is chosen from *The Forest*, a small collection of 15 poems, has been set to music and considered one of the treasured love lyrics in the English language. The poet sings praise of Platonic love in this poem. It is famous for its fresh imagery of "eyes", "kiss" and "wreath". Here changing of eyes represents exchanging of love between lovers; lover's kiss is considered as a divine drink while a wreath of roses as the messenger of love.

Drink to me[2] only with thine[3] eyes,
And I will pledge[4] with mine;
Or leave a kiss but[5] in the cup,
And I'll not look for wine.
The thirst that from the soul doth[6] rise
Doth ask a drink divine[7]:
But might I of Jove's nectar sup[8],
I would not change for thine[9].

I sent thee late[10] a rosy wreath[11],
Not so much honoring thee,
As giving it a hope[12] that there
It could not withered be[13].
But thou thereon didst only breathe[14],
And sent'st[15] it back to me;

Since when[16] it grows and smells, I swear,
Not of itself, but thee[17].

1616

Notes

1. This is a patchwork of five separate prose passages in the "Epistles of Philostratus" by Philostratus, a Greek sophist (3rd century A. D.). Jonson reworded the phrases into this classic lyric, in the ballad metre (the usual form of the folk ballad and its literary imitations, a quatrain in which the first and third lines have four stresses while the second and fourth have three stresses, usually only the second and fourth lines rhyme. The rhythm is basically iambic.) This lyric is written in a single stanza of sixteen alternate 8-syllable and 6-syllable lines of iambic meter with the even lines rhymed.
2. Drink to me: drink a toast to me.
3. thine: your.
4. pledge: toast.
5. but: only.
6. doth: does.
7. The thirst that from the soul doth rise, /Doth ask a drink divine: the thirst from the soul rises and asks a divine drink. drink divine: divine drink.
8. might I of Jove's nectar sup: might I sup of Jove's nectar. might I: if I might. of: some of. Jove: Jupiter, ruler of gods and men in Roman mythology. nectar: the drink of gods. sup: sip.
9. I would not change for thine: I would not exchange Jove's nectar for your wine (because your wine is more precious to me). Cf. Song of Solomon 7:9 in the Bible: "and your kisses like the best wine…"
10. late: lately.
11. rosy wreath: wreath of roses.
12. Not so much honoring thee, /As giving it a hope: not honoring thee, but rather giving it a hope. honoring: in order to honor. it: rosy wreath.
13. that there/It could not withered be: that it could not be withered there. that-clause is the appositive of hope. there: with you.

14. But thou thereon didst only breathe: but if you only breathe on it. didst breathe: did breathe, in subjunctive mood. thereon: on it.
15. sent'st: sent, in subjunctive mood.
16. when: then.
17. Not of itself, but thee: not by itself, but because of you. Not of itself: not by itself. but thee: but because of you.

诗歌赏析

这首短诗《致西丽娅》选自本·琼生的诗集《森林》(1616)，堪称爱情诗的典范，写得纯情甜美，深受年轻人的青睐。其祝酒的意象用得巧妙又出奇，不乏玄学思维，耐人回味。有人曾给它谱曲，传唱至今。

和文艺复兴时期的一般爱情诗热情奔放，追逐现世享乐不同，这首爱情诗歌咏的是柏拉图式的精神恋爱。诗人一开头就和所爱之人用眼波来祝酒。在诗人看来，眼神的交换就是爱的传递，对方留在杯沿的一吻比美酒还要香醇。灵魂深处确实涌起渴望，想饮一杯玉液琼浆，但是就算能喝到天神的酒，诗人也不愿拿恋人的酒来交换。诗人接着用玫瑰花环来传递真情。这样的玫瑰花环不同于一般，不是用来赞美恋人，而是寄予希望，希望恋人能够赋予花环永不凋谢的神奇力量。但是恋人仅仅在花环上吹了一口气，就送还了诗人。从此后，玫瑰花有了恋人的芳香，并且同恋人一起成长。玫瑰花是爱情的象征，诗人想表达恋人的美貌会永远存在，他们的爱情也将永葆新鲜。

恋人之间的眉目传情、亲吻和玫瑰花都是俗世爱情的象征，但是在本·琼生笔下，俗世的爱情信物得到了升华，变得神圣、永恒。从物质到精神，从世俗到神圣，一个传统的诗歌主题和几个普普通通的意象见证了诗人化腐朽为神奇的力量。

For Study and Discussion

1. What kind of love is described in the poem?
2. How does the poet portray the kiss of his love, directly or indirectly?
3. How precious is Celia's wine?
4. How does the speaker expect Celia to drink to him? Can we say such imagination is conceit?
5. Learn this poem by heart.

参考译文

致西丽娅

用你的眼神为我祝酒，
我也用眼神为你祝福；
你留下一个吻在杯口，
我就不会把美酒当作口福。
灵魂深处升出的渴求
的确愿喝神圣的美酒：
但即使我能品尝朱威的甘醇，
我也不愿拿它与你这杯交换！

我最近赠你一玫瑰花环，
并非全是为了向你献媚，
也有为它祈福的心愿，
愿它永不凋谢枯萎。
但你只对它闻了闻，
之后又把它送回。
此后它茁壮成长，
散发出的只是你的芳香。

（李正栓　译）

5. John Donne

John Donne（约翰·邓恩，1572—1631）was born into an old Roman Catholic family. When young, he received education in a Catholic atmosphere. His father died when John was only four. Because of the relationship with the Catholicism on his mother's side, his family members were persecuted. At a time when anti-Catholic feeling in England was near its height, his faith in Catholicism barred him from success. He studied at Oxford and Cambridge University as well as Lincoln's Inn for six years, but he was never given any academic degree. His early life was passed in dissipation and roguery. But later he turned saintly. John Donne quietly abandoned Catholicism some time during the 1590's. But he did not become an Anglican until 1615 when Donne finally overcame his scruples and entered ministry.

Donne read enormously in divinity, medicine, law and the classics. He wrote to display his learning and wit. He made his way in the world by wit, charm, learning, valor, and above all favour. His traveling also enriched his experiences. He traveled on the continent, esp., to Spain. With Raleigh and Essex he took part in two hit-and-run expeditions against Cadix and the Azores.

In 1598, John Donne was appointed private secretary to Sir Thomas Egerton, the Lord Keeper. He could sit in Elizabeth's last parliament and move in court circles: he seemed to march well worldly. But in 1601 he secretly married Lady Egerton's niece, Ann More, who was then 16 years old. Sir George More had John Donne imprisoned and dismissed from his post.

For about a dozen of years, he struggled at a series of make-shift employments to support his growing family. The middle years of Donne's life were a period of searching, uncertainty, and unhappiness. In 1615, Donne took divine orders and was promptly appointed Reader in Divinity at Lincoln's Inn. He soon became a great preacher. In 1621, he was made Dean of St. Paul's. He wrote very good sermons and continued to write sacred poetry until the very end of his life.

The poetry of Donne represents a sharp break with that written by his predecessors and contemporaries. Much Elizabethan verse is decorative and flowery in its quality. Its images adorn, its meter mellifluous. Images harmonize with images, and line swells almost predictably into line. Donne's poetry, on the other hand, is written very largely in conceits — concentrated images which involve an element of dramatic contrast, of strain, or of intellectual difficulty. In Donne's love poetry, one can not see the traditional flower images, cheeks like roses, lips like cherries, teeth like pearls or Cupid shooting the arrows of love. Donne's conceits in particular leap continually in a restless orbit from the personal to the cosmic and back again.

Donne's rhythms are colloquial and various. He likes to twist distorted not only ideas, but metrical patterns and grammar itself, esp. in the satires. In the lyrics, elegies and sonnets, the verse never fails of a complex and memorable melody.

Donne and his followers are known in literary history as the Metaphysical poets. They refer to a diverse group of 17th-century English poets whose work is notable for its ingenious use of intellectual and theological concepts in surprising conceits, strange paradoxes and far-fetched imagery. The leading Metaphysical poet was John Donne, whose colloquial, argumentative abruptness of rhythm and tone distinguishes his style from the conventions of Elizabethan love lyrics. Other poets to whom the label is applied include Andrew Marvell, Abraham Cowley, John Cleveland and the predominantly religious poets George Herbert, Henry Vaughan and Richard Crashaw.

Metaphysical poetry gained revival after H. J. C. Grierson published Donne's complete poems in 1912. Grierson did a great deal to make Donne's poetry more available to the modern reader. Almost at once it started to exert an influence on modern poetic practice. T. S. Eliot and many other critics helped a lot to make Donne an acknowledged master.

A Valediction: Forbidding Mourning[1]

The poem reveals Donne's affirmation of the constancy and eternity of true love. He provides a striking contrast between the earthly love and the spiritual love, of which he sings high praise of the latter. It is a typical work of the Metaphysical poetry, full of original conception, reasoning and far-fetched imagery. The comparison of two lovers' souls to the two legs of a pair of compasses has become a famous example of conceits.

As virtuous men pass mildly away[2],
And whisper to their souls to go,
Whilst[3] some of their sad friends do say
The breath goes now, and some say, No;

So let us melt[4], and make no noise,

No tear-floods, nor sigh-tempests move[5];
'Twere profanation[6] of our joys
To tell the laity[7] our love.

Moving of th' earth brings harms and fears,
Men reckon what it did and meant;
But trepidation of the spheres,
Though greater far, is innocent.[8]

Dull sublunary[9] lovers' love
(Whose soul is sense[10]) cannot admit[11]
Absence, because it[12] doth remove
Those things which elemented[13] it[14].

But we, by a love so much refined[15]
That ourselves know not[16] what it is,
Inter-assured of the mind[17],
Care less, eyes, lips, and hands to miss[18].

Our two souls therefore, which are one,
Though I must go, endure not yet[19]
A breach[20], but an expansion,
Like gold to airy thinness beat[21].

If they be two[22], they are two so[23]
As stiff[24] twin compasses[25] are two;
Thy soul, the fixed foot[26], makes no show
To move, but doth, if th' other do[27].

And though it in the center sit[28],
Yet when the other far doth roam,
It leans and hearkens[29] after it,
And grows erect[30], as that comes home[31].

Such wilt thou be to me, who must,
Like th' other foot, obliquely run[32];
Thy firmness makes my circle just,
And makes me end where I begun[33].

1633

Notes

1. This poem is written in nine quatrains of iambic tetrameter rhyming abab. Izaak Walton speculated that this poem was addressed to Donne's wife on the occasion of his trip to the Continent in 1611, but there is no proof of that. Donne was, however, apprehensive about that trip. Walton also heard that, while abroad, Donne had a startling vision of his wife holding a dead baby at about the time she gave birth to a stillborn child. If this is true, no love poem can be better than this one throughout history. Valediction: a poem of farewell.
2. As virtuous men pass mildly away: the poet compares the parting of lovers to death of virtuous men. pass mildly away: die quietly.
3. Whilst: while.
4. let us melt: the poet expresses his idea that the two lovers are one once and again in this poem. melt: imagery of alchemy. Cf. Line 21: "Our two souls therefore, which are one."
5. No tear-floods, nor sigh-tempests move: stir up no tear-floods, no sigh-tempests. They are both signs of parting between earthly lovers. Here tears are compared to floods, while sigh is compared to tempests, which are typical Metaphysical conceits (referring to an unusually far-fetched or elaborate metaphor or simile presenting a surprising juxtaposition of two apparently dissimilar things or feelings). move: stir up.
6. 'Twere profanation: it were desecration. 'Twere: it were.
7. the laity: the laymen as opposed to the clergy.
8. Moving of… innocent: earthquakes harm and terrify human beings, but the shaking of the outermost sphere, though a much more violent motion is neither destructive nor sinister. Moving of th' earth: referring to earthquakes.

reckon: know. trepidation of the spheres: shaking of the outermost sphere in the Ptolemaic universe. innocent: harmless.

9. sublunary: beneath the moon, therefore earthly, sensual, and subject to change. Stanza 4 introduces the sublunary love.
10. Whose soul is sense: whose essence is the senses. The earthly love is based on the five senses, is physical. Whose: the earthly love's. soul: essence. sense: the senses.
11. admit: tolerate.
12. it: referring to absence.
13. elemented: composed.
14. it: referring to sublunary love.
15. a love so much refined: a love that is greatly purified, referring to the spiritual love. refined: purified, the imagery of alchemy. Stanzas 5 and 6 introduce the spiritual love contrasted to the sublunary love, which is physical.
16. know not: do not know.
17. Inter-assured of the mind: referring to the combination of their souls.
18. Care less, eyes, lips, and hands to miss: don't care about missing eyes, lips, and hands. The normal order is "Care less to miss eyes, lips and hands". They enjoy a love (the spiritual love) which is so much refined that even though they don't know what it is, their spirits are mingled together, so they don't care about missing eyes, lips, and hands, which are symbols of earthly love.
19. endure not yet: yet do not suffer.
20. breach: breaking.
21. Like gold to airy thinness beat: like gold beat (=beaten) to airy thinness. Beaten gold, another image of alchemy, is also a famous Metaphysical conceit.
22. If they be two: Even though the lovers' souls be two. For the first time in this poem, the poet admits the two lovers may have two souls rather than one.
23. so: in such a way.
24. stiff: firm.

25. twin compasses: the two legs of a geometer's or draftsman's compasses, with which one draws circles. This simile is the most famous example of the Metaphysical conceits.
26. the fixed foot: the leg of compasses which is fixed.
27. but doth, if th' other do: but does move, if the other foot moves. doth: does. Th' other: the other foot, referring to the poet's soul.
28. though it in the center sit: though it sit in the center.
29. hearkens: listens.
30. erect: straight.
31. as that comes home: a pun, one meaning is when that foot comes back, the other is when the poet gets back home. In Stanza 8, the two legs of compasses draw circles together and go back to the original point at last. "Circle" represents consummation and eternity, which are the highest stage of love.
32. obliquely run: run aslant.
33. Thy firmness makes my circle just, /And makes me end where I begun: your firmness makes my circle full and makes me end where I began. Our mutual efforts make a full circle, which means the consummation and eternity of love are attained by mutual efforts of the two lovers. firmness: pun, one meaning is the firmness of the compass foot, the other is the constancy of the lover. just: full. begun: began.

诗歌赏析

奇思妙喻（conceit，亦译“奇喻”、“奇想怪喻”、“奇思妙想”）和似非而是的修辞（paradox）是邓恩诗歌的主要特点。新批评派从中汲取很多营养。邓恩运用奇思妙喻的最典型例子是《告别词：莫伤悲》中的圆规意象。这是邓恩于1611年出使巴黎前写给妻子Anne More的一首离别诗。

诗人在这首诗中用圆规的意象来形容忠贞不渝的爱情，将两个相爱的人比作圆规的两只脚，爱是基点。妻子守在家中，好比不动的圆心脚，而丈夫游走四方，为生活奔忙，恰似旋转不定的圆周脚。诗人用圆规紧紧相连的双脚，形象地比喻了夫妻福祸相倚、密不可分的关系，两者是统一的整体。家中的妻子是丈夫的牵挂，妻子的坚贞是丈夫的动力。丈夫无论离家多久，总是要返回妻子温暖的港湾，正如圆周脚画了一个圆后，还是返回起点，与圆心脚汇合。这个比喻给人耳目一新的感觉，乍一听，有点突兀，细想起来却很合逻辑，令人拍案叫绝。圆规的意象已成为玄学派奇想妙喻的经典。这首诗中的另一个意象也很经典："我们俩的灵魂溶成了一片，/尽管我走了，却不会破裂，/这种分离不过是一种延展，/像黄金打成了轻柔无形的薄页。"在这里，邓恩把夫妻之爱比作黄金，形容感情之纯；一时的分离只是爱情的延展，就像黄金被锻打成绵薄的金页，虽状似无形却紧紧相连。诗人还把眼泪比作洪水，叹息比作风暴，这种夸张的比喻显然受到了彼特拉克式诗风的影响。

For Study and Discussion

1. Comment on the relation of the various images to one another. Is there a development of some kind?
2. In what way could we say it is a representative work of the metaphysical poetry?
3. How do conceits contribute to the argument in this poem?
4. There is a central contrast in this poem between two kinds of love. What are they? What are their differences?

参考译文

告别词：莫伤悲

有德之人逝世，十分安详，
对自己的灵魂轻轻说，走，
这时候，一些悲伤的亲友讲，
他气息已断，有些说，还没有。

让我们熔化吧，默默无语，
不要泪流如洪水，叹息似风暴，
那将会亵渎我们的欢愉——
要是让我们的爱情被俗人知道。

地震带来恐惧和灾祸，
人们谈论它的含义和危害，
天体的震动虽然大得多，
对人类却没有丝毫的伤害。

世俗的恋人之爱
(它的本质是肉感)不允许
离别，因为离别意味着破坏
凡俗之爱的基本根据。

但我们经过提炼的爱情，
它是什么连我们自己也一无所知，
我们既然彼此信赖，心心相印，
对眼、唇、手就漠然视之。

我们俩的灵魂溶成了一片，
尽管我走了，却不会破裂，
这种分离不过是一种延展，
像黄金打成了轻柔无形的薄页。

我们的灵魂即便是两个，
那也和圆规的两只脚相同，
你的灵魂是圆心脚，没有任何
动的迹象，另只脚移了，它才动。

这只脚虽然在中心坐定，
如果另只脚渐渐远离，
它便倾斜着身子侧耳倾听，
待到另只脚归返，它就直立。

对于我，你就是这样；我像另只脚，
必须倾斜着身子转圈，
你坚定，我的圆才能画得好，
我才能终止在出发的地点。

(胡家峦 译)

The Flea[1]

This is one of Donne's famous poems, a representative work of metaphysical poetry. It describes the "physical love" with bold expression. The speaker is calm, trying to persuade the girl by using the image of marriage. Some critics say its theme is a kind of Carpe diem tradition. This poem is most famous for its conceit, which sounds far-fetched but reasonable and interesting when you think about it carefully. In sharp contrast to conventional Petrarchism, this poem uses a flea that has bitten both the man and the girl as the basic reference for its argument against the girls's resistance to the man. In common sense, the flea is a disgusting small, ugly insect. But in Donne's eyes, it is a symbol of love, a holy thing, a very sacred place in which a man and a girl are married. This image is bold, irritating but beautiful. This poem is full of dramatic quality. Donne also shows his powerful ability of reasoning in the poem.

Mark but this flea[2], and mark in this[3],
How little that which thou deniest me is[4];
Me it sucked first[5], and now sucks thee,
And in this flea our two bloods mingled be[6];
Thou know'st that this[7] cannot be said
A sin, or shame, or loss of maidenhead[8],
Yet this enjoys before it woo[9],
And pampered swells[10] with one blood made of two,
And this, alas, is more than we would do[11].

Oh stay[12], three lives in one flea spare[13],
Where we almost, nay more than married are[14].
This flea is you and I[15], and this
Our marriage bed and marriage temple is[16];
Though parents grudge[17], and you, we are met,
And cloistered[18] in these living walls of jet[19].
Though use make you apt to kill me[20],
Let not to that, self-murder added be,
And sacrilege[21], three sins in killing three[22].

Cruel and sudden, hast thou since
Purpled thy nail[23] in blood of innocence[24]?
Wherein[25] could this flea guilty be,

Except in that drop which it sucked from thee?
Yet thou triumph'st, and say'st that thou
Findst not thy self nor me the weaker now[26];
'Tis true; then learn how false fears be[27]:
Just so much honor, when thou yield'st to me,
Will waste, as this flea's death took life from thee.[28]

1633

Notes

1. This poem is chosen from *Songs and Sonnets* (《歌与短歌集》). It is written in three 9-line stanzas rhyming aabbccddd. Donne's love poems were written over nearly two decades, beginning around 1595. They were not published in Donne's lifetime but circulated widely in manuscript. The title *Songs and Sonnets* was supplied in the second edition (1635), which grouped the poems by kind, but neither this arrangement nor the more haphazard organization of the first edition (1633) is Donne's own.
2. Mark but this flea: only look at this flea. mark: look at, notice. but: only. flea: this insect afforded a popular erotic theme for poets all over Europe, deriving from a pseudo-Ovidian medieval poem in which a lover envies the flea for the liberties it takes with his mistress' body. The flea travels on the body of the female and comments on whatever it sees including the private parts.
3. mark in this: see in this flea. mark: see, notice. this: this flea.
4. How little that which thou deniest me is: how little what you deny me is. thou deniest: you deny.
5. Me it sucked first: It sucked me first. Donne is playing with words. At that time, "s" and "f" were spelt the same way.
6. in this flea our two bloods mingled be: our two bloods are mixed in this flea. Here it implies the mingling of bodies. mingled: mixed.
7. this: referring to the mingling of two bloods in the flea's body.
8. maidenhead: virginity.
9. before it woo: before it makes a proposal.
10. pampered swells: the flea's belly became bigger. It suggests pregnancy

here. pampered: overfed.

11. And this, alas, is more than we would do: we, alas, don't dare to hope for this consummation of our love, nevertheless, the flea accepts it freely.
12. stay: stop. Something happened between the first and second stanza. The girl caught the flea. This is quite like the scenes in plays when a person tries to save another one from death by shouting "刀下留人".
13. spare: save.
14. nay more than married are: we enjoy greater pleasures than those we can have after marriage. nay: or rather.
15. This flea is you and I: this flea is the symbol of our combination.
16. this/Our marriage bed and marriage temple is: this is our marriage bed and marriage temple. It is a metaphor. Here the flea's body is described as a very sacred place.
17. grudge: are unwilling.
18. cloistered: secluded as in a convent or monastery.
19. living walls of jet: black body of the flea. jet: black.
20. Though use make you apt to kill me: though custom makes you kill me by denying me sexual gratification. use: customs. apt to: inclined to.
21. sacrilege: disrespect to God.
22. three sins in killing three: the girl will commit three sins (murder, self-murder and sacrilege) in killing "I" (the speaker), yourself (the girl) and the flea.
23. Purpled thy nail: make your nail purple by killing the flea. In Lines 19-20, the girl has killed the flea, and her nail is made purple.
24. blood of innocence: it means the flea is innocent.
25. Wherein: in which respect.
26. Yet thou triumph'st, and say'st that thou / Findst not thy self nor me the weaker now: but you are the winner, and say that you don't find both you and me weaker than before (after killing the flea).
27. learn how false fears be: know how false the fears shown by the girls are. In some versions, "fears" are written as "tears".
28. Just so much honor, when thou yield'st to me, / Will waste, as this flea's death took life from thee: just so much honor will be useless since this

flea's death also takes the lives of both the man spaker and the girl.

诗歌赏析

邓恩运用奇思妙喻的另一个典型例子是《跳蚤》（*The Flea*）一诗。这首诗以跳蚤入诗，极富推理。全诗以口语体对话形式展开，就像一部三幕剧。诗中的说话人是一位男子，他想与他的恋人进一步温存，却遭到了她的拒绝。诗人便展开想象的翅膀，用玄学比喻，使诗中女子再也无法拒绝他们是一体的：他们化作跳蚤，跳蚤是他们的温床和殿堂，连跳蚤被杀也等同于他们失去生命。意象之奇特，想象之大胆，效果之绝妙，除邓恩别无二人能做此想。

For Study and Discussion

1. What does the image "the flea" signify? Do you think it is natural to connect love with a flea?
2. What is special about this image? How is it different from that of other love poems? Make some comparisons if you can.
3. Some critics say it is an erotic poem. What is your opinion?
4. What kind of love is described in the poem?
5. What is the tone of the speaker in the last stanza?
6. Learn the first stanza by heart.
7. Find as many articles commenting on this poem as you can.

参考译文

跳　蚤

你看吧，你看看这跳蚤，
你否认我的成分能有多少？
它先咬了我，此刻又咬了你，
我俩的血已在它里边融为一体；
要承认，这件事不能被说成是羞耻，
或罪过，也算不上你贞操的损失，
而它却未求婚就先得快意，
合我俩的血为一体，涨大它的腹肌，

唉，它做得远远超过我们自己。

啊，住手，饶过这跳蚤里的三个生命。
在它体内，我们不止是结了婚，
它是你是我，是我们的花烛温床，
是我们婚姻的殿堂；
尽管父母和你都不愿意，我们还是聚在一起。
同居于这乌黑的活墙里。
尽管习俗使你轻易杀我，
但不要把三个生命剥夺，
不要再加上自杀和渎圣的罪过。

你突然狠心地把毒手下，
用无辜者的血染紫了你的指甲？
这跳蚤只吸过你一口血，
这怎能算作一种罪过？
而你却得意洋洋地说：
你和我都不比从前弱；
不错，我因此全知：说你害怕是多么虚假！
你此时同意我，但跳蚤之死已把你生命夺下。
多少的道义全都浪费、白搭。

（李正栓　译）

from *Holy Sonnets*[1]

10

It is a representative work of Donne's religious poetry. The poem reveals the poet's belief in the triumph of resurrection over death. The speaker is addressing Death. His attitude is bold and defiant as he challenges Death's almighty power. Death is but a bodily rest. The soul exists forever. He is not afraid of it. In this poem, Death is not so powerful and terrifying as in the conventional poetry. Instead, Death himself shall die. It is another typical work of the Metaphysical poetry.

Death[2], be not proud, though some have called thee

Mighty and dreadful[3], for thou art[4] not so;
For those whom thou think'st thou dost[5] overthrow
Die not, poor Death, nor yet canst[6] thou kill me.
From rest and sleep, which but thy pictures be,
Much pleasure; then from thee much more must flow,[7]
And soonest our best men with thee do go,[8]
Rest of their bones, and soul's delivery.[9]
Thou art slave to fate, chance, kings, and desperate men,[10]
And dost with poison, war, and sickness dwell,[11]
And poppy or charms[12] can make us sleep as well
And better[13] than thy stroke[14]; why swell'st thou then[15]?
One short sleep past, we wake eternally
And death shall be no more; Death, thou shalt die.[16]

1633

Notes

1. This is chosen from *Holy Sonnets*, which consists of 26 religious sonnets. It is John Donne who broadened the sonnet into Religious themes, which is his great contribution to English poetry. This is a sonnet in the Petrachan pattern with the rhyme scheme of abbaabba cddcef.
2. Death: God of death.
3. Mighty and dreadful: powerful and terrible.
4. thou art: you are.
5. thou dost: you do.
6. canst: can.
7. From rest and sleep, which but thy pictures be, /Much pleasure; then from thee much more must flow: since much pleasure flow from rest and sleep, which are only your pictures, much more pleasure must flow from you (Death). which but thy pictures be: which are only your pictures. Cf. Act Ⅲ, Scene I in *Hamlet*: "To die, —to sleep, —No more."
8. soonest our best men with thee do go: our best men die soon. It is an idea that originated from a Greek proverb translated by Plautus: "Whom the gods love die young." with thee do go: die.

9. Rest of their bones, and soul's delivery: (death is) rest for their bones, and delivery for their souls. delivery: freedom. After death, they will have physical rest; their soul will be free from human troubles and enjoy freedom.
10. Thou art slave to fate, chance, kings, and desperate men: Death, you are controlled by destiny, opportunities, kings and lawless men who do things regardless of anything.
11. And dost with poison, war, and sickness dwell: and live with poison, war, and sickness. This line further illustrates the poet's idea that Death is not so powerful and terrifying. dost: do.
12. poppy or charms: opium or magic spells.
13. better: easier.
14. stroke: strike; attack.
15. why swell'st thou then?: why are you proud? swell'st: swell, puff with pride.
16. One short sleep past, … thou shalt die: shortly after we die, we will wake up and live forever. We shall have no death. Death, you shall die. It's a famous paradox. Be no more: die. Cf. Shakespeare's Sonnet 146: "So shalt thou feed on death, that feeds on men, /And death once dead, there's no more dying then."（于是，你将吃掉以人为食的死神，/ 死神一死，世上就不再有死亡发生。）

诗歌赏析

邓恩开辟了 17 世纪英国玄学派诗人包括赫伯特、克拉肖、沃恩在内写宗教诗的传统。邓恩的宗教诗包括 26 首《神圣十四行诗》和一些长诗。这些诗充满复杂难解的说理和心底的疑惑与恐惧，理性的分析和情感的宣泄奇特地结合在一起。似非而是的修辞是邓恩诗歌的特点之一。它是一种看似矛盾，其实逻辑合理、蕴意深厚的表达方式。这首诗是邓恩宗教诗的经典。最后一句"睡了一小觉之后，/我们便永远觉醒了，/再也不会有死亡，/你死神也将死去"使用似非而是的修辞方法，展示了邓恩对死亡的独到见解。死亡是暂时的，肉体死亡，而精神永生。

For Study and Discussion

1. What is the poet's belief in life after death? What did he compare death to?
2. Is Death mighty and powerful? Why yes? Why no?
3. Who is the listener of the speech made by the poet (speaker)?
4. In what way is this sonnet a work of the Metaphysical poetry?
5. Explain the paradox in the last two lines of this sonnet.

参考译文

死神你莫骄傲

死神，你莫骄傲，尽管有人说你
如何强大，如何可怕，你并不是这样；
你以为你把谁谁谁打倒了，其实，
可怜的死神，他们没死；你现在也还杀不死我。
休息、睡眠，这些不过是你的写照，
既能给人享受，那你本人提供的一定更多；
我们最美好的人随你去得越早，
越能早日获得身体的休息，灵魂的解脱。
你是命运、机会、君主、亡命徒的奴隶，
你和毒药、战争、疾病同住在一起，
罂粟与符咒和你的打击相比，同样，
甚至更能催我入睡；那你何必趾高气扬呢？
睡了一小觉之后，我们便永远觉醒了，
再也不会有死亡，你死神也将死去。

（杨周翰　译）

6. Robert Herrick

Robert Herrick (罗伯特·赫里克, 1591—1674), son of a prosperous London goldsmith, is thought to be the happiest of English poets. He attended Cambridge University where he received his B. A. in 1617 and his M. A. in 1620. He liked literature better than anything else, preferring to talk about literature and drink with Ben Jonson while polishing his verses. But under social pressure, he took orders in the church and moved unwillingly to Devonshire in the rough West Country.

He secreted poems as a hen laid eggs, making playful verses out of his pets, pleasures and momentary peeves. Paganism, which the Puritans did not quite notice at first, was a recurrent theme in his verses. At the top of his poetic bent, in "Corinna's Going A-Maying", Herrick produced a major lyric on the central theme of his life, the happy reconciliation of nature and nature's god.

In the storm of the Civil War, the Puritans dispossessed him. Then he went to London and published his poems in 1648. For the secular poems he entitled them as *Hesperides*, and for the sacred ones *Noble Numbers*. Because of the fatness of this volume containing 1200 poems, it was neglected, not to be restored to English literature till the 19th century. When King Charles came to power in 1660, his religious position was restored which brought him back to Dean Prior, where he first went and finally lived out his last years quietly until his death at the age of 83.

For him as well as Ben Jonson, life was a sacrament. Herrick brought to that sometimes portentous view of things a modesty and sense of proportion that are uniquely his own. Herrick was not directly concerned with the deeper questions of life. He customarily took up a light, even whimsical subject, and articulated his response to it with a delicate warmth and sureness of touch. The refinement of his poetic craftsmanship always reminds one of his early associations with the art of the jeweler and the goldsmith. His best poems are like richly worked miniatures. They give us that special pleasure of contemplating the small thing incomparably well.

Herrick belongs to the Cavalier poets, a group of English lyric poets who were active, approximately, during the reign of Charles I. This group includes Richard Lovelace, Sir John Suckling, Robert Herrick, Thomas Carew, and Waller. These poets virtually abandoned the sonnet form which had been the favoured medium for love poems for a century. They were considerably influenced by Ben Jonson. Their lyrics are light, witty, and elegant, for the most part, concerned with love. They show much technical virtuosity. Herrick's "To the Virgins, to Make Much of Time" is one of their good examples.

To the Virgins, to Make Much of Time[1]

The theme of this poem, "live for today" or "seize the day", belongs to a tradition known as "Carpe Diem" dating back to classical Greek and Latin poetry and particularly popular among the English Cavalier poets. The Carpe Diem theme is epitomized in the first line "Gather ye rosebuds while ye may" of the poem. It reflects on the brevity of life and the need to live for the moment.

Gather ye rosebuds while ye may,[2]
Old time is still a-flying;[3]
And this same flower that smiles today,
Tomorrow will be dying.[4]

The glorious lamp of heaven[5], the sun,
The higher he's a-getting[6],
The sooner will his race be run[7],
And nearer he's to setting[8].

That age is best which is the first,[9]
When youth and blood are warmer;[10]
But being spent, the worse, and worst
Times still succeed the former.[11]

Then be not coy[12], but use your time[13],
And while ye may, go marry[14];
For having lost but once[15] your prime[16],
You may forever tarry[17].

Notes

1. It is written in four quatrains of iambic lines with alternate 4 and 3 feet

rhyming abab while the odd lines have masculine rhymes and the even feminine. Virgins: maids. to Make Much of Time: to make good use of time.

2. Gather ye rosebuds while ye may: you should pick rosebuds while you have the opportunity. Gather: pick. ye: you. It is a famous line to show the Carpe Diem theme in Cavalier poetry. The first stanza implies the transience of time and beauty.
3. Old time is still a-flying: old time is always flying. still: always. a-flying: flying.

   Cf. Shakespeare's Sonnet 60: "Like as the waves make towards the pebbled shore, / So do our minutes hasten to their end, / Each changing place with that which goes before; / In sequent toil all forwards do contend." 宛如不息滔滔长波拍岸，/ 我们分分秒秒匆匆奔赴向前。/ 后浪推前浪，今天接明天，/ 奋发趋行，你争我赶。
4. This same flower that smiles today, /Tomorrow will be dying: Cf. Shelley's "Mutability": "The flower that smiles today/Tomorrow dies; /All that we wish to stay/Tempts and then flies."
5. The glorious lamp of heaven: a metaphor, referring to the sun.
6. a-getting: getting.
7. his race be run: finish the sun's race. Sun has a race every day.
8. nearer he's to setting: he is nearer to setting. In the second stanza, Herrick compares the journey of life to that of sun. Cf. Shakespeare's Sonnet 7:

And having climbed the steep-up heavenly hill,
Resembling strong youth in his middle age,
...
But when from highmost pitch, with weary car,
Like feeble age he reeleth from the day.
瞧它登上了陡峭的天峰，
宛如正当盛年的年轻人，
……
但当随倦乏的车辇越过了高峰，
他渐渐在远离白昼，如老迈之人。

Cf. Shakespeare's Sonnet 15: "at height decrease".

9. That age is best which is the first: that age which is the first is best, here referring to youth.
10. When youth and blood are warmer: when you are still young and enthusiastic.
11. But being spent, the worse, and worst / Times still succeed the former: but once (the youth) being spent, the later life, which always takes place of the former, will be worse and worse. still: always. The brevity of youth is introduced in the third stanza.
12. coy: shy.
13. use your time: make good use of your time.
14. go marry: go happy, enjoy yourself.
15. but once: just once.
16. prime: the best time of your life, youth.
17. tarry: delay. After three stanzas' persuasion, the poet suggests living for the present, echoing the theme in the first line of the poem. Cf. Spenser's Sonnet 70: Make hast therefore sweet love, whilest it is prime, /For none can call again the pass'ed time. 赶快吧，亲爱的，趁着春色尚在，/逝去的时光，谁也不能召回来。

诗歌赏析

《劝少女们利用好时光》是罗伯特·赫里克流传最广的诗，与马维尔的《致羞涩的姑娘》一诗主题相同，都是劝告人们趁青春年少，及时行乐，不过表现得更直接、更明白。与此意境相同的还有我国唐代杜秋娘的《金缕衣》："劝君莫惜金缕衣，劝君惜取少年时。花开堪折直须折，莫待无花空折枝。"李白也在他的《将进酒》中表达了同样的意愿："人生得意须尽欢，莫使金樽空对月。天生我材必有用，千金散尽还复来。"

这首诗篇幅短小，结构简单，但主题明确，逻辑严谨，很有说服力。前两个诗节分别用鲜花和太阳两个意象告诉我们盛开的花朵绚丽芬芳，终会凋谢；正午的太阳光彩夺目，终会西沉；第三节归结到人。人跟自然界的花儿和太阳一样，年轻时，风华正茂，血气方刚，但青春易逝，岁月无情。最后一节直奔主题，劝告少女们尽情享受爱情的甜蜜，莫要羞羞答答，因为红颜易老，时不我待。

“及时行乐”的主题已在无数诗人笔下演绎出万种风情，但赫里克这首《劝少女们利用好时光》因其言简意赅，清新明快，给人留下了美好的印象。

For Study and Discussion

1. The theme of this poem, “live for today”, belongs to a tradition known as “seize the day” that was typically Cavalier. Which lines in this poem best summarize this theme?

2. How do the images in this poem help convey the theme?

3. What is the tone of the poem?

4. Please name some other poems with the same idea either in English or Chinese poetry.

参考译文

劝少女们利用好时光

花开堪折直须折，
时光老人总飞驰；
今日花笑同一朵，
明日笑容会消逝。

太阳华灯天上悬，
越近高处路越短；
路程终点越临近，
越见匆匆向西沉。

青春年华最美好，
血气方刚热情高；
青春年华若虚度，
剩余时光失美妙。

故抓时间别羞怯，
能得悦时及时悦；
一旦错过好年华，
千古遗憾悔成河。

（李正栓　译）

7. George Herbert

George Herbert（乔治·赫伯特，1593－1633）was a religious poet of the Metaphysical school. He was born in a distinguished Welsh family. His father died when he was young. He was brought up by his mother, Magdalen Herbert, a friend of John Donne, and a lady eminent both for her piety and her love of letters.

George Herbert took his degrees with distinction at the University of Cambridge. His distinguished career resulted in his being elected Public Orator of the University which put him in a position to rise to high public office or to a prominent place at court. But he did not use his position as a stepping stone. He decided instead to become a minister. In 1626 he took a minor office in the church; in 1629 he married Jane Danvers; in 1630 he accepted the living of Bemerton near Salisbury; in 1633 he died there of consumption. Shortly after his death his volume of poems known as *The Temple*, which he completed and arranged during the three years of his ministry, was published by the friend to whom it had been left. His fame rests on this volume.

Herbert's poetry is quiet, graceful and neat. His argument and imagery are less dazzling than Donne's. His religious verse is full of resignation, humility and wise obedience. Herbert frequently makes use of emblematic images — verbal pictures or figures with a long tradition of moral or religious meaning attached to them. Herbert is never flashy, nor even strongly dramatic. The ancient forms are Herbert's chief delight. His poetry is always fresh, rich in traditional designs, open for the humblest person to enter. No matter what simplicity and directness Herbert shows, he is never short of a curious elaboration of expression, a deliberate juxtaposition of concepts and of images, an omission of logical steps, and a witty shift of tone. And these make up of the particular feature of Herbert's art and can be best exemplified in his sweetest song "Virtue".

Virtue[1]

The poet sings praise of good morality in the poem. In his view, all the things will die, only a sweet and virtuous soul can exist forever in the world. This poem conveys the most fantastic thoughts in the most concise and natural language, with clear structure and vivid images. Contrasted to the concept that all will die in the first three stanzas, the immortality of virtuous soul is revealed as its theme in the last stanza. Starting at a low pitch Herbert reaches the emotional climax at the end of the poem. Its language is repetitive, and its structure similar, but with an enriching of meaning at each image, this lyric is thus both plain and intense, clear on the first reading and yet densely packed with layers of meaning.

Sweet day, so cool, so calm, so bright,
The bridal[2] of the earth and sky:
The dew shall weep thy fall tonight,
For thou must die[3].

Sweet rose, whose hue, angry[4] and brave[5],
Bids the rash gazer wipe his eye[6]:
Thy root is ever in its grave,
And thou must die[7].

Sweet spring, full of sweet days and roses,
A box where sweets compacted lie[8];
My music[9] shows ye[10] have your closes[11],
And all must die[12].

Only a sweet and virtuous soul,
Like seasoned timber[13], never gives[14];
But though[15] the whole world turn to coal[16],
Then chiefly lives[17].

Notes

1. This poem is written in four quatrains rhyming abab. In each quatrain the first three lines are of 8 syllables while the last line is iambic dimeter. This is learned from Sappho, a famous lyric poet in 6th century B. C. In form, it is similar to a Chinese form called "三句半" (three sentences and a half). This short and exquisite poem probably is the best known of all his verses. Many succeeding poets have imitated "Virtue", but not one has excelled the original, nor can the English tongue produce a more exquisite passage than the few lines.
2. bridal: wedding. It's a metaphor; the poet compares the sweet day to the wedding of the earth and sky.
3. For thou must die: refrain of the first three stanzas with slight variations. In the first stanza, the poet puts forward an image of "sweet day" that will die.
4. angry: having the hue of anger, red.
5. brave: splendid, magnificent.
6. Bids the rash gazer wipe his eye: compels the rash gazer wipe his eye (to see you clearly). Bids: compels. the rash gazer: the impetuous men who look attentively (at the sweet rose).
7. And thou must die: in the second stanza, the poet uses an image of "sweet rose," another beauty in nature, to show it also will die.
8. A box where sweets compacted lie: a box full of perfumes. It is another metaphor; the poet compares the sweet spring to a box full of perfumes. sweets: perfumes. compacted: closely packed.
9. My music: my poem.
10. ye: you. Here it means the sweet spring.
11. closes: a musical term, concluding cadences in music. This expresses that Herbert intended his poem to be sung, as it has often been.
12. And all must die: In the third stanza, the poet uses the image of "sweet spring" that holds the beautiful images in the first two stanzas to show all beautiful things in the world will die.
13. seasoned timber: dried wood. The poet compares a sweet and virtuous soul

to seasoned timber, the best fuel. Obviously "seasoned timber" represents the wooden cross on which the Lord Jesus was nailed and put to death on Mount Calvary. Herbert sings high praise of "a sweet and virtuous soul". By likening "a sweet and virtuous soul" to "seasoned timber", he wishes that man with virtue could "chiefly live" as the cross of Christ that can get resurrection with Jesus. Herbert's "seasoned timber" offers a shock not because the simile is particularly original but because, unexpectedly, it juxtaposes the world of religion and the world of secularity.

14. gives: bends.

15. though: even though.

16. turn to coal: disappear, will be reduced to ashes at the Last Judgment. Cf. 2 Peter 3: 10 in New Testament: "But the day of the Lord will come like a thief, and then the heavens will pass away with a loud noise, and the elements will be dissolved with the fire, and the earth and everything that is done on it will be disclosed." coal: ashes.

17. chiefly lives: the subject is "a sweet and virtuous soul." Only a sweet and virtuous soul will live for ever. The title of this poem is "Virtue", but the poet does not mention it until the last stanza. It is typical of Herbert's style.

诗歌赏析

乔治·赫伯特，英国17世纪著名的宗教诗人、教士，生于一个古老而有威望的威尔士家族，毕业于剑桥大学。主要作品有宗教诗集《圣殿》（*The Temple*, 1633）。其中这首《美德》语调舒缓，文字浅显，但优美动人，蕴意深刻。

第一节写良辰。诗人在第一节开篇歌颂了白日的可爱：凉爽、明朗、静谧，是白日把天与地婚配成双。白日是新的开始，预示着希望，婚姻既暗指处子的纯洁又预示着新生。多么富有光明和希冀的景象啊！然而黑夜终将来临，露珠已开始为白日的陨落而哭泣，昼与夜、明与暗、天与地以及存在与消亡的对比也于无形中展开。

第二节写美景。诗人在第二节首先赞美了盛开的玫瑰花，它的美丽明艳动人，连莽撞的路人也驻足观望，拭目以待。但紧接着指出芬芳的玫瑰植根于坟墓，注定要消亡。这本身是一个奇喻。坟墓是死亡的象征。死亡孕育了生命，生命又注定要消亡，死死生生，生生死死，循环往复，以至无穷。它告诉我们生存和死亡相依相伴，密不可分，有生存就有死亡，这就是轮回，无法逃避。诗人也许想用芬芳艳丽的花朵象征火热的青春、创作的激情，然而岁月会洗刷所有粉饰，褪去一切铅华，死亡即是宿命。

第三节写包含良辰美景的春天。前面写了骄人的白昼和怒放的玫瑰都将消亡，那么世间其他事物呢？第三节做出了总结——可爱的春天犹如一个容器，盛满良辰和玫瑰，蕴藏着世间一切美好，然而它也逃不出“万物皆有尽”的自然规律，也会死亡。因为“我的音乐显示你也有终有尾”，所有的音乐都是跌宕起伏，有始有终的，再华美的乐章也有结尾。诗人在此得出结论：“世间一切都会死亡。”诗歌到这里仿佛可以结束了，有了完整的阐述、铺垫、展开和结论。然而，本诗的题目“美德”体现在哪里呢？

前三节尽是铺叙，最后一节才是真谛。诗人在最后一节点出了主题：“只有美好有德的灵魂，/像焙干的木材永不变形，/纵然是整个世界化为灰烬，/它仍然长存、永生。”这句诗引用了《圣经》中《新约·彼得后书》的寓言，到了最后审判日，一场大火会将一切烧毁，世界上的万物都会消失殆尽。但诗人认为美好有德的灵魂会永存不灭，即使世界末日的大火也无可奈何。赫伯特把美好有德的灵魂比作焙干的木材，颇具玄学派特色，很有创造性。灵魂怎能和木头相比呢？精神和物质又怎能相提并论？美好有德的灵魂让人肃然起敬，而木头只给人带来冰冷、生硬的感觉。但细细品味，竟是那样妥帖、契合。焙干的木材是最好的木料，坚韧、淳厚、永不变形，比喻美好有德的灵魂经过岁月的累积、生活的历练，历久弥坚，散发出恒久的光彩。诗人带着藐视一切的神气，将虔诚的心灵与整个世界相比，整个世界最后会化为灰烬，而美好有德的灵魂仍然长存、永生。如果说前三个诗节颂扬了大自然的美丽，哀悼了世上一切美好事物的最终凋亡，那么，最后一个诗节诗人将前三节的结论完全推翻，由死到生，从自然的美升华到灵魂的美，从物质美的灭亡到精神美的永生，达到全诗高潮。

诗人用白日、玫瑰、春天和干木这四个意象揭示了本诗的主题，告诉我们一个信念：世间万物，无论怎样奇丽芬芳，总不免消亡，唯美好有德的灵魂永存。《美德》的语言直白平易，意象清晰明了，结构简单重复。然而，看似简单的四个诗节每节都有矛盾，最后一节又与前三节形成矛盾，外弛而内张——前三节说明可爱的白日会被黑夜替代，芬芳的玫瑰终会凋谢，蕴藏一切美好的春天也会随季节的交替而逝去，揭示和印证了“万物皆有尽”的自然规律，好像与主题背道而驰。最后一节说明世间万物都会消亡，唯有美好有德的灵魂长存。深刻的蕴意在诗节之间相互印照、层层展现。

For Study and Discussion

1. In the last stanza, the poet compares the "sweet and virtuous" soul to "seasoned timber." Why is this image an effective one for the soul? How is this image related to the images of "rose" and "spring" used earlier in the poem?
2. Point out the poetic devices in the poem.
3. Analyze the structure of this poem. Where is the climax of this poem?
4. Explain how the poet reaches his goal by the successful use of four images "day", "rose", "spring" and "seasoned timber". Which one do you think is the most vivid and startling? Why?
5. Which stanza do you like best? Learn it by heart.

参考译文

美　德

可爱的白日，这么凉爽、明朗、静谧，
你把天和地婚配成双。
露珠会为你今夜坠落而哭泣，
因为你注定要消亡。

芬芳的玫瑰，你红艳似怒，
使急性子观者也拭目凝望。
但你总植根于坟墓，
这注定你要消亡。

可爱的春天，你充满良辰和玫瑰，
你是一只匣，里边凝藏芳香。
我的音乐显示你也有终有尾，
世间一切都会死亡。

只有美好有德的灵魂，
像焙干的木材永不变形，

纵然是整个世界化为灰烬，
它仍然长存、永生。

（李正栓　译）

Easter Wings[1]

It is an emblem poem whose shape presents the emblem picture. The lines, increasing and decreasing, imitate flight, and also the spiritual experience of falling and rising. By the shape of the poem, Herbert reinforces the divine meaning of Easter and the Christian theme of fall and rise. Early editions of Herbert printed this poem with the lines running vertically, making the wing shape more apparent.

Lord, who createdst[2] man in wealth and store[3],
Though foolishly he[4] lost the same[5],
Decaying more and more
Till he became
Most poor:
With thee
O let me rise
As larks, harmoniously,
And sing this day[6] thy victories:
Then shall the fall further the flight in me.[7]

My tender age[8] in sorrow did begin:
And still[9] with sicknesses and shame
Thou didst[10] so punish sin,
That I became
Most thin.
With thee
Let me combine,
And feel this day thy victory;
For, if I imp[11] my wing on thine,
Affliction shall advance the flight in me[12].

Notes

1. This poem is written in two 10-line stanzas rhyming ababacdcdc. It is a shaped verse, which represents, by the typographical shape of the poem on the page, some part of the subject. There are modern poets following this style.
2. createdst: created.
3. store: abundance.
4. he: referring to man.
5. the same: referring to the wealth and store.
6. this day: Easter day.
7. Then shall the fall further the flight in me: It originated from Romans 5: 20 in New Testament: "but where sin increased, grace abounded all the more."
8. tender age: childhood.
9. still: always.
10. didst: did.
11. imp: graft.
12. Cf. Isaiah 40: 31 in Old Testament: "but those who wait for the Lord shall renew their strength; they shall mount up with wings like eagles."

诗歌赏析

《复活节翅膀》(*Easter Wings*)选自《圣殿》。这首诗是一首图形诗(a pattern or shaped poem),即用图形来展现文本含义的诗歌形式。这首诗共分两节,原本是两节竖排,后改为两节横排,诗节的形状像两对翅膀,诗行由宽到窄,由窄到宽。它的形式象征了复活节的意义,同时形象地表达了诗歌主题——上帝创造了人类,而人类又因为罪恶失去乐园。不过这一堕落并非无法救赎,只要人类心向上帝,跟随上帝,定能弃恶从善,获得新生。

For Study and Discussion

1. What's the main idea of the poem?
2. Does the shape of the poem help express its meaning? How?
3. What "fall" is the poet referring to in Line 10?

4. How can a fall further a flight? Explain this paradox.

参考译文

复活节翅膀

造人的上帝给人丰裕生活，
但愚蠢的人把它丧失，
就因为日益堕落
最后竟至于
极落魄；
让我像
婉转的云雀
和你呀同上天堂
并歌唱今日你的胜利：
于是堕落更促我奋飞向上。

我尚未成熟便已开始忧愁；
而你还用病痛和羞耻
把罪孽如此惩处，
最后我终于
极消瘦。
哦请让
我同你一起
把你这胜利分享；
因为我倘把翼附于你，
痛苦磨难更促我奋飞向上。

（黄杲炘　译）

8. John Milton

John Milton（约翰·弥尔顿，1608—1674）is the greatest writer in the 17th century and one of the giants of English literature. He was born in London in 1608. His education began at St. Paul's School. Then he attended

Christ's College, Cambridge University, where he got B. A. in 1629 and M. A. in 1632. After graduation he did not enter the ministry as expected. He retired to his father's country house at Horton in Buckinghamshire where he did further reading for about six years (1632—1638). He read about everything that was ever written in English, Latin, Greek, Italian and Hebrew, studying literature, science, theology and music. He became famous as a poet for his two poems, *Comus* (1634), a masque and *Lycidas* (1637), the finest pastoral elegy in English, to memorialize Edward King. In 1638, he set out for a tour on the Continent. Late in 1639, hearing the news that the King and the Parliament broke, he returned to England.

Milton threw himself into the struggle for religious and political liberties. He wrote a series of pamphlets on marriage, freedom of press, the defence of English people. *Areopagitica* (1644) was a declaration of people's freedom of the press. In 1651, he published his pamphlet *Defence of the English People* and in 1654, *Second Defence of the English People* (1654). It was while he was engaged in this project that Milton went blind (1652). With the help of his family members, he completed his great epic *Paradise Lost* (1665), and then got it published (1667). Before his death Milton published two other works: *Paradise Regained* (1671) and *Samson Agonistes* (1671).

Milton is a great revolutionary poet of the 17th century. He is also an outstanding political pamphleteer of the Revolution period. He dedicated himself to the revolutionary cause. He made a strong influence on the later English poetry. Every progressive English poet since Milton has drawn inspiration from him.

Milton is a great stylist. His poetry has a grand style. That is because he made a lifelong study of classical and Biblical literature. His poetry is noted for sublimity of thought and majesty of expression. Milton is also difficult to read, because of his involved style with frequent inversions and very complicated sentence structure. His sentences are often long. Yet, to express his sublimity of thought, he wrote in a style that is unsurpassed in its sonority, eloquence, majesty and grandeur—the Miltonic style.

Milton is a great master of blank verse. He is the glorious pioneer to apply blank verse to nondramatic poetry. He used it as the main tool in his masterpiece *Paradise Lost*. His blank verse is rich in every poetic quality and never monotonous.

Methought I Saw My Late Espoused Saint[1] is written in a dream vision in 1658 in memory of his second wife, Katherine Woodcock. The poet uses several contrasts, such as day and night, life and death, to show his great happiness on seeing his wife in his dream and his deep sorrow while losing her in reality. He also uses allusions and paradox to show his deep love for his wife. Though a revolutionary poet, Milton also could be affectionate on lamenting his beloved. This poem exemplifies his profound poetic skills and great learning, which make it unique.

Methought[2] I Saw My Late Espoused Saint[3]

Brought to me like Alcestis[4] from the grave,
Whom Jove's great son[5] to her glad husband gave,
Rescued from death by force though pale and faint.
Mine[6], as whom[7] washed from spot of childbed taint[8],
Purification in the old law[9] did save[10],
And such, as yet once more I trust to have
Full sight of her[11] in Heaven without restraint[12],
Came vested all in white, pure as her mind[13].
Her face was veiled[14], yet to my fancied sight[15]
Love, sweetness, goodness, in her person shined[16]
So clear, as in no face with more delight[17].
But O, as to embrace me she inclined[18],
I waked, she fled, and day brought back my night.[19]

1658 1673

Notes

1. This poem is written in Italian sonnet form with the rhyme scheme of abba abba cdcdcd.
2. Methought: it seemed to me that.

3. my late espoused saint: the woman I lately married, now one of the blessed in heaven (saint). espoused: married. This saint refers to his second wife Katharine Woodcock who married him in 1656 and died in February 1658, three months after giving birth to a baby girl who followed the mother soon.
4. Alcestis: A Goddess in Greek Mythology, wife of Admetus, who sacrificed her life to save her husband and later she herself was also saved.
5. Jove's great son: Heracles, the son of Jove (Jupiter). It's Heracles that struggled with Death and brought Alcestis to life again. Professor Hu Jialuan of Peking University agrees to the belief that Heracles is the son of Zeus, the main god in Greek mythology; the Norton Anthology agrees to the belief that Heracles is Hercules, son of Jupiter the main god in Roman mythology. But the story of Alcestis is taken from Greek mythology. So we hold that whatever the name is, Heracles is the son of a main god. As the Roman mythology inherited a lot from the Greek mythology, the change of name here is of not too much importance on the condition that it is the son of main god who saved Alcestis from death.
6. mine: my wife.
7. as whom: as one whom.
8. washed from spot of childbed taint: washed from the bloodiness of childbed. taint: blood taint. Line 4 would read: "My wife, like the woman whom when washed from spot of childbed taint".
9. Purification in the old law: blood purification of women after childbirth as prescribed in the Mosaic Law (33 days after giving birth to a son, 66 days after a daughter. See Leviticus 12: 2-5). the old law: the Mosaic law.
10. save: rescue.
11. such, as yet once more I trust to have / Full sight of her: as such a one whom I trust to have full sight of yet once more.
12. without restraint: easily and freely. It implies that the poet will be free to see his wife while in heaven. Lines 3-7 constitute one complete sentence, which could read: my wife came vested all in white, pure as her mind, as one whom, when washed from spot of child-bed taint, Purification in the old law did save, as such a one whom I trust to have full sight of yet once

more in heaven without restraint.

13. vested all in white, pure as her mind: here Milton compares her wife's white clothes to her pure mind, thus the external and internal purity of her wife are combined together. vested: clothed.

14. Her face was veiled: her face was covered with a veil. Milton never saw what she looked like. When they got married, he was already blind.

15. my fancied sight: my imagination.

16. shined: shone.

17. as in no face with more delight: with more delight in her face than in any other.

18. inclined: bent over.

19. day brought back my night: a famous paradox in English poetry. To Milton, the day without his wife is like the night while the night with his wife is like the day. Cf. Shakespeare's Sonnet 43: "All days are nights to see till I see thee, /And nights bright days when dreams do show me thee." Cf. Milton's *Samson Agonistes*: "O dark, dark, dark, amid the blaze of noon, /Irrecoverably dark…/As in the land of darkness, yet in light, /To live a life half dead, a living death, /And buried; …"

诗歌赏析

弥尔顿的宏伟史诗让你看到一个革命者的胸怀。若是你据此认为他缺乏柔情，那就错了。他喜欢史诗般叙事，也不乏婉约柔情。《悼亡妻》便是绝妙例证。这首十四行诗是写给他的第二任妻子嘉德琳·胡德科克的。1656年与弥尔顿结婚的她温柔贤淑，婚后一年半就去世了。这更使弥尔顿充满思念。

这首诗采用意大利十四行诗的形式，层次分明，结构严谨。

引用典故是弥尔顿诗歌的一大特色，在这首诗中表现得淋漓尽致。

第一个四行诗中弥尔顿用希腊神话中忒萨吕王阿德莫托斯和新婚妻子阿尔塞斯蒂的故事来形容梦中与妻子相遇的狂喜之情。忒萨吕王结婚的当天忘了向女神献祭，于是女神要取走他的性命作为惩罚。这个时候，他新婚的妻子阿尔塞斯蒂勇敢地站出来，愿意替丈夫赴死。就在她刚死不久，朱庇特之子赫拉克里斯赶来，从死神的手中夺回了阿尔塞斯蒂。在诗人看来，梦中与妻子相遇的欣喜足以与忒萨吕王见到死而复生的妻子相比。他心爱的妻子婚后不久就死去了。梦超越了生死的界限，让他们得以相聚。

《旧约》中的摩西律法规定，妇女生子要经过33天的洁净礼，生女要经过66天的洁净礼。第二个四行诗中诗人把妻子形容成像经过基督教的洁净礼的女子一样圣洁无瑕。在第三个四行诗中，梦中的妻子蒙着面纱，全身素白。诗人与妻子结婚时，已经失明五年，从未见过妻子的真容。因此，梦中的妻子也只能以面纱示人，这既是诗人的巧妙处理，也是诗人的无奈。以衣服的纯白和爱妻心灵的纯洁比拟，形容妻子由内而外的纯洁。在弥尔顿看来，升入天堂的爱妻已经具备了神性的光辉，全身洋溢着爱的光彩，无人能及。

如果说前三个四行诗刻画了梦境的美丽，与妻子相聚的甜蜜，最后一个双偶句揭露了现实的严酷："但是，唉，正当她俯身要和我拥抱，/我醒了，她逃了，白昼带回了我的黑夜。"这首诗的最后一行是英语诗歌史上著名的似非而是的范例。经历了双目失明和失妻之痛的弥尔顿，时间观已与常人不同。有妻子的夜晚对诗人来说就是白昼，因为在梦里，诗人可以摆脱生死的桎梏，展开想象的翅膀，与妻子团圆，尽情欣赏妻子的容颜；失去妻子的白天，形同黑夜。因为白昼到来，现实是这样残酷——他双目失明，也失去了爱妻，王政复辟意味着诗人理想的破灭。黑白颠倒的时间观揭示了诗人内心极度的哀伤和凄凉。在《力士参孙》(1671)中，诗人借参孙之口再次抒发了自己心中的哀怨：

> 啊，黑暗呀，黑暗呀，黑暗呀，在正午烈日的强光里，
> 不可补救的黑暗呀……
> 虽在光天化日之下，如同在阴森森的境地，
> 半生半死，
> 而被埋在坟墓里；
> ……

（王佐良：《英国文学名篇选注》，269页，1983）

另外，弥尔顿还使用了对比、似非而是等修辞手法以及音韵手段，展示出非凡的诗歌技巧和广博的学识。诗中生与死、白昼与黑夜、现实与梦境的对比揭示了诗人夜晚时分，在梦中与妻子相遇的欢欣；白昼来临，诗人面对现实，失去妻子的苦痛。该诗用词考究，句式复杂，诗人频繁使用头韵、腹韵等音韵技巧，使语义、声音形成紧密结合的整体。尤其最后一行，连续使用单音节词，一字一顿，寄托了诗人脱离梦境，回到现实的沉痛心情以及对妻子深深的怀念和爱恋。

For Study and Discussion

1. Identify the rhyme scheme of this sonnet.
2. Point out the allusions in the poem.
3. How do you understand the last line of the poem?
4. What do you know about paradox in poetry?
5. Su Shi also has a poem in memory of his deceased wife Wang Fu. Try to find this *Ci*-poem and make a comparative study between the two.

参考译文

梦亡妻

我仿佛看到了婚后不久便进入天堂的妻
回到了我身边，像阿尔塞斯蒂从坟墓
被朱庇特伟大的儿子由死亡中抢救出，
交还她欣喜的丈夫，虽然她苍白无力。
我的妻，如同古戒律规定的净身礼
拯救的女子，洗清了产褥上的血污，
这样的她，我相信我必能再度
在天堂里无拘无束地细细瞻视，
她穿着和她心灵一样洁白的衣袍，
脸上蒙着面纱，但我好像看得真切，
爱、温柔、善良在她身上闪耀，
任何人脸上显不出这样的喜悦。
但是，唉，正当她俯身要和我拥抱，
我醒了，她逃了，白昼带回了我的黑夜。

（胡家峦　译）

When I Consider How My Light Is Spent[1]

This poem was written soon after Milton lost his sight in 1652 when he was 44. The theme of the poem is being rather than doing. In this poem, the poet expressed that he has intended to serve God with his talent, but God made him sightless. In the latter half of the poem he explains for himself that God does not need man's work or his gifts. They serve him best who can endure his suffering best. In this way, he had found the courage to live on in this dark and wide world.

When I consider how my light is spent[2],
Ere half my days[3], in this dark world and wide[4],
And that one talent[5] which is death to hide[6]
Lodged with me useless,[7] though my soul more bent[8]
To serve therewith my Maker[9], and present
My true account[10], lest he returning chide[11];
"Doth God exact daylabor, light denied?"[12]
I fondly ask;[13] but Patience to prevent
That murmur[14], soon[15] replies, "God doth not need
Either man's work or his own gifts; who best
Bear his mild yoke, they serve him best.[16] His state
Is kingly. Thousands[17] at his bidding speed
And post[18] o'er[19] land and ocean without rest:
They also serve who only stand and wait."[20]

1652? 1673

Notes

1. It is written in Italian or Petrarchan sonnet rhyming abba abba cde cde with the first octave, complaint of God, sorrow; the sestet, patience, calmness.
2. my light is spent: the literal meaning is that he has gone blind; the deep meaning is that life is spent. spent: extinguished. As spokesman of the Revolution, Milton got blind in answering Salmasius, the European scholar who was hired by Charles Ⅰ.
3. Ere half my days: before half of my days (the life expectancy is one hundred years according to Plato and the Bible). Milton was 44 when he got totally blind in 1652.
4. dark world and wide: dark and wide world.
5. And that one talent: And (when I consider) that one talent. talent: a pun, meaning both money and his literary talent. Lines 3-6 are in an allusion to

the Bible. In Matthew 25: 14-30, the servants who used their master's money (talents) to earn interest for him were praised, while the servant who buried the single talent he was given was deprived of it and cast into outer darkness.

6. which is death to hide: to hide which is death (to hide talent is same as death).
7. Lodged with me useless: (is) lodged with me useless. "useless" here is also a pun, meaning both useless and usury, the interest expected by the master.
8. though my soul more bent: though my soul (be) more bent. bent: eager.
9. to serve therewith my Maker: to serve my Maker with it. therewith: with which (talent). my Maker: God.
10. My true account: what I have done.
11. lest he returning chide: lest he, on returning, should chide.
12. Doth God exact day-labor, light denied?: Does God want (need) our day-labor when light is denied? exact: demand. Cf. John 9:4 in New Testament: "We must work the works of him who sent me, while it is day; night is coming when no man can work." Here the poet complains about God's unfairness to him.
13. I fondly ask: I foolishly ask, which is the main clause of the previous 7 lines. fondly: foolishly. The normal order of the whole sentence is: I fondly ask, "Doth God exact day-labour, light denied?" when I consider how my light is spent ere half my days in this dark and wide world and (how) that one talent, to hide which is death, (is) lodged with me useless, though my soul (be) more bent to serve therewith my Maker, and (to) present my true account, lest he, returning, (should) chide (me).
14. murmur: complaint.
15. soon: quickly.
16. who best/Bear his mild yoke, they serve him best: they who best bear his mild yoke serve him best. his mild yoke: the obligation and duty that God put on man. Cf. Matthew 11: 29-30 in New Testament: "Take my yoke upon you, and learn of me... For my yoke is easy, and my burden is light".
17. Thousands: thousands (of angels).
18. post: hasten, hurry up; travel quickly.

19. o'er: over.
20. They also serve who only stand and wait: They who only stand and wait also serve (God).

诗歌赏析

弥尔顿共写了23首十四行诗。他的十四行诗遵循意大利十四行诗的韵式，即大多采用abba abba cdcdcd（或cdecde），写得大气磅礴。激情澎湃处，往往采用跨行的形式，一气呵成，不留停顿。之前的十四行诗主要歌咏爱情。弥尔顿拓展了十四行诗的主题范围，加入了时事、志向等。1652年他因写《为英国人民声辩》，劳累过度，双目失明。弥尔顿有两首十四行诗谈到他的失明，其中一首就是写于1652年的《哀失明》。这首诗反映了他刚盲不久痛苦、矛盾的心情，只能寄托于宗教来平复自己内心的痛苦。

整首诗只有两句话：前七行半和后六行半各一句。第一句话表达诗人的苦闷和对上帝的抱怨。第二句话借基督教教义告诫自己要学会忍耐。诗人将基督教教义拟人化，并遵从其建议，选择忍耐。这首诗反映了诗人双目失明后心情的变化。作为一个具有豪迈心胸和昂杨斗志的革命诗人，失明对诗人意味着折断翅膀，不由得郁闷、颓丧，诗人不甘心就此沉沦，但是显然还没有找到与命运抗争的出路，因此，在诗歌末尾，他选择等待。这是一个革命者的不屈斗志也是面对不幸的无奈选择。

For Study and Discussion

1. What's the main idea of this poem?
2. What does "my light" mean? What's Milton's attitude towards his blindness?
3. How is the word "talent" used? Why is it "Death" to hide his talent?
4. How do you understand the one "wait", the last one of the whole sonnet?
5. What's Milton's attitude towards God?
6. Learn this sonnet by heart.

参考译文

哀失明

想到了在这茫茫黑暗的世界里，
还未到半生这两眼就已失明，

想到了我这个泰伦特，要是埋起来，
会招致死亡，却放在我手里无用，
虽然我一心想用它服务造物主，
免得报账时，得不到他的宽容；
想到这里，我就愚蠢地自问，
"神不给我光明，还要我做日工？"
但"忍耐"看我在抱怨，立刻止住我：
"神并不要你工作，或还他礼物。
谁最能服从他，谁就是忠于职守，
他君临万方，只要他一声吩咐，
万千个天使就赶忙在海陆奔驰，
但侍立左右的，也还是为他服务。"

（殷宝书　译）

9. Richard Lovelace

Richard Lovelace（理查德·洛夫莱斯，1618－1657）was a Cavalier poet. He came from an old and wealthy Kentish family. With his good looks and elegant manners, he created quite a stir when he went to study at Oxford University. After graduation he became a favourite courtier under King Charles Ⅰ and Queen Henrietta Maria. Naturally he was a firm supporter of the King during the Civil War. He was once imprisoned by the Parliamentary army. Then he left England for a time to fight with the French army against the Spanish. When he returned to England he was again put into prison. He lost all his wealth and died in poverty at the age of 39.

"To Althea" was supposed to have been written in prison. *Lucasta* was also prepared for print when he was in prison. His brother published his remaining verses, *Lucasta: Posthume Poems*. The poems of Lovelace epitomize what we think of as the Cavalier manner: witty, charming, graceful in a way that shows his poetic discipleship to Ben Jonson. At its best the poetry of

Lovelace is tinged with a slight element of desperation or melancholy which may remind us that behind a facade of gallantry and elegance, their careless, aristocratic lives were crumbling away. Their poems are always concerned with the passage of time in one way or another.

To Lucasta, Going to the Wars[1]

This poem is a well-known lyric which was written after Lovelace was put into prison in 1648. It seems a valediction that the poet made to his lover before leaving for war. It is not only an oath of love but a promise of his loyalty to the king. Though a representative work of the Cavalier poetry, it has some features of the Metaphysical. The comparisons are startling and unique.

Tell me not, sweet[2], I am unkind,
That from the nunnery[3]
Of thy chaste breast and quiet mind
To war and arms I fly.

True, a new mistress[4] now I chase,
The first foe in the field[5];
And with a stronger faith embrace
A sword, a horse, a shield.

Yet this inconstancy is such
As you too shall adore;
I could not love thee, dear, so much,
Loved I not honor more[6].

1649

Notes

1. This poem is chosen from *Lucasta*. It is written in three quartrains of alternate iambic tetrameter and trimeter rhyming abab.
2. sweet: sweetheart.

3. nunnery: a metaphor here to show the purity and chastity of his lover.
4. a new mistress: referring to "the first foe" in the next line.
5. The first foe in the field: alliteration. field: battlefield.
6. Loved I not honor more: if I did not love honor more.

诗歌赏析

《出征，致露卡丝塔》是诗人出征前赠给爱人的告别诗，既有恋人的柔肠，又有战士的豪情，解释了作者为何要告别爱人，奔赴战场。

全诗基本是抑扬格的节奏，隔行押韵，简洁生动、铿锵有力，格律规整又富有变化。开头就是一个有力的扬抑格"不要说我无情"。此外，诗人还用头韵和腹韵将中心词联系起来，环环相扣，如第二节的第二行中 first，foe 和 field 中连续出现三个［f］音，形成一个鲜明的头韵，突出强调第一个敌人。另外还有 a sword 与 a horse，honor 和 more 形成的腹韵等，使全诗形成一个整体，意义连续不断。

新奇的比喻是这首诗的显著特点。在第一节中，诗人将恋人的胸膛和心房比作庵堂，将精神与肉体结合起来，并神圣化。第二节诗人将敌人比喻为情人，即将战场上对敌人的穷追猛打与生活中对恋人的亲密关系类比，这种比喻大胆、新奇又耐人寻味。最后一节更是说出了"这样的负心连你也会崇仰"。这种似非而是的手法是玄学派的拿手好戏，但是骑士派的洛夫莱斯用起来同样游刃有余。诗人拥有甜蜜的爱情，但大战在即，诗人对他的选择做出了解释："亲爱的，我不能爱你更深，/ 如果我不更爱荣光。"在他心中，对国王的忠诚和对荣誉的珍惜要胜过个人的爱情，正所谓"舍小利，取大义"。

正如匈牙利诗人裴多菲所言："生命诚可贵，爱情价更高。若为自由故，二者皆可抛。"在诗人看来，为国增光的责任胜过对爱情的留恋。浪漫与现实，柔情与残酷，对国家的效忠及对爱情的忠贞巧妙地糅合在一起。

For Study and Discussion

1. What is the speaker's attitude toward going to the war?
2. What do you think of the comparison of a nunnery to his lover's breast and mind? Is it appropriate? Why or why not?
3. What do the last two lines of the poem mean?
4. Do you like this poem? Why or why not?
5. Learn this poem by heart.

参考译文

出征，致露卡丝塔

亲爱的，不要说我无情，
远离你那修道院一样
纯洁的酥胸和静谧的心境
我全身披挂，奔赴战场。

是的，我在追寻一个新的恋人，
我在战场遇见的第一个敌人；
我要用更加坚实的灵魂
去拥抱刀剑、战马和甲盾。

然而，这样的负心
连你也会崇仰，
亲爱的，我不能爱你更深，
如果我不更爱荣光。

（申玉革　译）

To Althea, from Prison[1]

This poem was also written in prison. The poet shows his longing for love and his loyalty to the king. The physical confinement and the spiritual freedom form a Metaphysical contrast. The line "Stone walls do not a prison make, / Nor iron bars a cage" has become a famous saying in English language.

When Love with unconfined wings
Hovers within my gates,
And my divine Althea brings[2]
To whisper at the grates;
When I lie tangled in her hair
And fettered to her eye,
The gods that wanton[3] in the air
Know no such liberty.

When flowing cups run swiftly round,
With no allaying Thames[4],
Our careless heads with roses bound[5],
Our hearts with loyal flames;
When thirsty grief in wine we steep[6],
When healths and drafts go free,
Fishes that tipple[7] in the deep[8]
Know no such liberty.

When, like committed linnets[9], I
With shriller throat shall sing
The sweetness, mercy, majesty,
And glories of my king[10];
When I shall voice aloud how good
He is, how great should be[11],
Enlarged[12] winds, that curl the flood,
Know no such liberty.
Stone walls do not a prison make,
Nor iron bars a cage;
Minds innocent and quiet take
That for an hermitage.[13]
If I have freedom in my love,
And in my soul am free,
Angels alone, that soar above,
Enjoy such liberty.

1649

Notes

1. It is written in four 8-line stanzas of alternate iambic tetrameter and trimeter rhyming ababcdcd.
2. my divine Althea brings: brings my divine Althea.
3. wanton: play about, play.
4. With no allaying Thames: with wine undiluted with water (from the river

Thames), no mixture of water (as from the river Thames) in the wine.
5. with roses bound: bound with roses.
6. thirsty grief in wine we steep: we steep thirsty grief in wine.
7. tipple: to drink constantly in small quantities.
8. the deep: (poetic) the sea.
9. committed linnets: caged birds, caged finches.
10. my king: Charles Ⅰ, in whose service the poet was "committed" to prison.
11. how great should be: how great he should be.
12. Enlarged: set free or released.
13. Minds innocent and quiet take/That for an hermitage: A prison may be suitable for quiet meditation. Minds innocent and quiet: innocent and quiet minds. That: the prison. an hermitage: a resting place.

诗歌赏析

在英国革命时期，诗人作为王室的忠实拥趸屡次征战沙场，但保王军还是被议会军打败，大势已去，而他也遭到囚禁。即便如此，他的心中依然不甘心失败。《狱中致奥西娅》一诗表达了他当时的心境：前三节表达了作者虽然身陷囹圄，但仍心系爱情、忠诚和国王，肉体的困囿与精神的自由形成玄学式的对比，对爱情的渴望和对国王的忠诚交织在一起。最后一节做出总结——囚室只是暂时的隐居地，困境总会过去，那时诗人定能像“翱翔天宇的安琪儿”自由而无拘，展示了作者不屈的灵魂。其中的警句：“石头砌不出牢狱，/钢铁也筑不起樊篱”已成为传唱的名句。

For Study and Discussion

1. What three kinds of liberty are described in this poem?
2. Note in the first three stanzas the comparison with something in nature. In what ways is the choice appropriate for each stanza?
3. How does the fourth stanza form a climax to the three stanzas that precede it?
4. What kind of idea is expressed in the last stanza? What is the image of the speaker?
5. Learn the last stanza by heart.

参考译文

狱中致奥西娅

当爱神盘旋在我的牢门，
用他那无拘的翅膀，
带来圣洁的奥西娅
窃窃私语在我的窗棂旁；
当我躺在她纠结的发间，
踯躅于她的眼眸，
天马行空的神仙，
也无福消受这样的自由。

当无忧的我们推杯换盏，
畅饮着玉液琼浆，
头上装饰着玫瑰花瓣，
忠贞的火焰在心中荡漾；
当我们把渴望和悲伤融入酒中，
当觥筹交错、自由自在，
深海遨游的鱼儿
也不知这自由从哪里得来。

如果我能像笼中的红雀，
用高昂的嗓音歌唱
国王的亲切、仁慈、
威仪与荣光；
如果我能大声称颂
他的无上仁德，至尊至大，
连席卷洪水的飓风，
也不如这般潇洒。

石头砌不出牢狱，
钢铁也筑不起樊篱，
纯洁的心儿安详而静谧，

只把它当作隐居地。
如果我能自由地爱，
我的灵魂也无拘，
那么，这样的自由啊，
只有翱翔天宇的安琪儿才配！

（申玉革　译）

10. Andrew Marvell

Andrew Marvell（安德鲁·马维尔，1621—1678）was born at Winead in Holderness，Yorkshire. Later his family moved to Hull. He attended Hull Grammar School and then went to Cambridge University. After graduating in 1638，he travelled in Europe for some years. Around 1650 he began to tutor young Mary Fairfax，daughter of Sir Thomas Fairfax，Lord General of Oliver Cromwell's Parliamentary army. In 1657，Marvell was appointed assistant to John Milton who was blind now. In his quiet way，he seemed to have been responsible for saving Milton from imprisonment and possible execution after the Restoration. In 1659，he was elected MP for Hull，and remained as MP for Hull until his death. He was devoted to the interests of Hull.

He wrote a lot of lyrics and satires. His "serious" verse was only published three years after his death，by his housekeeper Mary Palmer，who gave herself out to be his widow. Playful，casual，and witty in tone，always light on its metrical feet and exact in its diction，it displays depth and intellectual hardness in unexpected places；its texture is extraordinarily rich. One needs only glance at the famous "To His Coy Mistress" to see these qualities exemplified. All of Marvell's lyric poems were written by the early 1650's，although they were not published until 1681，when they seemed old-fashioned and out-of-date.

Like Donne，Marvell was largely forgotten during the 18th and 19th centuries. It was not until after the First World War，with Grierson's

Metaphysical Lyrics (1921) and T. S. Eliot's revaluation of the Metaphysical poets including Marvell that the modern high estimation of his poetry began to prevail. Eliot saw that Marvell's wit and magniloquence joined together the two great strands of the 17thcentury poetry, the Metaphysical poetry and Cavalier poetry.

To His Coy Mistress[1]

The poet tries to persuade his lady to seize the day and enjoy love, since time waits for no man and her beauty can not last long. At first it looks like a dozen other poems on the carpe diem theme, slight and sarcastic. But soon the images of worms, grave and the deserts of eternity stand out among the gorgeous compliments to his mistress. The surprising conceits and sound reasoning make the argumentation serious. The couplets of iambic tetrameter make the poem neat and compact. The motifs of time and space, love and death develop with the logical divisions of the poem.

Had we[2] but world[3] enough, and time,
This coyness, lady, were no crime.
We would sit down, and think which way
To walk, and pass our long love's day.
Thou by the Indian Ganges'[4] side
Shouldst rubies[5] find; I by the tide
Of Humber[6] would complain[7]. I would
Love you ten years before the Flood[8],
And you should, if you please, refuse
Till the conversion of the Jews[9].
My vegetable love[10] should grow
Vaster than empires and more slow;
A hundred years should go to praise
Thine[11] eyes, and on thy forehead gaze;
Two hundred to adore each breast,
But thirty thousand to the rest[12]:
An age[13] at least to every part,

And the last age should show your heart.
For, lady, you deserve this state[14],
Nor would I love at lower rate[15].
But at my back I always hear
Time's winged chariot hurrying near;[16]
And yonder[17] all before us lie
Deserts of vast eternity[18].
Thy beauty shall no more be found,
Nor, in thy marble vault[19], shall sound
My echoing song; then worms shall try
That long-preserved virginity,
And your quaint[20] honor[21] turn to dust,
And into ashes all my lust[22]:
The grave's a fine and private place,
But none, I think, do there embrace.
Now therefore, while the youthful hue
Sits on thy skin like morning dew[23],
And while thy willing soul transpires[24]
At every pore with instant fires[25],
Now let us sport us[26] while we may,
And now, like amorous birds of prey[27],
Rather at once our time devour[28]
Than languish in his slow-chapped[29] power.
Let us roll all our strength and all
Our sweetness up into one ball[30],
And tear our pleasures with rough strife
Thorough[31] the iron gates of life:
Thus, though we cannot make our sun
Stand still, yet we will make him run.[32]

ca. 1650—52　　　　1681

Notes

1. This poem is written in couplets of iambic tetrameter lines. Coy: shy.

2. Had we: If we had. It is in subjunctive mood.
3. world: space.
4. the Indian Ganges: a big river in India.
5. rubies: a kind of precious stones of deep red color.
6. Humber: a small river in the poet's hometown Hull. It is in the north of England. The poet's father died in it while trying to cross it in January, 1641.
7. complain: sing songs of plaintive love. Complains are poems of plaintive, unavailing love.
8. the Flood: the flood God made to get rid of the evil people. See Genesis 6—9.
9. the conversion of the Jews: Popular belief had it that the Jews were to be converted just before the last Judgment. The exaggerated offers in this stanza play off against conventional hyperbolic declarations of love in Petrarchan poetry. Here it implied that to make the Jew convert is impossible. People have to wait a very long time.
10. My vegetable love: my love that grows as slowly as the vegetables.
11. Thine: your.
12. to the rest: to the rest of your body.
13. An age: a long period of time.
14. state: dignity.
15. at lower rate: with emotion less than this.
16. But ... near: it has become a famous line in English poetry. Time's winged chariot: Time is imaged as flying fast in chariot with wings.
17. yonder: over there.
18. Deserts of vast eternity: refers to death.
19. in thy marble vault: in your tomb.
20. quaint: fastidious. It puns on "out of date" and queynte, a term for the female genitals.
21. honor: purity, chastity.
22. lust: desire, passion.
23. morning dew: an image that is transient. Here the poet wants to persuade his girl to seize the day and enjoy the happiness of love since her beauty and youth will disappear like the morning dew.

24. transpires: breathes forth.
25. instant fires: present, sudden enthusiasm.
26. sport us: make ourselves happy, enjoy ourselves.
27. like amorous birds of prey: like passionate raptors. It is a simile; the poet and his mistress are compared to passionate raptors who would rather take their time to enjoy love than wither under the destructive power of time.
28. our time devour: devour our time, that is, to make good use of time.
29. slow-chapped: slowly devouring. Time is envisaged as slowly chewing up the world and the people in it.
30. Let us roll all our strength and all/Our sweetness up into one ball: a famous conceit. Here the poet compares the strength and passions of the two lovers to a ball, which is full of beauty and strength.
31. Thorough: through.
32. though we cannot make our sun/Stand still: In the final lines, the speaker and his mistress triumphantly reverse their relation to time, eating it avidly like birds of prey instead of being eaten by it, forcing the sun to race after them instead of fruitlessly imploring it to stand still. See Joshua 10: 12, in which, the sun stood still for Joshua in his war against Gibeon; See the very different resolution in Donne's "The Sun Rising": "Busy old fool, unruly sun … Must to thy motions lover' seasons run?"

诗歌赏析

《致羞涩的姑娘》是马维尔的代表作。这首诗写得结构严谨，优雅动人。与赫里克写的《劝少女们利用好时光》主题相同，都是让人莫负青春，及时行乐，只争朝夕。"及时行乐"（Carpe Diem or Seize the day）出自古罗马诗人贺拉斯的《颂诗》，后来已成为一个常见的文学主题，在抒情诗中尤为多见。在表现这一主题的诗中，说者强调人生短暂，时光飞逝，劝听者（经常是说者的女友）抓紧时间，享受现时的欢乐。《致羞涩的姑娘》这首诗的大意是，一位青年男子劝说他热恋的姑娘不要羞涩，不要拖延，快快和他尽情地享受爱情的美妙，因为人生无常，青春易逝，还要面对死亡的威胁。马维尔在这里巧妙地运用了奇思妙喻、夸张手法和邓恩式的复杂说理。同样是"及时行乐"的主题，赫里克写得短小精悍，简洁有力，马维尔写得洋洋洒洒，荡气回肠，一样出色，一样精彩。

全诗采用三段论的方法，逻辑严密，结构谨严。第一部分，马维尔极尽夸张之能事，说明如果有足够的时间和空间，他们的爱情将如何缓慢发展。诗人将他们的爱情比喻为像植物般成长，又将爱情的发展比喻成辽阔帝国的扩展。如果有足够的时间和空间：

花一百年去称赞你的双眸，
还要久久地凝视你的额头。
用两百年去膜拜每一峰香乳，
但要花三万年欣赏其他各处。
至少要用一个时代去看每一个部位，
在最后一个时代你该敞开你的心扉。

有限的时空被诗人无限夸张，好像他们可以充分享受美妙的恋爱时光，不受局限。但是，第二部分，诗人话锋陡转，突出光阴飞逝，岁月如梭。身后时间的战车在飞驰，眼前等候他们的是永恒的沙漠，即死亡。如果这样的劝说还不能让姑娘动心，那么，请看吧，你一味地矜持会带来什么样的后果：

你的美再也无处可觅，
在你的大理石墓穴里，
我的歌再也不能回荡，
蛆把你久存童贞初尝。
你的矜持会化作泥土，
我的欲望会化为乌物。

在这里，贞操和蛆虫、荣誉和灰尘连在了一起，强烈的对比让每个人都不由得踯躅反思："这样做，值得吗?"最后，诗人使用温和的嘲讽"坟墓固然是很隐蔽的去处，也很好"，可是，坟墓葬送了世间一切美好：爱情、美貌和青春，"那里什么也得不到。"

因此，在第三部分，马维尔劝说恋人要珍惜美好的青春年华，尽情享乐。他把恋人比喻成相爱着的猛禽去"吞食"时间，尽情嬉戏，劝说恋人应趁激情洋溢，青春年少，尽情享受爱情的甜蜜，别等容颜老去，年华虚度，后悔不及；诗人又将恋人周围的桎绊比作铁铸的囚门，呼吁爱人们应该把恋情集结在一起，合成一球，以冲破铁门，夺取欢乐，这样才不枉青春一场。诗中对爱的表白坦率直露，表达了年轻人急于和女伴享受爱情的炽烈感情。这种“及时行乐”的思想是英国文艺复兴时期诗歌的主题之一。而诗中严密的说理和夸张的比喻又是玄学派诗歌的典型特点。

For Study and Discussion

1. Try to illustrate how the three divisions of the logical structure help to develop the theme of the poem. What's the tone of each division?
2. Comment on the imagery that Marvell chooses and develops in the poem. And tell how the speaker tries to persuade his mistress. Is his method efficient? What would you do, if you were the mistress?
3. T. S. Eliot said the poet expressed the passionate feeling with a tough reasonableness beneath the slight lyric grace. How do you understand this statement?
4. Compare this poem with Robert Herrick's "To the Virgins, to Make Much of Time". Tell how they are similar and different.

参考译文

致羞涩的姑娘

如果我们时间足够多，地域够广阔，
姑娘，你这样忸怩算不上什么罪过。
我们会坐着想想该漫步在哪条路上，
怎样度过长长的恋爱的白天的时光。
你可以去那印度的恒河
寻觅红宝石，我在亨伯
河畔低诉怨曲。我会在
上古洪水十年前起就把你爱。
你可以拒绝我，如果你乐意，
直到犹太人向其他宗教皈依。
我植物式的爱情会慢慢地长，
慢慢地突破辽阔帝国的边疆；
花一百年去称赞你的双眸，
还要久久地凝视你的额头。
用两百年去膜拜每一峰香乳，

但要花三万年欣赏其他各处。
至少要用一个时代去看每一个部位，
在最后一个时代你该敞开你的心扉。
因为姑娘啊，你值得这种礼遇，
我也不会以低于这礼遇来爱你。

但我听见身后生翼的车轮
总是在急匆匆地向我逼近。
在我们不远的正前边
沙漠横卧，无边无沿。
你的美再也无处可觅，
在你的大理石墓穴里，
我的歌再也不能回荡，
蛆把你久存童贞初尝。
你的矜持会化作泥土，
我的欲望会化为乌物。
坟墓幽静也很好，
但谁在里边拥抱？

所以现在趁光泽载着青春
像朝露一样紧紧贴着你身。
你那有情的内心迸发着火，
从每个汗毛孔里往外喷射，
那就让我们及时行乐吆，
像充满爱欲的捕食的鸟，
一下子吞食我们的时间，
不在他慢合的口中熬煎。
让我们把所有的爱和力
卷成一个结实的球形体，
吵闹着夺取我们的欢乐
把生活的钢铁囚门冲破：
这样虽不能让太阳停站，
我们却能让它一直向前。

（李正栓　译）

11. Alexander Pope

English neo-classical literature found first fine expression in poetry, of which Alexander Pope (亚历山大·蒲柏, 1688－1744) was a typical representative. He was born in London to a Catholic merchant's family. Because of a prejudice against the Catholic in the public schools and universities and his own physical weakness and deformity, he received little school education. When he was only sixteen, he wrote his *Pastorals*, and exhibited his genius as a poet. Being debarred by his Catholic faith from many official employments, he made up his mind to make letters his life work. A few years later *An Essay on Criticism* (1711) was published, which brought him fame. The publication of his *The Rape of the Lock* in 1714 made him well-known and honoured in England, which is a mock-heroic poem, dealing with a story of an insignificant quarrel between two prominent aristocratic families.

For the next twelve years he devoted himself to poetry and translation on Homer. He translated *The Iliad* (1715－1720) and *The Odyssey* (1725－1726), his translation was characterized by elegant and artificial language of his day, but Homeric strength and simplicity were lost. Then he wrote his *An Essay on Man* (1733－1734) and *The Dunciad* (1728－1743). His fame as a poet was firmly established, his work was successful financially. In his last years he was devoted to poetry, living peacefully in his villa at Twickenham on the Thames, where he was buried when he died in 1744.

An Essay on Criticism is Pope's chief contribution to literary criticism, written in heroic couplets. The poem contains 744 lines and is divided into three parts. He first deplores the dearth of true taste among the critics of his day and, urging the need to turn to nature for guidance, he praises highly the Ancients, especially Homer and Virgil, and declares that to follow nature is equivalent to follow the Ancients and their rules for literature. Next he warns the critics against various unsound critical standards and touches upon the current literary problems. Then he gives his advice on the laws of criticism to be observed and ends by eulogizing the great critics in history, including Aristotle and others.

Pope's mastery of the heroic couplet made it the perfect expression of the moral and intellectual values of an age that admired clarity and order. No writers except Shakespeare and Milton have given to English so many quotable lines and phrases as Pope. "Fools rush in where angels fear to tread;" "Hope springs eternal in the human breast;" "The proper study of mankind is man." His neat couplets are easy to remember, and his comments on life and learning are usually brief, clever and exact.

from *An Essay on Criticism*[1]

The following excerpt is taken from Part Ⅱ, Lines 289—336 of *An Essay on Criticism*, the poem that makes Pope famous, in which he advises the critics not to lay too much emphasis on the artificial conceits and the gaudy language.

Some to conceit[2] alone their taste confine,
And glittering thoughts struck out[3] at every line;
Pleased with a work where nothing's just[4] or fit,
One glaring chaos[5] and wild heap of wit[6].
Poets, like painters, thus unskilled to trace
The naked nature and the living grace[7],
With gold and jewels cover every part,
And hide with ornaments their want of art[8].
True wit is Nature to advantage dressed,[9]
What oft was thought, but ne'er so well expressed;
Something whose truth convinced at sight we find,
That gives us back the image of our mind.[10]
As shades more sweetly recommend the light,[11]
So modest plainness sets off sprightly wit;
For works may have more wit than does them good,
As bodies perish through excess of blood.

Others for language all their care express,[12]
And value books, as women men, for dress.
Their praise is still[13]—the style is excellent;
The sense they humbly take upon content.[14]
Words are like leaves; and where they most abound,
Much fruit of sense beneath is rarely found.[15]
False eloquence, like the prismatic glass,
Its gaudy colors spreads on every place;
The face of Nature we no more survey,
All glares alike, without distinction gay.[16]
But true expression, like the unchanging sun,
Clears and improves whate'er it shines upon;
It gilds all objects, but it alters none.
Expression is the dress of thought, and still
Appears more decent as more suitable.[17]
A vile conceit in pompous words expressed
Is like a clown[18] in regal purple[19] dressed:
For different styles with different subjects sort,[20]
As several garbs with country, town, and court[21].
Some by old words to fame have made pretense,[22]
Ancients in phrase, mere moderns in their sense.[23]
Such laboured nothings[24], in so strange a style,
Amaze the unlearn'd, and make the learned smile;
Unlucky as Fungoso[25] in the play,
These sparks[26] with awkward vanity display
What the fine gentleman wore yesterday;
And but so mimic ancient wits at best,
As apes our grandsires in their doublets dressed.[27]
In words as fashions the same rule will hold,
Alike fantastic if too new, or old:[28]
Be not the first by whom the new are tried,
Nor yet the last to lay the old aside.

1709 1711

Notes

1. It is written in heroic couplets (i. e. rimed couplets in iambic pentameter).
2. conceit: fantastic notion; pointed wit, ingenuity and extravagance, or affectation in the use of figures, especially similes and metaphors. The employment of conceits in poetry is the striking feature of the Metaphysical poetry represented by John Donne.
3. struck out: devised, invented.
4. just: proper.
5. chaos: confusion and disorder.
6. wit: fancy, imagination.
7. to trace/The naked nature and the living grace: to portray nature in its plainness and objects of charm derived from real life. "Nature" here refers to the objective world of reality.
8. want of art: lack of artistic skill.
9. True wit is Nature to advantage dressed: true wit is Nature dressed to advantage. "True wit" here refers to all good poetry. dressed: adorned. It's a famous line of Pope.
10. Something whose truth convinced at sight we find, /That gives us back the image of our mind: the normal order of the first line should be "something of whose truth we find ourselves convinced at sight." image: the imperfect notion of a thing. "Something" refers to "true wit" mentioned above. The two lines together mean: True wit, the truth of which is instantly convincing us, restores to us what we have only an imperfect notion of in our mind.
11. shades more sweetly recommend the light: i. e. the light looks brighter when set in contrast with the shades.
12. Others for language all their care express: others show all their care for language.
13. still: always.
14. upon content: on mere acquiescence, without examination.
15. where they most abound, /Much fruit of sense beneath is rarely found: where there are too many words, much sense is rarely expressed. "they"

refers to "words". Here Pope criticizes the poets who pay too much attention to words rather than contents.

16. gay: brilliant in colour.
17. Appears more decent as more suitable: the more suitable the expression, the more decent it ever appears. decent: proper, fit.
18. clown: an ignorant or ill-bred man.
19. purple: the colour in which the ancient European kings were usually dressed.
20. different styles with different subjects sort: different styles agree with (or are fit for) different subjects. sort: agree with.
21. country, town, and court: frequent scenes that occur in the eclogue, satire and epic respectively.
22. to fame have made pretense: have made pretense to fame.
23. Ancients in phrase, mere moderns in their sense: They are ancients when judged by their phrases, but they are mere moderns when judged by the ideas they express. In other words, they express their modern ideas quaintly in old phrases. phrase: language.
24. laboured nothings: much elaborated, meaningless expressions.
25. Fungoso: a character in Ben Jonson's comedy *Every Man out of His Humour* (1599), who is described as one "that follows the fashion far off like a spy. He buys clothes to imitate a spruce courtier, but fails, the fashion changing so fast that his money is thrown away".
26. sparks: men of fashion.
27. in their doublets dressed: dressed in their doublets. their: our grandsires'.
28. Alike fantastic if too new, or old: They are both fantastic whether the words used are too new or too old for the ideas.

诗歌赏析

《论批评》是蒲柏的成名作。发表这首诗时，蒲柏年仅 23 岁。这首长诗由英雄双韵体写成。英雄双韵体指两两押韵的抑扬格五音步诗行。英雄双韵体古已有之。乔叟、斯宾塞和马洛都用过，后来随着无韵诗的盛行，逐渐没落，17 世纪经过德莱顿的努力，又有所恢复，18 世纪古典诗人把它推向高峰。这种诗体的好处在于格律谨严，韵式工整，但是容易陷于机械、单调。蒲柏使英雄双韵体达到最高的艺术境界。一篇枯燥的文论作品，蒲柏把它处理成一首古典主义的艺术佳作，堪称音形意的完美结合。

这首 744 行的长诗共分三部分：第一部分（1—200 行）说明文学批评的重要性以及高明的批评家之养成；第二部分（201—559 行）列出批评的十大弊病（骄傲、浅学、枝节、挑剔或奉承、崇古或厚今、偏颇、怪僻、易变、党见、妒忌）及其原因；第三部分（560—774 行）论述文学批评的原则和欧洲批评史概况。本文出自原诗第二部分有关"枝节"的一段。蒲柏论述了批评家只注重局部而不顾全体之害，并举了两个例子说明何谓枝节：一是过分重视奇想怪喻；二是重视语言文字而忽视内容。针对每个弊病，他都提出了自己的意见和建议。这些文论思想非常值得借鉴。

蒲柏首先批评了 17 世纪玄学派诗人所倚重的奇想怪喻，指出诗人过分重视华丽的修辞就像蹩脚的画家，浓墨重彩只是为了掩盖画技的拙劣。他主张"真才气是把自然巧打扮，思想虽常有，说法更圆满"。文章中过多的修饰反而无益，就像人体，血液太多只有死路一条。wit 一词在本部分出现四次，起到穿针引线的作用。第一个 wit（wild heap of wit）和最后一个 more wit 均等同于第一行的奇想怪喻。中间两个 true wit 和 sprightly wit 指作者赞同的巧智，即做诗的智慧。

蒲柏又批判了批评界过分关注语言之弊病。有些人欣赏作品只关注风格是否奇巧就像女人只关注男人的外表。他提出，语言就像叶子，越繁茂的地方，反而结不出果实；语言是思想的外衣，真挚的表达像永恒不变的太阳，照亮一切物体，却从不改变它们的模样。同时，他进一步指出，诗人应该注意风格和主题的搭配。用华丽词语堆砌的不恰当比喻就像小丑披上了紫袍，装模作样、不伦不类。他还批评了有些诗人喜欢用古词来炫耀自己，指出将现代的思想用古旧的词语来包装就像猴子穿上了爷爷的马甲，搔首弄姿。

除了工整的形式，独到的见解，蒲柏还以其凝练、隽永的语言著称。他的很多诗行已成为英语中的格言警句，比如"真才气是把自然巧打扮，思想虽常有，说法更圆满"等。

For Study and Discussion

1. How much do you know about Neo-classicism?
2. What is the peculiar style of Pope's poems?
3. What is heroic couplet?

4. What are criticized in these lines?
5. How do you understand the last two lines?

参考译文

论批评

（节选：第 289—336 行）

有的诗人只偏爱奇思怪喻，
巧妙的构思突出于每行诗句。
满足于异想联翩和巧喻堆砌，
那样的作品不恰当也不合适。
整篇诗章遍用金玉铺砌堆成，
借装饰手段掩蔽艺术的无能。
写诗如同作画，似这般怎能描绘
大自然的真实面目和纯朴的妩媚？
真才气是把自然巧打扮，
思想虽常有，说法更圆满。
有的诗篇一看就知道写了真实的状况，
因为如实反映了我们脑海中的印象。
平易朴素才能施展机智，豪情奔放，
如同背景晦暗才能使光线格外明亮。
作品里奇思怪喻壅塞并没有好处，
人体的血液过多也会走上死路。
还有些诗人一心总在表达上苦盼，
书的好坏像女人看重男人的装扮，
他们的称颂一成不变：风格极佳，
对于文章的意思，却无法回答，
词语就像树叶子，越是生长茂盛，
那里，意义的果实就越无法生成，
空洞和虚幻的雄辩是块多棱镜片，
光怪的色彩被散射得波光涟涟，
自然的天然本色我们无法评判，
刺目的光线下，各自的特色全部打乱，

真挚的表达像永恒不变的太阳，
它照耀一切，一切就变得清晰而明亮，
将光芒镀上，却没有改变任何模样。
表达永远和思想，后者是物体前者是霓裳，
打扮愈是合体则身份愈显高尚。
卑微的巧智却用华丽的辞藻，
是丑陋的小丑却穿着帝王的皇袍，
不同的装束应适合迥然不同的臣民，
要适合农村、城镇人民，还有朝廷。
一些人用古旧的词语作为夸耀，
亘古的片言蠕动着现代的思潮，
如此的用心获得无益的徒劳，
取悦于无术，但为大方之家耻笑，
不幸的角色宛如福格所在剧本的表演，
翩翩的外表，而难堪虚荣在丢人现眼，
极力去装扮成昔日的绅士去充脸面，
模仿远古的智慧，效果就可想而知：
就像猴子穿着爷爷的马甲搔首弄姿。

（吕千飞　译　徐晓东补充）

12. Thomas Gray

Thomas Gray（托马斯·格雷，1716—1771）is remembered today chiefly as the author of "Elegy Written in a Country Churchyard." He was born in London, son of an exchange broker. Gray was the only surviving child in a family of eight. By keeping shop, his mother earned the money to send him through Eton and Cambridge. In 1738, he left Cambridge without taking a degree. After a 3-year Continental tour（1739—1741）with his former classmate and fellow writer, Horace Walpole, Gray settled in cloistered bachelor retirement at Cambridge, where he was a scholar of classical literature, a well-liked don, and a poet in residence. He enjoyed the quiet life of a Cambridge professor. On one occasion, however, a practical joke so shattered his nerves and disrupted the "noiseless tenor" of his ways that he moved to another of Cambridge's several colleges—a change which for him was a cataclysmic upheaval.

Although Gray's life was placid, his poetry was venturesome. Without discarding what he believed was good in the old, neoclassic tradition, he explored new and unfamiliar areas in poetry. His use of personification, high-flown allusions, and conventional poetic diction are representative of his ties to the earlier style. But while Pope reflected fashionable city taste, like Wordsworth and other Romantic poets, Gray turned to country life and humble people for inspiration. He dealt in honest and homely emotion and brought back into poetry the use of the first-person singular, considered a barbarism by the 18th century norms, which dictated suppression of the ego and concealment of emotion. Not only Gray's treatment of nature, but his interest in the past, in Celtic and Norse folklore and simple, primitive cultures, has been seen as a foreshadowing of themes that would find their fullest expression in the Romantic movement of the 19th century. But Gray can be appreciated on his own terms, free from theories about his preparing the way for the Romantic period.

Though a painstaking writer, Gray produced few poems. It took him nine years to complete *Elegy Written in a Country Churchyard* (1751). Samuel Johnson may have thought Gray dull, but most readers agreed with General Wolfe, who before the battle of Quebec in 1759, said of the "Elegy": "I would rather be the author of those lines than take Quebec."

Elegy Written in a Country Churchyard[1]

The term "elegy", first used to describe any serious meditative poem, is now used to refer to a poem that laments the death of a particular person. Gray's poem laments the passing of all people, but ends with an epitaph for a particular person, and is thus an elegy in both senses. In this poem, the humble lives of the innocent farmers are contrasted to the noble courses of the great men with fame and fortune. The poet concludes that they are equally conquered by death. The poem contains a number of memorable lines, though it is occasionally marred by artificial expressions of poetic dictions.

The curfew[2] tolls the knell of parting day,
The lowing herd[3] wind slowly o'er the lea[4],
The plowman homeward plods his weary way,
And leaves the world to darkness and to me.

Now fades the glimmering landscape on the sight,
And all the air a solemn stillness holds,[5]
Save[6] where the beetle wheels his droning flight,
And drowsy tinklings lull the distant folds[7];

Save that from yonder ivy-mantled tower
The moping[8] owl does to the moon complain
Of such, as wandering near her secret bower[9],
Molest[10] her ancient solitary reign[11].

Beneath those rugged elms, that yew tree's shade,
Where heaves the turf in many a moldering heap,
Each in his narrow cell forever laid,
The rude[12] forefathers of the hamlet sleep.

The breezy call of incense-breathing Morn[13],
The swallow twittering from the straw-built shed,
The cock's shrill clarion, or the echoing horn,[14]
No more shall rouse them from their lowly bed[15]

For them no more the blazing hearth shall burn,
Or busy housewife ply her evening care;
No children run to lisp their sire's return,
Or climb his knees the envied kiss to share.

Oft did harvest to their sickle yield,
Their furrow oft the stubborn glebe[16] has broke[17];
How jocund[18] did they drive their team[19] afield[20]!
How bowed the woods beneath their sturdy stroke!

Let not Ambition[21] mock their useful toil,
Their homely joys, and destiny obscure[22];
Nor Grandeur[23] hear with a disdainful smile
The short and simple annals of the poor.

The boast of heraldry[24], the pomp of power[25],
And all that beauty, all that wealth e'er gave[26],
Awaits alike the inevitable hour.[27]
The paths of glory lead but to the grave.

Nor you, ye proud, impute to these the fault,[28]
If Memory o'er their tomb no trophies[29] raise,
Where through the long-drawn aisle and fretted vault[30]
The pealing anthem swells the note of praise.

Can storied urn[31] or animated[32] bust
Back to its mansion[33] call the fleeting breath?
Can Honor's voice provoke[34] the silent dust[35],
Or Flattery soothe the dull cold ear of Death?

Perhaps in this neglected spot is laid
Some heart once pregnant with celestial fire[36];
Hands that the rod of empire[37] might have swayed[38],
Or waked to ecstasy the living lyre[39].

But Knowledge to their eyes her ample page
Rich with the spoils of time[40] did ne'er unroll;
Chill Penury repressed their noble rage[41],

And froze the genial[42] current of the soul.

Full many a gem[43] of purest ray serene,
The dark unfathomed caves of ocean bear:
Full many a flower[44] is born to blush unseen,
And waste its sweetness on the desert air[45].

Some village Hampden[46], that with dauntless breast
The little tyrant of his fields withstood;
Some mute inglorious Milton here may rest,
Some Cromwell[47] guiltless of his country's blood.

The applause of listening senates[48] to command,
The threats of pain and ruin to despise,
To scatter plenty o'er a smiling land,
And read their history in a nation's eyes,

Their lot[49] forbade[50]: nor circumscribed alone
Their growing virtues, but their crimes confined[51];
Forbade[52] to wade through slaughter to a throne,
And shut the gates of mercy on mankind,

The struggling pangs of conscious truth to hide,
To quench the blushes of ingenuous shame[53],
Or heap the shrine of Luxury and Pride
With incense kindled at the Muse's[54] flame.

Far from the madding crowd's ignoble strife,[55]
Their sober wishes never learned to stray;
Along the cool sequestered[56] vale of life
They kept the noiseless tenor[57] of their way.

Yet even these bones from insult to protect

Some frail memorial[58] still erected nigh,
With uncouth rhymes and shapeless sculpture decked[59],
Implores the passing tribute of a sigh.

Their name, their years, spelt by the unlettered Muse[60],
The place of fame and elegy supply:[61]
And many a holy text[62] around she strews,
That teach the rustic moralist to die.[63]

For who to dumb Forgetfulness a prey,
This pleasing anxious being e'er resigned,
Left the warm precincts of the cheerful day,
Nor cast one longing lingering look behind?

On some fond[64] breast the parting soul relies,
Some pious drops[65] the closing eye requires;
Even from the tomb the voice of Nature cries,
Even in our ashes live their wonted fires[66].

For thee[67], who mindful of the unhonored dead
Dost in these lines their artless tale relate;
If chance[68], by lonely contemplation led,
Some kindred spirit[69] shall inquire thy fate,

Haply some hoary-headed swain[70] may say,
"Oft have we seen him at the peep of dawn
Brushing with hasty steps the dews away
To meet the sun upon the upland lawn.

"There at the foot of yonder nodding beech
That wreathes its old fantastic roots so high,
His listless length[71] at noontide would he stretch,
And pore upon[72] the brook that babbles by.

"Hard by yon wood, now smiling as in scorn,
Muttering his wayward fancies he would rove,
Now drooping, woeful wan[73], like one forlorn,
Or crazed with care, or crossed in hopeless love[74]."
"One morn I missed him on the customed[75] hill,
Along the heath and near his favorite tree;
Another came; nor yet beside the rill[76],
Nor up the lawn, nor at the wood was he;"[77]

"The next[78] with dirges due in sad array
Slow[79] through the churchway path we saw him borne[80].
Approach and read (for thou canst read) the lay,
Graved on the stone beneath yon aged thorn[81]."

The Epitaph[82]

Here rests his head upon the lap of Earth
A youth[83] to Fortune and to Fame unknown.
Fair Science frowned not on his humble birth,[84]
And Melancholy marked him for her own.

Large was his bounty, and his soul sincere,
Heaven did a recompense as largely[85] send:
He gave to Misery all he had, a tear,[86]
He gained from Heaven ('twas all he wished) a friend.

No farther seek his merits to disclose,
Or draw his frailties[87] from their dread abode[88]
(There they[89] alike in trembling hope repose),
The bosom of his Father and his God.

ca. 1742—50 1751

Notes

1. This elegy is written in thirty-two quatrains of iambic pentameter rhyming abab. An elegy is a lyric poem of mourning, usually over the passing of life and beauty or a meditation on the nature of death, usually formal in language and structure, and solemn or even melancholy in tone. Here the country churchyard refers to that at Stoke Pogis in Buckinghamshire where Gray's mother lived. Gray and his mother were buried there.
2. curfew: an evening bell.
3. the lowing herd: the mooing cattle.
4. lea: grassland.
5. And all the air a solemn stillness holds: and a solemn tranquility prevails in the air. hold: control.
6. Save: except.
7. folds: sheepfolds.
8. moping: fretting.
9. bower: women's chamber.
10. Molest: trouble.
11. The first three stanzas provide the setting of the poem. The next four is to lament the persons buried in the churchyard and recall their lives in the world.
12. rude: uneducated.
13. incense-breathing Morn: morning that smells sweet with fragrant flowers.
14. the echoing horn: referring to the hunter's horn.
15. lowly bed: referring to the grave.
16. the stubborn glebe: the solid soil.
17. broke: broken.
18. jocund: joyful.
19. team: the domestic animals used for ploughing.
20. afield: to the field.
21. Ambition: it is personified here referring to persons with ambitions. The following Grandeur, Memory, Honor, Death, etc. are all used this way.
22. destiny obscure: obscure destiny.

23. Grandeur: persons of high social positions.
24. The boast of heraldry: the boastful display of their noble origin. heraldry: noble birth.
25. the pomp of power: the grand show of their political power.
26. gave: yielded.
27. Awaits alike the inevitable hour: equally waits for the unavoidable hour (of death). Cf. Shakespeare's *Cymbeline* 4.2: "Golden lads and girls all must, /As chimney-sweepers, come to dust."
28. Nor you, ye proud, impute to these the fault: Neither should you, the proud person, blame these poor peasants for the fault.
29. trophies: memorial sculptures, ornamental figures depicting the achievements of the dead.
30. fretted vault: arched ceiling ornamented by elaborate design. fretted: ornamented by elaborate design.
31. storied urn: an urn with an epitaph or pictures that tell the story of the deceased.
32. animated: lifelike.
33. mansion: referring to the dead body.
34. provoke: call forth.
35. the silent dust: referring to the dead. Cf. Genesis 3: 19: "You are dust, and to dust you shall return."
36. pregnant with celestial fire: filled with religious passion. There might be people who once held important religious positions.
37. rod of empire: the symbol of power, especially of rulers. There might be rulers, kings or statesmen among peasants.
38. swayed: wielded.
39. the living lyre: the symbol of poets and musicians. There might be poets or musicians among peasants.
40. spoils of time: the human experience and wisdom.
41. Chill Penury repressed their noble rage: cold poverty suppressed their worthy inspiration. penury: poverty. rage: inspiration.
42. genial: creative.
43. gem: the peasants are metaphorized as the jewelry buried in dark and deep

ocean.

44. many a flower: the peasants are metaphorized as flowers that no one will take notice of.
45. desert air: desolate air.
46. Hampden: referring to John Hampden (1594—1643), a popular hero who defied the king over unjust taxation in 1636. He was mortally wounded in a skirmish near Oxford.
47. Cromwell: Oliver Cromwell (1599—1658), leader of English bourgeois revolution in 1642—1649 who became Lord Protector of the Commonwealth in 1653—1658.
48. senates: referring to English parliament.
49. lot: fate.
50. forbade: to command, to despise, to scatter, and (to) read are all its objects.
51. nor circumscribed alone/Their growing virtues, but their crimes confined: (Their fate) not only limited their growing virtues, but confined their crimes.
52. Forbade: to wade, (to) shut, to hide, to quench and (to) heap are all its objects.
53. ingenuous shame: a natural sense of shame.
54. Muse: the poet's inspiring goddess.
55. Far from the madding crowd's ignoble strife: the following four stanzas show that even though they lived a quiet, obscure life, they should not be forgotten after their death. Thomas Hardy, the famous novelist in the 20th century, took the first five words as the title of one of his novels. ignoble: dishonourable.
56. sequestered: secluded.
57. tenor: continuous course.
58. frail memorial: simple tombstone.
59. decked: ornamented.
60. unlettered Muse: referring to the uneducated gravestone carver.
61. The place of fame and elegy supply: supply or take the place of fame and elegy.

62. holy text: the Scriptures.
63. That teach the rustic moralist to die: That teach the rustic moralist how to die (how to deal with death).
64. fond: affectionate.
65. drops: tears.
66. Even in our ashes live their wonted fires: Their usual spirit exists even after we die.
67. For thee: As for the poet Gray himself. The poet imagined his own death in the following six stanzas which are a complete sentence, with "swain" its subject.
68. chance: perchance.
69. kindred spirit: person like you.
70. hoary-headed swain: white-haired rustic.
71. listless length: listless body.
72. pore upon: focus his attention on.
73. woeful wan: sorrow and pale.
74. crossed in hopeless love: failed to win his love.
75. customed: accustomed.
76. rill: brook.
77. Hard by yon wood … was he: these eight lines were carved on Gray's tombstone as his epitaph.
78. The next: the next morning.
79. Slow: slowly.
80. borne: in his coffin.
81. thorn: hawthorn brush.
82. Epitaph: an inscription on a gravestone or a short poem written in memory of someone who has died. Many epitaphs are actually epigrams, or short witty sayings, and are not intended for serious use as monument inscriptions.
83. A youth: Thomas Gray himself, who was 28 when writing this poem.
84. Fair Science frowned not on his humble birth: his humble birth did not prevent him from having a good education. Science: general knowledge.
85. as largely: as generously.

86. He gave to Misery all he had, a tear: he gave all he had, a tear, to Misery. The implication is that all he possessed was sympathy he showed to the poor people.
87. draw his frailties: find faults with him.
88. dread abode: referring to his grave. dread: dreadful, for the bad person dreaded to be judged by God.
89. they: referring to both "his merits" and "his frailties".

诗歌赏析

这首诗是英国最著名的诗歌之一。全诗用抑扬格五音步写成，押 abab 韵，语言典雅，结构谨严，条理清楚，整齐划一，符合古典主义的特点。诗人一方面惋惜农民贫困的遭遇，惋惜他们不能发挥才干，成为伟人；另一方面又庆幸农民的无权正好使他们免于罪恶。这种消极无力的色彩又是以诗人为首的新的诗派——墓园诗派的诗歌特色。古典主义诗风与新的诗歌内容的完美结合使这首诗成为英语诗歌中的经典。

前三节重在设景。晚钟敲起了白日的丧钟，牛群哞哞地在草地上徘徊，疲惫的农人已开始归家，嗡嗡的甲虫，欲睡的羊群和月光下的猫头鹰更增加了安静、肃穆的气息。一日将尽，乡村一片静寂。

后四节点出墓中人。乡间的夜幕已经拉上，诗人想到那乡村墓园里坟墓中的农人，他们的人生已经谢幕了。诗人又想象着他们生前热闹的劳动场景、温馨的家居生活。他们或许没有雄心壮志，没有炫耀的门第，没有显赫的权势。他们活着时过着朴实无华的生活；死去后，也没有多少人去怀念他们。但是，死亡是任何人都不可避免的结局，荣誉和谄媚也不能阻止死神的脚步。

接下来的八节诗中，诗人指出，也许这些普通的农人中也有汉普顿、弥尔顿和克伦威尔那样的英雄好汉和诗才，可是贫寒的生活遏制了农人的发展，他们注定走过平凡的一生。因此，诗人发出了这样的感慨：

世界上多少晶莹皎洁的珠宝
埋在幽暗而深不可测的海底；
世界上多少花吐艳而无人知晓，
把芳香白白地散发给荒凉的空气。

这些带有浓郁浪漫主义诗风的诗行是格雷的名句，诉说了千古不灭的人生道理。或许他们的命运不济，不能铸就丰功伟绩，但是他们卑微的身份地位，也使他们不至于酿成大错，可以安然度过平凡的一生。这也算是一点安慰。

第20—23节，诗人表达了伤感无奈的情怀：虽然默然一生，默然离去，谁又愿意就此被人遗忘？诗人呼吁大家不要忘了这些离世的乡村父老。第24节以后，诗人联想到自己死后的光景，最后的“墓志铭”是他的人生写照，感情真挚，语言动人。

音调的考究是这首诗的一个重要艺术特色。全诗音韵和谐，流畅自然。诗人频繁使用长音，营造出一种缓慢、低沉、哀婉的氛围。有些地方又使用短音，表达一种无可挽回的情绪。音韵规整又富有变化，用词典雅又贴切动人。动植物、声、光、色彩等的描述烘托出栩栩如生的乡间景色。鲜明的生活气息与诗歌的死亡主题形成对比，增加了该诗忧郁、感伤的气氛。

For Study and Discussion

1. How does Gray use imagery and sound effect to establish the mood of his poem?
2. Although the poem identifies itself as an elegy, it does not memorialize any particular person. What does it memorialize? Provide at least two citations to illustrate your discussion.
3. What's the theme of this elegy?
4. Have you ever read other elegies? Compare the elegies you know with this one.
5. Learn the first and fourteenth stanzas by heart.

参考译文

墓畔哀歌

晚钟响起来一阵阵给白昼报丧，
牛群在草原上迂回，吼声起落，
耕地人累了，回家走，脚步踉跄，
把整个世界留给了黄昏与我。

苍茫的景色逐渐从眼前消退，
一片肃穆的寂静盖遍了尘寰，
只听见嗡嗡的甲虫转圈子纷飞，

昏沉的铃声催眠着远处的羊栏。

只听见常春藤披裹的塔顶底下
一只阴郁的枨枭向月亮诉苦，
怪人家无端走进它秘密的住家，
搅扰它这个悠久而僻静的领土。

峥嵘的榆树底下，扁柏的荫里，
草皮鼓起了许多零落的荒堆，
各自在洞窟里永远放下了身体，
小村里粗鄙的父老在那里安睡。

香气四溢的晨风轻松的呼召，
燕子从茅草棚子里吐出的呢喃，
公鸡的尖喇叭，使山鸣谷应的猎号
再不能唤醒他们在地下的长眠。

在他们，熊熊的炉火不再会燃烧，
忙碌的管家妇不再会赶她的夜活；
孩子们不再会“呀呀”地报父亲来到，
为一个亲吻爬到他膝上去争夺。

往常是，他们一开镰就所向披靡，
顽梗的泥板让他们犁出了垄沟；
他们多么欢欣地赶牲口下地！
他们一猛砍，树木就一棵棵低头！

“雄心”别嘲讽他们实用的操劳，
家常的欢乐，默默无闻的运命；
“豪华”也不用带着轻蔑的冷笑
来听讲穷人的又短又简的生平。

门第的炫耀，有权有势的煊赫，
凡是美和财富所能赋予的好处，
前头都等待着不可避免的时刻：
光荣的道路无非是引导到坟墓。
骄傲人，你也不要怪这些人不行，

"怀念"没有给这些坟建立纪念堂，
没有让悠长的廊道、雕花的拱顶
洋溢着洪亮的赞美歌，进行颂扬。

栩栩的半身像，铭刻了事略的瓮碑，
难道能恢复断气，促使还魂？
"荣誉"的声音能激发沉默的死灰？
"献媚"能叫死神听软了耳根？

也许这一块地方，尽管荒芜，
就埋着曾经充满过灵焰的一颗心；
一双手，本可以执掌到帝国的王芴
或者出神入化地拨响了七弦琴。

可是"知识"从不曾对他们展开
它世代积累而琳琅满目的书卷；
"贫寒"压制了他们高贵的襟怀，
冻结了他们从灵府涌出的流泉。

世界上多少晶莹皎洁的珠宝
埋在幽暗而深不可测的海底；
世界上多少花吐艳而无人知晓，
把芳香白白地散发给荒凉的空气。

也许有乡村汉普顿在这里埋身，
反抗过当地的小霸王，胆大，坚决；
也许有缄口的弥尔顿，从没有名声；
有一位克伦威尔，并不曾害国家流血。

要博得满场的元老雷动的鼓掌，
无视威胁，全不顾存亡生死，
把富庶、丰饶遍播到四处八方，
打从全国的笑眼里读自己的历史。

他们的命运可不许：既不许罪过
有所放纵，也不许发挥德行；
不许从杀戮中间涉登宝座

从此对人类关上仁慈的大门。

不许掩饰天良在内心的发作，
隐瞒天真的羞愧，恬不红脸；
不许用诗神的金焰点燃了香火
锦上添花去塞满“骄”“奢”的神龛。

远离了纷纭人世的勾心斗角，
他们有清醒的愿望，从不学糊涂，
顺着生活的清凉僻静的山坳，
他们坚持了不声不响的正路。

可是叫这些尸骨免受到糟蹋，
还是有脆弱的碑牌树立在近边，
点缀了拙劣的韵语、凌乱的刻画，
请求过往人顺便献一声惋叹。

无闻的野诗神注上了姓名、年份，
另外再加上地址和一篇诔词；
她在周围撒播了一些经文，
教训乡土道德家怎样去死。

要知道谁甘愿舍身喂哑口的“遗忘”，
坦然撇下了忧喜交织的此生，
谁离开风和日暖的明媚现场
而能不依依地回头来顾盼一阵？

辞世的灵魂还依傍钟情的怀抱，
临闭的眼睛需要尽哀的珠泪，
即使坟冢里也有“自然”的呼号，
他们的旧火还点燃我们的新灰。

至于你，你关心这些默默的陈死人，
用这些诗句讲他们质朴的故事，
假如在幽思的引导下，偶然有缘分，
一位同道来问起你的身世——

也许会有白头的乡下人对他说，

"我们常常看见他，天还刚亮，
就用匆忙的脚步把露水碰落，
上那边高处的草地去会晤朝阳。

"那边有一棵婆娑的山毛榉老树，
树底下隆起的老根盘错在一起，
他常常在那里懒躺过一个中午，
悉心看旁边一道涓涓的小溪。

"他转游到林边，有时候笑里带嘲，
念念有词，发他的奇谈怪议，
有时候垂头丧气，像无依无靠，
像忧心忡忡或者像情场失意。

"有一天早上，在他惯去的山头，
灌木丛，他那棵爱树下，我不见他出现；
第二天早上，尽管我走下溪流，
上草地，穿过树林，他还是不见。

"第三天我们见到了送葬的行列，
唱着挽歌，抬着他向坟场走去——
请上前看那丛老荆棘底下的碑碣，
（你是识字的）请念念这些诗句"：

墓 铭

这里边，高枕地膝，是一位青年，
生平从不曾受知于"富贵"和"名声"；
"知识"可没轻视他出身的微贱，
"清愁"把他标出来认作宠幸。

他生性真挚，最乐于慷慨施惠，
上苍也给了他同样慷慨的报酬：
他给了"坎坷"全部的所有，一滴泪；
从上苍获得了所求，一位朋友。

别再想法子表彰他的功绩，
也别再把他的弱点翻出了暗窖
（他们同样在颤抖的希望中休息），
那就是他的天父和上帝的怀抱。

（卞之琳　译）

13. William Blake

William Blake (威廉·布莱克, 1757—1827), "the most spiritual artist", was a major prophet of the Romantic Movement and of the revolt against the mechanical tyranny of the capitalist world. His achievement was a breakthrough into the Romantic Movement.

Blake was born on 28 November 1757, the son of a London Hosier. Blake received little formal education, but he was kept well supplied with books and prints of great paintings. His favorite studies were Shakespeare, Milton and Chatterton. When, at 10, he expressed the desire to be a painter. He was sent to a drawing school and then apprenticed to an engraver. His talent for sketching is seen in his illustrations not only of his own poems but also of Milton's *Paradise Lost*, Dante's *Divine Comedy*, Gray's poems and Young's *Night Thoughts*. But he never got rich in this trade and remained poor all his life.

Some objectors of Blake called him mad man. He was not, but as a child, he did often say words of near madness, claiming to have seen a tree filled with angels, the prophet Ezekiel, or God at his window. Maybe this eccentricity helped to shape him into a poet.

His first collection of poems is *Poetical Sketches* (1783), in which he showed contempt for classicist rule of reason and a strong sympathy for the freshness of Elizabethan poetry. "Without contrast," wrote Blake, "there is no progression." His *Songs of Innocence* (1789) and *Songs of Experience* (1794) which contain some of the most beautiful lyrics in the English language, clearly show this idea. In the *Songs of Innocence*, Blake depicts the happy condition of a child before it knows anything about the pains of existence. In the *Songs of Experience* the poems are pictures of neediness and distress and show sufferings of the poor. The salvation is to come through passionate revolt, through revolution. Blake's style is symbolic, with which, he shows his progressive democratic ideas.

Blake was one of the revolutionary thinkers of that time. His support of the French Revolution (1789) was lifelong. The greatness of Blake lies in his mastery, in art and verse, of an extreme and moving simplicity. William Wordsworth thus commented on Blake: "There is something in the madness of this man which interests me more than the sanity of Lord Byron or Walter Scott." Blake was called a forerunner of the Romantic Movement. His lyric poetry displays the characteristics of the romantic spirit. What's more, Blake's revolutionary passion was very much similar to that of Shelley, esp. in imagery and symbolism.

Blake was a representative poet of Pre-romanticism, which was a general term applied by modern literary historians to a number of developments in late 18th century culture that are thought to have prepared the ground of Romanticism in its full sense. In various ways, these are all departures from the orderly framework of neoclassicism and its authorized genres.

When old, he gave up poetry and devoted himself to painting and engraving. In 1827, this good, honest, great, "crazy" poet and painter died in obscurity and poverty.

London[1]

This is taken from *Songs of Experience*. In this poem, the poet wanders in the street of London and sees different scenes of misery. From the description of the miserable living conditions of the poor people, Blake shows his sympathy to the poor and his hatred to the ruling class. The famous critic Oliver Elton once called it "the mightiest brief poem".

I wander thro'[2] each charter'd street[3],
Near where the charter'd Thames[4] does flow,

And mark[5] in every[6] face I meet
Marks[7] of weakness, marks of woe.

In every cry of every Man,
In every Infant's cry of fear,
In every voice, in every ban[8],
The mind-forg'd manacles[9] I hear:

How the Chimney-sweeper's[10] cry
Every blackning Church[11] appalls[12],
And the hapless Soldier's sigh
Runs in blood down Palace walls.[13]

But most[14] thro' midnight streets I hear
How the youthful Harlot's[15] curse
Blasts[16] the new-born Infant's tear,
And blights with plagues the Marriage hearse[17].

1794

Notes

1. It is written in four quatrains of iambic tetrameter rhyming abab.
2. thro': through.
3. charter'd street: a street on which certain persons are given special privileges. charter'd: chartered, granted certain privileges according to a charter.
4. charter'd Thames: the Thames on which certain persons are given special privileges to make voyages. Thames: a river in Southeast England flowing east through London to the North Sea.
5. mark: notice.
6. every: this word is repeated several times in this poem to emphasize no one can escape the miserable life in London.
7. Marks: signs.
8. ban: the various meanings of ban are relevant (political and legal prohibition,

curse, public condemnation) as well as "banns" (marriage proclamation).

9. mind-forg'd manacles: fetters shaped by the minds, implying that the common people suffered both physically and spiritually. mind-forg'd: mind-forged.

10. Chimney-sweeper: person who sweep the chimney, usually little boys.

11. blackning Church: a pun, referring to the dirty church covered by dust on the surface, and the evils that religion has done to common people. blackning: blackening.

12. appalls: frightens greatly, shocks.

13. And the hapless Soldier's sigh/Runs in blood down Palace walls: a synaesthesia; hearing the unfortunate soldier's sigh, the poet thinks of the blood that the soldier sheds for the ruling class. hapless: unfortunate.

14. most: most of all.

15. Harlot's: prostitute's.

16. Blasts: makes…dry.

17. And blights with plagues the Marriage hearse: and converts the marriage coach into a funeral hearse with deadly disease. blights: destroys. plagues: deadly contagious disease including sexual disease. the Marriage hearse: an oxymoron. The poet is comparing the wedding to a funeral.

诗歌赏析

威廉·布莱克是英国18、19世纪之交的重要诗人兼版画家。他一生支持法国大革命，同情劳苦大众，对统治阶级持批评的态度，他的诗歌充满象征主义和神秘主义倾向。他的长诗《天真的预言》（*Auguries of Innocence*）的开头四行在中国家喻户晓：

To see a world in a grain of sand
And a heaven in a wild flower,
Hold infinity in the palm of your hand
And eternity in an hour.
一沙一世界，一花一天堂。
无限掌中置，刹那成永恒。

（徐志摩　译）

《伦敦》韵律工整，节奏铿锵。全诗由四个四行诗组组成，几乎每行都是工整的抑扬格四音步，押 abab 韵。但个别地方也有变化。从抑扬格到扬抑格，韵律随着情绪的变化起伏跌宕。频繁使用的长音和双元音表达了诗人沉重、压抑的情感。头韵的使用使诗歌主题在回旋中得以不断加强。

这首诗从诗人漫步伦敦街头时所看所听入手，描述了伦敦城里老百姓受苦受难的辛酸场面，对统治阶级的剥削、压迫进行了不同层面的控诉。

第一节通过独占的泰晤士河边的每一条独占的街道上的每一张虚弱痛苦的脸，从经济角度揭露了统治阶级对劳苦大众的摧残，尤其是身体上的摧残。第二节诗人从每个人、每个婴儿的每种声音、每条禁令里听到的精神的镣铐声说明老百姓经受的不仅是肉体的摧残还有精神的折磨。every 的五次重复增加了诗歌的感染力，强调无人幸免这悲惨的命运。第三节通过哭喊的扫烟囱小孩和不幸的士兵的形象实现了整首诗从抽象到具象，从整体到个体的转变。教堂代表宗教，宗教本来是用来保护劳苦大众的，可是那些穷人家的孩子们还要打扫漆黑的教堂。扫烟囱小孩的哭喊让黑心的教士们心惊胆战！黑暗的教堂说明了教会的腐败。士兵本来是保家卫国，为国家的神圣荣誉而战的，而英国连年的殖民扩张，导致伤兵无数。伤员回国后得不到安置，不得不流浪街头。不幸士兵的叹息血流宫墙，展示了那些年轻士兵对战争的失望及对军队和政府的血泪控诉。最后一节中年轻妓女的形象触目惊心。年轻女孩是青春美丽的象征，新生儿预示着希望，婚姻是幸福的殿堂。如今，年轻女孩沦为妓女。她在深夜街头的诅咒让新生儿不敢哭泣，让婚车变成灵柩。诗人一针见血地指出爱情被玷污、希望不再、无可救药的社会现实。

他从画家的角度，用丰富的视觉和听觉意象，勾勒出强烈的画面感，通过代表性的人物，从政治、经济、军事、宗教等各个角度揭露了英国社会的种种罪恶，并描绘了下层人民的苦难生活。

除了丰富的音韵手段和意象效果外，诗人还运用了丰富的修辞手法。最突出的手法是反复。全诗开始两行“独占”的重复，说明英国社会经济制度对老百姓的迫害。同类主题词的重复如哭喊、诅咒、虚弱、痛苦、恐惧等多方面展示了老百姓穷困潦倒的生活状态。全诗 every 共出现七次，强调人人如此，悲惨的命运无人能逃避。第三节中的黑暗的教堂分明使用了双关：一方面指尘土的堆积；另一方面指教会的邪恶、腐败。而“叹息如血流过宫墙”则使用了通感的手法，把听觉的叹息和视觉的鲜血以及触觉的流动感联系起来，形成鲜明的感官刺激，让人把士兵的悲惨命运和他们曾经付出的鲜血以及政府的无道联系起来。最令人触目惊心的是诗歌的最后两个词，即婚姻和灵柩的并举。婚姻是幸福的殿堂，可是诗人却将它与灵柩放在一起。在这样的社会里，年轻的妓女流浪在街头，爱情被诅咒，婚姻就意味着坟墓，普通人的幸福根本无法实现！

For Study and Discussion

1. Why does the poet use "every" many times? What effect does it produce?
2. This poem is famous for its vivid images. Which image strikes you most? Why?
3. What's the tone of this poem?
4. What effect is achieved in capitalizing words like Infant, Church, Soldier and Harlot?
5. Is this the kind of London you expected? What should London be like?

参考译文

伦 敦

我徘徊在每条被独占的街上，
靠近那也被独占的泰晤士河，
注意到那被遇见的每张脸上
都把衰弱和痛苦的烙印铭刻。

从每个男女的每一次呼喊声，
从每个婴孩害怕的哭叫，
从每个声音里，从每一条禁令
都能听到心灵铸的镣铐。

听扫烟囱孩子的叫喊
震惊着每座熏黑的教堂。
不幸兵士的悲叹
像鲜血冲下堵堵宫墙。

但我常听见在深夜的街头
年轻妓女在不停地诅咒。
那声音吓得新生儿眼泪不敢流，
妓女带来瘟疫，使婚车变成灵柩。

（李正栓　译）

The Sick Rose[1]

This poem is difficult for it is full of symbols. It is brief but suggestive and meaningful. There are many interpretations of the poem. Rose has many implied meanings, such as nature, love or society, so as the other symbols.

O Rose, thou art sick[2].
The invisible worm[3]
That flies in the night
In the howling storm

Has found out thy bed
Of crimson joy,
And his dark secret love
Does thy life destroy.

1794

Notes

1. This poem is written in two quatrains of combined iambic and anapestic feet with the even lines rhymed.
2. thou art sick: you are sick.
3. invisible worm: an image of evil force which cannot be seen.

诗歌赏析

这首短诗充分体现了布莱克诗歌的象征主义和神秘主义倾向。批评界对这首诗还没有一个统一的理解。在文艺复兴时期的文学中，玫瑰一直都是美丽、爱情的象征，然后布莱克以他独特的方式赋予这一传统的意象以新的内涵。

从表面来看，诗中描绘了一个自然现象：暗夜中，一只看不见的虫子借着暴风雨的遮蔽摧残了一朵玫瑰。但是，这首诗显然没有这么简单。玫瑰可以理解为爱情。看不见的虫子是邪恶力量的象征，暗夜、暴风雨是邪恶的屏障，绯红色充满欢欣的花床意味着感官享乐，也是邪恶的目的所在。它用黑暗、隐秘的爱猎取了玫瑰的爱情，玫瑰也因此凋零。亦即纯真的爱情如果没有道德的约束，只图感官享乐，最终只能消亡。诗歌借此对不健康的爱进行谴责。玫瑰也可以指爱人、社会等。简单的句式、丰富的意象使这首诗充满了想象的空间。

For Study and Discussion

1. What do "the sick rose" and "the invisible worm" symbolize in this poem?
2. What ideas and associations are connected with rose, worm and other images in this poem?
3. What's your interpretation of this poem?
4. Please recite the poem.

参考译文

病玫瑰

哦，玫瑰，你病了。
无形的虫
横飞在暗夜里
在咆哮的暴雨中

发现你的床
充满猩红的欢乐，
他那黑暗私密的爱
把你生命剥夺。

（李正栓　译）

The Chimney Sweeper[1]

This poem is chosen from *Songs of Innocence*. In another volume *Songs of Experience*, there is a poem with the same title. But they are quite different. In this poem, Blake expresses his optimistic idea toward life: though the chimney-sweepers suffer a lot, if they work hard enough, God will save them.

When my mother died I was very young,
And my father sold me while yet my tongue

Could scarcely cry "weep! weep! weep! weep!"[2]
So your chimneys I sweep & in soot I sleep.

There's little Tom Dacre, who cried when his head
That curl'd like a lamb's back[3], was shav'd[4], so I said,
"Hush, Tom! never mind it, for when your head's bare,
You know that the soot cannot spoil your white hair."

And so he was quiet, & that very night,
As Tom was a-sleeping[5] he had such a sight!
That thousands of sweepers, Dick, Joe, Ned, & Jack,[6]
Were all of them lock'd up[7] in coffins of black[8];

And by came an Angel[9] who had a bright key,
And he open'd the coffins & set them all free;
Then down a green plain, leaping, laughing they run,
And wash in a river and shine in the Sun.

Then naked & white, all their bags left behind,
They rise upon clouds, and sport in the wind.
And the Angel told Tom, if he'd be a good boy,
He'd have God for his father & never want[10] joy.

And so Tom awoke; and we rose in the dark
And got with our bags & our brushes to work.
Tho' the morning[11] was cold, Tom was happy & warm;
So if all do their duty, they need not fear harm.

1789

Notes

1. It consists of six quatrains of combined iambic and anapestic meters rhyming aabb.
2. weep: the child's lisping attempt at the chimney sweeper's street cry,

"Sweep! Sweep!"

3. That curl'd like a lamb's back: that curled hair on the boy's head is like that of a lamb.
4. shav'd: shaved.
5. a-sleeping: sleeping.
6. Dick, Joe, Ned, & Jack: common names for children.
7. lock'd up: locked up.
8. in coffins of black: in the black chimneys.
9. by came an Angel: an Angel came by.
10. want: lack.
11. Tho' the morning: though the morning.

诗歌赏析

这首诗选自布莱克的《天真之歌》。在18世纪，穷人家的小孩子，有时候甚至只有四五岁，就被雇佣来爬上狭窄的烟道，去清扫烟囱，直到从出口爬出来喊一声"扫啊!"这一过程才算结束。因为烟囱大多窄而小，只有小孩子才能钻进去，有些烟囱刚刚熄火，还有烫伤的危险，这种悲惨的状况一直持续到1788年国会通过一个法案，规定八岁以下的孩子不得扫烟囱，扫烟囱的孩子每周必须沐浴一次，雇主不得逼迫孩子进入未熄火的烟囱等。诗歌借用扫烟囱小孩童真的语言揭露生活的不幸，但是基调不是悲观的。这首诗语言简单，蕴意丰富。汤姆、杰克等都是普通人的名字，因为只有穷人家的孩子才会扫烟囱。把孩子的卷发比作羊羔毛，也就是说孩子们就是上帝的羔羊。羔羊是纯洁、温顺的象征。梦里的黑棺材是对他们悲惨命运的控诉。黑黑的烟囱对这些孩子来说就像棺材一样，随时会夺取他们的性命。但是孩子们知道，只要听上帝的话，他们就有美好的未来。穷人家的孩子看不到生活的希望，只能借用宗教来安慰自己，无奈中暗藏悲愤。托姆的美梦和结尾处冰冷的现实形成巨大的反差，具有反讽的效果。

For Study and Discussion

1. Which words tell you the misery of the chimney sweepers?
2. How is innocence shown through the poem?
3. Do you agree with the statement "if all do their duty, they need not fear harm"? Give your reason.

4. This poem is famous for its irony. Which irony strikes you most?

参考译文

扫烟囱孩子

我母亲死的时候，我还小得很，
我父亲把我拿出来卖给了别人，
我当时还不大喊得清："扫呀——扫！"
我就扫你们烟囱，晚上在烟灰里睡觉。

有个小托姆，头发卷得像小羊头，
剃光的时候，哭得好伤心，好难受，
我就说："小托姆，不要紧，光了脑瓜，
大起来煤屑就不会糟蹋你白头发。"

他就安安静静了，当天夜里，
托姆睡着了，事情就来得稀奇，
他看见千千万万的扫烟囱小孩
阿猫阿狗全都给锁进了黑棺材。

后来来了个天使，拿了把金钥匙，
开棺材，放出了孩子们（真是好天使！）
他们就边跳，边笑，边跑过草坪，
到河里洗了澡，太阳下晒得亮晶晶。

光光的，白白的，把袋子都抛个一地，
他们就升上了云端，在风里游戏；
"只要你做个好孩子，"天使对托姆说，
"上帝会做你的父亲，你会永远快乐。"

托姆就醒了；屋子里黑咕隆咚，
我们就起来拿袋子、扫帚去做工。
大清早尽管冷，托姆的心里可温暖；
所以，只要尽责，不必担心受伤害。

（卞之琳　译）

The Chimney Sweeper[1]

This is taken from *Songs of Experience*. It describes a little chimney sweeper's miserable life in the form of a dialogue and discloses ironically the relation of his life to God, King and his family in his own words. In this poem, God is no longer a Savior, but the Maker of his sufferings, together with King and his family.

A little black thing[2] among the snow
Crying "'weep[3], 'weep," in notes of woe!
"Where are thy father & mother? say?"
"They are both gone up to the church to pray."

"Because I was happy upon the heath[4],
And smil'd among the winter's snow;
They clothed me in the clothes of death[5],
And taught me to sing the notes of woe[6].

"And because I am happy, & dance & sing,
They think they have done me no injury,
And are gone to praise God & his Priest & King,
Who make up a heaven of our misery."[7]

1790—92 1794

Notes

1. This poem consists of three quatrains of combined iambic and anapestic feet with the first stanza rhyming aabb and the other two abab.
2. a little black thing: a little boy who is a chimney-sweeper (chimney-sweeping has made him look black).
3. 'weep: a pun, meaning "to sweep" and "to weep".
4. heath: the open field in the countryside.
5. the clothes of death: the black clothes. In England, black is the symbol of death.

6. the notes of woe: to cry "'weep!"
7. Who make up a Heaven of our misery: who build a Heaven upon our misery. "Who" refers to "God and His Priest and King". The poet criticizes the religion and the government.

诗歌赏析

这首诗选自《经验之歌》。诗人不再寄希望于宗教和社会，对18世纪英国社会中惨无人道的社会现象进行了强烈谴责。全诗从一个孩子的视角，用孩子天真、质朴的语言，揭露了扫烟囱小孩所受的压迫。对照手法的运用是这首诗的鲜明特色。当孩子在烟囱里哭泣时，他的父母去教堂感谢上帝；童年时孩子在野地里无忧无虑地玩耍，现在父母却让他穿上黑衣扫烟囱；因为孩子难掩天性，依然会唱歌跳舞，父母就以为他的生活充满欢欣。可是，最后，孩子一针见血地揭露出真相：他们的天堂建立在我们的痛苦之上！

For Study and Discussion

1. Compare this poem with "The Chimney Sweeper" taken from *Songs of Innocence*. Comment on the changes of tone.
2. Comment on how contrast is used in this poem.
3. Is it fit for the parents to go to the church to praise God while the children suffer?

参考译文

扫烟囱孩子

风雪里一个满身乌黑的小东西
"扫呀，扫"的在那里哭哭啼啼！
"你的爹娘上哪儿去了，你讲讲？"
"他们呀都去祷告了，上了教堂。"

"因为我原先在野地里欢欢喜喜，
我在冬天的雪地里也总是笑嘻嘻，
他们就把我拿晦气的黑衣裳一罩，
他们还教我唱起了悲伤的曲调。"

"因为我显得快活，还唱歌，还跳舞，
他们就以为并没有把我害苦，
就跑去赞美了上帝、教士和国王，
夸他们拿我们苦难造成了天堂。"

（卞之琳　译）

14. Robert Burns

Robert Burns（罗伯特·彭斯，1759－1796）was born in a poor peasant's family at Alloway, Ayrshire, Scotland. He had to help his father on the farm when he was still a child. He received little formal education. He got acquainted with English and Scottish classics as well as popular, old Scottish songs and ballads and legends from his mother and grandmother. In 1775, when he was sixteen and already the principal labourer on the farm, he started to write poems. In 1784 his father died and the family met financial problems. Being the eldest son, Burns had to support the family. In 1786 when he was about to emigrate to Jamaica for a living, he found himself famous with the publication of *Poems, Chiefly in Scottish Dialect*. He was once invited to Edinburgh, but he soon found himself not suitable for that society. Burns went back home, and kept living there for the rest of his life. He died of heart disease in 1796, when he was only 37 years old.

Burns was a poet of the labouring people. He came from the people, worked as the people and wrote for the people. He was the national poet and national hero of Scotland. Most of his poems and songs were written in Scottish dialect. He was also one of the greatest song writers in the world. He had a deep knowledge and an excellent mastery of the old Scottish song tradition. He learned a lot from it and used many such elements in his poems. This was the main factor of his great success. Many of his lyrics were set to music and sung in the world. "*Auld Lang Syne*" was the most popular one.

The range and variety of Burns' poetry are most impressive, from the lyric to the narrative, dramatic, and satiric, from politics to love, nature and patriotism. Every year on January, 25, the Scottish people will drink whisky, eat Scottish puddings, and sing his songs to commemorate his birth. It has become a traditional festival for Scottish people in the world.

A Red, Red Rose[1]

This poem is one of Burns' popular love lyrics. The poet describes the deep love of the speaker for a girl. He compares the girl to a red, red rose and the sweet melody. He lists several impossible things to show his constant love for her. With the simple language, clear form and masterly poetic skills, Burns expressed the young man's true love for his beloved. This was also set to music and was sung widely.

O my Luve's[2] like a red, red rose[3],
That's newly sprung[4] in June;
O my Luve's like the melodie[5]
That's sweetly played in tune[6].

As fair art thou[7], my bonie lass[8],
So deep in luve am I;
And I will love thee still[9], my Dear,
Till a'[10] the seas gang[11] dry.

Till a' the seas gang dry, my Dear,
And the rocks melt wi'[12] the sun:
O I will love thee still, my Dear,
While the sands o' life shall run.[13]

And fare thee weel[14], my only Luve!
And fare thee weel, a while!
And I will come again, my Luve,
Tho'[15] it were ten thousand mile!

1794 1796

Notes

1. This poem is written in the form of ballad stanza, rhyming on the second and fourth lines of each stanza with alternate lines of four and three feet. Ballad stanza or meter is the usual form of the folk ballad and its literary imitations, consisting of a quatrain in which the first and third lines have four stresses while the second and the fourth have 3 stresses. Usually only the second and fourth lines rhyme. The meter is basically iambic.
2. Luve's: love is. Luve: Scottish dialect, love.
3. a red, red rose: here the poet compares his love to the red, red rose. The repetition of "red" makes "rose", the popular image in English poetry, unique. It may imply three meanings, that is, the beauty of the flower, the beauty of the girl and the deep love of the speaker toward his beloved. Besides, the red, red rose is also an expression of defamiliarization. It made the image fresh.
4. newly sprung: recently blossomed.
5. melodie: melody. Here the poet compares his love to the sweet melody which displays the sweet voice or the dynamic beauty of the girl.
6. in tune: in harmony.
7. fair art thou: you are beautiful.
8. bonie lass: pretty girl.
9. still: always.
10. a': all.
11. gang: Scottish dialect, go.
12. wi': with.
13. While the sands o' life shall run: In ancient times time was measured by the sandglass, so "while the sands o' life shall run" means as long as there are sands in the sandglass, that is, as long as I live. sands o' life: sands of life.
14. fare thee weel: farewell to you, goodbye. weel: Scottish dialect, well.
15. Tho': though, even though.

诗歌赏析

《一朵红红的玫瑰》是彭斯根据苏格兰民谣创作的一首脍炙人口的爱情诗篇。该诗语言朴素，音韵优美，修辞巧妙，构思新颖，歌颂了坚贞不渝的纯真爱情。

音乐美是彭斯诗歌的旗帜。他不仅把心爱的姑娘形容为乐曲，而且诗行间音韵和谐，旋律优美，达到了形式与内容的完美统一。全诗共四节，用民谣体的形式写成，即每节四行，其中奇数行为四音步，偶数行为三音步，格律基本上是抑扬格；前两节的韵脚为abcb，后两节的韵脚为abab；读起来铿锵有力，抑扬顿挫，表达出诗人对爱情忠贞不渝的决心。头韵和腹韵的使用也加强了该诗的节奏感。另外诗歌在结构、措辞上的重复、对称等，也产生了回旋往复、一唱三叹的音乐效果。

这首诗经久传唱的原因还在于明喻、重复、夸张等修辞的成功运用。

首先诗人把爱人比喻为红红的玫瑰，独具匠心。红红的玫瑰不仅给人一种光鲜照人的感觉，它还是热情、奔放的象征，暗示了爱人的健康与活力以及诗人对姑娘火一般热烈的爱情。另外，这个平常的意象在彭斯的笔下，通过陌生化的形式产生了奇崛的效果。它清新自然，富有新意，极富视觉冲击力和想象空间；它既是声音的延长，也是情感的延伸，让人产生无穷的回味。其次，把爱人形容为乐曲，那种律动美、气质美跃然纸上；乐曲还可以理解为恋人的话语。在诗人眼里，恋人一举手一投足都是风景！那么和谐完美、青春靓丽！从玫瑰到乐曲，从外在到内涵，一个生动光鲜、活泼可爱的农村少女形象脱颖而出。

彭斯在他的爱情诗中还大量使用了重复的手法以加强语言的表现力和深化主题。Luve（古体）是诗中反复出现的字眼，在短短的4个诗节中，出现了7处之多，分别代表了"爱人""爱情"和动词"挚爱"，这一中心词的不断出现强化了主题；诗歌中间部分"大海干枯水流尽"的重复则把全诗分为两个部分：前一部分仅涉及恋人；后一部分引入大海、岩石、太阳，为两人的爱情提供了广阔的宇宙背景。两个部分既对照鲜明，又联系密切，形成密不可分的整体。最后，"离别"（fare thee weel）的重复表达了热恋中的年轻人分别时的依依不舍。词、短语、句子的重复很有层次感，让人不觉俗套并能深刻体会到说话者真挚、火热的情感。

诗人在第三节中用海枯石烂的夸张手法表达了对爱人的铿锵誓言，用不可能发生的自然现象表现主人公对爱情的坚贞不渝，这样的爱情宣言让人想到中国的古老民歌，如汉乐府《上邪》："上邪！我欲与君相知，长命无绝衰。山无陵，江水为竭，冬雷震震，夏雨雪，天地合，乃敢与君绝。"而敦煌曲子词《菩萨蛮·枕前发尽千般愿》中也有："枕前发尽千般愿，要休且待青山烂。水面上秤锤浮，直待黄河彻底枯……"三者同为民歌民谣，有异曲同工之妙，恐怕这也是中国读者喜欢这首诗的原因。

这首诗语言直白，感情真挚，毫不矫揉造作。诗人的情感如滔滔的江水奔流而下，一泻千里。另外，本诗丝毫不带功利性的爱情诉求，在当今社会读起来还有一种荡涤心灵的感受。比起 18 世纪新古典主义充满说教气息的英雄双偶句与伤感主义忧郁的诗风，彭斯的诗充满了乡土气息和民族特色，简单易懂，给人耳目一新的感觉。

For Study and Discussion

1. What do you think of the two images in the first stanza? In what ways are they vivid and effective?
2. What do you know about the speaker's beloved according to the two similes?
3. Burns uses many poetic devices in this poem. How many can you find out? How do they relate to the theme of the poem?
4. What do you think of the poet's love for his beloved?
5. Learn this poem by heart.

参考译文

一朵红红的玫瑰

呵，我的爱人像一朵红红的玫瑰，
六月里迎风初开；
呵，我的爱人像一支甜甜的乐曲，
演奏得合弦又合拍。

我的好姑娘，你是那么美，
我的爱是这么深；
亲爱的，我要永远地爱你，
直到大海干枯水流尽！

直到大海干枯水流尽，
直到太阳把岩石化作灰尘：
呵，亲爱的，我将永远地爱你，
只要我一息犹存。

再见吧，我惟一的爱，
让我们暂时地分离！
亲爱的，我一定要回来，
哪怕是远行千里万里！

（李正栓　译）

Auld Lang Syne[1]

Burns is a great song writer. Many of his lyrics were set to music and sung in the whole world. This poem is the most popular one. The poem sings high praise of friendship, usually sung before parting. It became the theme song of the movie *Waterloo Bridge* (《魂断蓝桥》) in 1931, thus becoming more famous. Its Chinese version is《友谊地久天长》. The poet recalls the happy scenes the old friends once experienced; from then on they had departed and gone through many hardships. But neither time nor distance could hold back the everlasting friendship between them.

Should auld acquaintance be forgot
And never brought to mind?
Should auld acquaintance be forgot,
And auld lang syne!

Chorus

For auld lang syne, my dear,
For auld lang syne,
We'll tak[2] a cup o' kindness[3] yet
For auld lang syne.

And surely ye'll[4] be[5] your pint-stowp[6]!
And surely I'll be mine!

And we'll tak a cup o' kindness yet,
For auld lang syne.

Chorus

We twa hae[7] run about the braes[8]
And pou'd[9] the gowans fine[10];
But we've wander'd many a weary fitt[11],
Sin[12] auld lang syne.

Chorus

We twa hae paidl'd[13] in the burn[14]
Frae morning sun till dine;[15]
But seas between us braid[16] hae roar'd,
Sin auld lang syne.

Chorus

And there's a hand, my trusty fiere[17]!
And gie's[18] a hand o' thine!
And we'll tak a right gude-willie-waught[19],
For auld lang syne.

Chorus

For auld lang syne, my dear,
For auld lang syne,
We'll tak a cup o' kindness yet
For auld lang syne.

1788 1796

Notes

1. Auld Lang Syne: Scottish dialect for old long since, long long ago. Auld: old. Lang: long. Syne: since. This poem is also written in ballad stanza.
2. tak: take.
3. a cup o' kindness: a cup of wine for friendship.

4. ye'll：you'll.
5. be：pay for.
6. pint-stowp：pint-cup，a kind of big cups.
7. twa hae：two have.
8. braes：slopes，small hills.
9. pou'd：pulled.
10. gowans fine：fine gowans. gowans：wild daisies. fine：beautiful.
11. wander'd many a weary fitt：wandered a lot with weary feet. fitt：foot.
12. Sin：since.
13. paidl'd：paddled.
14. in the burn：in the rivulet，in the brook. i'：in. burn：brook，rivulet，small river.
15. Frae morning sun till dine：from morning to evening，from day to night. dine：dinner.
16. braid：broad.
17. fiere：friend，fellow.
18. gie's：give us.
19. gude-willie-waught：a deep draught of wine for good will，a cordial drink.

For Study and Discussion

1. What's the theme of this poem?
2. Why is this song world-famous?
3. Are there popular songs on friendship in Chinese poetry? If any，which do you prefer? Give your reason.
4. Please learn to sing this song.

参考译文

过去的好时光

老朋友怎能遗忘掉，
永不再放心上？
老朋友怎能遗忘掉，
还有过去的好时光？

为了过去的好时光，亲爱的，
为了过去的好时光，
让我们干一杯友谊的酒，
为了过去的好时光。

请举起你的那杯酒，
我也举起我的，
我们喝一杯友谊的酒，
为了过去的好时光。

我们俩曾游遍山岗，
并把野菊来采摘；
我们已历尽苦和辛，
远离过去的好时光。

我们俩曾蹚溪又过河，
从早到日悬天中央；
如今大海将我们分隔，
远离过去的好时光。

老朋友，我已伸出我的手，
请你也伸手相握，
让我们干一杯友谊的酒，
为了过去的好时光。

为了过去的好时光，亲爱的，
为了过去的好时光，
让我们干一杯友谊的酒，
为了过去的好时光。

（李正栓　译）

My Heart's in the Highlands[1]

This is one of the best known poems of Burns. In this poem he pours out his deep love for his homeland — the Highlands. It shows the poet's pure patriotic feeling. Burns is such a genius in language that he has admirable faculty of expressing himself with passionate emotion in simple and musical verse. This poem is characterized by its appealing musical quality. Burns uses alliteration, repetition and many parallel constructions to stress his sentiment for his homeland.

My heart's in the Highlands[2], my heart is not here,
My heart's in the Highlands a-chasing[3] the deer—
A-chasing the wild deer, and following the roe[4];
My heart's in the Highlands, wherever I go.

Farewell to the Highlands, farewell to the North[5],
The birth place of Valour[6], the country of Worth[7];
Wherever I wander, wherever I rove,
The hills of the Highlands for ever I love.

Farewell to the mountains high cover'd with snow;
Farewell to the straths[8] and green Valleys below;
Farewell to the forests and wild-hanging woods[9];
Farwell to the torrents and loud-pouring floods.

My heart's in the Highlands, my heart is not here,
My heart's in the Highlands a-chasing the deer
Chasing the wild deer, and following the roe;
My heart's in the Highlands, wherever I go.

Notes

1. This poem is written in four 4-line stanzas of irregular iambic and anapestic feet rhyming aabb.
2. the Highlands: the mountainous Northern area of Scotland.
3. a-chasing: chasing.
4. roe: a small kind of deer.
5. the North: here also referring to the Highlands, the hometown of Burns, in Scotland.
6. Valour: heroism, bravery.

7. Worth: virtue, high morality.
8. straths: (Scotch) wide, flat river valleys.
9. wild-hanging woods: wild woods on the slopes or hills.

For Study and Discussion

1. How does Burns show his patriotic feeling in this poem?
2. Repetition is frequently used in this poem. What's the function of repetition?
3. Are there any other devices to promote the theme of the poem?
4. Learn the first three stanzas of this poem.

参考译文

我的心在高原

我的心在高原，我的心不在这里；
我的心在高原，追逐着鹿群遍地，
追逐户外野鹿，跟踪着长幼牝鹿，
我的心在高原，不管我漂流何处。

再见吧，高原！再见吧，北方！
你是品德的家园、勇士的故乡；
不管我流浪何处，不管我何处浪迹，
高原的群山永远在我的心底。

再见吧，银装素裹的高山；
再见吧，绿色的山谷与河滩；
再见吧，参天的森林和丛生的野树，
再见吧，汹涌的激流和轰鸣的流瀑。

我的心在高原，我的心不在这里；
我的心在高原，追逐着鹿群，
追逐户外野鹿，跟踪着长幼牝鹿，
我的心在高原，不管我漂流何处。

（李正栓　译）

15. William Wordsworth

William Wordsworth (威廉·华兹华斯, 1770—1850), one of the greatest poets of England and the world, was born in a lawyer's family. He became an orphan at the age of 14. He was brought up by relatives who sent him to school at Hawkshead in the beautiful Lake District in Northwestern England. The beauty of nature attracted him greatly. Nature became his best teacher. The flowers, hills, stars, birds and all things of nature were of greater fascination. So he early developed and cherished a love for nature.

He attended Cambridge University where he spent four years, beginning from 1787. Influenced by the young republicans there, he was politically enthusiastic about and sympathetic with the French Revolution (1789). He visited France twice, the first time in 1790, the second time in 1792. Of course, his poems of this period were more or less full of democratic ideas.

In 1795, Wordsworth and his sister, Dorothy settled at Racedom in Somersetshire, where they enjoyed the nature, where they, in 1797, made friends with Coleridge, with whom Wordsworth collaborated and published the *Lyrical Ballads* (1798) which marked the break with classicism and the beginning of the Romantic revival in England.

Wordsworth had his own principle of poetry. He declared that "all good poetry is the spontaneous overflow of powerful feelings". He appealed directly to individual sensations, i.e. pleasure, excitement and enjoyment as the foundation in the creation and appreciation of poetry. Poetry "takes its origin from emotion recollected in tranquility". The function of poetry lies in its power to give an unexpected splendor to familiar and commonplace things, to "incidents and situations from common life". As to language used in poetry, he advocated using the language of the common people. Imagination was very important in poetic creation. All these principles were stated in the *Preface* to the second edition of *Lyrical Ballads*, which served as the manifesto of the

English Romantic Movement in poetry.

Romanticism is a movement that flourished in literature, philosophy, music and art in Western culture during most of the 19th century, beginning as a revote against classicism. There have been many varieties of Romanticism in many different times and places. Many of the ideas of English Romanticism were first expressed by William Wordsworth and Samuel Taylor Coleridge. It prevailed in England during the period 1798 — 1832. Romanticists expressed the ideology and sentiment of those classes and social strata that were discontent with and opposed to the development of capitalism. They split into two groups. The elder group or the Lake poets are represented by Wordsworth, Coleridge and Southey. The younger group is represented by Byron, Shelley and Keats.

William Wordsworth expressed the deepest aspirations of English Romanticism. He saw nature and man with new eyes. His poetry is distinguished by the simplicity and purity of his language. It was his theory that the language spoken by the peasants when purified from its defects was the best of all. His whole work is an attempt to communicate that new vision.

With the establishment of the Jacobin dictatorship (May 1793—July 1794) and the rise of Napoleon (November 1799—April 1814) in France, Wordsworth lost his former political fervor and changed his attitude toward the Revolution. He retired to the northern Lake District and later accepted the office of a distributor of stamps and was made poet laureate. He died when he was 80 in 1850.

Wordsworth wrote a great many poems, fresh in imagination, simple, plain and vivid in language but profound in meaning. He was especially good at writing about nature and common people. Hence he was called the poet of nature. He was also referred to as one of the Lake Poets because he lived in the Lake District. His major works, to mention a few here, include *Lucy Poems* (1799), "I wandered lonely as a cloud" (1804), "The Solitary Reaper" (1805) and his long poem *The Preclude* (1850). He also wrote a lot of sonnets.

I Wandered Lonely as a Cloud[1]

In this poem, Wordsworth sings praise of the beauty of nature and its influence upon people. "Dance" appears four times, once in each stanza, serving as a clue to the theme of the poem. Key words like "joyful", "gay", "jocund" reflect the bliss that the happy scene in nature gives him. Wordsworth's poetic idea that "poetry should take its origin from emotion recollected in tranquility" is also shown in this poem.

I wandered lonely as a cloud[2]
That floats on high[3] o'er vales[4] and hills,
When all at once[5] I saw a crowd[6],
A host[7], of golden daffodils;
Beside the lake, beneath the trees,
Fluttering and dancing[8] in the breeze.

Continuous[9] as the stars that shine
And twinkle on the milky way[10],
They stretched in never-ending[11] line
Along the margin of a bay[12]:
Ten thousand saw I at a glance[13],
Tossing their heads in sprightly[14] dance.

The waves beside them danced[15]; but they
Out-did the sparkling waves in glee:[16]
A poet could not but be gay,
In such a jocund company:[17]
I gazed—and gazed—but little thought[18]
What wealth the show to me had brought:[19]

For oft[20], when on my couch I lie[21]
In vacant or in pensive mood,[22]
They flash upon that inward eye[23]
Which is the bliss of solitude;[24]
And then my heart with pleasure fills[25],
And dances with the daffodils.

1804 1807

Notes

1. This poem is written in four 6-line stanzas of iambic tetrameter rhyming ababcc. It was written in 1804 and printed in 1807. Dorothy Wordsworth described the original experience in her *Grasmere Journals* for April 15, 1802: "When we were in the woods beyond Gowbarrow Park we saw a few daffodils close to the waterside... But as we went along there were more and ye more; and at last, under the boughs of the trees, we saw that there was a long belt of them along the shore, about the breadth of a country turnpike road. I never saw daffodils so beautiful. They grew among the mossy stones about and about them; some rested their heads upon these stones as on a pillow for weariness; and the rest tossed and rolled and danced and seemed as if they verily laughed with the wind that flew upon them over the lake; they looked so gay, ever glancing, ever changing."
2. I wandered lonely as a cloud: "wander", "lonely", "a cloud" are all words to describe the loneliness of the speaker. wander: walk aimlessly.
3. on high: high in the sky.
4. o'er vales: over small valleys.
5. all at once: suddenly.
6. a crowd: a large group.
7. A host: a great number.
8. Fluttering and dancing: tossing the head and shaking the body.
9. Continuous: countless.
10. the milky way: a broad belt of faint light, consisting of countless stars shining like a river across the sky at night. Here the long belt of daffodils is just like the milky way.
11. never-ending: endless.
12. the margin of a bay: the edge of a lake.
13. Ten thousand saw I at a glance: I saw ten thousand (of daffodils) at a glance.
14. sprightly: lively, joyfully.
15. The waves beside them danced: the waves (in the lake) beside them rose and fell.

16. but they / Out-did the sparkling waves in glee: but they danced more joyfully than the shining wave. Out-did: did more or better than; excelled. sparkling: shining. glee: cheer, delight.
17. A poet could not but be gay, / In such a jocund company: A poet could only be happy with such a joyful companion. jocund: cheerful, joyful.
18. little thought: thought little.
19. What wealth the show to me had brought: what wealth the show had brought to me. wealth: value, benefit. show: beautiful scene.
20. oft: often.
21. when on my couch I lie: when I lie on my couch.
22. In vacant or in pensive mood: in an unthinking or seriously thoughtful mood.
23. They flash upon that inward eye: the golden flowers suddenly appear in my mind. that inward eye: a metaphor, referring to the soul or mind.
24. Which is the bliss of solitude: which is the great happiness when I am alone. Cf. his "Tintern Abbey": "But oft, in lonely rooms, and 'mid the din / Of towns and cities, I have owed to them/In hours of weariness, sensations sweet, / Felt in the blood, and felt along the heart; /And passing even into my purer mind, /With tranquil restoration…"
25. my heart with pleasure fills: my heart fills with pleasure.

诗歌赏析

华兹华斯曾在《抒情歌谣集》中指出，诗歌是“强烈情感的自然流露”，但诗人在激情中往往写不出好诗来，诗歌应该描绘那些“宁静中回忆起来的情感”。这首诗正是这样的一个范例。1802 年 4 月 15 日，华兹华斯和妹妹多萝西漫步湖畔，忽然看到林间一片水仙，在微风中摇曳生姿。这一美景给诗人留下了深刻的印象。两年后诗人写这首诗时，那景象依然清晰。这首诗抒发了诗人对自然的赞美、热爱之情，并体现了自然对人的影响：大自然的美丽能够整饬人类内心的无序，能驱走人的寂寞与惆怅。全诗形式工整，音韵和谐，与内容相得益彰。

这首诗分四节，每节有六行，每行由四个抑扬格四音步组成，押 ababcc 韵。这首诗用词简练又不乏机巧。“舞蹈”一词出现四次，每个诗节一次，构成全诗的主线，通过水仙、湖波和诗人心灵的舞蹈巧妙地把三者紧密地连接起来，暗示人与自然的和谐。另外，这首诗中频繁出现喜悦、欢快等词汇，直接表达了诗人看到自然美景的欣喜感受以及自然赋予诗人的巨大财富。

除了巧妙的用词外，诗人还擅长使用各种形象生动的比喻性语言。诗人一开头将自己比作天上漫游的孤云，将一个形单影只的旅人形象鲜明地勾勒出来。正在这时，诗人看到了一丛丛、一簇簇的水仙灿若银河的繁星闪现在自己面前。于是，诗人的内眼（即心灵）受到触动，不由地和欢快的水仙一起跳起舞来。孤云一般的旅人和灿若繁星的水仙本是一组相对的概念，通过心灵的舞蹈完美地结合起来，从而实现了人与自然的统一。

华兹华斯所处的时代是浪漫主义的鼎盛时期。浪漫主义诗人十分推崇想象力，他们所歌颂的大自然是永恒的美的体现者。同时，华兹华斯的作品还具有一定的个人主义和理想主义色彩。在华兹华斯的诗中，物我是分离的，情即是情，景即是景。描写完自然景物之后，华兹华斯总是回到自我意识当中，大自然只是他表达心情的客体，主位在诗人的心中。这首诗的前两节主要写景，最后两节开始抒情——“有这样欢乐的侣伴，/ 诗人怎能不心花怒放？”“我的心就充满欢乐，/ 随着那些水仙起舞婀娜。”与我国南朝时期的山水诗人谢灵运如出一辙，即山水景物描摹独立于性情之外，先抒见闻再发感慨。另外，他靠着长期政府津贴和遗产，舒适地生活在风光明媚的湖区。行吟湖畔、陶醉于自然风光的华兹华斯像高空飞翔的鸟儿，居高临下，俯视着大地，从中寻觅自己需要的东西。他以旁观者的身份，表达对农人穷苦生活的同情，从未真正融入到他生活的环境当中。

同样是自然诗人，我国晋代的陶渊明则不同。在陶渊明的田园诗中诗人的意趣与自然意象达到混化无迹，与自然呈现出水乳交融般的和谐。在陶渊明眼中，自然即是诗。其物我混化的至高境界在“采菊东篱下，/ 悠然见南山。/ 山气日夕佳，/ 飞鸟相与还。/ 此中有真意，/ 欲辩已忘言。”诗行中得到了很好的表达。农业生活的经历，赋予了陶渊明的田园诗强烈的现实主义精神。他以写实的手法，于自然中见自然，把自己于自然中得到的乐趣融入其中，真正达到了天人合一、情景交融的理想状态。

从平淡无奇的事物中悟出不平凡的哲理并升华为诗，是华兹华斯的诗歌特色和他重要的一条诗学原理。于平凡中见真趣，也是陶渊明诗歌的风格。但相同的基调之下，他们的诗作也彰显了不同的个性。这主要是由二者不同的文化背景及经历造成的。

For Study and Discussion

1. The poet compares himself to a lonely cloud. Talk about the image of "loneliness" in this poem.
2. "Dance" appears four times in this poem. What's the function of the repetition of dance?
3. In what way are the daffodils like the stars in the Milky Way?
4. What is the meaning of the last stanza? What poetic idea is reflected here?

参考译文

我独自漫游像一朵浮云

我独自漫游像一朵浮云，
高高地飘浮在山与谷之上，
突然我看见一簇簇一群群
金色的水仙在开放：
靠湖边，在树下，
随风起舞乐开花。

它们连绵不断，像银河中
的群星闪烁、眨眼，
它们展延无限成远景
沿着湖湾的边沿：
一瞥眼我看见成千上万，
它们欢快摇首舞翩翩。

近旁的波浪跳着舞；但水仙
欢快的舞姿远远胜过闪光的波浪；
有这样欢乐的侣伴，
诗人怎能不心花怒放？
我凝视着——凝视着——当时并未领悟
这景色给我带来的是何等财富：

常常是，当我独卧榻上，
或是沉思，或是茫然，
它们在我心田闪亮
这是我独处时的欢乐无限；
于是我的心就充满欢乐，
随着那些水仙起舞婀娜。

（李正栓 译）

She Dwelt among the Untrodden Ways[1]

It is a lament for a deceased girl. Though the girl is quite common and plain to others, she is innocent and unique in the speaker's mind. Though she was ignored by others, she is important to the speaker. The key words "untrodden", "none", "few", "unknown", "only" suggest the solitude of the girl.

She dwelt[2] among the untrodden[3] ways
Beside the springs of Dove[4],
A Maid whom there were none to praise
And very few to love:

A violet by a mossy stone
Half hidden from the eye!
—Fair[5] as a star, when only one
Is shining in the sky.

She lived unknown, and few could know
When Lucy[6] ceased to be[7];
But she is in her grave, and, oh,
The difference to me!
1799 1800

Notes

1. The poem is the first poem of *Lucy Poems* (1799). It is written in three

quatrains of alternate four and three iambic feet rhyming abab.
2. dwelt：lived.
3. untrodden：seldom-visited，never be stepped on.
4. Dove：a river in the English Midlands. There are several rivers by this name in England，including one in the Lake District.
5. Fair：beautiful.
6. Lucy：a common name for girls in England.
7. ceased to be：a euphemism for “died”.

诗歌赏析

这首诗是华兹华斯描写农家女孩的《露茜组诗》中的第一首，采用民谣体诗节的形式写成。

第一节用“人迹罕至”、“无人称赞”、“无人爱恋”勾勒出一个乡下女孩的整体形象——普通、单纯、默默无闻。第二节用青苔石旁的紫罗兰和天上唯一的星两个鲜明的意象表达了对姑娘的赞美。紫罗兰是开放在路边的普通野花，诗人用紫罗兰而不用红玫瑰来形容心中的女孩，说明姑娘的默默无闻、兰心蕙质。青苔石旁的紫罗兰说明姑娘出淤泥而不染的特质。青苔石旁普通的紫罗兰和天上闪烁的孤星构成鲜明的对比。虽然在世人眼中，姑娘只是普通的繁花一朵，但是在诗人心目中她却卓尔不群，拥有至高无上的地位。一个明喻和一个暗喻构成了姑娘在世人眼里和诗人心中的强烈对比。第三节诗人做出了总结：她的生死在世人眼里无关紧要，但是对诗人来说却有着天壤之别。最后一行“对我，就不同了”短促而有力量。诗人用低调陈述的方式表达了心中的沉痛，是这首短诗中最有力的一行。

这首诗简洁明快，意象鲜明，富含音韵手段和声音效果。首先，诗歌用传统的形式、纯朴的语言来展现一个普普通通的女孩，构成形式与内容的契合。其次，很多头韵、腹韵的使用使这首诗读起来朗朗上口。

For Study and Discussion

1. What qualities of Lucy are implied in the first stanza?
2. What do the comparisons in the second stanza suggest about Lucy?
3. The final line ends with “me”. How does this sudden introduction of the speaker intensify the loss of Lucy?
4. What do you think of the last line of the poem? Is it powerful? Why or why not?

5. Compare this poem with Burns' "*A Red, Red Rose*" and make comments.
6. Learn the second stanza by heart.

参考译文

她住在人迹罕至的地方

她住在人迹罕至的地方，
就在多佛小溪旁，
无人曾将这少女称赞，
也没几人把她放在心上。

青苔石旁紫罗兰，
怀抱苔石半遮面！
——她美丽，像一颗孤星
独自个儿在夜空闪现。

她活着，无人知晓，
她死了，没几人知道；
但她现在孤坟之中，
对我，就不同了。

（李正栓　译）

The Solitary Reaper[1]

This poem is one of the rare poems not based on Wordsworth's own experience. Wordsworth said that it was suggested by a passage in Thomas Wilkinson's *Tour of Scotland* (1824), which he had seen in MS: "Passed by a female who was reaping alone, she sang in Erse (the Gaelic language of Scotland) as she bended over her sickle, the sweetest human voice I ever heard. Her strains were tenderly melancholy, and felt delicious long after they were heard no more." The poem describes a solitary Highland girl working and singing in nature. He uses many key words like "melancholy", "plaintive", "unhappy" and "sorrow" to describe her song, while loneliness is the core of her image.

Behold her, single in the field,
Yon[2] solitary Highland[3] Lass!
Reaping and singing by herself;
Stop here, or gently pass!
Alone she cuts and binds the grain,
And sings a melancholy strain[4];
O listen! for the Vale profound
Is overflowing with the sound.

No Nightingale did ever chaunt[5]
More welcome notes[6] to weary bands
Of travelers[7] in some shady haunt[8],
Among Arabian sands[9]:
A voice so thrilling ne'er[10] was heard
In spring-time from the Cuckoo-bird,
Breaking the silence of the seas
Among the farthest Hebrides[11].

Will no one tell me what she sings?[12]—
Perhaps the plaintive numbers[13] flow
For old, unhappy, far-off things,
And battles long ago:
Or is it some more humble lay,[14]
Familiar matter of to-day?
Some natural sorrow, loss, or pain,
That has been, and may be again?

Whate'er[15] the theme, the Maiden
As if her song could have no ending;
I saw her singing at her work,
And o'er the sickle bending[16]; —
I listened, motionless and still;
And, as I mounted up the hill,

The music in my heart I bore,
Long after it was heard no more.
Nov. 5, 1805 1807

Notes

1. This poem contains four 8-line stanzas of combined iambic and anapestic feet rhyming ababccdd.
2. Yon: yonder, over there.
3. Highland: belonging to the Highlands or the northern part of Scotland.
4. strain: melody.
5. chaunt: chant, sing.
6. welcome notes: pleasant music or songs.
7. weary bands/Of travelers: tired companies of travelling merchants.
8. some shady haunt: some place in the shade.
9. Arabian sands: Arabian Desert.
10. ne'er: never.
11. Hebrides: a group of islands off the northwestern coast of Scotland.
12. Will no one tell me what she sings: Wordsworth wants others to tell him what she sings because he does not understand Erse, the language in which she sings (a language in the Highlands).
13. the plaintive numbers: the mournful singing. numbers: songs.
14. lay: short lyric for singing.
15. Whate'er: whatever.
16. o'er the sickle bending: bending over the sickle.

诗歌赏析

这首诗和《咏水仙》一样，同样先写景后抒情，诗人同样是居高临下，高高在上（山丘之上）。第一节先声夺人，开篇就用你看（behold her）吸引读者的注意力，接着用 single，solitary，by herself 和 alone 几个关键词勾勒出一个孤独的在田间劳作的农家少女形象。然后用你听（O listen）调动读者的听觉，去关注姑娘的歌声。第二节中，诗人由少女的歌声联想到阿拉伯沙漠上夜莺的歌唱以及赫布里底群岛上杜鹃的鸣叫，不仅烘托出姑娘歌声的婉转而且使空间得到了扩展。第三节，诗人展开对姑娘吟唱内容的猜想——过去、现在还是将来？时间也从遥远的过去延伸到未来。第四节写这首歌对诗人的影响：虽然诗人已远去，但这首歌在他的心中久久回荡。这首诗反映了华兹华斯“用老百姓日常生活中的事件或场景入诗”的创作理念。

For Study and Discussion

1. Paint a word picture of the highland girl as the poet or speaker saw her. Describe her singing.
2. Why did the speaker say "Will no one tell me what she sings?"
3. What did the speaker think the song might be about?
4. What was the most vivid impression of the reaper which the speaker carried away with him?
5. What poetic idea is reflected in this poem?

参考译文

孤独的刈麦女

你看，那边高原上孤独的少女，
独自个儿在这田野里！
她自己一人，边收割边哼着小曲；
停下吧，要么就悄悄地绕过去！
孤独一人，她又收割又绑捆，
唱出的曲调有些哀婉伤心；
啊，听！那深深的峡谷
也把她的歌声洒布。

阿拉伯沙漠，
在偶见的绿荫，对疲惫的旅人，
夜莺会唱出甜美的歌，
但怎么也超不过这少女的唱吟；
在遥远的赫布里底群岛，
听到啼叫报春的布谷鸟
打破辽阔海域的沉寂，
却也赶不上少女的歌声醉人心迷。

就没人告诉我她唱的是什么？——
也许只是些伤感事，
也许是些遥远过去不幸的生活，
也许是古老的战场怨曲。
也许唱的是更普通的曲子，
唱的是当今的生活琐事。
也许诉说着自然的伤感、损失和痛苦，
这些事曾经发生以后也会反复。

不管这少女唱的主题是什么，
仿佛这歌声无头无尽远流长；
我见她边唱歌儿边工作，
我见她弯腰运镰收割忙。
我凝神贯注啊静静地听，
我登高后仍听见那歌声。
那乐声在我这儿长存，
久未听见，却仍留于心。

（李正栓　译）

16. Samuel Taylor Coleridge

Samuel Taylor Coleridge（塞缪尔·泰勒·柯勒律治，1772—1834）was born in rural Devonshire, he was the son of a clergyman and the youngest of the fourteen children. He first attended school in London and then at Cambridge University in 1791. In 1794 he left Cambridge without taking a degree.

As a young man he held radical views on politics and religion. He had been fired to wild enthusiasm by the French Revolution. During the summer of 1794 he met Robert Southey. They two set about planning a small Utopian community in America. Coleridge named it "Pantisocracy" (equal rule by all). But both of them were dreamers without any means to put their plans into practice.

In 1797 he met Wordsworth, and thus began the happiest and most productive time of Coleridge's life. The two poets published their *Lyrical Ballads*. The first poem in this collection is Coleridge's masterpiece, "The Rime of the Ancient Mariner". His specific role in *Lyrical Ballads* was "directed to persons and characters supernatural".

In 1798 Coleridge went to Germany with Wordsworth and Dorothy, the latter's sister. At the University of Gottingen, he began his lifelong study of Kant and other German philosophers. Coleridge played an important role in introducing the advances of German philosophy to English poets and thinkers.

Coleridge is a great poet. He wrote with excellent style and techniques. He is a medievalist, fond of the unusual and supernatural things. His imaginative power is intense and his language melodious. His early poetry shows the influence of Thomas Gray and William Blake, especially of the latter. In his later poems his imagination is bridled by thought and study.

Coleridge was also a literary critic, good at giving lectures. He was the first critic of the Romantic school. Between 1808 and 1815 he delivered a series of lectures on Shakespeare, which were later collected in his *Notes and Lectures on Shakespeare*. His most important prose work is *Biographia Literaria, or Sketches of My Literary Life and Opinions* (1817), which afforded the new Romantic poetry a new principle of criticism. According to Coleridge, the critic's task was not to judge but to appreciate and interpret. Just like Wordsworth he became conservative in thinking in his later years.

from *The Rime of the Ancient Mariner*[1]

The poem is one of the masterpieces of the Romantic poetry. The theme of the poem is about sin and salvation, depravation and redemption. It tells a strange story in the form of ballads. Three guests are on their way to a wedding party, but one of them is detained by an ancient mariner. The mariner tells him of his adventures on the sea. When his ship sails towards the South Pole, an albatross comes through the snow-fog and alights on the rigging. The mariner shot it. Then misfortune falls on the ship. The whole crew, with the exception of the mariner, die of thirst as a punishment for the act of inhospitality.

The spell breaks only when the mariner repents his cruelty. The atmosphere, the beauty of music and imagery make the poem stand alone of its kind.

Part 1

An ancient Mariner meeteth three gallants bidden to a wedding-feast, and detaineth one.

It is an ancient Mariner
And he stoppeth[2] one of three[3].
"By thy long grey beard and glittering eye[4],
Now wherefore[5] stopp'st thou me?"

The Bridegroom's doors are opened wide,
And I am next of kin[6];
The guests are met, the feast is set:[7]
May'st[8] hear the merry din."

He holds him with his skinny hand,
"There was a ship," quoth[9] he.
"Hold off![10] unhand me, grey-beard loon!"
Eftsoons[11] his hand dropt[12] he.

The wedding guest is spellbound by the eye of the old sea-faring man, and constrained to hear his tale.

He holds him with his glittering eye—
The wedding-guest stood still,
And listens like a three years' child:
The Mariner hath his will.[13]

The wedding-guest sat on a stone:
He cannot choose but hear;
And thus spake on that ancient man,
The bright-eyed Mariner.[14]

"The ship was cheered, the harbor cleared[15],
Merrily did we drop[16]
Below the kirk[17], below the hill,
Below the light house top.

The Mariner tells how the ship sailed southward with a good wind and fair weather, till it reached the line.

The sun came up upon the left[18],
Out of the sea came he!
And he shone bright, and on the right
Went down into the sea.

Higher and higher every day,
Till over the mast at noon[19]—"
The wedding-guest here beat his breast,
For he heard the loud bassoon[20].

The wedding guest heareth the bridal music; but the mariner continueth his tale.

The bride hath paced into the hall,
Red as a rose[21] is she;
Nodding their heads before her goes
The merry minstrelsy.

The wedding-guest he[22] beat his breast,
Yet he cannot choose but hear;
And thus spake[23] on that ancient man,
The bright-eyed Mariner.

The ship driven by a storm toward the south pole.

"And now the storm-blast came, and he[24]
Was tyrannous and strong:
He struck with his o'ertaking wings,
And chased us south along.

With sloping masts and dipping prow,
As who[25] pursued with yell and blow
Still[26] treads the shadow of his foe,
And forward bends his head,
The ship drove fast, loud roared the blast,
And southward aye[27] we fled[28]

And now there came both mist and snow,
And it grew wondrous[29] cold:
And ice, mast-high, came floating by,
As green as emerald.

The land of ice, and of fearful sounds Where no living thing was to be seen.

And through the drifts[30] the snowy clifts[31]
Did send a dismal sheen[32]:
Nor shapes of men nor beasts we ken[33] —
The ice was all between.

The ice was here, the ice was there,
The ice was all around:
It cracked and growled, and roared and howled,[34]
Like noises in a swound[35]!

Till a great sea-bird, called the Albatross, came through the snow-fog, and was joy and hospitality.

At length did cross an Albatross[36],
Thorough[37] the fog it came;
As if it had been a Christian soul,
We hailed it in God's name[38].

It ate the food it ne'er had eat[39],
And round and round it flew.
The ice did split with a thunder-fit;
The helmsman steered us through!

And lo! the Albatross proveth a bird of good omen, and followeth the ship as it returned northward through fog and floating ice.

And a good south wind sprung[40] up behind;
The Albatross did follow,
And every day, for food or play,
Came to the mariner's hollo!

In mist or cloud, on mast or shroud[41],
It perched for vespers nine[42];

Whiles[43] all the night, through fog-smoke white,
Glimmered the white moon-shine."

The ancient Mariner Inhospitably killeth The pious bird of Good omen.

"God save thee, ancient Mariner!
From the fiends, that plague thee thus! —
Why look'st thou so?" —With my cross-bow
I shot the Albatross[44].

1797 1798

Notes

1. This excerption is the first part of "The Rime of the Ancient Mariner", the first poem in *Lyrical Ballads*, which consists of seven parts written in ballad form rhyming abcb with several exceptions of more than four lines in a stanza.
2. stoppeth: stops.
3. one of three: the numbers of 3, 7 and 9 appear frequently in this poem to stress the mysterious and supernatural atmosphere of the story.
4. glittering eye: this image appears several times in Lines 13, 20, 40, and 228, etc., seeming to have a magic power.
5. wherefore: why.
6. next of kin: near relative.
7. The guests are met, the feast is set: "met" and "set" form an internal rhyme, which is frequently used in this poem.
8. May'st: you may.
9. quoth: (archaic) said.
10. Hold off: get away.
11. Eftsoons: (archaic) at once.
12. dropt: dropped.
13. He holds him … hath his will: the Mariner has gained control of the will of the wedding guest by his bright eyes.
14. Mariner: maniner here should be pronounced as "marinere", to rhyme with "hear".

15. cleared: passed beyond.
16. drop: to put out to sea with the ebbing tide.
17. kirk: church.
18. upon the left: the sun rose to the left of the ship.
19. Till over the mast at noon: the ship had reached the equator.
20. bassoon: a musical instrument, implying that the wedding has begun.
21. Red as a rose: the image of rose is often used by poets to describe the beauty of a girl, here the bride. Cf. Robert Burns' "A Red, Red Rose": "O my Luve's like a red, red rose, /That's newly sprung in June." The beautiful young face of the bride is contrasted to the gloomy old face of the mariner.
22. The wedding-guest he: pleonasm, the wedding-guest.
23. spake: (archaic) spoke.
24. he: the storm is personified here.
25. As who: as one who.
26. Still: always.
27. aye: always.
28. Stanza 12 contains six lines other than four to suggest the hard journey of the ship.
29. wondrous: extremely.
30. drifts: mists.
31. the snowy clifts: the icebergs. clifts: cliffs.
32. a dismal sheen: an oxymoron, a gloomy brightness.
33. Nor shape of men nor beasts we ken: we saw no living things. ken: (archaic) saw.
34. It cracked and growled, and roared and howled: the poet used several onomatopoetic words to describe the terrible noise made by the icebergs.
35. swound: (archaic) swoon.
36. Albatross: a sea-bird of good omen in western culture.
37. Thorough: through.
38. We hailed it in God's name: we welcomed the Albatross with great joy and hospitality.
39. eat: old form of "eaten".

40. sprung：sprang.
41. shroud：rope of the rigging，rope supporting the mast.
42. vespers nine：nine evenings.
43. Whiles：(archaic) while.
44. I shot the Albatross：the first 5 parts of the poem all end with the Albatross to show its great influence on the mariner.

诗歌赏析

《古舟子咏》是柯勒律治与华兹华斯合作的浪漫主义诗集《抒情歌谣集》的第一首。该诗通过老水手射杀信天翁而遭受的种种磨难和最终因忏悔而获得救赎的故事，表现了罪恶和拯救、堕落和再生的道德寓意。也有人说这首诗表现了诗人的生态意识和思想。诗中充满神秘主义和超自然色彩——传统民谣体诗节、头韵和古词的使用烘托了古老的氛围；3、7、9 等奇数词、老水手慑人的眼神和信天翁的魔咒等塑造出神秘、超自然的气氛。这首诗共七部分，这里节选的是第一部分。

开局突兀。一个老水手拦住了婚礼的三个宾客中的一个，开始讲述他的故事。婚礼上轻松喜庆的气氛和老水手紧张的叙述产生了鲜明对比。随着故事的发展，读者不由地深陷其中。诗歌的声音、语言、结构等也形成一种内在的张力，与紧张、神秘的故事氛围相互映衬。

头韵作为英国诗歌最古老的韵式，在这首诗中此起彼伏，与悠远的故事氛围相得益彰。此外，这首诗频繁使用行内韵，如第二节中“The guests are met，the feast is set，”第六节中“The ship was cheered，the harbor cleared，”第七节“And he shone bright，and on the right”等。英国诗歌中很少有一首诗如此集中地使用行内韵，这首诗堪称英国诗歌中行内韵的范本。

词语的重复和句式的排比也是这首诗的一个特点，如第十五节冰的重复和排比句式突出了冰雪茫茫的肃杀气氛，一连串的拟声词形容冰雪呼啸的场景。这样的场景与柳宗元的《江雪》中描写的“千山鸟飞绝，万径人踪灭”的景致别无二致。

诗歌为了展现古朴、遥远的气氛，采用民谣体诗节的形式，然而第十二节脱离了民谣体固有的四行诗节的节奏变为六行诗节，用诗行的拖沓来形容船只在暴风雨驱赶下向南方艰难行进的场景，同样体现了形式与内容的统一。

最后一节在老水手的讲述中忽然插入一句问话“你怎么啦?”通过刻画老水手紧张的面部表情，渲染出紧张的气氛，表现老水手射杀信天翁的罪过，为后续的惩罚做出铺垫。

另外，诗人还使用了明喻、矛盾修饰法（如阴霾的光亮）等，加强诗歌效果。如此繁复的诗歌手段的运用，造就了柯勒律治瑰丽的诗歌色彩。读者为这首诗的神秘性所吸引，为其音乐性所震撼，为诗中严肃的宗教意义所触动。

For Study and Discussion

1. Describe the atmosphere of the poem. Cite words, phrases, and vivid images that contribute to the atmosphere.
2. Do you think the Albatross takes on a religious significance? If so, what's that?
3. To what extent does the presence of the wedding guest influence your own response to the poem?
4. Choose one stanza you like best and learn it by heart.

参考译文

古舟子咏

第 1 章

他是一个年迈的水手，
从三个行人中他拦住一人。
"凭你的白须和闪亮的眼睛，
请问你为何阻拦我的路程？"

新郎家的大门已经敞开，
而我是他的密友良朋；
宾客已到齐，宴席已摆好：
远远能听到笑语喧阗。

他枯瘦的手把行人抓住，
喃喃言道，"曾有一艘船。"
"走开，撒手，你这老疯子！"
他随即放手不再纠缠。

但他炯炯的目光将行人慑住——
使赴宴的客人停步不前，

像三岁的孩子听他讲述：
老水手实现了他的意愿。

赴宴的客人坐在石头上，
不由自主地听他把故事讲；
就这样老水手继续往下说，
两眼闪烁着奇异的光芒。

“船在欢呼声中驶出海港，
乘着落潮我们愉快出航，
驶过教堂，驶过山岗，
最后连灯塔也消失在远方。

“只见太阳从左边升起，
从那万顷碧波的汪洋里！
它终日在天空辉煌照耀，
然后从右边落进大海里。

“它每天升得越来越高，
正午时直射桅杆的顶极——”
赴宴的客人捶打着胸膛，
当听到巴松管嘹亮的乐曲。

这时新娘已跨进大门，
她如鲜红的玫瑰一样漂亮；
行吟诗人们走在她前面，
摇头摆尾快乐地歌唱。

赴宴的客人捶打着胸膛，
但不由自主听他把故事讲；
就这样老水手继续往下说，
两眼闪烁着奇异的光芒。

“这时大海上刮起了风暴，
它来势凶猛真叫人胆寒：
它张开飞翅追击着船只，
不停地把我们向南驱赶。

"桅杆弓着身，船头淌着水，
像有人在背后追打叫喊，
却总是躲不开敌人的影子，
只好低着头任其摧残，
船儿在疾驶，狂风在呼啸，
我们一个劲儿往南逃窜。

"接着出现了浓雾和冰雪，
天气奇寒，冻彻骨髓：
如樯的冰山从船旁漂过，
晶莹碧绿，色如翡翠。

"冰山射出惨淡的光芒，
在漂流的云雾中若明若灭：
四周既无人迹也无鸟兽——
只有一望无垠的冰雪。

"这儿是冰雪，那儿是冰雪，
到处都是冰雪茫茫：
冰雪在怒吼，冰雪在咆哮，
像人昏厥时听到隆隆巨响！

"终于飞来了一头信天翁，
它穿过海上弥漫的云雾，
仿佛它也是一个基督徒，
我们以上帝的名义向它欢呼。

"它吃着从未吃过的食物，
又绕着船儿盘旋飞舞。
坚冰霹雳一声突然裂开，
舵手把我们引上了新途！

"南来的好风在船后吹送；
船旁紧跟着那头信天翁，
每天为了食物或玩耍，
水手们一招呼它就飞进船中！

"它在桅索上栖息了九夜；
无论是雾夜或满天阴云；
而一轮皎月透过白雾
迷离闪烁，朦朦胧胧。"

"上帝保佑你吧，老水手！
别让魔鬼把你缠住身！——
你怎么啦？"——"是我用箭，
射死了那头信天翁。"

（顾子欣　译）

17. George Gordon Byron

George Gordon Byron（乔治·戈登·拜伦，1788—1824）was born in an impoverished noble family in London. But at the age of 3, shortly after his father died, he was taken by his mother to Scotland. Although a handsome boy, Byron was born with a clubfoot. He struggled all his life with the physical and psychological effects of his deformity.

At ten, Byron became the sixth Lord Byron by the death of his great uncle. He was educated in Harrow, and then in Cambridge University. It was at Cambridge that Byron began to write poetry. In 1807 Byron published his first volume of poems *Hours of Idleness*. The volume was sharply attacked in the influential *Edinburgh Review*, and Byron responded in 1809 with his first important poem, a biting satire in the 18th century manner, called *English Bards and Scotch Reviewers*.

In the same year, Byron set out on a tour to Europe, which he recounted in the first two cantos of *Childe Harold's Pilgrimage*. It was published on his return to England in 1812, which was enormously successful. As Byron himself recalled, "I awoke one morning and found myself famous." He became the greatest literary and social celebrity of London. His reputation grew still further with the publication of a series of Romantic verse narratives with exotic, oriental settings: *The Giaour* (1813), *The Corsair* (1814), and *Lara* (1813). His unhappy marriage in 1815 and the scandal related to it made him leave England on April 25, 1816.

Byron resumed his travels in Europe, living first at Geneva in Switzerland, where he became close friends with Shelley and where he produced a magnificent third canto of *Childe Harold*. Then he moved to Venice at the end of 1816, where he began his greatest work, the satirical epic *Don Juan* (1818—1823). In 1824 he went to Greece. He organized and led an expedition to help liberate the country from Turkey. He was stricken with a severe fever in the swamps of Missolonghi and died on April 19, 1824, shortly after his thirty-sixth birthday. He is still regarded in Greece as a national hero.

Byron wrote a lot of short lyrics. All of them are beautifully written. The best-known pieces are "*She Walks in Beauty*", "*When We Two Parted*", "*On This Day I Complete My Thirty-Sixth Year*!" He also wrote some poetic dramas such as the philosophical *Manfred* (1817) and the mysterious *Cain* (1821), and some political satirical poems.

Byron is one of the most excellent representatives of English Romanticism. He was one of the most influential poets of his time. His literary career was closely linked with the struggle and progressive movements of his age. He opposed oppression and slavery, and had an ardent love for liberty. He praised the people's revolutionary struggles in his works. His poems are favorites of the British workers and the labouring people of other countries. Byron's influence has shown itself in the works of the Chartist Poets in England and the progressive poets in many other countries.

Some of his poems were translated into Chinese in the early years of the 20th century and influenced the young people who pursued freedom and democracy.

She Walks in Beauty[1]

This poem is chosen from *Hebrew Melodies* (1815), a collection of lyrics that Byron composed to accompany the musician Isaac Nathan's settings of traditional synagogue chants. Byron wrote the lines the morning after he had met his beautiful young cousin by marriage, Mrs. Robert John Wilmot, who wore a black gown brightened with spangles. In the poem, Byron describes the harmonious beauty of the lady.

1

She walks in beauty, like the night
Of cloudless climes and starry skies[2];
And all that's best of dark and bright
Meet in her aspect[3] and her eyes:
Thus mellow'd[4] to that tender light
Which heaven to gaudy day denies[5].

2

One shade the more, one ray the less,[6]
Had half impair'd[7] the nameless grace[8]
Which waves in every raven tress,
Or softly lightens o'er her face;[9]
Where thoughts serenely sweet express
How pure, how dear their dwelling place.[10]

3

And on that cheek, and o'er that brow,
So soft, so calm, yet eloquent[11],
The smiles that win[12], the tints that glow[13],
But tell of days in goodness spent,[14]
A mind at peace with all below[15],
A heart whose love is innocent!

June 1814 1815

Notes

1. It is written in three 6-lined stanzas of iambic tetrameter rhyming ababab.
2. cloudless climes and starry skies: regions where the sky is cloudless and starry. "cloudless climes" and "starry skies" both form alliteration, while "climes" and "skies" assonance. climes: areas with certain weather condi-

tions.

3. aspect: appearance; facial expression.
4. mellow'd: mellowed, softened.
5. to gaudy day denies: denies to (refuses to give) gaudy day. gaudy: too bright.
6. One shade the more, one ray the less: one more piece of darkness or one less piece of brightness. It is the most shining line of this poem.
7. Had half impair'd: would have half impaired. impair'd: destroyed.
8. the nameless grace: grace beyond description.
9. Which waves in every raven tress, / Or softly lightens o'er her face: which appears in the waves of her long, black hair or is gently expressed on her face. which: her beauty. raven tress: long, black hair. o'er: over.
10. Where thoughts serenely sweet express / How pure, how dear their dwelling place: where serenely sweet thoughts express how pure, how dear their dwelling place (is). Where: on her face. their dwelling place: mind, spirit.
11. eloquent: meaningful.
12. The smiles that win: the smiles that are attractive.
13. the tints that glow: the shades of color that are shining (on the face).
14. But tell of days in goodness spent: just tell of days spent in doing good things.
15. all below: all the things in the world.

诗歌赏析

拜伦在一次聚会上遇见了身穿孝服的威尔莫特夫人，她的美貌给诗人留下了很深的印象。这首诗歌颂了威尔莫特夫人的和谐美。很难想象一个针砭时弊、言语犀利，擅长讽刺的诗人也能写出如此婉约的颂扬女性美的诗歌。

诗歌的题目“她走在美的光影中”先声夺人，展示了女主人的动态美。第一节诗给大家描述了该女子的整体印象：“她走在美的光影中，如夜空一般，/皎洁无云，星光灿烂。”暗夜与星光的对比反衬出女子恬静与娴雅的美。“明与暗的色泽在她的脸庞和眼神里交汇”，这样的光彩连白日都不可企及。诗人在第二节诗中用一句经典的对偶形容女子：“多一道阴影，少一抹光晕，/都会令她失却难言的风韵。”这一形容与战国末期楚辞作家宋玉笔下的美女有异曲同工之妙。宋玉在《登徒子好色赋》中云："东家之子，增之一分则太长，减之一分则太短，着粉则太白，施朱则太赤……"接下来，诗人开始描述女子的内在美。由表及里，由外而内，从外表美到心灵美，由动态美到静态美，诗人用短短的三节诗勾勒出一个理想的贵族女子形象。

这首诗歌音韵优美、形式工整，充满了音乐美和形式美，和诗歌内容相得益彰。全诗由三个抑扬格四音步的六行诗节构成，隔行押韵，抑扬顿挫；头韵、腹韵在诗行间起起落落。诗人很注意遣词造句，用词典雅，与女主人公的贵妇身份契合。"柔和"、"甜蜜"、"宁静"等主题词不断在诗行间出现以形容女子恬静、柔美。

For Study and Discussion

1. The lady being praised is compared to the night. What particular aspects of the night are singled out in the comparison?
2. How does the poet describe the lady's beauty in a balance of opposites?
3. What's the sound effect of this poem?
4. Find other poems describing woman's beauty and compare them.
5. Find other Chinese versions of this poem and compare them.

参考译文

她走在美的光影中

1

她走在美的光影中，如夜空一般，
皎洁无云，星光灿烂，
白昼黑夜的色泽精粹，
在她的玉容秋波里交汇，
凝聚成一片柔雅情调，
浓艳的白昼也无法从上苍得到。

2

多一道阴影，少一抹光晕，
都会令她失却难言的风韵，

美涌动于她的每一缕秀发，
温柔地映照着她的脸颊，
甜蜜而安详的思绪在表达，
哦，那思想的寓所，纯洁而高雅。

3

那面容，那眉宇，
温柔，安详，似蕴含千言万语，
那醉人的微笑，那生辉的容颜，
诉说着她在温馨中度过的芳年，
宁静的心境能容下人间万象，
圣洁的心灵里珍藏着爱的琼浆。

（刘若兰　译）

The Isles of Greece[1]

The poem sings praise of the Greek glory in the past of defeating the Persian invaders several times and laments the humiliated state of Greek at the moment. By sharp contrast between the past and the present, the poet calls upon the Greeks to fight for their liberation. It is among Byron's most effective poems on national freedom.

1

The isles of Greece, the isles of Greece!
Where burning Sappho loved and sung[2],
Where grew the arts of war and peace[3],
Where Delos[4] rose, and Phoebus[5] sprung[6]!
Eternal summer gilds them yet,
But all, except their sun, is set.[7]

2

The Scian and the Teian muse,[8]
The hero's harp, the lover's lute,[9]
Have found the fame your shores refuse:[10]

Their place of birth alone is mute
To sounds which echo further west
Than your sires' 'Islands of the Blest'[11].

3

The mountains look on Marathon[12]—
And Marathon looks on the sea;
And musing there an hour alone,
I dream'd that Greece might still be free;
For standing on the Persian's grave,[13]
I could not deem myself a slave.

4

A king[14] sate[15] on the rocky brow[16]
Which looks o'er sea-born[17] Salamis[18];
And ships, by thousands, lay below,
And men in nations; —all were his!
He counted them at break of day—
And when the sun set where were they?[19]

5

And where are they? And where art thou,
My country? On thy voiceless shore
The heroic lay[20] is tuneless now—
The heroic bosom beats no more!
And must thy lyre, so long divine,
Degenerate into hands like mine?

6

'T is something, in the dearth of fame[21],
Though link'd among a fetter'd race,
To feel at least a patriot's shame,
Even as I sing, suffuse[22] my face;

For what is left the poet here?[23]
For Greeks a blush—for Greece a tear.

7

Must we but weep o'er days more blest?
Must we but blush? — Our fathers bled.
Earth! render back from out thy breast
A remnant of our Spartan dead[24]!
Of the three hundred grant but three,
To make a new Thermopylae[25]!

8

What, silent still? and silent all?
Ah! no; — the voices of the dead
Sound like a distant torrent's fall,
And answer, "Let one living head,
But one arise, —we come, we come!"
'T is but the living who are dumb.

9

In vain—in vain; strike other chords[26];
Fill high the cup with Samian[27] wine!
Leave battles to the Turkish hordes,
And shed the blood of Scio's vine[28]!
Hark! rising to the ignoble call—
How answer each bold Bacchanal[29]!

10

You have the Pyrrhic dance[30] as yet:
Where is the Pyrrhic phalanx[31] gone?
Of two such lessons, why forget
The nobler and the manlier one?
You have the letters Cadmus[32] gave—

Think ye he meant them for a slave?

11

Fill high the bowl with Samian wine!
We will not think of themes like these!
It made Anacreon's song[33] divine:
He served—but served Polycrates[34]—
A tyrant; but our masters then
Were still, at least, our countrymen.

12

The tyrant of the Chersonese[35]
Was freedom's best and bravest friend;
That tyrant was Miltiades[36]!
Oh![37] that the present hour would lend
Another despot of the kind!
Such chains as his were sure to bind[38].

13

Fill high the bowl with Samian wine!
On Suli's rock, and Parga's shore[39],
Exists the remnant of a line[40]
Such as the Doric mothers[41] bore;
And there, perhaps, some seed is sown,
The Heracleidan blood[42] might own.

14

Trust not for freedom to the Franks—
They have a king who buys and sells;[43]
In native swords, and native ranks,
The only hope of courage dwells:
But Turkish force, and Latin fraud,[44]
Would break your shield, however broad.

15

Fill high the bowl with Samian wine!
Our virgins dance beneath the shade —
I see their glorious black eyes shine;
But gazing on each glowing maid,
My own the burning tear-drop laves,[45]
To think such breasts must suckle slaves.

16

Place me on Sunium's[46] marbled steep,
Where nothing, save[47] the waves and I,
May hear our mutual murmurs sweep;
There, swan-like, let me sing and die:
A land of slaves shall ne'er be mine—
Dash down you cup of Samian wine!

Notes

1. This song, included in the third canto of Byron's *Don Juan* is different from the rest of the poem metrically, consisting of sixteen 6-line stanzas of iambic tetrameter, with a rhyme scheme of ababcc.
2. burning Sappho ['sæfəu] loved and sung: passionate Sappho loved and sang. Sappho: an ancient Greek poetess (c. 600 B. C.) of Lesbos, known for her passionate love lyrics. sung: sang.
3. the arts of war and peace: military and political achievements.
4. Delos ['di: lɔs]: a small Greek island in the southwest Aegean Sea, supposed to be the site of the oracle of Apollo.
5. Phoebus ['fi: bəs]: Apollo, the Greek sun-god.
6. sprung: sprang.
7. But all, except their sun, is set: but all their past glories are no more, only the sun still shines upon them. Cf. Byron's *Childe Harold's Pilgrimage*: "Greece! Change thy lords, thy state is still the same; /Thy glorious day is o'er, but not thy years of shame."

8. The Scian and the Teian ['ti：ən] muse：referring to Homer and Anacreon. "Muse" here means poet. Scian：of Scio or Chios in the Grecian Archipelage，claimed to have been the birthplace of Homer. Teian：of Teos in ancient Ionia，where the poet Anacreon was born.
9. The hero's harp，the lover's lute：also referring to Homer who wrote epics and Anacreon who wrote love lyrics.
10. Have found the fame your shores refuse：have elsewhere received the honor which Greece itself failed to give.
11. your sires' 'Islands of the Blest'：according to the ancient Greek mythology，the Islands of the Blest (the blessed people) were supposed to lie in the Western Ocean，where the human beings who were the favorites of the gods dwelt after their death，in everlasting joy. "your sires" refer to the ancient Greeks who held the above superstitious belief. sires'：(archaic) ancestors'.
12. Marathon：the plain of Marathon，the site of a famous battle in 490 B. C.，where the Greeks won a big victory over the invading Persians.
13. Persian's grave：graves of the Persian soldiers killed in the battle of Marathon.
14. A king：referring to Xerxes (519 B. C.？—465 B. C.)，the king who led the Persians to invade Greece in 480 B. C.
15. sate：(archaic) sat.
16. on the rocky brow：on the edge of the cliff.
17. sea-born：rising out of the sea.
18. Salamis：an island off the southwest coast of Greece. The Greeks defeated the Persian invaders near Salamis in a naval battle，480 B. C.
19. And when the sun set where were they?：referring to the destruction of all the Persians at the naval battle of Salamis.
20. lay：a narrative to be sung；a song.
21. in the dearth of fame：in these days when there is a lack of great events and great men. dearth：lack.
22. suffuse：overspread with colour，redden.
23. For what is left the poet here?：what is left for the poet to do here?
24. Spartan dead：the dead Spartan warriors，referring to the Spartans in

ancient Greece, who were known to be great fighters.

25. Thermopylae [θəˈmɔpəliː]: the famous battle at Thermopylae (a narrow mountain pass in East Greece) where three hundred Spartans resisted heroically the Persian invaders in 480 B. C.

26. strike other chords: play some other musical composition, implying here "to deal with some other themes".

27. Samian: of Samos, an island in the Aegean Sea.

28. blood of Scio's vine: referring to wine. Scio is known for its grapes, oranges and lemons. See Note 8.

29. bold Bacchanal: drunken reveller; worshipper of Bacchus, the god of wine.

30. Pyrrhic dance: war dance of the ancient Greeks of quick, light movement. It is said to have been so named from Pyrrhicus, the inventor.

31. Pyrrhic phalanx: a military formation of the ancient Greeks, consisting of a body of heavy infantry armed with long spears and short swords, standing in line close behind one another, generally 8 men deep.

32. Cadmus: a semi-mythological personage, to whom are ascribed the introduction of the Greek alphabet from Phoenicia and the invention of writing.

33. Anacreon's song: the song of a Greek lyric poet of Teos, Anacreon (572 B. C. ? —488 B. C. ?) who lived chiefly at Samos and Athens.

34. Polycrates: a tyrant of Samos and a friend of Anacreon ("tyrant", in ancient Greece, was a person who had absolute power in a certain state).

35. The tyrant of the Chersonese [ˈkəːsəniːs]: referring to Miltiades (540 B. C. ? —489 B. C.), an Athenian general famous for his decisive victory over the Persians at Marathon in 490 B. C. He later became the absolute ruler of the Peninsula of the Dardanelles. "Chersonese", from the Greek word "Chersonesos", meaning "Peninsula", here refers to the peninsula of the Dardanelles, now Gallipoli.

36. Miltiades [milˈtaiədiːz]: see the above note.

37. Oh: I wish.

38. to bind: to unite (the Greeks).

39. Suli's rock, and Parga's shore: Suli, a mountain stronghold in Epirus, Greece; Parga, a seacoast town in Greece.

40. a line: a line of descent.

41. Doric mothers：brave Spartan mothers（the Dorians were one of the four divisions of the Greek race，Spartans being their chief representatives）.
42. Heracleidan blood：descendants of Hercules，a man of superhuman strength in Greek mythology.
43. Trust not for freedom to the Franks-/They have a king who buys and sells：do not depend on foreign countries to obtain freedom for you（i. e. the Greeks），they have a king who buys and sells the interests of others for his own profit. “the Franks” normally refers to France，but here obviously refers to western European countries in general.
44. Latin fraud：dishonesty or deceitfulness of the Latin countries. Here the Latin countries are similar to “the Franks” mentioned immediately above.
45. My own the burning tear-drop laves：the burning tear-drop laves my own. My own：my own eyes. laves：washes.
46. Sunium：now Cape Colennam in South Attica，Greece.
47. save：except.

诗歌赏析

《哀希腊》是一首讴歌自由、反抗压迫的革命抒情诗，选自拜伦代表作《唐璜》的第三章。此诗常单独出现。拜伦以一位希腊诗人的名义吟唱了这首歌。拜伦与希腊的情愫由来已久，在《恰尔德·哈罗德游记》和《邪教徒》中多有吟唱。拜伦自己后来也投身于希腊的民族解放事业当中，出钱出力，亲自带队，最后染病而亡，迄今还被希腊人尊为民族英雄。鲁迅对拜伦在希腊的壮举推崇备至，希望成为一个像拜伦一样“所遇常抗，所向必动，贵力而尚强，尊己而好战”的离经叛道的革命战士。

这首诗回顾了古希腊历史上数次与入侵的波斯人大战并取得胜利的辉煌，联想到希腊受人奴役的现状，呼吁希腊人重现昔日辉煌。诗人不断用过去和现在对比，让人猛醒。全诗层次分明，格律工整，由 16 个六行诗节组成，每个诗行为抑扬格四音步，押 ababcc 韵，读起来铿锵有力。另外，这首诗用典颇多，古希腊人名和地名频频出现，不熟悉希腊历史文化的读者会产生理解障碍。但是，对于希腊人来说，正是这些展现昨日辉煌的具体事例才能激励和刺激希腊人奋起反抗侵略，捍卫祖国尊严，赢得独立。

For Study and Discussion

1. Discuss the tone of the poem.
2. Try to appreciate the technique of contrast in this poem.
3. Mark out the allusions in this poem. How do they serve the theme?
4. How does Byron try to arouse the patriotic feeling of the Greek people?
5. Learn the first stanza by heart.

参考译文

哀希腊

1

希腊群岛呵，美丽的希腊群岛！
火热的莎弗在这里唱过恋歌；
在这里，战争与和平的艺术并兴，
狄洛斯崛起，阿波罗跃出海波！
永恒的夏天还把海岛镀成金，
可是除了太阳，一切已经消沉。

2

开奥的缪斯和蒂奥的缪斯，
那英雄的竖琴，恋人的琵琶，
原在你的岸上博得了声誉，
而今在这发源地反倒喑哑，——
呵，那歌声已远远向西流传，
远超过你祖先的海岛乐园。

3

起伏的山峦望着马拉松，
马拉松望着茫茫的海波；
我独自在那里冥想了一刻，
梦见希腊仍旧自由而欢乐；
因为当我在波斯墓上站立，

我不能想象自己是个奴隶。

4

一个国王高高坐在山头上，
瞭望着萨拉密挺立于海外，
千万只战船停靠在山脚下，
还有多少队伍——全由他统率！
他在天亮时把他们数了数，
但在日落时他们到了何处？

5

呵，他们而今安在？还有你呢，
我的祖国？在无声的土地上，
英雄的颂歌如今喑哑了，
那英雄的心也不再激荡！
难道你一向庄严的竖琴，
竟至沦落到我的手里弹弄？

6

也好，置身在奴隶民族里，
尽管荣誉都已在沦丧中，
至少，一个爱国志士的忧思，
还使我作歌时感到脸红；
因为，诗人在这儿有什么能为？
为希腊人含羞，对希腊国落泪。

7

我们难道只对好日子哭泣
和惭愧？——我们的祖先却流血。
大地呵！把斯巴达人的遗骨
从你的怀抱里送回来一些！
哪怕给我们三百勇士的三个，
让色茅霹雳的决死战复活！

8

怎么，还是无声？一切都沉寂？
不是的！你听那古代的英魂
正像远方的瀑布一样喧哗，
他们回答："只要有一个活人
登高一呼，我们就来，就来！"
噫！倒只是活人不理不睬。

9

算了，算了；试试别的调子；
斟满一杯萨摩斯的美酒！
把战争留给土耳其野人，
让开奥的葡萄的血汁倾流！
听呵，每一个酒鬼多么踊跃
响应这一个不荣誉的号召！

10

你们还保有庇瑞克的舞艺，
但庇瑞克的方阵哪里去了？
这是两课：为什么你们偏把
那高尚而坚强的一课忘掉？
凯德谟斯给你们造了字体——
难道他是为了传授给奴隶？

11

斟满一杯萨摩斯的美酒！
让我们且抛开这样的话题！
这美酒曾使阿那克瑞翁
发为神圣的歌；是的，他屈于
波里克瑞底斯，一个暴君，
但这暴君至少是我们国人。

12

克索尼萨斯的一个暴君
是自由的最忠勇的朋友，
那暴君是密尔蒂阿底斯！
呵，但愿现在我们能够有
一个暴君和他一样精明，
他会团结我们不受人欺凌！

13

斟满一杯萨摩斯的美酒！
在苏里的山中，巴加的岸上，
住着一族人的勇敢的子孙，
不愧是斯巴达的母亲所养，
在那里，也许种子已经播撒，
是赫拉克勒斯血统的真传。

14

别相信西方人会带来自由，
他们有一个作买卖的国王；
本土的利剑，本土的士兵，
是冲锋陷阵的唯一希望；
但在御敌时，拉丁的欺骗，
比土耳其的武力还更危险。

15

呵，斟满一杯萨摩斯的美酒！
树荫下舞蹈着我们的姑娘，
我看见她们的黑眼睛闪耀；
但是，望着每个鲜艳的女郎，
我的眼就为火热的泪所迷：
这乳房难道也要哺育奴隶？

16
让我登上苏尼阿的悬崖，
在那里，将只有我和那海浪
可以听见彼此的低语飘送，
让我像天鹅一样歌尽而亡；
我不要奴隶的国度属于我——
干脆把那萨摩斯酒杯打破！

（查良铮 译）

18. Percy Bysshe Shelley

Percy Bysshe Shelley（珀西·比希·雪莱，1792—1822）is a contradictory and challenging figure. His writing was at once the most passionate and intense of all the Romantic poets, and yet the most intellectual, the fullest of philosophical speculation and technical experiment. He made brilliant innovations and experiments in poetic language, and he wrote "The Defense of Poetry" (1821), a magnificent essay on the meaning and importance of poetry.

Like Byron, Shelley was born of an upper-class family. They called him "mad Shelley". At Eton, Shelley first became determined to fight against the forces of injustice and oppression in life. In 1810 he went to Oxford University, where he wrote a pamphlet called *The Necessity of Atheism* (1811), for which he was expelled from the university and disowned by his father. An ill-starred marriage with Harriet Westbrook followed, and after that came the quixotic attempt to arouse Ireland to struggle for national independence.

Returning to London, Shelley joined the circle of the radical social philosopher William Godwin and published his first important poem, *Queen Mab* (1813), a long allegorical work. In 1814 Shelley fell in love with William Godwin's daughter Mary. In 1816 Harriet drowned herself and a great scandal arose. Like Byron, Shelley felt himself an alien and an outcast in his own country. He completed another important long poem *The Revolt of Islam* (1817). In 1818, soon after he and Mary were married, they left England for Italy, where Shelley spent the rest of his life.

During the few years in Italy, Shelley produced an astonishing amount and range of magnificent poetry. In 1818 he began the philosophical drama, *Prometheus Unbound*, his masterpiece. In 1819 he completed *Prometheus Unbound* and wrote his great "*Ode to the West Wind*". In 1820 he produced a political lyric *The Mask of Anarchy*. The year 1821 saw the publication of *Adonais*, Shelley's great elegy on the death of John Keats. In 1822 he completed *Hellas*, a lyrical drama about the Greek war of liberation against the Turks. In addition to these major works, Shelley wrote in each of these years many of the intense, beautifully crafted shorter lyrics for which he is so well known. On July 8, 1822, he was drowned when sailing in a small boat along the coast of Italy. Shelley's ashes were buried in the Protestant cemetery at Rome, near the grave of Keats.

Shelley loved the people and hated their oppressors and exploiters. He called on the people to overthrow the rule of tyranny and injustice and prophesied a happy and free life for mankind. He stood for his social and political ideal all his life. He and Byron are justifiably regarded as the two great poets of revolutionary romanticism in England.

Ode to the West Wind[1]

This poem was one of Shelley's great lyrics, written in Italy in 1819. Shelley expresses his political ideas through the west wind. It is divided into five stanzas. The first three stanzas describe the west wind's influence on the autumn leaves on the earth, the clouds in the sky and the waves in the sea respectively. In the fourth stanza, Shelley longs to identify himself with the objects of the wind's power. In the last stanza, the poet discovers his true relationship to the west wind — they are one. He shows his active and optimistic spirit in this part represented by the last line of the poem "If Winter comes, can Spring be far behind?"

1

O wild West Wind[2], thou breath of Autumn's being[3],

Thou, from whose unseen presence the leaves dead
Are driven[4], like ghosts from an enchanter fleeing,[5]

Yellow, and black, and pale, and hectic red,[6]
Pestilence-stricken multitudes[7]: O Thou,
Who chariotest to their dark wintry bed

The winged seeds,[8] where they lie cold and low,
Each like a corpse within its grave, until
Thine azure sister of the Spring[9] shall blow.

He clarion[10] o'er the dreaming earth, and fill
(Driving sweet buds like flocks to feed in air[11])
With living hues and odours plain and hill:[12]

Wild Spirit, which art[13] moving everywhere;
Destroyer and Preserver;[14] hear, O hear!

2

Thou on whose stream, 'mid the steep sky's commotion,
Loose clouds like Earth's decaying leaves are shed,[15]
Shook[16] from the tangled boughs of Heaven and Ocean,[17]

Angels of rain and lightning:[18] there are spread[19]
On the blue surface of thine aery[20] surge,
Like the bright hair uplifted from the head

Of some fierce Mænad[21], even[22] from the dim verge
Of the horizon to the zenith's height[23],
The locks of the approaching storm[24]. Thou Dirge

Of the dying year,[25] to which this closing night
Will be the dome of a vast sepulchre[26],

Vaulted with all thy congregated might[27]

Of vapours[28], from whose[29] solid atmosphere
Black rain and fire and hail will burst: O hear!

3

Thou[30] who didst waken from his[31] summer dreams
The blue Mediterranean, where he lay,
Lulled by the coil[32] of his crystalline streams,

Beside a pumice isle[33] in Baiæ's bay[34],
And saw in sleep old palaces and towers
Quivering within the wave's intenser day[35],

All overgrown with azure moss and flowers
So sweet, the sense faints picturing them![36] Thou
For whose path the Atlantic's level powers[37]

Cleave[38] themselves into chasms, while far below
The sea-blooms and the ooze woods which wear
The sapless foliage of the ocean, know

Thy voice, and suddenly grow grey with fear,
And tremble and despoil themselves:[39] O hear!

4

If I were a dead leaf thou mightest bear;[40]
If I were a swift cloud to fly with thee;
A wave to pant beneath thy power, and share

The impulse of thy strength, only less free
Than thou, O Uncontrollable! If even
I were as in my boyhood, and could be

The comrade of thy wanderings over Heaven,[41]
As then,[42] when to outstrip thy skiey speed[43]
Scarce seemed a vision[44]; I would ne'er have striven

As thus with thee in prayer in my sore need.[45]
Oh! lift me as a wave, a leaf, a cloud!
I fall upon the thorns of life[46]! I bleed!

A heavy weight of hours[47] has chained and bowed
One too like thee:[48] tameless, and swift, and proud.

5

Make me thy lyre, even as the forest is[49]:
What if my leaves[50] are falling like its own[51]!
The tumult of thy mighty harmonies

Will take from both a deep, autumnal tone,[52]
Sweet though in sadness. Be thou, Spirit fierce,
My spirit! Be thou me, impetuous one![53]

Drive my dead thoughts over the universe
Like withered leaves to quicken a new birth!
And, by the incantation[54] of this verse,

Scatter, as from an unextinguished hearth
Ashes and sparks[55], my words among mankind!
Be through my lips to unawakened Earth

The trumpet of a prophecy![56] O Wind,
If Winter comes, can Spring be far behind?[57]

1819 1820

Notes

1. "Ode to the West Wind" was begun in 1819 according to Shelley's own note: "This poem was conceived and chiefly written in a wood that skirts the Arno, near Florence, and on a day when that tempestuous wind, whose temperature is at once mild and animating, was collecting vapors which pour down the autumnal rains, … attended by that magnificent thunder and lightning peculiar to the Cisalpine regions." This ode is written in a complicated fusion of the sonnet and terza rima with an interlocking rhyme scheme (aba bcb cdc ded ee) of four 3-line groups and a final couplet.
2. wild West Wind: notice the alliteration in these words.
3. thou breath of Autumn's being: thou (are) breath of Autumn's being (a metaphor). Autumn is personified. being: life, existence.
4. from whose unseen presence the leaves dead/Are driven: from whose unseen presence the dead leaves are driven. whose: your. presence: existence. It means the west wind cannot be seen but can be felt.
5. like ghosts from an enchanter fleeing: like ghosts fleeing from an enchanter (a simile). In the first stanza, the poet uses four figures of speech — alliteration, metaphor, personification and simile to describe the power of the West Wind.
6. hectic red: feverish red.
7. Pestilence-stricken multitudes: referring to the dead leaves. Pestilence-stricken: attacked by fatal disease.
8. O Thou, / Who chariotest to their dark wintry bed / The winged seeds: you carry the winged seeds in your chariot to their dark wintry bed. chariotest: (archaic) chariot. bed: earth.
9. Thine azure sister of the Spring: the west wind in spring which will bring blue sky to Italy.
10. clarion: horn; a high, shrill trumpet. The clarion and the corpse in Line 8 are both in allusion to the Bible. Cf. Corinthians 15: 52 in the New Testament: "For the trumpet will sound, and the dead will be raised imperishable…"
11. Driving sweet buds like flocks to feed in air: sweet buds get nourishment in

the air. Here the West Wind is compared to the shepherd.

12. and fill/With living hues and odours plain and hill: and fill plain and hill with living hues and odours. living hues and odours: fresh color and sweet smells.
13. art: are.
14. Destroyer and Preserver: you are both a destroyer to destroy old things and a preserver to preserve the new things indicating life and hope. The west wind is considered as the "destroyer", for driving the last signs of life from the trees; it is considered as the "preserver", for scattering the seeds which will come to life in the spring.
15. Thou on whose stream, 'mid the steep sky's commotion, /Loose clouds like Earth's decaying leaves are shed: Thou, loose clouds are shed like earth's decaying leaves, on whose stream, mid the steep sky's commotion. Thou: loose clouds. whose stream: air current brought by the West Wind. mid: amid. steep: high. commotion: the changing state. shed: scattered.
16. Shook: shaken.
17. the tangled boughs of Heaven and Ocean: implying that the line between the sky and stormy sea is indistinguishable, the whole space from the horizon to the zenith being covered with trailing storm cloud.
18. Angels of rain and lightning: the messengers that can bring rain and lightning, here referring to the loose clouds.
19. there are spread: there are (the locks of the approaching storm) spread.
20. aery: airy.
21. Mænad: a very frenzied woman in Greek mythology, a female worshipper who danced frenziedly in the worship of Dionysus (Bacchus), the Greek god of wine and vegetation.
22. even: just.
23. zenith's height: the highest point on the celestial sphere.
24. The locks of the approaching storm: referring to the loose clouds. approaching: coming.
25. Thou Dirge / Of the dying year: thou (are) dirge of the dying year. Thou: the West Wind. Dirge: funeral song. The west wind in autumn predicts the end of the year. Here the dying year symbolizes all the traditional, old

things.

26. the dome of a vast sepulchre: the ceiling of a big tomb.
27. thy congregated might: your gathered power.
28. vapours: clouds.
29. whose: referring to vapours'.
30. Thou: the West Wind.
31. his: Mediterranean's.
32. coil: noise of the tide.
33. a pumice isle: an isle near Naples, Italy, which is formed by deposits of lava from Vesuvius, a volcano nearby.
34. Baiæ's bay: a favorite resort of the ancient Romans on the coast of Campania, at the western end of the Bay of Naples, the locale of imposing villas built in the glory days of imperial Rome. Their ruins are reflected in the waters of the bay.
35. wave's intenser day: the translucency of the water is intenser than the dazzling daylight above its surface. "day" here refers to the daylight.
36. So sweet, the sense faints picturing them: so sweet that the sense faints in describing them.
37. the Atlantic's level powers: the waves of the Atlantic Ocean moving on its flat surface. powers: waves with power.
38. Cleave: break apart.
39. far below/…/And tremble and despoil themselves: the plants at the bottom of the ocean also fall under the influence of the west wind which announces the change of the season. despoil: strip (themselves) of (their leaves).
40. thou mightest bear: you might carry (here and there).
41. be/The comrade of thy wanderings over Heaven: run with the wind in the sky.
42. As then: as in my boyhood.
43. to outstrip thy skiey speed: to go faster than your flying speed in the sky. skiey: (poetic) airy and ethereal.
44. vision: dream.
45. As thus with thee in prayer in my sore need: praying to you, in my great need, in this way (the two lines below are the poet's prayer to the west

wind). As thus: in this way.

46. the thorns of life: trouble or hardship of life.
47. A heavy weight of hours: a heavy burden of time.
48. One too like thee: here the poet compares himself to the West Wind. One: the poet himself. thee: the West Wind.
49. even as the forest is: just as the forest is (thy lyre).
50. my leaves: the pessimistic ideas of the poet, my dead thoughts.
51. like its own: like the forest's own (leaves).
52. The tumult of thy mighty harmonies/Will take from both a deep, autumnal tone: the tumult of thy mighty harmonies will take a deep autumnal tone from both my depressed feeling and the falling leaves. thy mighty harmonies: your powerful music (sound of the West Wind). both: the poet and the forest.
53. Be thou, Spirit fierce, /My spirit! Be thou me, impetuous one: I wish you, the fierce and impetuous Spirit, become my spirit! impetuous: courageous, brave.
54. incantation: spell.
55. as from an unextinguished hearth/Ashes and sparks: as ashes and sparks from and unextinguished hearth.
56. The trumpet of a prophecy: the trumpet that announces a new age.
57. If Winter comes, can Spring be far behind: a rhetorical question, also a famous line showing Shelley's optimistic idea towards life.

诗歌赏析

《西风颂》写于1819年秋天的一个傍晚，当时雪莱在意大利佛罗伦萨附近阿诺河畔的树林里遇上风暴有感而发。这首诗是雪莱最著名的政治抒情诗，西风是革命力量的象征。全诗分为五节，主要的意象就是西风。字里行间丰富的象征性语言为这首诗赋予了多重内涵。

首先，这首诗是英国诗歌中形式表达内容的典范。全诗共分五部分，每部分十四行，由四个三行诗组和一个双偶句组成，诗歌形式是英国十四行诗和意大利但丁体的复杂融合。格律为抑扬格五音步，韵式aba bcb cdc ded ee。这种连环抱韵和双偶句结合的押韵格式生动形象地表现了西风在空中回旋飞舞，最后飘然落地的运动；诗中多跨行和跨节诗句，表达了西风狂放不羁的形象和诗人狂傲不驯的灵魂，做到了形式与内容的统一。

诗人在第一节中生动介绍了西风对陆地的影响。诗歌一开头就用顿呼的方式赞美西风是秋之生命的呼吸。Wild West Wind 中接连三个 w 的重复形成头韵，用来比拟呼呼的风声。西风被赋予破坏者和保护者的角色——作为破坏者，它以摧枯拉朽般的力量横扫一切鬼魅般的叶子；作为保护者，它把种子送到了地下，促成了来年新生命的诞生。落叶代表一切旧的东西或思想，种子则预示着新的力量及生命。

第二节描绘了西风对天空的影响。天上的云朵作为雨和电的使者，就像地上的枯叶一般被西风从海天之间吹散；西风奏起了残年的挽歌！西风带来了黑雨、冰雹和火焰。“山雨欲来风满楼”，狂热的革命风暴正在凝聚，革命形势一触即发，旧的王朝行将就木，新的时代即将到来！

第三节描写西风对海洋的作用。西风把蓝色的地中海从沉睡中唤醒，将海底的草木吓得战栗、枯萎。沉睡的地中海或许指英国昏昏的民众。梦中的古老殿堂楼阁就是古代文明的象征。海底的花木指被革命力量所吓倒的保守派。

在描述了西风在陆地、天空、海洋的作用之后，诗人在第四节渴望自己也能像落叶、乱云和波浪一样，被西风带起，随着西风奔放的力量，自由无拘。诗人曾经也像西风一样桀骜不驯，可是如今，诗人已失却了往日的自在，跌坐在生活的荆棘之上，鲜血淋漓！

最后一节，诗人化被动为主动，希望与西风合二为一，期待自己的诗歌拥有西风的力量，打破旧秩序，迎来新思想，把革命的理想向全世界散播。最后一句“要是冬天已经来了，西风啊，春日怎能遥远？”充满了革命乐观主义精神，已经成为英诗的名句。

For Study and Discussion

1. In what way is the West Wind both a destroyer and a preserver?
2. The speaker's relation to the wind develops in a dramatic way during the course of the poem, particularly in Stanzas 4 and 5. Explain his relation to the wind at the end of Stanza 4? How does this change in Stanza 5?
3. What does the West Wind symbolize?
4. What's the main idea of each stanza?
5. There are not a few Chinese translations of this poem. Make a comparative study of some of them and try to give your comment.
6. Please learn the last stanza by heart.

参考译文

西风颂

1

哦，狂暴的西风，秋之生命的呼吸！
你无形，但枯死的落叶被你横扫，
有如鬼魅碰到了巫师，纷纷逃避：

黄的，黑的，灰的，红得像患肺痨，
呵，重染疫疠的一群：西风呵，是你
以车驾把有翼的种子催送到

黑暗的冬床上，它们就躺在那里，
像是墓中的死穴，冰冷，深藏，低贱，
直等到春天，你碧空的姊妹吹起

她的喇叭，在沉睡的大地上响遍，
(唤出嫩芽，像羊群一样，觅食空中)
将色和香充满了山峰和平原：

不羁的精灵呵，你无处不远行；
破坏者兼保护者：听吧，你且聆听！

2

没入你的激流，当高空一片混乱，
流云像大地的枯叶一样被撕扯
脱离天空和海洋的纠缠的枝干，

成为雨和电的使者：它们飘落
在你的磅礴之气的蔚蓝的波面，
有如狂女的飘扬的头发在闪烁，

从天穹最遥远而模糊的边沿
直抵九霄的中天，到处都在摇曳
欲来雷雨的卷发。对濒死的一年

你唱出了葬歌，而这密集的黑夜
将成为它广大墓陵的一座圆顶，
里面正有你的万钧之力在凝结；

那是你的浑然之气，从它会迸涌
黑色的雨、冰雹和火焰：哦，你听！

3

是你，你将蓝色的地中海唤醒，
而它曾经昏睡了一整个夏天，
被澄澈水流的回旋催眠入梦，

就在巴亚海湾的一个浮石岛边，
它梦见了古老的宫殿和楼阁
在水天映辉的波影里抖颤，

而且都生满青苔，开满花朵，
那芬芳真迷人欲醉！呵，为了给你
让一条路，大西洋的汹涌的浪波

把自己向两边劈开，而深在渊底
那海洋中的花草和泥污的森林
虽然枝叶扶疏，却没有精力；

听到你的声音，它们已吓得发青：
一边颤栗，一边自动萎缩：哦，你听！

4

唉，假如我是一片枯叶被你浮起，
假如我是能和你飞跑的云雾，
是一个波浪，和你的威力同喘息，

假如我分有你的脉搏，仅仅不如
你那么自由，哦，无法约束的生命！
假如我能像在少年时，凌风而舞

便成了你的伴侣，悠游于天空
（因为呵，那时候，要想追你上云霄，

似乎并非梦幻)，我就不致像如今
这样焦躁地要和你争相祈祷。
哦，举起我吧，当我是水波、树叶、浮云!
我跌在生活的荆棘上，我流血了!
这被岁月的重轭所制伏的生命
原是和你一样的：骄傲、轻捷而不驯。

5

把我当作你的竖琴吧，有如树林：
尽管我的叶落了，那有什么关系!
你巨大的合奏所振起的乐音
将染有树林和我的深邃的秋意：
虽忧伤而甜蜜。呵，但愿你给予我
狂暴的精神！奋勇者呵，让我们合一。
请把我枯死的思想向世界吹落，
让它像枯叶一样促成新的生命!
哦，请听从这一篇符咒似的诗歌，
就把我的话语，像是灰烬和火星
从还未熄灭的炉火向人间播散!
让预言的喇叭通过我的嘴唇
把昏睡的大地唤醒吧！要是冬天
已经来了，西风呵，春日怎能遥远?

(查良铮　译)

A Song: "Men of England"[1]

This poem was written at a time of turbulent unrest, after the return of troops from the Napoleonic Wars had precipitated a great economic depression. The "song" expressing Shelley's hope for a proletarian revolution, was originally planned as one of a series for workers. It has become a hymn of the British labor movement. In this lyric, the capitalist society is divided into two hostile classes: the bourgeoisie and the proletariat. Shelley calls upon the working class to fight against their rulers and exploiters.

Men of England, wherefore[2] plough
For the lords who lay ye[3] low?
Wherefore weave with toil and care
The rich robes your tyrants wear?

Wherefore feed and clothe and save
From the cradle to the grave?
Those ungrateful drones[4] who would
Drain your sweat—nay, drink your blood?

Wherefore, Bees of England[5], forge
Many a weapon, chain, and scourge[6],
That these stingless drones may spoil[7]
The forced produce of your toil?[8]

Have ye leisure, comfort, calm,
Shelter, food, love's gentle balm?
Or what is it ye buy so dear
With your pain and with your fear?[9]

The seed ye sow, another reaps;
The wealth ye find, another keeps;
The robes ye weave, another wears;
The arms ye forge, another bears.

Sow seed—but let no tyrant reap:
Find wealth—let no impostor heap:
Weave robe—let not the idle wear:
Forge arms—in your defence to bear.

Shrink to your cellars, holes, and cells—

In halls ye deck[10] another dwells.
Why shake the chains ye wrought[11]? Ye see
The steel ye tempered glance on ye.[12]

With plough and spade and hoe and loom
Trace[13] your grave and build your tomb
And weave your winding-sheet[14]—till fair
England be your Sepulchre.

1819 1839

Notes

1. This song contains eight quatrains rhyming aabb with each line of four accented syllables.
2. wherefore: (archaic) why.
3. ye: (archaic) you.
4. drones: the male of the honey-bees that do no work, referring here to the parasitic class in human society.
5. Bees of England: here referring to the laboring people in England.
6. scourge: whip.
7. spoil: plunder.
8. The forced produce of your toil: the products of your labor which are produced under compulsion.
9. Or what is it ye buy so dear/With your pain and with your fear: i. e. what is the recompense you obtain at the high price of your sufferings and anxieties?
10. deck: decorate.
11. wrought: (archaic) made.
12. The steel ye tempered glance on ye: the sword you forged is flashed on your face.
13. Trace: map out.
14. winding-sheet: shroud.

For Study and Discussion

1. What is the theme of the poem?

2. Is it a satiric poem? Why or why not?
3. Discuss the rhetorical devices used in the whole poem. What are their functions?

参考译文

给英国人民的歌

英国人民呵，何必为地主而耕？
他们一直把你们当作贱种！
何必为你们的昏暴的君王
辛勤地纺织他豪富的衣裳？

何必把那些忘恩负义的懒虫
从摇篮到坟墓都好好供奉？
吃饭，穿衣，救命，一股脑儿承担，
而他们却要榨干你们的血汗！

为什么，英国的工蜂呵，要熔锻
那么多武器，锁链和钢鞭，
因而使无刺的雄蜂便于劫夺
你们被迫劳动而得的收获？

你们可有闲暇、舒适和平静？
可有住宅、食粮、爱情的温存？
不然，你们整天在痛苦和害怕，
究竟为什么要付这么高的代价？

你们撒的种子，别人拿收成；
你们找到的财富，别人留存；
你们织的衣袍，别人穿戴；
你们铸的武器，别人取过来。

播种吧——但别让暴君搜刮；
寻找财富吧——别让骗子起家；
纺织吧——可别为懒人织锦衣；
铸武器吧——保护你们自己。

钻进你们的地窖、洞穴、陋室里，
你们装饰的大厦已有别人安居。
为什么要摆脱你们制的锁链？
看，你们铸的剑把你们看管！

就用耕犁、织机、铁铲和铁锄，
规划和建筑你们的坟墓；
织好你们的尸衣吧，就让
美丽的英国作你们的墓场。

（查良铮　译）

A Song[1]

This is a minor poem of Shelley often ignored by most readers and critics. But it is most intense in feeling. With concrete and vivid images, the poet displays an atmosphere of sorrow. In the second stanza, the mournful scene is displayed both from the visual and acoustic angles.

A widow bird[2] sat mourning[3] for her love
Upon a wintry bough[4];
The frozen wind[5] crept on above
The freezing stream[6] below[7].

There was no leaf upon the forest bare[8],
No flower upon her ground[9],
And little motion in the air
Except the mill-wheel's sound.

Notes

1. This is a short poem written in two quatrains rhyming abab. Cf. 南朝民歌《子夜四时歌·冬歌》：“寒鸟依高树，枯林鸣悲风。为欢憔悴尽，那得好颜容？”
2. A widow bird: a female bird without companion.
3. mourning: grieving.

4. wintry bough: bough in the winter. A wintry bough usually has no leaves. Here both a bird without companion and a bough without leaves show a woeful state.
5. frozen wind: here the poet uses the wind that was frozen to show the cold weather.
6. freezing stream: stream is becoming frozen.
7. below: in contrast to "above" in the third line. The images above and below are all of coldness.
8. the forest bare: the bare forest.
9. No flower upon her ground: there is no flower in the forest.

For Study and Discussion

1. How does the setting help express the meaning of the poem?
2. Appreciate the contrast in the last stanza.
3. This poem is famous for its images. Compare this poem with the famous Chinese poem《天净沙·秋思》。
4. Learn this poem by heart.

参考译文

歌

孤鸟栖枯树，
失伴多凄苦；
头上寒风爬，
脚下溪凝固。

树林叶落尽，
地上花不存。
空中无声响，
唯闻水车吟。

（李正栓　译）

19. John Keats

John Keats (约翰·济慈, 1795—1821) was a brilliant figure of active romanticists in England. He was born in London in 1795, the son of a stable-keeper. At 15, he was made an apprentice to a surgeon and apothecary. Then he studied medicine at hospitals, but he soon decided to devote his life to poetry. It is Leigh Hunt, a well-known literary critic and political radical, who encouraged Keats to take him seriously as a writer.

Keats published a long mythological poem entitled *Endymion* in 1818, which was severely attacked by the reviewers. In January 1819 Keats took a vacation from London and spent a few days with some very good friends near the southern coast of England. Keats wrote one of his greatest poems, *The Eve of St. Agnes*, which marks the beginning of one of the most extraordinarily productive periods in all of English literature. In less than 9 months, from January to September, Keats produced an astonishing sequence of masterpieces: "*La Belle Dame Sans Merci*", 6 great odes including "*To Autumn*", "*Ode On Melancholy*", "*Ode to a Nightingale*" and "*Ode on a Grecian Urn*" (The last 2 odes have generally been considered jointly as the height of Keats' poetic achievement), *Lamia*, and a group of magnificent sonnets. During the last few months of 1819 Keats finished another long poem *Hyperion*.

But Keats' career was to be cut tragically short just as he was beginning to realize his full potential. The first clear signs of the tuberculoses he had always feared became apparent in February 1820. He weakened rapidly during the spring and summer. His close friend, the painter Joseph Severn, persuaded him to spend the autumn and winter in Italy. Keats went as advised but could not recover. He died in Rome on February 23, 1821.

Keats learned the art of poetry mainly from the poets of the English Renaissance such as Spenser, Shakespeare and Milton. The artistic aim in his poetry was always to create a beautiful world of imagination as opposed to the sordid reality of his day. He sought to express beauty in all his poems. His leading principle is: "Beauty is truth, truth beauty." He is a voice through which beauty expresses itself. He is part of the nature which he describes. He expresses the delight which comes not only through the eye and the ear but also through the senses of touch, taste and smell. His poetry is distinguished by sensuousness and the perfection of form. So he has always been known as a sensuous poet. His ability to appeal to the senses through language is virtually unrivaled. Some of his poems touch upon the burning political problems of his day. He shows his dissatisfaction with the capitalist society and describes the sufferings of the poor people.

To Autumn[1]

This is one of John Keats' best poems. Through concrete images and colors the poem gives us a vivid description of the beauty of autumn scene. It has three stanzas. The first stanza shows the ripeness before harvest from the senses of sight, smell and touch, presenting a beauty of colour. The second stanza describes different scenes of harvest, focusing on the activities of the labouring people and creating a beauty of work. The last stanza describes the world of insects and birds after harvest in autumn from the sense of hearing, presenting a beauty of sound. In short, in the three stanzas, he respectively describes the autumn colour, the autumn people and the autumn sound. The poet shows us his deep love for autumn, the season of ripeness and warmth.

1

Season of mists and mellow fruitfulness,
Close bosom-friend of the maturing sun[2];
Conspiring[3] with him how to load and bless
With fruit[4] the vines that round the thatch-eves[5] run;
To bend with apples the moss'd[6] cottage-trees,
And fill all fruit with ripeness to the core;
To swell the gourd, and plump the hazel shells
With a sweet kernel; to set budding more,

And still more, later flowers for the bees,
Until they think warm days will never cease,
For summer has o'er-brimm'd their clammy cells.[7]

2

Who hath not seen thee oft amid thy store[8]?
Sometimes whoever seeks abroad[9] may find
Thee sitting careless[10] on a granary floor,
Thy hair soft-lifted by the winnowing wind[11];
Or on a half-reap'd furrow sound asleep,
Drows'd[12] with the fume of poppies[13], while thy hook[14]
Spares[15] the next swath and all its twined flowers:
And sometimes like a gleaner thou dost keep
Steady thy laden head[16] across a brook;
Or by a cyder-press[17], with patient look,
Thou watchest the last oozings[18] hours by hours.

3

Where are the songs of Spring? Ay,[19] where are they?
Think not of them, thou hast thy music too, —
While barred clouds[20] bloom the soft-dying day,
And touch the stubble-plains[21] with rosy hue[22];
Then in a wailful[23] choir the small gnats mourn
Among the river sallows[24], borne aloft
Or sinking[25] as the light wind lives or dies[26];
And full-grown lambs loud bleat from hilly bourn[27];
Hedge-crickets sing; and now with treble[28] soft
The red-breast whistles from a garden-croft[29];
And gathering swallows[30] twitter in the skies.
Sept. 19, 1819 1820

Notes

1. It is written in three 11-line stanzas of iambic pentameter lines rhyming

ababcde cdde/dcce. Two days after this serene and gracious ode was composed, Keats wrote to a friend: "I never liked stubble-fields so much as now — Aye, better than the chilly green of the spring. Somehow a stubble-plain looks warm in the same way that some pictures look warm — this struck me so much in my Sunday's walk that I composed upon it."

2. the maturing sun: the sun that matures the living things.
3. conspiring: planning.
4. bless / With fruit: endow with fruit.
5. thatch-eves: thatch-eaves.
6. moss'd: mossed.
7. For summer has o'er-brimm'd their clammy cells: for summer has made their cells overfilled with honey. o'er-brimm'd: overfilled. The first stanza has only one sentence. Syntactically it is a sentence with a subject but without a predicate. Through plentiful visual images we are deeply impressed by the beauty of various ripe plants.
8. store: the things harvested.
9. whoever seeks abroad: anyone who goes to the open fields. seek: (archaic) resort to. abroad: outdoors.
10. careless: without care.
11. winnowing wind: wind that fans the chaff from the grain.
12. Drows'd: made sleepy.
13. poppies: sort of plants, which are often seen in wheat fields in England.
14. hook: scythe.
15. Spares: leaves… uncut.
16. thy laden head: your head which is laden with gleaning.
17. cyder-press: cider-press.
18. oozings: the juice discharged from the cider-press.
19. Ay: yes.
20. barred clouds: stripes of clouds.
21. stubble-plains: stubble fields.
22. hue: colour.
23. wailful: sorrowful, lamentable.
24. sallows: willows.

25. aloft/Or sinking: rising or falling.
26. lives or dies: rises or falls.
27. bourn: domain.
28. treble: the high-pitched voice.
29. garden-croft: a piece of land enclosed for a garden.
30. gathering swallows: swallows that are returning home.

诗歌赏析

与传统中国诗歌中的悲秋情结不同，济慈的《秋颂》旨在歌颂秋天的丰硕、秋收的快乐。济慈无愧其“感官诗人”的称号，在这首诗里充分调动丰富的官感，从视觉、触觉、听觉等几个方面，分别写秋色、秋人和秋声，勾勒出一幅美好的秋日画面。

第一节用一系列果实累累的秋日景色，着重塑造秋收前的丰硕；第二节用几个鲜明的劳动者形象塑造出忙碌的秋收景象；第三节用田野里的虫鸣鸟叫衬托出秋收后大地的静谧。从秋色、秋人到秋声，随着画面的切换和时间的推移，一幅丰满的秋日景色立体化地呈现在读者面前。这首诗充分道出了贫病交加的济慈的乐观主义情绪和对生活的热爱。

For Study and Discussion

1. The poem consists of three stanzas. What specific aspect of autumn is described in each stanza? What's the central idea of each stanza?
2. What poetic devices are used in this poem?
3. Appreciate the visual imagery in the first two stanzas and the auditory imagery in the last.
4. Please try to find some Chinese poems on autumn. Comment on how Chinese poets present autumn to readers.

参考译文

秋　颂

1

雾气霭霭、果实香醇的季节，
你是令万物成熟的太阳的密友；

你与他密谋策划如何将毛屋檐下的一切
葡萄藤蔓挂上累累的珠球；
使屋前长满青苔的树弯腰挂果，
所有果实填满熟味，直到心里；
让葫芦涨大；让榛子鼓壳，
把甜核塞进；为蜜蜂一次又一次
催放晚开的花朵，
直到它们认为日子会永远暖和，
因为夏日早已填满它们的粘巢。

2

谁不常见你伴着谷仓？
有时人们出门便能发现
你无忧无虑坐在打谷场上，
簸谷的微风把你的发丝轻掀；
或见你酣睡于收割一半的田垄，
罂粟花香使你沉迷，
你镰刀停歇在下一畦及其萦绕的花旁；
有时你像拾穗人头顶
谷穗袋蹚过小溪；
有时见你在榨果机旁耐心凝视，
一连几小时地瞧着徐徐榨出的汁浆。

3

春天的歌曲安在？它们安在？
还是不想它们吧，你也有自己的音乐，
慢慢逝去的白日被波云斜照回来，
用胭脂红涂抹残梗仍存的田野，
此时，河柳下群群飞虫哀音同奏
一会儿高飞于空，
一会儿低落，随着微风的起与灭；
群羊在山圈里大声咩叫；
篱下的蟋蟀竞相争雄；

从园中传出知更鸟柔尖的叫声；
还有那归巢的群燕在天空呢喃不歇。

（李正栓　译）

Ode to a Nightingale[1]

In this poem, Keats not only expresses his raptures upon hearing the beautiful songs of the nightingale and his desire to go to the ethereal world of beauty together with the bird, but shows his deep sympathy for the poor and his keen understanding of human miseries in the society in which he lived. Through the contrast of the joys of the "immortal bird" with the miseries of the "hungry generations", one can see clearly the poet's inner contradiction between the ugly social reality all around him and his vain wish to leave it or forget it. By saying the word "forlorn", the poet ends the poem with an acute sense of pain. The central symbol of the poem is the song of the nightingale.

1

My heart aches, and a drowsy numbness pains
My sense, as though of hemlock[2] I had drunk,
Or emptied some dull opiate to the drains[3]
One minute past[4], and Lethe-wards[5] had sunk:
'Tis not[6] through envy of thy happy lot[7],
But being too happy in thine happiness, —
That thou, light-winged Dryad[8] of the trees,
In some melodious plot
Of beechen green[9], and shadows numberless,
Singest of summer in full-throated ease[10].

2

O, for a draught of vintage![11] that hath been
Cool'd a long age in the deep-delved earth[12],
Tasting of Flora[13] and the country green,
Dance, and Provencal song[14], and sunburnt mirth[15]!
O for a beaker full of the warm South,[16]

Full of the true, the blushful Hippocrene,[17]
With beaded bubbles[18] winking[19] at the brim,
And purple-stained mouth;
That I might drink, and leave the world unseen,
And with thee fade away into the forest dim.[20]

3

Fade far away, dissolve, and quite forget
What thou among the leaves hast never known,
The weariness, the fever, and the fret
Here, where men sit and hear each other groan;
Where palsy shakes a few, sad, last gray hairs,
Where youth grows pale, and spectre-thin[21], and dies;
Where but to think is to be full of sorrow
And leaden-eyed despairs[22],
Where Beauty cannot keep her lustrous[23] eyes,
Or new Love pine at them[24] beyond to-morrow.[25]

4

Away! away! for I will fly to thee,
Not charioted by Bacchus[26] and his pards[27],
But on the viewless wings of Poesy,
Though the dull brain perplexes and retards:
Already with thee! tender is the night,[28]
And haply[29] the Queen-Moon is on her throne,
Cluster'd around by all her starry Fays[30];
But here[31] there is no light,
Save[32] what from heaven is with the breezes blown
Through verdurous[33] glooms and winding mossy ways.[34]

5

I cannot see what flowers are at my feet,
Nor what soft incense[35] hangs upon the boughs,

But, in embalmed darkness, guess each sweet[36]
Wherewith[37] the seasonable month[38] endows[39]
The grass, the thicket, and the fruit-tree wild;
White hawthorn, and the pastoral eglantine[40];
Fast fading violets cover'd up in leaves;
And mid-May's eldest child[41],
The coming musk-rose, full of dewy wine,
The murmurous haunt of flies on summer eves.[42]

6

Darkling[43] I listen; and, for many a time
I have been half in love with easeful Death,
Call'd him soft names in many a mused rhyme[44],
To take into the air my quiet breath[45];
Now more than ever seems it rich to die,
To cease upon the midnight with no pain,
While thou art pouring forth thy soul abroad[46]
In such an ecstasy!
Still[47] wouldst thou sing, and I have ears in vain—
To thy high requiem[48] become a sod.[49]

7

Thou wast[50] not born for death, immortal Bird![51]
No hungry generations tread thee down;
The voice I hear this passing night was heard
In ancient days by emperor and clown[52]:
Perhaps the self-same song that found a path
Through the sad heart of Ruth[53], when, sick for home,
She stood in tears amid the alien corn[54];
The same that oft-times[55] hath
Charm'd magic casements[56], opening on the foam
Of perilous seas, in faery lands forlorn[57].

8

Forlorn! the very word is like a bell
To toll me back from thee to my sole self[58]!
Adieu! the fancy[59] cannot cheat so well
As she is fam'd[60] to do, deceiving elf[61].
Adieu! adieu! thy plaintive anthem[62] fades
Past the near meadows, over the still stream,
Up the hill-side; and now 'tis buried deep
In the next valley-glades:
Was it a vision, or a waking dream?
Fled is that music: —Do I wake or sleep?[63]
May 1819 1819

Notes

1. This poem is written in eight 10-line stanzas of iambic pentameter rhyming ababcdecde, with the exception of the eighth line which has only three feet. It is generally known to be written after the poet had an actual experience of listening to a nightingale's singing one day in his friend's house in Hampstead.
2. hemlock: a high poisonous umbelliferous plant.
3. emptied some dull opiate to the drains: drank up to the last drop some sleep-inducing drug containing opium. to the drains: to the last drop in the cup.
4. One minute past: one minute ago.
5. Lethe-wards: towards Lethe [ˈliθi], the river of forgetfulness, in the underworld, according to the ancient Greek mythology.
6. 'Tis not: it is not.
7. lot: fate.
8. Dryad [ˈdraɪəd]: a nymph inhabiting a tree and watching over it, here referring to the nightingale.
9. plot/Of beechen green: piece of land green with beech trees. plot: piece of land.
10. in full-throated ease: (sing) loudly and freely. In the first stanza, the poet is overcome by the song and almost loses himself, so powerful is its effect.
11. for a draught of vintage: Here the poet expresses his desire to have a drink

of wine. vintage: (poetic) wine.

12. in the deep-delved earth: deep underground. deep-delved: deep-dug.
13. Flora: the goddess of Spring and flowers in Roman mythology, here referring to flowers.
14. Provencal song: the poetry of the troubadours, the court poets of Provence, in south-eastern France in the 12th century. Provencal: the language spoken in Provence.
15. sunburnt mirth: referring to the mirth of the people in southern Europe where the sun's rays are stronger.
16. O for a beaker full of the warm South: here again the poet expresses his wish for a drink of wine. beaker: large drinking cup. the warm South: referring to wine brewed in the warm south in Europe.
17. the blushful Hippocrene [hipəu'kri:ni:]: the red wine. Hippocrene: a fountain on Mount Helicon, the residence of Apollo and the Muses in Greek mythology. Its waters were supposed to impart poetical inspiration.
18. beaded bubbles: bubbles like beads.
19. winking: twinkling, sparkling.
20. In the second stanza, he imagines a drink that might take him out of himself completely and carry him off into the nightingale's retreat.
21. spectre-thin: thin like a ghost. spectre: ghost.
22. leaden-eyed despairs: despairs that make human eyes lose sparkles.
23. lustrous: charming.
24. them: her lustrous eyes.
25. The third stanza turns back to the sadness of the world.
26. Bacchus: god of wine in Roman mythology, who was fabled to have driven a team of tigers or lynxes round the world.
27. pards: (archaic) leopards, substituted by poetic licence for the tigers or lynxes of the Bacchus legend.
28. tender is the night: the famous American novelist Francis Scott Fitzgerald (1896—1940) took this line as the title of one of his novels in 1934.
29. haply: perhaps.
30. Fays: (archaic) fairies.
31. here: referring to the human world.

32. Save: except.
33. verdurous: green-foliaged.
34. The poet's attempted flight to that world takes another form in the fourth stanza — "poesy". At this point the poem takes an unexpected turn, almost a somersault, for after proclaiming that the poet is "Already with thee!" as if he could at a leap join moral hopes to an eternal being, "a Queen Moon," he falls back into a world of time and change, a world in which "there is no light."
35. soft incense: referring here to scented blossoms. incense: scent.
36. But, in embalmed darkness, guess each sweet: but in the scented darkness, try to distinguish the several odours. embalmed: perfumed.
37. Wherewith: with which.
38. the seasonable month: the month of the season, here referring to May.
39. endows: gives, provides.
40. eglantine: sweet brier or honeysuckle.
41. mid-May's eldest child: the earliest flowers in May, here referring to the musk-rose in Line 49.
42. The murmurous haunt of flies on summer eves: the sound of flies in the summer evenings. The wood in which the poet finds himself in the fifth stanza is one where flowers bloom and die and seasons come and go. There he is conscious of his mortality and is drawn by the fantasy of dying to the nightingale's music.
43. Darkling: in darkness.
44. mused rhyme: meditated poetic lines. mused: meditated.
45. breath: life.
46. abroad: outside.
47. Still: always.
48. requiem: a hymn sung for the peaceful rest of the soul of the dead, according to Christian belief.
49. In the sixth stanza, Keats imagines a death which is an ecstatic conclusion, but then acknowledges that if he were dead the song would go unheard.
50. wast: (archaic) were.
51. immortal Bird: referring to the nightingale.

52. by emperor and clown: by all persons high and low. clown: peasant.
53. Ruth: the name of a woman in "The Book of Ruth" in the Old Testament of the Christian Bible. After the death of her husband in a great famine, she went voluntarily to live with her mother-in-law in a foreign country. But here the poet assumes that she was sad at heart while she gleaned the ears of corn in a strange land.
54. corn: wheat.
55. oft-times: often.
56. Charm'd magic casements: bewitched magic windows, here referring to the person behind the window. It is in an allusion to a legend that talks about a beautiful princess who was confined in a castle by magic and who waited for a person to rescue her.
57. in faery lands forlorn: in faery forlorn lands. faery: fairy. forlorn: remote. In the seventh stanza, the poet believes that the nightingale's song can go beyond time and space. It is immortal.
58. my sole self: my lonely self.
59. fancy: imagination.
60. fam'd: famed, famous.
61. deceiving elf: referring to fancy.
62. anthem: hymn.
63. In the last stanza, the poet is pulled back to reality by the word "forlorn", but he is not sure he is awake or not.

For Study and Discussion

1. Please identify the many allusions in the poem.
2. What is the speaker's mental and emotional state at the opening of the poem? Why is he in this state? What emotions are aroused in him by the song of the nightingale?
3. What's the implied meaning of "forlorn" in this poem?
4. In what way does the speaker feel betrayed by fancy or imagination at the end of the poem?
5. How may this ode be read as a poem in which the self has an adventure of the imagination?

参考译文

夜莺颂

1

我的心在痛，困盹和麻木
刺进了感官，有如饮过毒鸩，
又像是刚刚把鸦片吞服，
于是向着列斯忘川下沉：
并不是我嫉妒你的好运，
而是你的快乐使我太欢欣——
因为在林间嘹亮的天地里，
你呵，轻翅的仙灵，
你躲进山毛榉的葱绿和阴影，
放开了歌喉，歌唱着夏季。

2

唉，要是有一口酒！那冷藏
在地下多年的清醇饮料，
一尝就令人想起绿色之邦，
想起花神、恋歌、阳光和舞蹈！
要是有一杯南国的温暖
充满了鲜红的灵感之泉，
杯沿明灭着珍珠的泡沫，
给嘴唇染上紫斑；
哦，我要一饮而悄然离开尘寰，
和你同去幽暗的林中隐没：

3

远远地、远远地隐没，让我忘掉
你在树林中从不知道的一切，
忘记这疲劳、热病和焦躁，
这使人对坐而悲叹的世界；

在这里，青春苍白、消瘦、死亡，
而“瘫痪”有几根白发在摇摆；
在这里，稍一思索就充满了
忧伤和灰眼的绝望，
而“美”保持不住明眸的光彩，
新生的爱情活不到明天就枯凋。

4

去吧！去吧！我要朝你飞去，
不用和酒神坐文豹的车驾，
我要展开诗歌的无形羽翼，
尽管这头脑已经困顿、疲乏；
去了！呵，我已经和你同往！
夜这般温柔，月后正登上宝座，
周围是侍卫她的一群星星；
但这儿却不甚明亮，
除了有一线天光，被微风带过
葱绿的幽暗和苔藓的曲径。

5

我看不出是哪些花草在脚旁，
什么清香的花挂在树枝上；
在温馨的幽暗里，我只能猜想
这个时令该把哪种芬芳
赋予这果树、林莽和草丛，
这白枳花和田野的玫瑰，
这绿叶堆中易谢的紫罗兰，
还有五月中旬的娇宠，
这缀满了露酒的麝香蔷薇，
它成了夏夜蚊蚋的嗡吟的港湾。

6

我在黑暗里倾听；呵多少次

我几乎爱上了静谧的死亡，
我在诗里用尽了好的言辞，
求他把我的一息散入空茫；
而现在，哦，死是多么富丽：
在午夜里溘然魂离人间，
当你正倾泻着你的心怀
发出这般的狂喜！
你仍将歌唱，但我却不再听见——
你的葬歌只能唱给泥土一块。

7

永生的鸟呵，你不会死去！
饥饿的时代无法将你蹂躏；
今夜，我偶然听到的歌曲
曾使古代的帝王和村夫喜悦。
或许这同样的歌也会激荡
露丝忧郁的心，使她不禁落泪，
站在异邦的谷田里想着家；
就是这声音常常
在失掉了的仙域里引动窗扉：
一个美女望着大海险恶的浪花。

8

呵，失掉了！这句话好比一声钟
使我猛省到我站脚的地方！
别了！幻想，这骗人的妖童，
不能老要弄它盛传的伎俩。
别了！别了！你怨诉的歌声
流过草坪，越过幽静的溪水，
溜上山坡；而此时，它正深深
埋在附近的溪谷中：
噫，这是个幻觉，还是梦寐？
那歌声去了：——我是睡？是醒？

（查良铮　译）

Ode on a Grecian Urn[1]

This ode was written in May, 1819, almost at the same time as "*Ode to the Nightingale*". Here the speaker of the poem meditated on a Greek vase which, as a relic of ancient culture, caught his imagination. On the surface of the vase there was an ornamental band of sculpture with figures of trees, pipes and lovers on it. Though quiet forms, they possessed the beauty, significance and eternity of art which appealed to Keats. Keats shows his immense admiration for lasting beauty in the world of art, which is contrasted to the transience of human love and happiness.

1

Thou still unravish'd bride of quietness,
Thou foster-child of silence and slow time,[2]
Sylvan historian[3], who canst thus[4] express
A flowery tale more sweetly than our rhyme:
What leaf-fring'd legend[5] haunts about thy shape
Of deities or mortals[6], or of both,
In Tempe[7] or the dales of Arcady[8]?
What men or gods are these? What maidens loth[9]?
What mad pursuit? What struggle to escape?
What pipes and timbrels? What wild ecstasy?

2

Heard melodies are sweet, but those unheard
Are sweeter;[10] therefore, ye soft pipes, play on;
Not to the sensual ear[11], but, more endear'd,
Pipe to the spirit ditties of no tone:[12]
Fair youth, beneath the trees, thou canst not leave
Thy song, nor ever can those trees be bare;
Bold lover, never, never canst thou kiss,
Though winning near the goal[13]—yet, do not grieve;
She cannot fade, though thou hast not thy bliss,

For ever wilt thou love, and she be fair!

3

Ah, happy, happy boughs! that cannot shed
Your leaves, nor ever bid the spring adieu;[14]
And, happy melodist, unwearied,
For ever piping songs for ever new;
More happy love! more happy, happy love!
For ever warm and still to be enjoy'd,
For ever panting, and for ever young;
All breathing human passion far above,
That leaves a heart high-sorrowful and cloy'd,
A burning forehead, and a parching tongue.[15]

4

Who are these coming to the sacrifice[16]?
To what green altar, O mysterious priest,
Lead'st thou that heifer lowing at the skies[17],
And all her silken flanks with garlands drest?[18]
What little town by river or sea shore,
Or mountain-built with peaceful citadel,[19]
Is emptied of this folk, this pious morn[20]?
And, little town, thy streets for evermore
Will silent be; and not a soul to tell
Why thou art desolate, can e'er return.

5

O Attic shape![21] Fair attitude[22]! With brede
Of marble men and maidens overwrought,[23]
With forest branches and the trodden weed;
Thou, silent form, dost tease us out of thought
As doth eternity:[24] Cold Pastoral![25]
When old age shall this generation waste,

Thou shalt remain, in midst of other woe
Than ours, a friend to man, to whom thou say'st,
"Beauty is truth, truth beauty," —that is all
Ye know on earth, and all ye need to know.[26]

1819 1820

Notes

1. This poem is written in five 10-line stanzas of iambic pentameter rhyming abab cdedce with variations in the sestet. Grecian: of Greek.
2. The first two lines refer to the urn which, as a work of art, has been wedded to quietness and brought up by silence and slow time, and therefore, suffers no change, implying that in contrast to the transitoriness of human life, art is immortal. unravish'd: not seized or carried away by force. Here it means the secret of the urn has not yet been disclosed. slow time: time moves slowly so far as the urn is concerned.
3. Sylvan historian: referring to the urn that recounts the story of the pastoral life as represented by the figures on the urn. Sylvan: of the woods.
4. thus: in pictures.
5. leaf-fring'd legend: legend that is leaf-fringed because the sculpture on the urn has a border of leaves about it and therefore suggests a woodland scene.
6. deities or mortals: gods or men.
7. Tempe: a beautiful valley in Greece, anciently regarded as sacred to Apollo.
8. the dales of Arcady: the valleys of Arcadia, a pastoral district in ancient Greece often used as a symbol of the pastoral ideal.
9. loth: loath, unwilling.
10. Heard melodies are sweet, but those unheard / Are sweeter: a famous line of Keats. Cf. 白居易的《琵琶行》:"此时无声胜有声。"
11. sensual ear: the ear of senses, as opposed to that of the spirit or imagination.
12. Pipe to the spirit ditties of no tone: play on the pipe to serve as musical accompaniment to the songs which exist only in spirit and therefore are toneless.
13. Though winning near the goal: though getting near to the act of kissing his beloved.

14. nor ever bid the spring adieu: never say goodbye to spring (the leaves of the trees will never fall, as if spring will stay with them forever). adieu: (French) farewell.
15. All breathing human passion far above…a parching tongue: i. e. the images of men and maidens on the urn and their dramatic actions are far above the human passion which brings great agony as the poet himself often experienced in the world. breathing: living. cloy'd: made weary by excess.
16. sacrifice: the offering of the life of a person or an animal to pay homage to a god.
17. that heifer lowing at the skies: the young cow offered as sacrifice, crying out to the skies.
18. all her silken flanks with garlands drest: both sides of the cow's body which are as smooth as silk are decorated with wreaths of flowers.
19. citadel: fortress.
20. this pious morn: this morning for religious devotion.
21. Attic shape: referring to the urn as a work in ancient Greek art form. Attic: of Attica, a region of Greece in which Athens was located.
22. attitude: the pose struck by a figure in statuary or painting.
23. With brede/Of marble men and maidens overwrought: adorned with sculptured men and maidens that are cold and hard as if made of marble. brede: (archaic) embroidery or braiding. overwrought: adorned all over.
24. Thou, silent form, dost tease us out of thought/As doth eternity: though a silent form, you (the urn) do puzzle us and lead us to transcend human thoughts as does something that is immortal, implying that silent as the urn is, it is pregnant with meaning and communicates a wonderful message to the poet.
25. Cold Pastoral: i. e. the pastoral scene represented by the sculpture on the urn lacks the warmth of reality.
26. "Beauty is truth, truth beauty," —that is all/Ye know on earth, and all ye need to know: it has become a famous saying representing Keats' aesthetic ideas.

For Study and Discussion

1. What does the urn represent? What is the poet really talking about in the poem?
2. What do the first two lines refer to?
3. How is the world of the urn compared with the real world in the poem?
4. How do you interpret "Cold Pastoral"?
5. Please comment on the epigram "Beauty is truth, truth beauty."
6. Please learn the second stanza by heart.

参考译文

希腊古瓮颂

1

你委身"寂静"的、完美的处子，
受过了"沉默"和"悠久"的抚育，
呵，田园的史家，你竟能铺叙
一个如花的故事，比诗还瑰丽：
在你的形体上，岂非缭绕着
古老的传说，以绿叶为其边缘，
讲着人或神！腾佩或阿卡狄？
呵，是怎样的人或神！在舞乐前
多热烈的追求！少女怎样地躲避！
怎样的风笛和鼓铙！怎样的狂喜！

2

听见的乐声虽好，但若听不见
却更美；所以，吹吧，柔情的风笛；
不是奏给耳朵听，而是更甜，
它给灵魂奏出无声的乐曲；
树下的美少年呵，你无法中断
你的歌，那树木也落不了叶子；
鲁莽的恋人，你永远、永远吻不上，

虽然够接近了——但不必心酸
她不会老，虽然你不能如愿以偿，
你将永远爱下去，她也永远秀丽！

3

呵，幸福的树木！你的枝叶
不会剥落，从不曾离开春天；
幸福的吹笛人也不会停歇，
他的歌曲永远是那么新鲜；
呵，更为幸福的、幸福的爱！
永远热烈，正等待情人宴飨，
永远热情地心跳，永远年轻；
幸福的是这一切超凡的形态；
它不会使心灵餍足和悲伤，
没有炽热的头脑，焦渴的嘴唇。

4

这些人是谁呵，都去赴祭祀？
这作牺牲的小牛，对天鸣叫，
你要牵它到哪儿，神秘的祭司？
花环缀满着它光滑的身腰。
是从哪个傍河傍海的小镇，
或哪个静静的堡寨的山村，
来了这些人，在这敬神的清早？
呵，小镇，你的街道永远恬静；
再也不可能回来一个灵魂
告诉人你何必是这么寂寥。

5

哦，希腊的形状！唯美的观照！
上面缀有石雕的男人和女人，
还有林木和践踏过的青草；
沉默的形体呵，你像是"永恒"

使人超越思想：呵，冰冷的牧歌！
等暮年使这一世代都凋落，
只有你如旧；在另外的一些
忧伤中，你会抚慰后人说：
"美即是真，真即是美"，这就包括
你们所知道和该知道的一切。

（查良铮　译）

On First Looking into Chapman's Homer[1]

This poem is one of Keats' best known sonnets. The poet expresses his ecstasy upon discovering the great poetry of Homer. Keats' former schoolteacher, Charles Cowden Clarke, introduced him to Homer in the robust translation by the poet and dramatist George Chapman (1557—1634) in 1815. They read through the night, and Keats walked home at dawn. This sonnet reached Clarke by the ten o'clock mail that same morning. In the poem, Keats makes good use of analogies, metaphors and similes to express his excitement.

Much have I travell'd in the realms of gold[2],
And many goodly states and kingdoms[3] seen;
Round many western islands have I been[4]
Which bards in fealty to Apollo hold.[5]
Oft[6] of one wide expanse[7] had I been told
That deep-brow'd Homer ruled as his demesne;[8]
Yet did I never breathe its pure serene[9]
Till I heard Chapman speak out loud and bold:
Then felt I like some watcher of the skies[10]
When a new planet swims into his ken[11];
Or like stout[12] Cortez[13] when with eagle eyes
He star'd at the Pacific—and all his men[14]
Look'd at each other with a wild surmise—
Silent, upon a peak in Darien.

Oct. 1816　　　1816

Notes

1. It is written in Petrachan sonnet consisting of an octave and a sestet, rhyming abba abba cdcdcd.
2. the realms of gold: a metaphor, referring to the great literature.
3. many goodly states and kingdoms: also referring to the great literature. goodly: magnificent.
4. Round many western islands have I been: I have been round many western islands. western islands: imaginary islands in the western ocean, supposed by the ancient Greeks to be very happy and pleasant places. Here the term is used as a metaphor to refer to the realms of great poetry.
5. Which bards in fealty to Apollo hold: the lyric poets who are loyal to Apollo hold these islands. Which: the western islands. bards: the ancient lyric poets. in fealty to: loyal to. Apollo: god of poetry in Greek mythology.
6. Oft: often.
7. one wide expanse: a big realm.
8. That deep-brow'd Homer ruled as his demesne: referring to Homer's great epics. deep-brow'd: meditative, as indicated by a well-developed forehead. Homer: an ancient Greek poet. demesne: domain.
9. pure serene: clear expanse of air, here referring to the pure and clear style of Homer. serene: a clear and bright sky.
10. watcher of the skies: astronomer.
11. ken: scope of sight.
12. stout: big and fat.
13. Cortez: Hernand Cortez (1485—1547), the Spanish conqueror of Mexico. Actually it was another Spanish explorer Vasco Balboa (1475—1519), not Cortez, who caught his first sight of the Pacific from the heights of Darien, in Panama. Keats confused them two.
14. his men: his followers.

For Study and Discussion

1. What's Keats' feeling on reading Chapman's translation of Homer?
2. How does the metaphor of travel is used in this poem?

3. How do you understand the two similes in the sestet?
4. Please explain the change of tone in this sonnet. When and where does it happen?

参考译文

初读查普曼译荷马史诗有感

我游历过许多黄金的国度，
见过不少美好的城邦和王国，
还去过许多西方的岛屿，
那是诗人膜拜阿波罗的圣地。
我常听说有一片广阔无垠的地域，
浓眉的荷马在那里称王；
可我却从未领略过它纯净的空气，
直到我听见查普曼的声音无畏而高昂：
于是我的情感犹如一位观象家，
当他发现一颗新星游入视野；
或像考蒂兹用锐利如鹰的双眼
凝视着太平洋，而他的队员
在惊讶的揣测中面面相觑，
沉默无言——呆立在达利安山巅。

（查良铮　译）

On the Grasshopper and Cricket[1]

Keats sings praise of the beauty of nature in this poem. He compares the nature's song, represented by the grasshopper and the cricket's, to poetry. By comparison and contrast, by vivid sound effects, the poet makes the common imagery of two insects fresh and naive. This sonnet and "To Autumn" combine to show Keats' optimism and his idea that the poetry of life never dies.

The poetry of earth is never dead:
When all the birds are faint with the hot sun[2],
And hide in cooling trees[3], a voice[4] will run

From hedge to hedge about the new-mown mead[5];
That is the Grasshopper's—he takes the lead
In summer luxury,[6]—he has never done
With his delights;[7] for when tired out with fun[8]
He rests at ease beneath some pleasant weed.
The poetry of earth is ceasing never:
On a lone winter evening, when the frost
Has wrought[9] a silence, from the stove there shrills
The Cricket's song, in warmth increasing ever[10],
And seems to one in drowsiness half lost[11],
The Grasshopper's among some grassy hills.

Notes

1. It is written in Italian sonnet rhyming abbaabba cdecde.
2. faint with the hot sun: lazy or sleepy because of the hot sun.
3. hide in cooling trees: hide themselves in trees for coolness.
4. voice: referring to the sound produced by the vibrations of its wings. The same is true with the cricket.
5. mead: (poetic) meadow. "mead" and "dead" in the first line form an eye rhyme.
6. he takes the lead / In summer luxury: he plays the leading role in the many pleasures that summer can offer.
7. he has never done / With his delights: his delights never come to an end. done: finished.
8. tired out with fun: exhausted because of playing.
9. wrought: (archaic) worked.
10. in warmth increasing ever: in ever increasing warmth.
11. one in drowsiness half lost: one half lost in drowsiness.

For Study and Discussion

1. Comparison and contrast frequently appeared in this poem. How do they serve the theme?
2. Keats used vivid sound effect to display the state of the two insects. Please

give some examples to explain it.

3. How is this sonnet structured? It can be clearly divided into two parts. What's their relationship?
4. Why of all creatures are the grasshopper and the cricket singled out to represent the poetry of earth?
5. Please learn this sonnet by heart.

参考译文

蝈蝈与蟋蟀

大地的诗歌永不间断：
当鸟儿因酷日而懒洋洋
在树上藏身乘凉，新刈的草地上
另一种声音便飘荡在篱笆之间；
那是蝈蝈在唱，它率先
享受盛夏的喜悦，不停地唱，
喜不自禁；直到要累了不能再唱，
便心里舒适，憩息在欢乐的草丛间。
大地的诗歌永远不停：
当孤寂冬夜里，冰霜冻结，
万籁俱寂，炉边却响起了
蟋蟀的歌声，音量随室温而升，
对醺醺欲睡者
仿佛是蝈蝈在草坡上鸣叫。

（李正栓　译）

20. Elizabeth Barrett Browning

Elizabeth Barrett Browning (伊丽莎白·巴雷特·勃朗宁，1806—1861) is one of the best women poets. She was born in a rich family. Her early life was shadowed by illness and affliction. She started writing poetry at an early age and showed sympathy for all human misery. In *The Cry of the Children* (1843), she voices the humanitarian protest against the practice of employing childlabour in mines and factories.

Before she met Robert Browning and married him in 1846, she was a better-known poet than he was. After her marriage and removal to Italy her health improved, and her art greatly strengthened. In 1850 her *Sonnets from the Portuguese*, a series of 44 sonnets celebrating their love came out. Browning thought them "the finest sonnets in any language since Shakespeare". Mrs. Browning was deeply interested in the struggle of Italy to shake off her bondage to Austria, as is shown by her *Casa Guidi Windows* (1851). In 1857 appeared her most ambitious work, *Aurora Leigh*, a kind of versified novel of modern English life, with a social reformer and humanitarian of aristocratic lineage as hero and a young poetess, in large part a reflection of Mrs. Browning's own personality, as heroine. The interest in public problems also appears in Mrs. Browning's *Poems before Congress* (1860), and in her *Last Poems* (1862).

Mrs. Browning's technique is uncertain, and she never freed herself from her Characteristic faults of vagueness and unrestraint. But her sympathy for noble causes, the elevation and ardor of her moods of personal emotion, and the distinction of her utterance at its best, tempt us to overlook her technical limitations. She shares her husband's strenuousness and optimism, but she speaks always from the feminine vantage ground. Her characteristic note is that of intimate, personal feelings.

from *Sonnets from the Portuguese* 43[1]

This is a famous lyric poem by Elizabeth Barrett Browning. The poet shows her passionate love for her husband Robert Browning by listing eight ways how she loves him. The most powerful line appears at the end of the poem: if God choose her, the poet would love her husband better after death.

How do I love thee? Let me count the ways. [2]
I love thee to the depth and breadth and height
My soul can reach, when feeling out of sight

For the ends of Being[3] and ideal Grace[4].
I love thee to the level of everyday's
Most quiet need, by sun and candlelight[5].
I love thee freely, as men strive for Right;
I love thee purely, as they turn from Praise.
I love thee with the passion[6] put to use
In my old griefs, and with my childhood's faith.
I love thee with a love I seemed to lose
With my lost saints—I love thee with the breath,
Smiles, tears, of all my life! —and, if God choose,
I shall but love thee better after death.

1845—1847 1850

Notes

1. It is written in Italian sonnet form with the rhyme scheme of abbaabba cdcdcd.
2. Let me count the ways: the poetess lists eight ways of how she loved him.
3. feeling out of sight / For the ends of Being: probing into infinity to find the purpose of the existence of the Universe. feeling… for: probe into. out of sight: beyond the range of physical reality. Being: existence.
4. Grace: Mercy of God.
5. by sun and candlelight: (I love thee) as the day needs sun and the night needs candlelight.
6. passion: referring to the passion in extreme suffering.

诗歌赏析

《葡萄牙十四行诗》由 44 首十四行诗组成爱情诗集，诗中表达了勃朗宁夫人对丈夫的深情。本诗是其中的第 43 首。全诗以一个问句开始——“我究竟怎样爱你?”然后，诗人自问自答，列数了爱情的八种方式。诗人采用了灵魂、阳光、蜡烛、笑容、眼泪、呼吸、生命和死亡等意象把自己对爱人的感情娓娓道来，情真意切。全诗共 14 行，其中“我爱你”出现了九次，“爱”字出现十次。读者不由地随着她的笔触，在她的爱情世界里徜徉。

诗人首先把她的爱情定位于灵魂所能达到的深度、宽度和广度，把她的爱与生命的极致和神的恩赐相提并论，以示爱情的深厚、宽广与无限。正当我们对“灵魂”、“生命的极致”、“神的恩赐”这些抽象的概念感到无从衡量、无从把握的时候，诗人又把她的爱拉到了地上，“我爱你就像平日里最寻常的需要，就像白日需要阳光，夜晚需要蜡烛。”多么朴素的表达！可是，谁能想象如果白日没有阳光，夜晚缺少了蜡烛，我们的生活会是什么模样？她的爱自然而生，就像人类追求平等的权利；她的爱不求回报，不为功利，就像人们做好事不求赞誉。

“我爱你用我旧日苦难中所经历的情感以及旧日的信仰。”诗人认为她的爱情之炽烈不亚于曾经的苦难带给她的煎熬；她对爱情的忠实不亚于儿时的信仰。旧日的苦难或许指她幼年坠马，从此卧病在床并且充满孤独、寂寞的经历。诗人早年曾经崇拜过基督教的圣徒。如今，她对丈夫的感情，就像早年对圣徒一样虔诚。此时，她的爱仿佛充满了神性的光辉。“我爱你，用我生命的全部呼吸、欢笑和眼泪。”爱情已经融入她的生命，就像呼吸、欢喜与哀愁一样，与她毫厘不分。活着，爱情是她生命的一部分。死了以后呢？全诗的高潮出现在最后一句：“如果上帝允许，死后我将更加爱你。”如此出人意料又情真意切！

从世俗到神圣，从生存到死亡，从具体到抽象，勃朗宁夫人完成了她对爱情的所有定位。这首诗措辞简单、感情纯朴、真挚感人！这位卧床多年，39岁刚刚赢得爱情的女诗人用她真挚纯朴的情感打动了无数读者的心！

For Study and Discussion

1. Study Mrs. Browning's handling of traditional sonnet form. Does she follow the Shakespearean pattern?
2. How does the poet define her love in the poem?
3. What do you think of the poet's attitude toward love?
4. How do you understand the last line of the poem?
5. Find out the figures of speech used in this poem and appreciate them.
6. Which lines do you like best? Why?

参考译文

我是怎样地爱你

我是怎样地爱你？让我逐一细算。
我爱你尽我的心灵所能及到底

深邃、宽广和高度——正像我探求
玄冥中上帝的存在和深厚的神恩。
我爱你的程度，就像日光和烛焰下
那每天不用说的需要。我不假思虑地
爱你，就像男子们为正义而斗争；
我纯洁地爱你，像他们在赞美前低头。
我爱你以我童年的信仰；我爱你
以满怀热情，就像往日满腔的辛酸；
我爱你，抵得上那似乎随着消失的圣者
而消逝的爱慕。我爱你以我终生的
呼吸、微笑和泪珠——假使是上帝的
意旨，那么，我死了我还要更加爱你！

（方　平　译）

21. Alfred Tennyson

Alfred Tennyson（艾尔弗雷德·丁尼生，1809－1892），for more than 50 years，was recognized among his contemporaries as the greatest poet of Victorian England. He was born and bred in a country clergyman's family in the village of Somersby in Lincolnshire. He began to write poetry before he was ten，and in 1827，when he was 18，he and his brother Charles published anonymously *Poems by Two Brothers*. More than half of the poems in this volume were written by him，and these poems were strongly influenced by Byron and Scott.

Also in 1827 Tennyson went to study at Cambridge University where he made friends with Arthur Henry Hallam，a highly gifted and charismatic young writer. In 1830 the two friends travelled together in Europe，and Hallam became engaged to Tennyson's sister Emily. In the same year Tennyson published *Poems，Chiefly Lyrical*，the first volume of verse that appeared under his own name. Though not a critical success，it was a clear reflection of his development as a poet during the years at Cambridge. Tennyson was absolutely shattered in 1833 by the news that his friend Hallam had died suddenly in Vienna. The immediate effect of his grief and of the other setbacks he had suffered was a period in Tennyson's life sometimes referred to as the "ten years" silence.

Tennyson returned to public notice in 1842 with the publication of *Poems* in two volumes. This collection firmly established his reputation and initiated the fifty-year period in which he was the major figure in Victorian poetry. In 1850 he published *In Memoriam*, a sequence of elegiac and meditative poems recalling the experience of Hallam's death. His most ambitious project, *Idylls of the King* (1869—1872), is a series of poetic narratives based on the legend of King Arthur and the Round Table. In 1883 he was made a peer of the realm and was thus accorded the title of Lord. He died in 1892, with a reputation among all classes of readers that grew until it eventually exceeded Byron's in the early years of the 20th century.

Tennyson's poetic output is vast and extremely varied. He wrote lyrics, dramatic monologues, plays, long poetic narratives, elegies and poems commemorating specific occasions. Tennyson has a total mastery of the sounds and rhythms of the English language. Tennyson has a genius for evoking moods and states of mind in his poems. He is able to create a sense of nostalgia, a wistful longing for the past or for remote experiences. No English poet surpasses Tennyson at linking descriptions of nature or setting to state of mind. Some of his poems deal with the main political, religious and scientific issues of his day. His poems reflect his conservative ideas and idealization of the bourgeois social reality.

Tennyson was made poet laureate in 1850 when Wordsworth died. As a man he was intensely private and introspective, and some of his greatest work as an artist depends upon the creation of very personal and subjective moods or states of mind. In the largest sense it is this division in Tennyson between his public and private selves, between social and purely artistic commitments, that makes him such a central figure in the Victorian Age.

Break, Break, Break[1]

This poem was written in 1842, in memory of Arthur Hallam, the poet's close friend who died at the age of 22 in Vienna in 1833. The poem is full of contrasts—sense vs. sensibility; hardness of nature in contrast to the weakness of the poet's heart; the joyful scene of the fisherman's boy and of a sailor lad vs. the sorrowful state of his mind; the going on of natural things vs. the great change in the poet's life. By the sharp contrast between the outer world and the inner world, it displays the poet's great sorrow over Hallam's death.

Break, break, break,[2]
On thy cold gray stone, O Sea![3]
And I would[4] that my tongue could utter
The thoughts that arise in me.

O, well for[5] the fisherman's boy,
That he shouts with his sister at play!
O, well for the sailor lad,
That he sings in his boat on the bay!

And the stately ships go on[6]
To their haven under the hill;
But O for[7] the touch of a vanished hand[8],
And the sound of a voice[9] that is still[10]!

Break, break, break.
At the foot of thy crags, O Sea!
But the tender grace of a day that is dead[11]
Will never come back to me.

1834 1842

Notes

1. It is written in four quatrains with the second and the fourth lines rhymed in each.

2. Break, break, break: a pun referring to both the sound of the tide hitting the rock and the great sorrow in the poet's broken heart.
3. On thy cold gray stone, O Sea: the repetition of "O" shows the deep sorrow in the poet's heart.
4. I would: I wish.
5. O, well for: it would be well for.
6. the stately ships go on: implying that people's everyday life is going on. stately: dignified.
7. O for: how I wish for.
8. a vanished hand: referring to the hand of Hallam.
9. a voice: referring to the voice of Hallam.
10. still: silent.
11. the tender grace of a day that is dead: referring to the happy memory of the past when his friend Hallam was with him.

诗歌赏析

这首诗发表于1842年，是丁尼生为怀念亡友哈勒姆而创作的。哈勒姆是诗人在剑桥大学的同窗，也是其妹妹的未婚夫。诗人与哈勒姆结下了深厚的友谊，好友的猝然离世给他带来了很大的打击。丁尼生为此写了很多首诗，并出了一部诗集《悼念》，于1850年出版。这首诗由四个四行诗节组成，多抑扬格和抑抑扬格音步，偶行押韵。

对照是这首诗最显著的特点。第一节的"冲激"是一个双关语。它一方面指波涛拍击岩石的声音，另一方面指好友逝去后诗人破碎的心灵。灰冷、坚硬的岩石和诗人脆弱的心灵形成对比，展现出大自然的冷酷无情。第二节中渔家孩子在嬉戏，年轻水手正歌唱。他们的轻松、快乐与诗人内心的郁结形成强烈的反差，更加重了诗人的伤感。如果说前两节的对照是暗含在诗句当中的，最后两节则直接将外部世界与诗人的内心世界进行对比。一艘艘船只庄严地进入港口，而诗人再也摸不到朋友消失了的手，听不到亡友沉寂了的声音；大海依然在冲击悬崖下的海岸，而那些和朋友一起度过的美好日子再也回不来了。外部世界的一切如旧，而诗人的生活因朋友的去世发生了巨大的变化。

这首诗的另一个特点是重复。开篇 break，break，break 连着三个单音节词的重复，一字一顿，表现了诗人沉痛的心情。短句 break，break，break 在第一节和最后一节重复出现，意味深长。第一节的重复侧重诗人心中的沉痛，最后一节的重复形容生活的无情。惊涛依旧拍岸，而诗人的生活发生了巨变。

另外，诗歌的音韵也表达了诗人的哀愁。全诗多双元音，形成幽怨、哀愁的氛围。这首诗堪与雷振邦的《怀念战友》相媲美。《怀念战友》歌词如下：

天山脚下是我可爱的故乡，
当我离开它的时候，
就像那哈密瓜断了瓜秧。
白杨树下住着我心上的姑娘，
当我和她分别后，
就像那都达尔闲挂在墙上。
瓜秧断了哈密瓜依然香甜，
琴师回来都达尔还会再响，
当我永别了战友的时候，
好像那雪崩飞滚万丈。
啊亲爱的战友，
我再不能看到你雄伟的身影和和蔼的脸庞。
啊亲爱的战友，
你也再不能听我弹琴听我歌唱。

For Study and Discussion

1. What's the tone of this poem?
2. How does the title serve the theme of the poem?
3. How does the setting intensify the speaker's mood? What feelings arise in the speaker as he looks out at the sea breaking endlessly against the shore? What effect do the joyful scenes in the second stanza bring to the whole poem?
4. How does the sound effect serve the theme of the poem?
5. Please appreciate the use of contrast in this poem.
6. Learn the first stanza by heart.

参考译文

冲激，冲激，冲激

冲激，冲激，冲激，
大海呀，冲击你灰冷的石岩！
但愿我的舌端能道出
我内心涌起的思念。

若像那渔家儿童该多好，
他在和妹妹一起玩耍喊叫！
若像那青年水手该多好！
他在海湾里荡桨歌唱多美妙！

还有，一艘艘庄严的船舶
朝它们山下的港口驶近；
多么想得到那只消逝了的手的触摸，
还有那已不作声响的嗓音。

冲激，冲激，冲激，
大海呀，冲击你悬崖的脚下！
但那逝去的温文尔雅
将永远回不到我这里。

（李正栓　译）

The Eagle: A Fragment[1]

In this short poem, Tennyson describes the state of an eagle by vivid images: the blue sky and the lonely lands, the high mountain and the deep sea, the sun and the eagle. The eagle, as the central image of the poem, is isolated from others both in space and in mind. The first three lines describe a peaceful scene, while the last three reverse the former impression by the sudden falling of the eagle. Both static and dynamic features of the eagle are displayed. Though brief, it provides profound connotations.

He clasps[2] the crag[3] with crooked[4] hands;
Close to the sun in lonely lands,
Ringed with the azure world[5], he stands.

The wrinkled sea beneath him crawls:
He watches from his mountain walls,
And like a thunderbolt[6] he falls.

Notes

1. It is written in two triplets rhyming aaa.
2. clasps: grasps firmly.
3. crag: high and steep rough rock.
4. crooked: bent. Pay attention to the alliteration of "clasp", "crag" and "crooked" in the first line.
5. the azure world: referring to the sky. azure: blue.
6. thunderbolt: a flash of lightening from which thunder is heard.

For Study and Discussion

1. What qualities of natural power and grandeur does the eagle possess in Tennyson's poem?
2. What rhetorical device is used strikingly in the first two lines?
3. How do you interpret the eagle's situation "close to sun"?
4. What element of contrast or tension can you find between the two stanzas of the poem? Pay attention to Line 3 which ends with the words "he stands", and Line 6 which ends with the words "he falls."
5. The last line forms a kind of climax to the poem. How does it do so?
6. Please learn the poem by heart.

参考译文

鹰

他弯曲的利爪紧紧抓住陡壁峭岩，
在太阳近旁，身处寂寞高山，

周围是蔚蓝世界，他屹立山巅。

看脚下：海浪滚滚水不平，
从山崖峭壁他把一切收入眼中，
他突然从上坠落，犹如夏日雷霆。

（李正栓　译）

Crossing the Bar[1]

This is a symbolic poem with the bar as the central symbol. Tennyson draws an analogy between the experience of a sailor embarking at evening on a long voyage across the sea and that of one's approaching death. Although not the last poem written by Tennyson, "Crossing the Bar" appears, at his request, as the final poem in all collections of his work.

Sunset and evening star,
And one clear call for me!
And may there be no moaning of the bar[2],
When I put out to sea,

But such a tide as moving seems asleep,
Too full for sound and foam,[3]
When that which drew from out the boundless deep
Turns again home.[4]

Twilight[5] and evening bell,
And after that the dark!
And may there be no sadness of farewell,
When I embark;

For though from out our bourne[6] of Time and Place
The flood may bear me far,
I hope to see my Pilot[7] face to face
When I have crossed the bar.

1889

Notes

1. It is written in four quatrains rhyming abab with the odd lines in five iambic feet, the even lines in three. Crossing the bar: implying death.
2. moaning of the bar: mournful sound of the ocean beating on a sand bar at the mouth of a harbor.
3. Too full for sound and foam: the tide is too full to produce any sound or foam.
4. When that which drew from out the boundless deep / Turns again home: the ebb and flow of the tide referring to the life and death of humans. The same idea was expressed in the American poet Longfellow's "The Tide Rises, the Tide Falls" in 1879, 10 years earlier than this poem.
5. Twilight: dusk.
6. bourne: boundary.
7. Pilot: referring to God. The poet compares life to journey, a traditional comparison in English poetry. Cf. Spenser's Sonnet 34: "Lyke as a ship that through the Ocean wyde, / By conduct of some star doth make her way…"

For Study and Discussion

1. What's the overall tone of this poem? How do the images of "tide" and "sea" contribute to the tone?
2. What particular details help define the real subject of the poem?
3. Why is "Pilot" in Line 15 capitalized? What's the implication of this word?
4. What's the denotation and connotation of the word "bar"?
5. What is the poet's attitude towards death as reflected in this poem?

参考译文

越过海滩

太阳沉没，晚星闪烁，
一个清晰的呼声在召唤我！
愿海滩不要哀泣呜咽，
当我出海的时刻。

浑然流动的潮水似已睡去，
潮太满了，反而无声无息，
从无边的海洋里汲取的，
如今又复归去。

暮色茫茫，晚钟轻轻，
接着是黑暗降临！
但愿不要有诀别的悲痛，
当我启航的时辰；

虽然潮水会把我带到无限遥远，
越出我们的时间、空间，
我希望见到领航人，面对着面，
当我越过了海滩。

（飞　白　译）

22. Robert Browning

Robert Browning（罗伯特·勃朗宁，1812—1889）was born in 1812 in Camberwell, an attractive suburb only 3 miles from central London. He was a son of a clerk of the Bank of England. Although Browning attended a boarding school, he was also tutored at home. Browning began writing poetry at a very early age. Though his early poems and plays (including his first book of poetry *Pauline*, 1833) were not so successful, he discovered during these years that his real ability as a writer lay in adapting the techniques of dramatic writing to poetry. His development is reflected in a remarkable series of poetic pamphlets called *Bells and Pomegranates*, written between 1841 and 1846. Included in these pamphlets is *Pippa Passes*, the most interesting of his early poetic plays. Browning met Elizabeth Barrett in 1845. They got married secretly in 1846 and then they went to Italy where they lived until her death in 1861.

It was while living in Italy that he published his honest volume of poems, *Men and Women* (1885). This collection reflects Browning's intense interest in the Italian Renaissance, and it displays his complete mastery of the poetic form through which he was to achieve his greatest success, the dramatic monologue. In Browning's dramatic monologues, the imagined speakers rather than Browning himself, often based on famous figures from history or art but sometimes entirely Browning's own invention—utter their thoughts to the implied listeners. Previous writers of the 19th century, Byron and Tennyson, for example, had written in this form, but it was Browning who explored its possibilities to the full. When Elizabeth Barrett Browning died in 1861, Browning returned to London and began working on *Dramatis Personae* (1864), another collection of the dramatic monologues. He also wrote *The Ring and the Book* (1868—1869), his longest and most ambitious work, in which the principle of dramatic monologue extended to project a single murder story from ten different points of view. He died at the age of 77, and was buried in Westminster Abbey.

Browning is thought to be the most important Victorian poet after Tennyson. During much of his own career, however, he was better appreciated by the readers of a younger generation than by his immediate contemporaries. Browning was an adventurous and experimental poet, and his verse seemed to open new possibilities to younger Victorians who felt that Tennyson had done all that could be done with traditional subjects and forms. Toward the end of his career, Browning came to be revered by a wide range of readers, many of whom insisted on making him the voice of wise and reassuring optimism.

Two aspects of Browning's poetry are particularly significant for understanding his influence on 20th-century poetry and his appeal to readers today. First, there is Browning's interest in what we may loosely call psychology, in the conscious and unconscious workings of the human mind. Second, Browning's importance derives from his stylistic experimentation. Following the example of Donne and his own desire to break with the traditional decorum of most English poetry, Browning makes deliberate use of rough colloquial diction and word order, of surprising and even grotesque rhymes, and of harsh rhythms and metrical patterns. Browning's general purpose in exploring these uses of language was to bring his poetry more closely in touch with the irregular, unpredictable, and often distorted movements of his speakers' minds. Browning opened up new possibilities and helped prepare the way for some of the best poetry of our own era.

Home-Thoughts, from Abroad[1]

This poem reveals the poet's nostalgic feeling while he was staying abroad. The poem begins with the beautiful scene of England presented by vivid visual and aural images and ends suddenly with a central contrast to show Browning's love for his homeland.

1

Oh, to be in England
Now that April's there,[2]
And whoever wakes in England
Sees, some morning, unaware,
That the lowest boughs and the brushwood sheaf
Round the elm-tree bole[3] are in tiny leaf
While the chaffinch[4] sings on the orchard bough
In England—now!

2

And after April, when May follows,
And the whitethroat[5] builds, and all the swallows!
Hark,[6] where my blossomed pear-tree in the hedge
Leans to the field and scatters on the clover
Blossoms and dewdrops—at the bent spray's edge—
That's the wise thrush[7]; he sings each song twice over,
Lest you should think he never could recapture[8]
The first fine careless[9] rapture!
And though the fields look rough with hoary[10] dew,
All will be gay when noontide wakes anew
The buttercups, the little children's dower
—Far brighter than this gaudy melon-flower!

Notes

1. The poem contains two stanzas of different lengths in combined couplets and interchanging rhymes.
2. Oh, to be in England / Now that April's there: oh, how wonderful it would be in England now that April is there!
3. bole: trunk of a tree.
4. chaffinch: a small song bird.
5. whitethroat: a bird with a white spot around the throat.
6. Hark: (poetic) listen.
7. thrush: a song bird.
8. recapture: reexperience.
9. careless: without care.
10. hoary: grey or white.

诗歌赏析

这首诗写于勃朗宁旅居意大利时。诗人看到意大利的春日景色，想起英国四五月间美丽的自然风光，有感而发。全诗只有短短两节，诗节参差不齐，诗行长短不一，表达了诗人激动的心情。

诗人开篇先发出感叹："呵，要在英格兰该多好!"接着用丰富的视觉和听觉意象描述了英格兰四、五月间的美景。四月里，榆树低低的枝干和周围低矮的灌木丛已经冒出了嫩芽，而苍头燕雀正在果树枝头鸣唱。诗人在第二节描写了英格兰五月的光景。白喉鸟在筑巢，所有的燕子都飞回来了！大家可以想象群鸟纷飞，叽叽喳喳，忙着筑巢的热闹景象。多么生机盎然的春日风光！你看！在篱笆里芬芳的梨树枝伸出篱笆外，俯向田野，在三叶草上洒满了露珠和花瓣。你听！低矮的枝桠上机灵的画眉鸟在歌唱，它每首歌都唱两遍，恐怕旁人不知道它能再次体会初次鸣叫的无拘无束和狂喜。虽然挂着灰白露珠的大地还是显得突兀不平，但是当正午的阳光把孩子们珍爱的金凤花唤醒，所有的一切都会变得欢快。

在诗篇的末尾，纯粹的自然景物描摹加入抒情成分。一想起故乡，诗人的心情就变得欢畅，笔下的一切也随之雀跃。最后一句直接抒发了诗人对故乡的深情："金凤花，小孩子们喜用这花弄成嫁妆 /——比炫丽甜瓜花还鲜亮!"金凤花是家乡孩子们的宠物，甜瓜花代表意大利。这一鲜明的对比反映了诗人的心声——"月是故乡明"。

For Study and Discussion

1. What is the significance of the word "unaware" in Line 4?
2. What's the main idea of this poem?
3. What's symbolic meaning of the final contrast in the poem between the bright buttercups and this gaudy melon flower? What do they symbolize respectively?
4. Appreciate the visual and aural images in this poem.
5. Find more poems or songs expressing home-thoughts, either in English or Chinese.

参考译文

异域乡思

1

呵，要在英格兰该多好！
那里正是四月，
一朝早醒就会不知不觉看见
英格兰春天的风景：
连最矮的树枝和灌木林丛
在榆树周围也已嫩芽葱葱，
果园枝头的苍头燕
正欢唱鸣叫在英格兰！

2

四月去后五月随，
白喉筑巢燕子回！
听，我围篱内开花的梨树
俯向田野，洒香于苜蓿与朝露，
就在弯曲枝桠的顶头——
是机灵的画眉在唱：每首歌他连唱两遍，
唯恐你以为他不能再次

捕捉初次美妙无忧的欢娱！
尽管田野因白露显得不齐整，
一切会欢闹，当正午再次唤醒
金凤花，小孩子们喜用这花弄成嫁妆
——比炫丽甜瓜花还鲜亮！

（李正栓　译）

My Last Duchess[1]

This is one of the best known dramatic monologues written by Browning. The poem is based on incidents in the life of Alfonso Ⅱ, Duke of Ferrara in Italy, whose first wife, Lucrezia, a young woman, died in 1561 after three years of marriage. Following her death, the duke negotiated through an agent to marry a niece of the Count of Tyrol. The duke's monologue is addressing this agent. From his conversation the readers know what the situation is, both past and present, and see the personality of both the duke and his wife.

Ferrara

That's my last Duchess painted on the wall,
Looking as if she were alive. I call
That piece a wonder, now: Fra Pandolf's[2] hands
Worked busily a day, and there she stands.
Will't[3] please you sit and look at her? I said
"Fra Pandolf" by design[4], for never read
Strangers like you that pictured countenance[5],
The depth and passion of its earnest glance,
But to myself they turned (since none puts by
The curtain I have drawn for you, but I[6])
And seemed as they would ask me, if they durst[7]
How such a glance came there; so, not the first
Are you to turn and ask thus. Sir, 'twas not
Her husband's presence only, called that spot
Of joy into the Duchess' cheek[8]: perhaps
Fra Pandolf chanced to say, "Her mantle laps

Over my lady's wrist too much,"[9] or "Paint
Must never hope to reproduce the faint
Half-flush that dies along her throat[10]": such stuff
Was courtesy,[11] she thought, and cause enough[12]
For calling up that spot of joy. She had
A heart—how shall I say? —too soon made glad,
Too easily impressed; she liked whate'er
She looked on, and her looks went everywhere.
Sir, 't was all one![13] My favor at her breast,[14]
The dropping of the daylight in the West,
The bough of cherries some officious fool[15]
Broke in the orchard for her, the white mule
She rode with round the terrace—all and each
Would draw from her alike the approving speech,
Or blush, at least. She thanked men—good! but thanked
Somehow—I know not how—as if she ranked
My gift of a nine-hundred-years-old name
With anybody's gift.[16] Who'd stoop to blame
This sort of trifling?[17] Even had you skill
In speech— (which I have not) —to make your will
Quite clear to such an one[18], and say, "Just this
Or that in you disgusts me; here you miss,
Or there exceed the mark[19]" —and if she let
Herself be lessoned so, nor plainly set
Her wits to yours,[20] forsooth,[21] and made excuse
—E'en then would be some stooping;[22] and I choose
Never to stoop. Oh sir, she smiled, no doubt,
Whene'er I passed her; but who passed without
Much the same smile? This grew; I gave commands;
Then all smiles stopped together.[23] There she stands
As if alive.[24] Will't please you rise? We'll meet
The company below,[25] then. I repeat,
The Count your master's known munificence

Is ample warrant that no just pretense
Of mine for dowry will be disallowed;[26]
Though his fair daughter's self, as I avowed
At starting[27], is my object. Nay, we'll go
Together down, Sir.[28] Notice Neptune, though,
Taming a sea horse, thought a rarity,[29]
Which Claus of Innsbruck cast in bronze for me![30]

1842

Notes

1. Although it is written in heroic couplets, we hardly notice this regularity of form because the language of the poem is so colloquial and natural that it gives the impression of actual speech.
2. Fra Pandolf: Brother Pandolf, an imaginary painter who painted the portrait of the duchess now hung on the wall.
3. Will't: will it.
4. by design: on purpose.
5. that pictured countenance: that face in the picture (or painting).
6. since none puts by / The curtain I have drawn for you, but I: since no one draws the curtain that I have drawn for you, except me.
7. durst: dared.
8. called that spot / Of joy into the Duchess' cheek: caused that happy smile (or blush) to appear on the face of the duchess. that spot of joy: that mark which indicates joy.
9. Her mantle laps / Over my lady's wrist too much: Her cloak covers up too much of my lady's wrist. "Her" and "my lady" both refer to the duchess.
10. the faint / Half-flush that dies along her throat: the indistinct half-redness on her face that spreads down to her throat.
11. such stuff / Was courtesy: such nonsensical talk was a compliment paid to her.
12. cause enough: enough cause.
13. 't was all one: it was all the same, i. e. all the things enumerated below produced the same effect on her.

14. My favor at her breast: the present given by me and worn by her at her breast.
15. some officious fool: some obliging person. "fool" is used here sarcastically to refer to some silly person who may be in love with the duchess or may simply try to please her by giving her a bunch of flowers.
16. she ranked / My gift of a nine-hundred-years-old name / With anybody's gift: she considers the title of the Duchess of Ferrara (which I gave her by marrying her) as no better than a simple gift given to her by someone of no importance. "nine-hundred-years-old name" refers to the Duke's family being an ancient family with a long history of 900 years.
17. Who'd stoop to blame / This sort of trifling: who would lower oneself to find fault with this kind of frivolous behaviour.
18. such an one: referring to the duchess.
19. here you miss, / Or there exceed the mark: in this respect you don't do enough (to please me) and in that respect you go too far.
20. if she let/Herself be lessoned so, nor plainly set/Her wits to yours: if she let herself be admonished in this way, and do not argue with you.
21. forsooth: (archaic) indeed.
22. E'en then would be some stooping: even in that case it would mean that I should be lowering my dignity.
23. This grew; I gave commands; / Then all smiles stopped together: as the duchess began to show more affection to everybody, I ordered that she should be put to death and she died. This grew: this developed and became more serious.
24. There she stands / As if alive: here the duke is referring to the portrait of his "last duchess" on the wall.
25. We'll meet/The company below: we shall meet the others downstairs.
26. no just pretense/Of mine for dowry will be disallowed: i. e. the count will not refuse to allow his fair claim for a dowry for the count's daughter (if he were to marry her). pretense: claim. disallow: refuse to allow.
27. At starting: at the beginning (of our interview).
28. Nay, we'll go / Together down, Sir: here the duke politely suggests that he and the envoy walk downstairs together abreast of each other, obviously

after the latter has insisted on the duke's precedence.

29. Notice Neptune, though, / Taming a sea horse, thought a rarity: though, look at the bronze statue of Neptune taming a sea horse, which is considered as a rare and precious work of art. Naptune: the god of sea in Roman mythology.

30. Claus of Innsbruck: an imaginary sculptor, who comes from Innsbruck, the capital of Tyrol in Austria.

For Study and Discussion

1. What passages in the Duke's monologue suggest that he is an intelligent, cultivated Renaissance nobleman? What passages suggest that he is egotistical, tyrannical and ruthless?
2. According to the Duke, what was his last duchess like?
3. What can you get from the phrass "Looking as if she were alive"?
4. At the end of "My Last Duchess", the Duke asks the envoy to notice another work of art, a bronze sculpture showing "Neptune… / Taming a sea horse…" (Lines 54－55) What does this work of art suggest about the theme of the poem as whole?
5. Who is the mock listener in this poem? What's the function of his existence in this poem?

参考译文

我的前公爵夫人

墙上的这幅画是我的前公爵夫人，
看起来就像她活着一样。如今，
我称它为奇迹：潘道夫的手笔
经一日忙碌，从此她就在此站立。
你愿坐下看看她吗？我有意提起
潘道夫，因为外来的生客（例如你）
凡是见了画中描绘的面容、
那真挚的眼神的深邃和热情，
没有一个不转向我（因为除我外

再没有别人把画上的帘幕拉开），
似乎想问我可是又不大敢问：
是从哪儿来的——这样的眼神？
你并非第一个人回头这样问我。
先生，不仅仅是她丈夫的在座
使公爵夫人面带欢容，可能
潘道夫偶然说过："夫人的披风
盖住她的手腕太多"，或者说：
"隐约的红晕向颈部渐渐隐没，
这绝非任何颜料所能复制。"
这种无聊话，却被她当成好意，
也足以唤起她的欢心。她那颗心——
怎么说好呢？——要取悦容易得很，
也太易感动。她看到什么都喜欢，
而她的目光又偏爱到处观看。
先生，她对什么都一样！她胸口上
佩戴的我的赠品，或落日的余光；
过分殷勤的傻子在园中攀折
给她的一枝樱桃，或她骑着
绕行花圃的白骡——所有这一切
都会使她同样赞羡不绝，
或至少泛起红晕。她感激人，好的！
但她的感激（我说不上怎么搞的）
仿佛把我赐她的九百年的门第
与任何人的赠品并列。谁愿意
屈尊去谴责这种轻浮举止？即使
你有口才（我却没有）能把你的意志
给这样的人儿充分说明："你这点
或那点令我讨厌。这儿你差得远，
而那儿你超越了界限。"即使她肯听
你这样训诫她而毫不争论，
毫不为自己辩解，——我也觉得
这会有失身份，所以我选择

绝不屈尊。哦，先生，她总是在微笑，
每逢我走过；但是谁人走过得不到
同样慷慨的微笑？发展至此，
我下了令：于是一切微笑都从此制止。
她站在那儿，像活着一样。请你起身
客人们在楼下等。我再重复一声：
你的主人——伯爵先生闻名的大方
足以充分保证我对嫁妆
提出任何合理要求都不会遭拒绝；
当然，如我开头声明的，他美貌的小姐
才是我追求的目标。别客气，让咱们
一同下楼吧。但请看这海神尼普顿
在驯服海马，这是件珍贵的收藏，
是克劳斯为我特制的青铜铸像。

（飞　白　译）

Meeting at Night[1]

It is a poem about the night meeting of two young lovers, but nothing is told directly, one can only infer something about love from a series of images. The word "love" even does not appear in the poem. The gray sea, the long black land, the yellow half-moon and the blue spurt of the lighted match arouse our sense of sight. The warm sea smell of the beach appeals to both our sense of smell and touch while a tap at the pane, quick sharp scratch, and a voice less loud sparks our sense of hearing. By engaging the reader's senses, the poet is able to attract their attention and convey his feelings about love.

1

The grey sea and the long black land;
And the yellow half-moon large and low;
And the startled little waves that leap
In fiery ringlets[2] from their sleep,
As I gain the cove with pushing prow,[3]
And quench its speed[4], i'[5] the slushy[6] sand.

2

Then a mile of warm sea-scented beach;
Three fields to cross till a farm appears;
A tap at the pane, the quick sharp scratch
And blue spurt of a lighted match,
And a voice less loud, thro' its joys and fears,
Than the two hearts beating each to each!

Notes

1. It is written in two 6-line stanzas of combined iambic and anapestic meters with 4 stresses in each line. The rhyme scheme is abccba.
2. ringlets: ripples.
3. As I gain the cove with pushing prow: as I reach the prow and push the small bay.
4. quench its speed: stop the moving of the boat.
5. i': in.
6. slushy: muddy.

For Study and Discussion

1. Please identify each image and its significance in the poem.
2. What does the image of the pushing prow suggest?
3. What do you think of the sound effect of the poem?
4. Find other poems to describe the private meeting of lovers at night.
5. Please learn the poem by heart.

参考译文

深夜幽会

1

海，灰暗；地，漫长、漆黑；
半轮黄月，大而低垂；
细浪从梦中惊醒，

在火一般的涟漪中闪动。
我驾急行的小舟抵达海湾，
船头扎进充满泥沙的海滩。

2

之后，走过一里散发温暖海香的沙滩，
又穿过三块田地，直到一农庄出现；
轻叩窗户；急速的刺啦声响，
蓝光闪过，火柴点亮。
柔声细语，透露出惊与喜。
两颗心怦怦地狂跳在一起。

（李正栓 译）

Parting at Morning[1]

This poem is sometimes taken as a whole with "Meeting at Night". The night meeting of young lovers is romantic and sweet, but they have to part in the morning and meet their duties and anxieties—all they have to face in the reality. This poem is both an aubade and a valediction.

Round the cape of a sudden came the sea,
And the sun looked over the mountain's rim[2]:
And straight was a path of gold[3] for him[4],
And the need of a world of men for me.

Notes

1. It is written in one quatrain rhyming abba of combined iambic and anapestic meters with the first two lines five stresses, the last four.
2. rim: a raised edge, mountain's rim.
3. a path of gold: the path the golden sun shines upon.
4. for him: for the sun.

For Study and Discussion

1. How do punctuation and sentence structure affect the poem in terms of image creation?

2. What is particular about the image of the sun in comparison with the image of the speaker?
3. How do you understand the last two lines?
4. Please learn this poem by heart.

参考译文

清晨离别

绕过海岬，大海忽现，
旭日从山后露脸俯瞰。
太阳的前程金光灿烂，
我要去和世人周旋。

（王式仁　译）

23. Matthew Arnold

Matthew Arnold (马修·阿诺德, 1822—1888) was born in Middlesex, southeast England. His father, Dr. Thomas Arnold, was an important religious and educational reformer who became headmaster of the Rugby School, one of the most prestigious private schools in England. Arnold was deeply influenced by his father's ideas, but he also showed a certain rebellious defiance of his father's rigorous principles. When Arnold left Rugby to attend Oxford University in 1841, he assumed the style of an aristocratic wit and dandy famous for his elegant, colorful clothes and flippant manner. He did not work particularly hard at Oxford, and only by desperate last-minute cramming did he manage a respectable performance on his final examinations. But underneath the casual manner that Arnold cultivated as a young man were a wide-ranging intellect and a sensitive, brooding imagination. Even before he abandoned his youthful dandyism, Arnold was beginning to write poems that would surprise his closest friends and family with their meditative intensity and their power of symbolic suggestion. In 1851 Arnold became a government inspector of schools, a position he held for over thirty years. The job was a demanding one and left him with less free time for his own writing than was enjoyed by other major Victorian writers. Yet Arnold wrote continually throughout these years.

Arnold's career as a writer may be divided roughly into four phases. Most of his poems appeared during the 1850s: a volume entitled *The Strayed Reveller and Other Poems* (1849) was followed by additional volumes in 1852 and 1853. During the 1860s the focus of his writing shifted from poetry to literary and social criticism. In 1865 the first series of his *Essays in Criticism* was published, and in 1869, *Culture and Anarchy*, a fierce attack on middle-class materialism and narrow-mindedness, considered by many to be his finest work. In the 1870s Arnold devoted himself mainly to writing about education and religion. Finally, in the 1880s he returned to literary criticism and wrote the second series of his *Essays in Criticism*, published soon after his death in 1888.

Matthew Arnold is important both as a poet and as a critic. In his poetry, Arnold confronts more directly than either Tennyson or Browning the central Victorian problem of remaining human in the dehumanizing atmosphere of a modern industrial society. In his critical essays, Arnold tries to provide answers to the questions about modern life that he poses but leaves for the most part unanswered in his poems.

Many of his best poems convey a melancholy, pessimistic sense of the dilemmas of modern life, without offering any secure source of hope, joy and permanent value. Today his poetry seems distinctively expressive of mid-Victorian anxiety because it avoids offering optimistic answers to the doubtful questions it raises.

Dover Beach[1]

This poem represents Arnold's view on the spiritual unrest of his time. It is written in dramatic monologue. On a moonlight night, with his wife, he enjoyed a moment of calmness on the Dover Beach, while the flinging in and flinging out of the pebbles made him think of the rise and fall of human faith. The form of the poem also serves its meaning. The long or short poetic lines resemble the ebb and flow of the tide and thoughts, while the sound pattern reflects the speaker's different moods, calm or unease.

The sea is calm tonight.
The tide is full, the moon lies fair
Upon the straits[2]—on the French coast the light
Gleams and is gone; the cliffs of England[3] stand,
Glimmering and vast, out in the tranquil bay.
Come to the window, sweet is the night air![4]
Only, from the long line of spray
Where the sea meets the moon-blanched land[5],
Listen! you hear the grating[6] roar
Of pebbles which the waves draw back, and fling,
At their return, up the high strand,
Begin, and cease, and then again begin,
With tremulous cadence slow[7], and bring
The eternal note of sadness[8] in.

Sophocles[9] long ago
Heard it[10] on the Aegean[11], and it brought
Into his mind the turbid[12] ebb and flow
Of human misery[13]; we
Find also in the sound a thought,
Hearing it by this distant[14] northern sea.

The Sea of Faith[15]
Was once, too, at the full, and round earth's shore
Lay like the folds of a bright girdle furled.[16]
But now I only hear
Its melancholy, long, withdrawing roar,
Retreating, to the breath
Of the night wind, down the vast edges drear[17]
And naked shingles[18] of the world.

Ah, love, let us be true
To one another! for the world, which seems
To lie before us like a land of dreams,
So various, so beautiful, so new,
Hath really neither joy, nor love, nor light,
Nor certitude, nor peace, nor help for pain;[19]
And we are here as on a darkling[20] plain
Swept with confused alarms of struggle and flight,
Where ignorant armies clash by night.

ca. 1851 1867

Notes

1. The poem is written in four stanzas of irregular lengths and rhythms.
2. straits: straits of Dover, a crossing between England and France.
3. the cliffs of England: referring to the white steep cliffs on the bank of the Straits of Dover.
4. sweet is the night air: Cf. John Keats' "Ode to the Nightingale": "tender is the night..."
5. the moon-blanched land: land that is made white by the moonlight.
6. grating: making harshly sound.
7. tremulous cadence slow: tremulous slow cadence. This *adj.* + *n.* + *adj.* structure is know as Miltonic structure in which the two adjectives before and after both modify the noun.
8. The eternal note of sadness: the basic tone of the poem. Here the change from the calm, beautiful night scene to the poet's inner world is achieved.
9. Sophocles ['sɔfəkli:z]: a famous Athenian tragedian (496? —406 B. C.) in the golden age of Greek drama, from whose story *Oedipus the King*, Freud created the term Oedipus Complex.
10. it: referring to the eternal note of sadness.
11. Aegean: Aegean sea, an arm of the Mediterranean Sea.
12. turbid: not clear.
13. human misery: the central idea of the poem.

14. distant: far away (from the Aegean Sea).
15. The Sea of Faith: here faith is compared to the ebb and flow of the sea tide.
16. Lay like the folds of a bright girdle furled: Lay furled like the folds of a bright girdle. It means at high tide the sea envelops the land closely; at ebb tide, as the sea retreats, it is unfurled and spread out.
17. the vast edges drear: another Miltonic structure, the vast drear edges.
18. naked shingles: referring to the barren state of modern culture. shingles: beaches covered with pebbles.
19. Hath really neither joy, nor love, nor light, /Nor certitude, nor peace, nor help for pain: the poet thinks that the Industrial Revolution has taken away the religious spirit of England and made it a wasteland of spirit.
20. darkling: (poetic) in the dark.

诗歌赏析

这首诗写于1851年，是诗人和新婚的妻子在多佛海滩度蜜月时的随想。维多利亚时期工业和自然科学发展迅猛，传统的宗教思想受到严重打击，社会思想一度混乱。这首诗用戏剧独白的形式写成，反映了当时人们在时代转型时期焦虑不安的思想状态。诗人假设的场景是：独白者在多佛海边的旅馆内一边依窗远眺，一边对他妻子讲话。

第一节诗以宁静的大海、涨满的潮水和皎洁的明月起首，一幅风平浪静、月朗星稀的祥和画面。说话者让爱人到窗边欣赏这美景。可是紧接着，便听到了远处海水拍击海岸的声音，时起时落，带来了永恒的悲音。这永恒的悲音是全诗的基调。这悲音古希腊悲剧家索福克勒斯也曾在爱琴海边听到过。他从中听到了人类苦难的潮汐，我们也从中听到深意。从古到今，从爱琴海到北海，人类的苦难从未停息。

第三节中诗人把信仰比作大海，并对英国古今的信仰进行了对比。信仰之海曾经有过满潮，像一根闪亮的腰带把世界的海岸环绕。可是现在只有退潮的咆哮，只留下阴郁的海岸和光秃秃的卵石。信仰之海的满潮指英国人民曾经有过虔诚的信仰。退潮指在自然科学和工业发展的冲击下，人们混乱不堪的思想现状。而阴郁的海岸和光秃秃的卵石指的就是当时人们思想的荒芜和信仰的缺失。

最后，诗人得出结论：“亲爱的，让我们彼此忠诚。”因为这个世界虽然看上去光怪陆离，可是已经没有了爱，没有欢乐和光明，没有肯定、和平以及对痛苦的救助。在这个乱世之中，只有恋人彼此的忠诚是最值得信赖和依赖的精神慰藉。

该诗的中心比喻是将人类的信仰比作潮汐。除了文字的比喻，诗人还通过声音、形式将这一比喻层层加强。诗行长短不一，韵脚参差不齐，多跨行现象，就像潮水的涨落和诗人难平的思绪。诗歌的意象从清风、明月、潮水开始，到最后的黑暗、战争、搏杀戛然而止，从古代到当代，从宁静到喧嚣，预示着诗人对当时英国现状的不满。

For Study and Discussion

1. What is the basic tone of the whole poem? Try to find out some key words to show the tone.
2. What do you think of the sound pattern of this poem? What's the significance of this pattern?
3. What mood is created by the description of the moonlit sea in the opening lines of the poem? Where does this mood change?
4. Why does Arnold mention Sophocles in his poem?
5. In what way does the sea resemble Faith?
6. Study carefully the imagery that Arnold places at the end of the poem. Why does Arnold think of himself and the person he loves as being situated "on a darkling plain"? What is suggested by the idea of "ignorant armies" clashing "by night"?

参考译文

多佛海滩

今夜大海平静，
潮水正满，月色朗朗，
临照海峡，——法国海岸上
微光渐隐，而英国的峭壁高竖，
在宁静的海湾里显出巨大模糊的身影。
到窗边来吧，晚风多么甜！
可是你听！月光漂白了的陆地
与大海相接处，那一条长长的浪花线

传来磨牙般的喧声，
这是海浪卷走卵石，然后转回头来，
又把它们抛到高高的海滩之上，
涌起，停息，再重新涌起，
以缓慢而颤动的节拍
送来永恒的悲哀的音响。

索福克勒斯很久以前
在爱琴海边听过这喧声，
在他心中引起了人类苦难的
浊浪滚滚的潮汐，
我们在此遥远的北海边聆听，
也在此声听到了深意。

信仰之海
也曾有过满潮，像一根灿烂的腰带
把全球的海岸围绕。
但如今我只听得
它那忧伤的退潮的咆哮久久不息，
它退向夜风的呼吸，
退过世界广阔阴沉的边界，
只留下一滩光秃秃的卵石。

啊，爱人，愿我们
彼此真诚！因为世界虽然
展开在我们面前如梦幻的国度，
那么多彩、美丽而新鲜，
实际上却没有欢乐，没有爱和光明，
没有肯定，没有和平，没有对痛苦的救助；
我们犹如处在黑暗的旷野，
斗争和逃跑构成一片混乱与惊怖，
无知的军队在黑夜中互相冲突。

（飞　白　译）

24. Christina Georgina Rossetti

Christina Georgina Rossetti (克里斯蒂娜·乔治娜·罗塞蒂, 1830—1894) was the younger sister of Dante Gabriel Rossetti (1828—1882), an artist and the founder of the Pre-Raphaelite Brotherhood. She was born in London in 1830, the youngest child of Gabriel Rossetti, an Italian patriot who fled to England for refugee in 1824. Like her brothers and sister, she was educated mostly at home where she met politicians, artists, and writers, many of which, like her parents, were exiles from Italy. She was the model for many paintings by her brother Dante and his artist friends. Her first verses, written when she was 12, were printed by her grandfather. At 19 some of her poems were printed by her brothers in *The Germ*, the magazine of the Pre-Raphaelite Brotherhood.

Her collection *Goblin Market and Other Poems* (1862), illustrated by her brother Dante, received public recognization. *The Prince's Progress and Other Poems* was published four years later. The collection of her earlier writings for children, *Sing-Song, a Nursery Rhyme Book*, appeared in 1872, and *A Pageant and Other Poems* in 1881. Her later works in prose and verse are mostly religious. She died in London on December 29, 1894.

Christina Rossetti's work ranges from poems for children to love lyrics, sonnets and religious poetry. Her poetry is remarkable for its simplicity and singing quality. The recurring theme in her love poems is the unhappy or frustrated love. Her religious poetry often shows a strong sense of duty. Frequently suffering from ill health, Christina wrote poetry that was often melancholy and concerned with thoughts of death. However, she could also be sprightly and fanciful in her writing.

Remember[1]

This poem is chosen from *The Goblin Market and Other Poems* (1862), in which the poet expresses her love for her fiancé. The poet first asks her beloved to remember her after her death, and then wishes him to forget her as long as he shall be happy. These ideas seem contradictory to each other but reasonable. Its language is simple, its structure clear; yet, with not a word of love mentioned, the poet makes this poem passionate and moving to the core.

Remember me when I am gone away,
Gone far away into the silent land;[2]
When you can no more hold me by the hand,
Nor I half turn to go yet turning stay.[3]
Remember me when no more day by day
You tell me of our future that you planned:
Only remember me; you understand
It will be late to counsel[4] then or pray.
Yet if you should forget me for a while
And afterwards remember, do not grieve:
For if the darkness and corruption[5] leave
A vestige of the thoughts that once I had,
Better by far[6] you should forget and smile
Than that you should remember and be sad.

Notes

1. It is written in Italian sonnet rhyming abbaabba cddece.
2. Gone far away into the silent land: (Euphemism) dead.
3. Nor I half turn to go yet turning stay: referring to her reluctance to part with her love and die.
4. counsel: give advice.
5. corruption: putrescence of the body.
6. Better by far: I shall think it better.

诗歌赏析

这首诗选自《妖怪市场》(1862)，表达了罗塞蒂对她的恋人詹姆斯·科林森(James Collinson)的爱。诗人因患日益恶化的疾病而时常陷入对死亡的沉思，她把这种对于死亡的沉思与她的爱情纠缠在一起。

这首诗用意大利十四行诗的形式写成，逻辑结构也符合意大利十四行诗的传统，即转折点发生在第九行，也就是六行诗节的开始。诗人在前八行三次重复地表示“请记着我”，但是后六行又希望恋人忘记她——“我宁愿你能忘记我并露出微笑，/ 也不愿你把我记住而惨惨凄凄。”诗人的语气很平淡，似乎在平静地对恋人表达自己的希冀。诗歌的主题是死亡，但诗人没有直接提到死亡，而是委婉地用“离开，去那寂静的国度”，表达了对死的忌讳；而“你再也不能把我的手紧握”，“无休无止地描绘未来的生活”表现出对生的恋恋不舍。

没有哭泣，没有恐惧，宁静中一丝淡淡的伤感。也许，这就是罗塞蒂面对死亡的态度。

For Study and Discussion

1. What does “the silent land” symbolize?
2. Explain the structure of this sonnet. How does it serve the development of the poem?
3. How do you understand the contradictory ideas expressed in the poem? Is this contradiction reasonable? Why or why not?
4. Interpret the meaning of the last two lines.

参考译文

记住我

记住我，当我离开这世界后，
远离这世界，去那寂静的国度；
那时你再也不能把我的手握住，
我也不能再转身犹疑，欲走还留。
记住我，当你不能再夜以继昼
把我们未来的生活给我描述。
只祈求记住我；你心里清楚
到那时已来不及忠告或祈求。
不过如果你一时把我忘掉，
之后又把我记起，你别悲哀，

因为黑暗和腐败
还留一些我曾有过的思念痕迹，
我宁愿你能忘记我并露出微笑，
也不愿你把我记住而惨惨凄凄。

（李正栓　译）

25. Thomas Hardy

Thomas Hardy（托马斯·哈代，1840—1928），novelist and poet, is one of the representatives of English critical realism at the turn of the 19th century. He was born in Dorset, an agricultural district in the south of England. Son of an architect, he followed his father's profession. In 1861 he went to London for further study and to practice his profession. Today Thomas Hardy is better known as a novelist than as a poet. In 1868 he submitted his first novel to a publisher. It was rejected, but Hardy was encouraged to try again, and in 1871 a second novel, *Desperate Remedies*, was published. Another novel *Under the Greenwood Tree* appeared the following year, and Hardy gave up his profession as an architect to devote full time to his writing. His career as a novelist extended from 1871 to 1896. After the hostile public response to his last novel, *Jude the Obscure* (1896), he devoted the final thirty years of his life almost exclusively to poetry.

His first collection, *Wessex Poems*, was published in 1898. Between 1903 and 1908 appeared *The Dynasts*, a vast epic-drama based upon the Napoleonic Wars. When he died in 1928, he was widely admired. His ashes were buried in Westminster Abbey, but in accordance with his wishes, his heart was removed and buried in the parish churchyard of his native village in Dorsetshire.

Hardy's best poems usually present situations that illustrate his concern with circumstances or forces beyond human control. Hardy is often described as a gloomy pessimist who believed in the impersonal and generally negative power of fate. But it is important to recognize that while the sadness in

Hardy's writing is sometimes attributed to causes remote from human will and consciousness, more often it springs from within, from our own insatiable desires, emotions, and illusions. And while the prevailing mood in Hardy's poetry is somber, there is also a very rich and positive feeling for the ancient landscape and cultural roots of rural England, for patterns of life so old that they come to seem archetypal.

In style, Hardy's poems create an impression of plainness or ruggedness, in keeping with his rural background and his lack of extensive formal education. But the colloquial directness of his language is very much a matter of conscious selection and craft. Even Hardy's frequent use of archaic words or of homely diction is part of a deliberate reaction against the ornate, elaborate language of some late-Victorian verse. Hardy's poetry may appear to lack sophisticated complexity and glamour, but its surface simplicity is deceptive. Its deep integrity will consistently reward a reader who is free of presumptions about what fine poetry should be.

The Darkling Thrush[1]

This poem was written on the last day of the 19th century, i. e. December 31, 1900. The vocabulary and imagery of the poem are directed mainly toward creating a sense of the bleakness and sadness of the winter landscape, which reflect the poet's bewilderment at the turn of the century.

I leant upon a coppice gate[2]
When Frost was spectre-gray[3],
And Winter's dregs[4] made desolate
The weakening eye of day[5].
The tangled bine-stems[6] scored the sky[7]
Like strings of broken lyres,
And all mankind that haunted nigh[8]
Had sought their household fires.

The land's sharp features seemed to be
The Century's corpse[9] outleant[10],

His crypt[11] the cloudy canopy[12],
The wind his death-lament[13].
The ancient pulse of germ[14] and birth
Was shrunken hard and dry,
And every spirit[15] upon earth
Seemed fervourless as I.

At once a voice arose among
The bleak twigs overhead
In a full-hearted evensong[16]
Of joy illimited;
An aged thrush, frail, gaunt, and small,
In blast-beruffled plume,[17]
Had chosen thus to fling his soul[18]
Upon the growing gloom.

So little cause for carolings[19]
Of such ecstatic sound
Was written[20] on terrestrial[21] things
Afar or nigh[22] around,
That I could think there trembled through
His happy good-night air[23]
Some blessed[24] Hope, whereof he knew
And I was unaware.

1900, 1901

Notes

1. This poem is chosen from *Poems of the Past and Present* (1902). It is written in four 8-line stanzas rhyming ababcdcd with the odd lines in iambic tetrameter, while the even lines in iambic trimeter. Darkling: in the dark.
2. coppice gate: gate leading to a small wood or thicket.
3. spectre-gray: gray or white as a ghost. spectre: ghost.
4. dregs: last remains.

5. The weakening eye of day: the dimming sun. the eye of day: referring to sun.
6. tangled bine-stems: twining stems of shrubs.
7. scored the sky: marked the sky with lines.
8. nigh: near.
9. Century's corpse: the century was compared to a corpse for the poem was written on December 31, 1900, the last day of the 19th century.
10. outleant: leaning out (of its coffin).
11. crypt: underground chamber or vault under a church, used as a burial place.
12. canopy: referring to the sky.
13. death-lament: dirge.
14. germ: seed or bud.
15. every spirit: every breath of life.
16. evensong: evening song.
17. In blast-beruffled plume: with his feathers ruffled by the wind.
18. fling his soul: pour out all his emotional energy.
19. carolings: singing joyously.
20. written: marked.
21. terrestrial: earthly.
22. Afar or nigh: far or near.
23. air: music, melody.
24. blessed: blissful.

诗歌赏析

本诗写于1900年12月31日，恰是世纪之交。作为诗人，他对自然的感悟向来很深，对于时令的变化、时间的迁移，更是敏感之至。此时此刻，诗人位于这个时空的交叉点上，回首往事，一片黑暗，未来也是一片茫然，但当时的他毕竟有着美好的憧憬。此诗是诗人写给新世纪的献词，包含着诗人情感的曲折变化。全诗共分四节，每节八行，抑扬格，韵脚基本采取ababcdcd形式，整齐优美。

第一节诗描写了一幅暗淡、凄凉的冬景，为全诗定下了悲观的基调，这是诗人为19世纪末期的英国描绘的一幅画面。这一节里哈代使用了鬼魂

(spectre)、残渣(dregs)、暗淡(weakening)、破旧(broken)等字眼，突显旧世纪的衰败景象，落日、残冬宣示着死亡，破旧竖琴又让人倍感曲终人散的凄凉，字里行间饱含着诗人的伤心失望。第二节诗继续描绘凄凉的冬景，并明确指出19世纪已惨然告终。诗人用“本世纪的尸体”的比喻正面提出了世纪交替这一时间主题，暗示时间的流逝和不可避免的死亡。诗人在这两节诗里用一连串的景物和意象，渲染出一种世纪末的萧瑟气氛——远望大地如一具尸体，苍穹是阴沉的，寒风奏着哀歌，世上一切生灵都没有一点生机——悲观的情绪也宣泄得淋漓尽致。

然而第三节诗人笔锋一转，描写了一只欢唱的老画眉，使人精神为之一振。画眉的欢唱暗示新的世纪可能会带来一点生机，但是这只预示着希望的鸟儿又是那样的纤弱憔悴，行将就木，顶着急风，羽毛已被吹乱却还在暮色中歌唱，让人在看到希望的同时不免心情沉重。尽管如此，画眉的欢唱毕竟稍稍冲淡了前两节诗中的悲观基调，把全诗向前推进了一步。

第四节表现了诗人对画眉优美的歌声感到迷惑不解，但又觉得其中隐含着一线希望。画眉的欢歌给全诗阴郁的基调涂上了一抹亮色，也给大家带来了一丝希望。诗人在奏响了19世纪的哀歌之后，对20世纪充满了惶惑，希望或许有，只是自己还不甚了解，静观以待吧，一副消极观望的漠然态势。

综观全诗，作者在前两节用一连串死气沉沉的意象展现出一幅静态的世纪荒原的荒凉景象，极富视觉冲击力。第三、四节在肃杀的气氛中加入了一只欢歌的画眉，虽然是只孱弱、老朽的画眉，也让人精神一抖，更增添了听觉的感受。这一前一后静态与动态的对比，视觉上的凄凉景象与听觉上的欢歌鸟语的差异，展示了诗人的内心矛盾。19世纪已悲惨落幕，未来究竟是什么样子？英国明天的出路到底在哪里？20世纪会不会给人带来希望？哈代感到迷茫和困惑。这首《薄暮听画眉》既表现了作者对旧世纪的伤心失望，又表达了诗人对新世纪的向往。

For Study and Discussion

1. What is the setting of the poem?
2. Give examples to show how Hardy's language give to the wintry scene a dreariness that is more than just visual or physical.
3. Discuss the imagery of this poem.
4. There is a mental change in this poem. Where does it happen? Why?
5. What's the poet's attitude towards the past century? And the coming century?

参考译文

薄暮听画眉

我倚着灌木林的篱门，
这时天寒地冻光照惨白，
残冬使暗淡的太阳
显得分外凄凉。
交织的藤蔓划破长空，
恰如破旧竖琴的纷乱丝弦。
漫游此间的常客不再流连，
躲在家中的炉边。

远望大地起落分明，
好像本世纪的陨体横陈，
阴沉的苍穹是它的墓穴，
寒风是它的哀歌。
自古迄今的生息的脉动
而今微弱停滞，
世上的一切生灵
都和我一样死气沉沉。

忽然响起一声啼叫，
来自头顶上空赤裸的枝条，
像倾心歌唱的夜曲，
无限快乐，无限欢欣。
一只老画眉纤弱憔悴，
急风拂乱它的羽毛，
竟在此时倾吐心灵，
对着愈渐浓重的幽冥。

画眉为何唱出这样迷人的歌声，
几乎无人能够说清，
把原因写在世间万物之上，
不论远在天边还是近在咫尺。

我能想到它欢乐的晚安曲中，
震荡着某种神圣希望，
对此画眉早已知晓，
我却不解它的由衷。

（李广成　译）

26. Gerard Manley Hopkins

Gerard Manley Hopkins（杰拉德·曼利·霍普金斯，1844－1889）was born into a large and very religious English family. He was often unhappy while attending the Highgate School in northwest London. In 1863 he went to study classics at Oxford University, and there his brilliant intellect and imagination began to flower. He was a student of Walter Pater, the eloquent late-Victorian spokesman for artistic experience as the only stable source of value in the modern world. And he was influenced by the Oxford movement, which sought to revive the ritualistic and dogmatic traditions of the Church of England. The original leader of the Oxford movement, John Henry Newman, had left the church of England in 1845 to become a Roman Catholic. After a period of deep religious turmoil, Hopkins himself, under Newman's sponsorship, joined the Catholic Church in 1866.

In 1868 he entered the Society of Jesus, one of the most intellectually demanding and disciplined orders of the Church. Before becoming a Jesuit, Hopkins burned all the poems he had written up to that time, feeling that his artistic interests were incompatible with strict devotion to his religious obligation. He did not begin to write poetry again until 1875 or 1876, and even then he resisted his friend's suggestion that he publish at least some of his work. In 1877 he became an ordained priest and served in a number of parishes, including one in a depressing working class district of Liverpool. In 1884 he was appointed Professor of Classics at University College, Dublin. Hopkins died in Dublin of typhoid fever in 1889. His poems were finally published in 1918 by his close friend, the poet Robert Bridges.

Although not widely read or appreciated until the 20th century, Hopkins is in many respects a deeply characteristic Victorian writer. He is, to be sure, a remarkable experimenter and innovator in the rhythm, vocabulary, and formal arrangements of English verse. As much as any other Victorian poet, including Browning, Hopkins has influenced the direction of modern English and American poetry. Yet in his expressions of intense spiritual anxiety and in his passionate devotion to the unique particularized beauty of the natural world, he is very much a 19th century poet. To read Hopkins well, we must learn to value the Victorian dimension of his writing as well as its advanced, forward-looking modernity.

The Windhover[1]

The central image of the poem is a falcon in flight. Hopkins first introduces that the falcon makes him aware of Christ's power and glory in spite of its humility, and then he concludes the poem with the implication of the martyrdom of Christ. The falcon is the symbol of Christ whose majesty and grandeur are displayed by various ways in this poem like language, color images and sound effects. It is a religious poem on the whole.

To Christ our Lord

I caught this morning morning's minion[2], king—
dom of daylight's dauphin[3], dapple-dawn-drawn Falcon, in his riding
Of the rolling level underneath him steady air, and striding
High there, how he rung upon the rein[4] of a wimpling[5] wing
In his ecstasy! then off, off forth on swing,
As a skate's heel sweeps smooth on a bow-bend: the hurl and gliding
Rebuffed the big wind. My heart in hiding
Stirred for a bird, —the achieve of, the mastery of the thing!

Brute beauty and valour and act, oh, air, pride, plume, here
Buckle![6] AND the fire that breaks from thee then, a billion

Times told lovelier, more dangerous, O my chevalier![7]

No wonder of it: sheer plod makes plough down sillion[8]
Shine, and blue-bleak embers, ah my dear,
Fall, gall[9] themselves, and gash gold-vermilion.

1877 1918

Notes

1. It is a sonnet written in Italian form rhyming aaaaaaaa bcbcbc. Windhover: kestrel, a small European hawk noted for hovering in the air.
2. minion: favorite, darling.
3. dauphin: a prince who is heir to the French throne.
4. rung upon the rein: circled at the end of a rein.
5. wimpling: rippling.
6. Buckle: the verb can be read as imperative or indicative. All three meanings are relevant: to prepare for action, to fasten together, to collapse.
7. chevalier: knight.
8. sillion: ridge between two plowed furrows.
9. gall: break the surface of.

诗歌赏析

茶隼是一种体型较小的鹰，因擅长迎风翱翔且姿态优美，又称风鹰。《风鹰》是霍普金斯宗教抒情诗的代表作，写得流光溢彩、绚丽辉煌。这首诗由意大利十四行诗的形式写成，但是又不受形式的局限。前八行押“ing”韵，一韵到底，展现了风鹰在空中翱翔的气势；后六行隔行押韵，与诗人变化的心境契合。

前八行主要描述了风鹰在空中飞行的动态美。风鹰被喻为日光王国的太子，他庄严、高贵，“骑着”（riding，第 2 行）身下滚滚的大气层，用翻滚的翅膀做“缰绳”（rein，第 4 行），“跨行”（striding，第 3 行）、盘升，活像一位勇猛的骑士。描写风鹰迅疾的飞腾时，绵密的头韵就像一张密密的网让人几乎不能呼吸（第 1、2 行）；形容风鹰舒缓的翱翔时，又用了一系列的长音和双元音（第 6 行）。这些细致的遣词造句以及跨行设计就像风鹰不拘的飞翔，时而急促，时而缓和，充满动感和张力。在风鹰，这大自然的宠儿面前，诗人自愧弗如，谦卑的灵魂也为之悸动。

前八行诗人用一个通韵和一系列跨行诗句以及绵密的头韵塑造了风鹰飞翔的气势，后六行一开始诗人又用一连串的单音节词如疾风骤雨般表达了对风鹰的仰慕和赞叹。然而，从“弯折”（buckle，第10行）开始，语意发生了变化。如果说前面的诗行中，风鹰的壮美、雄俊、自由和骄傲暗含了基督的精神和气质，从buckle起，诗人开始直接赞美基督。“弯折”象征着基督的蒙难。风鹰作为自然的统治者，固然气势不凡，然而“我的骑士”（即我主基督）因其历经凶险的自我牺牲精神，更加可爱。单纯的劳作会将铁犁磨光，阴冷的灰烬也会迸出金黄朱红。基督的崇高神性在风鹰的雄浑、壮美和耶稣的苦难、隐忍当中得到了完美体现。

神无处不在；万物都秉承上帝之形象而存在。这就是霍普金斯宗教诗的主旨。

For Study and Discussion

1. In the first eight lines, how is the speaker affected by his sight of the bird as it hovers and wheels in flight? What does he mean by "My heart in hiding/ Stirred for a bird"?
2. What is the symbolic meaning of the windhover?
3. How do the details of the images suggest both the paradoxical qualities of Christ and the physical appearance of the bird?
4. Discuss the alliterations used in the poem. Appreciate other sound effects produced in the poem.
5. Compare this poem with Tennyson's "The Eagle" and Ted Hughes' "Hawk Roosting".

参考译文

风　鹰

献给我主基督
清晨，在日光王子的国度，我看到，
那黎明的宠儿，直面斑斓彩霞的风鹰，
跨着滚滚劲风，羽翅甩动着缰绳，
于狂喜中，尽兴盘升，纵情驰骋，
尔后，它振翅冲向天际，隐没在远方。

犹如冰刀掠过弯道，它傲对疾风，激升缓降。
我隐匿着的心不觉为之悸动，
为它的胜利，为它那主宰一切的力量。

雄俊，骁勇，奋动，啊，流云，傲骨，翅膀，
在此融为一体！然而，与你骤然分开的火，描述着
千百倍美丽，凶悍的你，啊，我高贵的勇将！

这不足为奇：真正的劳作会使垄间铁犁
闪光发亮，使灰冷的余烬，啊，亲爱的，
散落，绽裂，露出一片猩红金黄。

（王继辉　译）

Pied Beauty[1]

The theme of the poem is that the entire universe is God's glory and reflection. Hopkins was a priest who saw God's hand in all. Hopkins begins and ends this poem by directing our attention to the source of the "pied beauty" in the world, that is, God. This is an example of Hopkins' sprung rhythm. Hopkins placed strongly accented syllables against unaccented ones to produce greater tension and emphasis within each line.

Glory be to God for dappled things—
For skies of couple-colour as a brinded[2] cow;
For rose-moles all in stipple[3] upon trout that swim;
Fresh-firecoal chestnut-falls[4], finches' wings;
Landscape plotted and pieced—fold, fallow, and plough;[5]
And all trades, their gear and tackle and trim.[6]

All things counter[7], original, spare[8], strange;
Whatever is fickle, freckled (who knows how?)
With swift, slow; sweet, sour; adazzle, dim;[9]
He fathers-forth[10] whose beauty is past change:
Praise him.

1877　　1918

Notes

1. It is written in two stanzas with the first stanza of six lines rhyming abcabc, the second of 5 lines rhyming decdc. Pied: of two or more colors in blotches, variegated.
2. brinded: streaked with dark, brownish orange in color with streaks of gray.
3. stipple: dots or small spots.
4. Fresh-firecoal chestnut-falls: freshly fallen chestnuts, bright as coals.
5. Landscape plotted and pieced—fold, fallow, and plough: the fields are either lying fallow or plowed for cultivation, thus appear like patches of different colors.
6. their gear and tackle and trim: their equipment.
7. counter: contrary.
8. spare: rare.
9. With swift, slow; sweet, sour; adazzle, dim: with slow (countering with) swift; sweet (countering with) sour; adazzle (countering with) dim. adazzle: dazzling.
10. fathers-forth: creates everything.

For Study and Discussion

1. What kind of beauty in the natural world is Hopkins celebrating in this poem? What specific examples are given to show the beauty?
2. Who is that source? In what way is his own beauty unlike that of the natural world "He fathers-forth" (Line 10)?
3. The look and sound of individual words in "Pied Beauty" are important aspects of the poem's meaning. What do "dappled" (Line 1), "couple-colour" (Line 2), and "stipple" (Line 3) have in common? What other words in the poem can you relate to these through their look and sound? (Notice "plotted" in Line 5, for example)
4. In what sense is Hopkins imitating in language the "pied beauty" he celebrates in nature?
5. What does Hopkins mean by "All things counter"? How are they part of the "pied beauty"?

参考译文

斑驳之美

事物陆离斑驳，光荣归上帝——
因为有炫彩天空像牛身的花斑；
因为有水中鳟鱼身上玫瑰红点；
有栗子落下如旺火；有雀儿的双翼，
有分片成块土地——或起伏，或轮种，或耕翻；
各行各业，用具，吊车，设备齐全。

一切相对，新奇，独特，怪异；
变动的都带斑点（谁有知如何？）
快必有慢；酸必有甜；暗必有明；
万物生于他，他的美常在不易：
要赞他真灵。

（周珏良　译）

27. William Butler Yeats

William Butler Yeats（威廉·巴特勒·叶芝，1865－1939）was born in Dublin，Ireland，the eldest son of a painter. He spent part of his childhood in Sligo，on the northwest coast of Ireland. There he became acquainted with traditional Irish legends and folklore. His father moved the family between Dublin and London，where Yeats attended school and spent much time reading，pursuing his interests in Irish legends and Romantic idealism and occult philosophies. Mixed into his thought were the mysticism of Blake，the Romantic idealism of Shelley，and the aesthetic ideas of the Pre-Raphaelites.

He was particularly interested in making the Irish people conscious of their past and in resurrecting a heroic ideal by which they could live. The beautiful Maud Gonne, whom Yeats met in 1889, drew him into the Irish National movement. Together with Lady Gregory who shared his interest in Irish legend, he founded the world famous Abbey Theatre, which played a great part in the revival of Irish drama.

Maud Gonne's marriage to John MacBride, in 1903, marked an important change in Yeats' life. Disappointed in love, he was resolved to make great poetry out of his experience, seeking "perfection of the work" instead of "perfection of the life", as he called it in a late poem. Yeats was working to toughen his poetry and to bring it more into touch with the language and preoccupations of the modern world. He was working to simplify his style, to rid it of Romantic vagueness, and to bring it close to the rhythms of everyday speech. His aim was to write poems "as cold and passionate as the dawn". In his aims and practice, and rejection of late Victorian poetic modes, Yeats gave impetus to the Modernist movement in poetry, in which Ezra Pound, T. S. Eliot, Edith Sitwell and others sought a fresh language, new rhythms, and an extension of poetic subjects.

Throughout his poetic career, Yeats sought to unify his experience of the world and gain for his poems a central illuminating vision comparable to that of Dante and Shelley, one that would pull together the thousand separate fragments of everyday life. He sought that vision in the mysticism of Blake and occult philosophies, drawing these various ideas together in his philosophical and historical book, *A Vision*, published in 1925. He saturated his poetry with these ideas, constructing in various volumes of poetry a composite portrait of a complex modern being. No single poem revealed Yeats' personality completely. Each poem provided some insight into a moment of thought or feeling. At the same time, these poems took the pulse of current thought and feeling.

He became a senator in the Irish Free State in 1922. In 1923, he was awarded the Nobel Prize for literature. In his lifetime, he wrote 11 volumes of poetry, 26 plays, 9 books of prose and many other kinds. By the time of his death in 1939, Yeats had become the leading poet of his age, who had taught "the free man how to praise", as W. H. Auden wrote of him in his great elegiac poem, *In Memory of W. B. Yeats* (1939).

When You Are Old[1]

This poem was written in 1891 for Maud Gonne (1866—1953), an actress and Irish revolutionist, for whom Yeats cherished a lifelong love. By sharp contrast between his love and others', Yeats shows his deep admiration for her and regret for the passing of love. Though short and simple, it is passionate and moving.

When you are old and gray and full of sleep,
And nodding by the fire, take down this book[2],
And slowly read, and dream of the soft look
Your eyes had once, and of their shadows deep;

How many loved your moments of glad grace,
And loved your beauty with love false or true,
But one man loved the pilgrim soul in you,
And loved the sorrows of your changing face[3];

And bending[4] down beside the glowing bars[5],
Murmur, a little sadly, how Love[6] fled
And paced upon the mountains overhead
And hid his face amid[7] a crowd of stars.

1891　　　　1892, 1899

Notes

1. This poem is written in three quatrains of iambic pentameter rhyming abba.
2. this book: the book of poetry Yeats wrote for Maud Gonne.
3. changing face: the face getting old.
4. bending: referring to the bending of her body or the hunchback when she is old.
5. the glowing bars: referring to the fireplace.
6. Love: personification, referring to a man who loved her.
7. amid: among.

诗歌赏析

《当你老了》是叶芝献给他的意中人毛德·冈的一首诗。毛德·冈是一位美丽的女演员，1889年叶芝对她一见钟情，然而这段感情注定是叶芝的一厢情愿。毛德·冈多次拒绝叶芝的追求，并最终嫁给了一位爱尔兰军官。尽管如此，叶芝对她的爱始终不渝、一往情深。这种难以排解的痛苦和无望折磨着叶芝，促使他写下了许多真挚的爱情诗歌。《当你老了》是其中的名篇。这首诗写于1891年，诗人刚刚27岁，毛德·冈也只有26岁，诗歌模拟恋人在迟暮之年对爱情经历的回想，写得情真意切，婉转动人。诗人不幸，诗之幸。多位诗人如邓恩、济慈均如此。

第一节诗塑造了一个诗人想象中的场景。恋人垂垂老矣，头发花白，睡意昏沉，颤巍巍地取下诗人写给她的情诗，在炉边阅读，不由地想起自己的青春时光。nodding（第2行）可以理解为打盹，也可以理解为老年人不能自控的点头；slowly read（第3行）既表示老人缓慢的举动，也有诗人的主观愿望，希望恋人能慢慢阅读，仔细品味诗中的深意。

第二节中诗人将自己与其他人的爱情进行对比。恋人年轻时，有很多追求者。他们或是真情，或是假意，爱过她快乐时刻的魅力和她的青春美貌。只有一个人爱她朝圣般的灵魂和容颜变化中的深沉。这个人当然指诗人自己。changing face（第8行）既指随着时光流逝恋人容颜的衰老，也指恋人因不同情绪带来的表情变化，与上文欢乐时的魅力相对。毛德·冈是一位激进的爱尔兰民族主义者，她像基督徒朝圣一样虔诚地投入到爱尔兰民族事业当中。诗人爱毛德·冈，并用文人的方式支持她忠诚的事业，为爱尔兰文艺复兴做出了巨大的贡献。别人爱她的外表，诗人爱她的内心；别人只爱她的青春美貌，诗人对她的爱，无论岁月流逝，容颜变迁，始终如一。诗人的爱与他人的爱形成鲜明对比。

第三节又回到假想中的未来。恋人老了，弯着腰，在炉火边有点忧伤地喃喃自语，爱情怎样逃离，爬上了头顶的山巅，把脸庞隐在星星中间，变成一个星座，好似被封为神，栖息于天堂。bending（第9行）既可以指俯下身来，也可以指恋人佝偻着背的老年形象。诗人付出的感情即便没有回报，依然默默地隐在群星之间守望着爱人。叶芝对毛德·冈无奈又难舍的爱恋，不言自明。这一节的love以大写形式出现，说明诗人的爱之深、情之切虽然不能打动恋人，但是已经感动了爱神，从而以他的形象永远存在。

这首诗写恋人暮年的回想，时态也不断从现在到过去游移，红颜难敌岁月的磨砺，青春随时光消逝，然而不变的是诗人对爱的坚守。尽管这首诗全篇用第二人称，我们依然可以从字里行间感受到诗人的存在。在现实生活中，诗人的爱情不能实现，恋人决绝的态度让他绝望。诗人希望，穿过岁月的时空，这段感情仍然能够带给恋人一份温情和追念。

这首诗由三个四行诗组成，语言简单、流畅。工整的抑扬格五音步，节奏缓慢、悠扬，abba 的韵式让人想到诗人始终如一的爱情。中外爱情诗多姿多彩，或激昂奔放，或含蓄内敛，多歌咏青春爱情的浓烈。然而，这首诗独辟蹊径，从恋人老年的回想出发，对爱情进行回顾，加上深沉、舒缓的基调，幽怨、哀伤的情愫，成为爱情诗中别具一格的佳作。

For Study and Discussion

1. What book do you think the speaker is asking the woman to read?
2. What does the phrase "pilgrim soul" tell you about the woman?
3. Please analyze the contrast in the second stanza. What's the difference between his love and that of others?
4. What evidence can you find to show that the speaker's love was not reciprocated and was finally withdrawn?
5. Why is the word "Love" capitalized in the last stanza?

参考译文

当你老了

当你老了，满头白发，充满睡意，
在火炉旁打盹时，你取下这本书，
慢慢地读，慢慢回忆你昔日眉目
的柔和还有你眼中那深深的忧郁；

多少人爱过你美好温雅的时光，
多少人或真或假爱过你的美貌，
只有一人爱过你那圣洁的灵魂，
还爱你日渐衰老的容颜的哀伤；

在散发柔光的炉火旁，你弯着身躯，
有些凄然，低声诉说，爱如何消散，
如何爬上头顶上的山巅，
把自己的脸藏在繁星紧簇的天宇。

（李正栓　译）

The Lake Isle of Innisfree[1]

The poem is one of Yeats' best known lyrics. Written in 1893, it is one of the poet's early work under the influence of the Pre-Raphaelites in the late 19th century England. Tired of the life of his day, Yeats sought to escape into an ideal "fairy land" where he could live calmly as a hermit and enjoy the beauty of nature. In his opinion, the best remedy for the emptiness of his age seemed to lie in a return to the simplicity of the past. The poem is closely-woven, easy, subtle and musical.

I will arise and go now,[2] and go to Innisfree,[3]
And a small cabin build there, of clay and wattles[4] made:
Nine bean-rows will I have there, a hive for the honey-bee,
And live alone in the bee-loud glade[5].

And I shall have some peace there, for peace comes dropping slow,[6]
Dropping from the veils of the morning to where the cricket sings[7];
There midnight's all a glimmer, and noon a purple glow,
And evening full of the linnet's wings[8].

I will arise and go now, for always night and day
I hear lake water lapping with low sounds by the shore[9];
While I stand on the roadway[10], or on the pavements grey,
I hear it in the deep heart's core[11].

1890, 1892

Notes

1. The poem consists of three quatrains of iambic pentameter rhyming abab.

2. I will arise and go now: Cf. Luke 15: 18 in New Testament: "I will get up and go to my father."
3. Innisfree: an inlet in the lake in Irish legends. Here it refers to a place for hermitage. In his autobiography Yeats writes: "I had still the ambition, formed in Sligo in my teens, of living in imitation of Thoreau on Innisfree... and when walking through Fleet Street [in London] very homesick I heard a little tinkle of water and saw a fountain in a shop-window which balanced a little ball upon its jet, and began to remember lake water. From the sudden remembrance came my poem *Innisfree*, my first lyric with anything in its rhythm of my own music."
4. wattles: a construction of poles interwined with twigs or branches.
5. the bee-loud glade: an open place in the wood where bees buzz loudly.
6. peace comes dropping slow: peace comes slowly like the dropping of water.
7. where the cricket sings: here the cricket's singing is to intensify the quietness of Innisfree. Cf. Keats' "On the Grasshopper and Cricket": "On a lone winter evening, when the frost/Has wrought a silence, from the stove there shrills / The cricket's song."
8. full of the linnet's wings: referring to the fact that lots of linnets fly here and there.
9. lapping... by the shore: flowing against the shore.
10. the roadway: the symbol of city, so as the pavement in the same line.
11. in the deep heart's core: at the bottom of my heart.

For Study and Discussion

1. What is the poet's attitude toward life in this poem?
2. What does Innisfree symbolize in the poem?
3. This poem is famous for its vivid images. Discuss the imagery used in this poem.
4. Interpret the contrast in this poem.
5. Find similar poems in Chinese poetry and make a comparative study of them.

参考译文

茵尼斯弗利岛

我要起身，现在就走，去茵尼斯弗利岛，
用泥土和枝条建造一个小屋，
种上九架芸豆，为蜜蜂建一蜂巢，
在蜜蜂高唱的林间幽居独处。

在那儿我会有安宁，安宁慢慢来到，
从晨曦的面纱降落到蟋蟀歌唱的地方；
那里午夜一片闪光，中午有紫霞燃烧，
暮色中也到处飞舞着红雀鸟的翅膀。

我要起身，现在就走，因为我日夜都听到
湖水轻声地拍打着湖滨；
不管站在路上，还是在灰色的人行道，
在心灵深处我总听到水拍湖滨的声音。

（李正栓　译）

28. Wystan Hugh Auden

Wystan Hugh Auden（威斯坦·休·奥登，1907—1973）was born in a middle-class family in York and educated at Gresham's School, Holt, and Christ Church, Oxford. His first poems were published in 1928, and early in his career he became a friend of T. S. Eliot, whose ideas on poetry influenced his work. He was also a friend and colleague of Stephen Spender (1909—1995), Louis MacNeice (1907—1963), and C. Day Lewis (1904—1972), who shared with Auden an interest in politics and who saw them bringing new techniques and attitudes to the United States. They were called the "Auden Group", with Auden as the leader. He became an American citizen in 1946 and made his living teaching and writing poetry. In 1956, once again back in England, he was elected Professor of Poetry at Oxford University, a post he held until 1961.

Auden's early poems were concerned with revealing the ills of his native country and were intended to shock their readers. He often combined deliberate irreverence with verbal craftsmanship to awaken what he saw as the complacent middle class to the hollowness of their society and the need for reform. It was his impatience with the limits imposed by English society that prompted Auden to move to the United States. To some extent, Auden must have felt that Europe was slowly dying and that his residence in a young nation would bring with it new life. Like Eliot, Auden later in his life returned to the formal practice of Christianity, having grown disenchanted with the socialism he had professed in his youth. His later poetry, though often as satirical as the early poems had been, became increasingly concerned with religious themes.

Auden wrote three ambitious long poems: *For the Time Being* (1944), a Christmas oratorio in which he explores the modern significance of the Nativity; *The Sea and the Mirror*, written and published in the mid-forties, a discourse in poetic form on the relationship between life and art, which takes the form of a commentary on Shakespeare's *The Tempest* (1611); and *The Age of Anxiety* (1947), a work that presents four individuals attempting to find a way out of their spiritual dilemmas. Toward the end of his life, Auden's poetry tended to become mellower, reflecting a spirit that was less urgent in its denunciation of evil. His poetry never lost its moral quality, however, nor did it abandon its concern with the troubles of the modern world.

Auden's poetry has been praised for its vitality, variety, and originality. He imposes new and unexpected patterns on a wide range of forms—from archaic ballads to street-corner blues. Perhaps Auden's most important contribution to the 20th century poetry is his experimentation in many verse forms and meters, combining an off-hand informality with remarkable technical skill.

Musee des Beaux Arts[1]

This poem was written in 1939 when Auden visited the Museum of Fine Arts in Brussels, and saw *Icarus* by the Flemish painter Pieter Brueghel (1525—

1569). It is basically about the painting *Icarus*, but the theme is human suffering and human being's indifference to others' tragic fates in the world. The irregularity of the lengths and rhymes reinforces the depressing atmosphere that the poem displays.

About suffering they were never wrong,
The Old Masters[2]: how well they understood
Its human position; how it takes place
While someone else is eating or opening a window or just walking dully along;
How, when the aged are reverently, passionately[3] waiting
For the miraculous birth[4], there always must be
Children who did not specially want it to happen, skating
On a pond at the edge of the wood:
They[5] never forgot
That even the dreadful martyrdom[6] must run its course[7]
Anyhow in a corner, some untidy spot
Where the dogs go on with their doggy life and the torturer's[8] horse
Scratches its innocent behind on a tree.[9]

In Brueghel's *Icarus*[10], for instance: how everything turns away
Quite leisurely from the disaster; the ploughman may
Have heard the splash, the forsaken cry,
But for him it was not an important failure; the sun shone
As it had to on the white legs disappearing into the green
Water; and the expensive delicate ship that must have seen
Something amazing, a boy falling out of the sky,
Had somewhere to get to and sailed calmly on.

Dec. 1938 1940

Notes

1. It is written in two stanzas with no regular lengths and rhymes. Musee des Beaux Arts: (French) Museum of Fine Arts.
2. Old Masters: classical painters in general sense.

3. reverently, passionately: piously, enthusiastically.
4. miraculous birth: referring to the birth of Jesus.
5. They: the Old Masters.
6. the dreadful martyrdom: referring to the martyrdom of Jesus.
7. run its course: finish its running.
8. torturer: the murderer, the slaughter.
9. Scratches its innocent behind on a tree: suggesting people's indifference. Behind: buttocks, hips.
10. *Icarus*: Icarus was the son of Daedalus, the cunning craftsman of ancient legend. They flew on artificial wings fastened to their shoulders with wax, but Icarus ventured too near the sun, which melted the wax, and so he fell and perished. In one corner of Brueghel's painting, Icarus' legs are seen disappearing into the sea, his wings having melted.

诗歌赏析

奥登是英国 20 世纪的一位重要诗人。他与另外三位牛津诗人路易斯、麦克尼斯和司班德一起被称为艾略特之后的“奥登一代”。他们在政治上有“左”倾思想，反对法西斯和弗郎哥；题材上是城市性或工业性的；在诗法上受艾略特的影响，具有鲜明的现代风格。奥登在 1939 年参观布鲁塞尔的皇家美术馆时，看到一幅 16 世纪画家勃鲁盖尔的名画《伊卡洛斯的坠落》，有感而发，写成此诗。他以诗咏画，描写了人类对他人的苦难和死亡视若无睹的漠然态度。

诗人在一开头就指出以勃鲁盖尔为代表的古典画家洞悉苦难在人类生活当中的位置，并接连列举了三个重大事件以及人们的反应。苦难发生时，有人在吃饭，有人在开窗，有人在无聊地走动；婴儿奇迹般诞生时，老人们虔诚、热切地期待，孩子们并不希望它发生，依然在林边池塘上溜冰；可怕的殉难发生时，“某个角落里，一块不干净的去处，/ 狗照样过着狗的生活，刽子手的马 / 在树上来回蹭着它那无辜的屁股。”诗人将可怕的殉难与狗儿的生活以及马蹭屁股并置在一起，产生强烈的反讽。不同的人或动物对这些重大事件的态度形成互文，即人们对这些特殊事件持冷漠的态度。

第二节诗人以勃鲁盖尔的名画《伊卡洛斯的坠落》为例，说明人类的冷漠由来已久。伊卡洛斯是希腊神话中的艺术家代达罗斯的儿子。他和父亲想用蜡粘起来的翅膀飞回家乡，但在飞的过程中，伊卡洛斯忘乎所以，不顾父亲的劝告，离太阳太近，翅膀上的蜡融化后坠海而死。在勃鲁盖尔这幅名画上，远处是海天相接，一片寂静，几艘船在海面上漂荡；近处，耕夫赶着牛车刚从田里归来，牧羊人放牧着群羊从此路过，一派忙忙碌碌的生活景象。太阳依旧光芒四射，而画面的一角，伊卡洛斯的一双腿正从海面上消失。婴儿奇迹般地诞生和可怕的殉难显然指的是耶稣的降临和殉难。诗人试图揭示，从古希腊开始，到基督教文明，人类对悲剧的冷漠从未改变。

形式表达内容也是这首诗的特点。这首诗由两节构成，诗行长短和节奏毫无规律，就像琐碎的日常生活一样。有的诗行拖沓、冗长（如第 4、12 行），凸显特殊事件发生时，人们的生活一如既往；描写老年人时，诗人连续使用多音节词（第 5 行的 reverently，passionately），与老人缓慢、迟滞的节奏契合。另外，诗人用口语化的形式、幽默的嘲讽探讨严肃的人生话题，进一步加深了全诗的主旨。

For Study and Discussion

1. What's the relationship between the painting *Icarus* and the theme of the poem?
2. Can you find the hints of Christianity in this poem?
3. The poem juxtaposes ordinary events and extraordinary ones. What does the poet want to show by this juxtaposition?

参考译文

美术馆

说到苦难，他们从未看错，
古代那些大师：他们深切体认
苦难在人世的地位；当苦难降临，
别人总是在进食或开窗或仅仅默然走过；
当长者正虔诚地、热烈地等，
等奇迹降临，总有孩子们
不特别期待它发生，正巧
在林边的池塘上溜冰：
大师们从不忘记
即使可怖的殉道也必须在一隅
独自进行，在杂乱的一隅

一任狗照常过狗的日子，酷吏的马匹
向一棵树干摩擦无辜的后臀。

例如布鲁果的《伊卡瑞斯》，众人
都悠然不顾那劫难，那农夫可能
听见了水波溅洒，呼救无望，
但是不当它是惨重的牺牲；阳光灿照，
不会不照见白净的双腿没入碧湛
的海波；那豪华优雅的海舟必然看见
一幕奇景，一童子自天而降，
却有路要赶，仍安详地向前航行。

（余光中　译）

29. Dylan Thomas

World War Ⅱ produced a series of poets like Dylan Thomas whose response to the catastrophe was emotionally intense and often highly rhetorical. This group of poets is sometimes referred to as the "New Apocalypse". Dylan Thomas（迪伦·托马斯，1914－1953）was a Welsh poet, short-story writer, and playwright, renowned for the unique brilliance of his verbal imagery and for his celebration of natural beauty.

He was born in Swansea, Wales. After grammar school he went to London where, in 1934, his first book of poetry, *Eighteen Poems*, was published. At this early age, he revealed unusual power in the use of poetic diction and imagery. The volume won him immediate critical acclaim. Thematically, these poems and virtually all that followed seem obscure because they contain elements of surrealism and personal fantasy. But the freshness and vitality of Thomas' language draw the reader into the poems and reveal the universality of the experiences with which they are concerned. This introspective tendency is less apparent in *Deaths and Entrances* (1946) and *In Country Sleep* (1951), which are generally regarded as containing his finest writing.

Thomas' other works include *Twenty-five Poems* (1936) and *The Map of Love* (1939), containing both poetry and prose. *A Portrait of the Artist as a Young Dog* (1940) is a group of autobiographical sketches, and *Adventures in the Skin Trade* (published posthumously, 1954) contains an unfinished novel and other prose pieces. During World War Ⅱ (1939—1945) Thomas wrote scripts for documentary motion pictures.

After the war Thomas was a literary commentator for BBC radio. *Under Milk Wood* (published posthumously, 1954), a play for voices, was originally written for radiobroadcast. When Thomas read it for its first public performance in Cambridge, Massachusetts, in 1953, it was still unfinished. The work became his most famous piece. It evokes the lives of the inhabitants of Llareggub, a small, Welsh seaside town. Noted for his readings of his own verse, Thomas became legendary in the United States, where he gave many lecture tours and gained a wide following. Nevertheless, his last years were shadowed by an increasingly tragic view of his own tempestuous life. His death in New York City on November 9, 1953, was brought on by alcoholism.

Do Not Go Gentle into That Good Night[1]

Written in 1951, this poem was one of Thomas' most popular poems. By listing four kinds of people's ways of leaving, the poet asks his father not to accept death passively, but to be brave and struggle for life. The subject of death is displayed in different ways as in "night", "close of day", "dying of the light", "dark", etc.

Do not go gentle into that good night[2],
Old age should burn and rave[3] at close of day[4];
Rage, rage against the dying of the light[5].

Though wise men[6] at their end know dark is right,
Because their words had forked no lightning[7] they
Do not go gentle into that good night.

Good men, the last wave by, crying how bright
Their frail deeds might have danced in a green bay,
Rage, rage against the dying of the light.

Wild men who caught and sang the sun in flight,
And learn, too late, they grieved it on its way,
Do not go gentle into that good night.

Grave men,[8] near death, who see with blinding sight[9]
Blind eyes could blaze like meteors[10] and be gay,
Rage, rage against the dying of the light.

And you, my father, there on the sad height,
Curse, bless, me now with your fierce tears, I pray.
Do not go gentle into that good night.
Rage, rage against the dying of the light.

1951 1952

Notes

1. It is written in an intricate poetic form, villanelle, of five 3-line stanzas rhyming aba plus a final quatrain rhyming abaa. Villanelle is a traditional 19-line form first in Italy, then popular in France in the late 16th century.
2. that good night: referring to death.
3. rave: to speak wildly.
4. at close of day: before dying. The following phrases "at their end", "the last wave by" and "on the sad height" all refer to this.
5. light: symbol of life.
6. wise men: scholars or philosophers.
7. forked no lightning: produced no forklike lightning.
8. Grave men: a pun, referring to both the serious men and the men approaching death.

9. blinding sight: an oxymoron; a dying person is doomed to have a weakening sight but may have great insight that can penetrate the nature of life.
10. meteors: shooting stars.

诗歌赏析

迪伦·托马斯生于威尔士海港斯温西，父亲是中学校长。托马斯在中学时代就开始写诗，20 岁离家去伦敦，专门从事写作。托马斯诗歌的主题是探索人生经历中的重大问题：出生、死亡、爱情、童年的天真、老年的坚韧等，他不做抽象评论，而是具体形象地写出感受。托马斯不是一个宗教主义诗人，但他的诗作却带着明显的宗教色彩。他常常赋予自然现象以宗教意义。他的作品联想丰富，形象奇特，比喻生动，感情炽热，特别讲究音韵效果。

本诗是托马斯在 1945 年他父亲得了不治之症，即将去世时写的，于 6 年后发表。诗中表达了死亡的必然性，同时也对死亡发出了强烈抗议，希望他的父亲不要无声无息地与他永诀。本诗采用了一种不常见的田园诗形式：十九行二韵体。第一节的一、三两行在全诗中不断重复，是全诗力量的集中表现，也是主题之所在。

“那美好的夜晚”是死亡的象征。死亡像夜晚一样，带给人宁静、安宁，但是死亡也和夜晚一样，神秘、幽暗、不可预知。诗人在第一节中就直奔主题，呼吁他的父亲不要被动地接受死亡，要勇于和死亡抗争。从第二节开始，诗人历数了四种人反抗死亡的例子及原因。最后一节，直接跟父亲对话，并再次重复贯穿全诗的两个叠句，让父亲不要被动地接受死亡，要勇敢地与死神对抗。诗人希望父亲诅咒他，因为他也无力与死神对抗；祝福他，因为他祈愿父亲与死神勇敢抗争。最后一节重复第一节的一、三行：“不要驯顺地走进那个良夜。愤怒，愤怒的抗拒阳光的泯灭。”首尾呼应，展示了作为儿子的拳拳之心。全诗温柔的哀伤与说服和疾风骤雨般的反抗情绪糅合在一起，动人心弦。

For Study and Discussion

1. What's the poet's attitude towards his father and death?
2. What's the function of the refrain in this poem?
3. What's the tone of this poem? Find examples to show this tone.
4. Interpret the line “Blind eyes could blaze like meterors”.

参考译文

不要温顺地走进那个美好的夜里

不要温顺地走进那个美好的夜里，
老年人应该在日暮时燃烧和咆哮；
愤怒、愤怒地抗拒光明的离去。

明智的人临终时懂得黑暗是正理，
因为语言已经无法划出闪电，
也不温顺地走进那美好的夜里。

善良的人，当最后一波卷过，哭泣
他们苍白的业绩本可以灿烂地在海湾舞蹈
愤怒、愤怒地抗拒光明的离去。

狂野的人抓住并歌咏过飞奔的太阳，
现在徒知，他们曾使它一路悲怆，
也不温顺地走进那个美好的夜里。

严肃的人，濒临死亡，用炫目的视觉
看到盲眼可以灿若流星，欢快、闪耀，
愤怒、愤怒地抗拒光明的离去。

而您，我的父亲，在那悲伤的顶点，
用您奔涌的热泪诅咒、祝福我吧，我祈祷。
不要温顺地走进那个美好的夜里。
愤怒、愤怒地抗拒光明的离去。

（申玉革　译）

30. Philip Larkin

In contrast to Dylan Thomas' group is "The Movement" — a group of poets educated at Oxford University including Kingsley Amis (1922—1995), Donald Davie (1922—1995) and Thom Gunn (1929—2004), who are strongly influenced by W. H. Auden. They are concerned with creating a less intense and

colloquial experience and the changes in everyday English life. Philip Larkin (菲利普·拉金, 1922—1985) was one of the best poets of this group.

Larkin was born in Coventry, educated at its King Henry VIII School and at St. John's College, Oxford. For many years he was a librarian of the Hull University Library. He wrote the poems of his first book, *The North Ship* (1945), under Yeats' strong enchantment. Larkin found his own voice distinct in *The Less Deceived* (1955), influenced by Hardy. Like Hardy, he wrote novels, *Jill* (1946), and *A Girl in Winter* (1947), and his poems have a novelist's sense of place and skill in the handling of direct speech. His other poems mainly appeared in *New Lines* (1956) and *The Whitsun Weddings* (1964).

No other poet presents the welfare-state world of post-imperial Britain so vividly, so unsparingly, and in the last analysis so tenderly. Much has been written of Larkin's Hardyesque pessimism, his depiction of loneliness, age and death. However, the many negatives in his poems imply positives, out of reach of the ironic and self-deprecating speaker, but available perhaps to others more fortunate, elsewhere. His output was small, but his four volumes of poetry and his controversial anthology *The Oxford book of Twentieth Century English Verse* (1973) testify to the continuing vitality of a native English tradition, the tradition of Chaucer, Wordsworth and Hardy, distinct from (and, in Larkin's view, oppose to) the imported modernist tradition of Eliot and Pound.

The Whitsun Weddings[1]

This is one of the best known poems by Philip Larkin, published in the 1964 collection of the same name. Larkin describes a stopping-train journey through East Yorkshire from Paragon Station, Kingston upon Hull (where Larkin was a librarian at the university) to Kings Cross, London on a hot Whitsun Saturday afternoon in the late 1950s. At each stop, Larkin becomes aware the train is being joined by parties of newly-weds.

That Whitsun, I was late getting away:
Not till about
One-twenty on the sunlit Saturday
Did my three-quarters-empty train pull out[2],
All windows down, all cushions hot, all sense
Of being in a hurry gone. We ran
Behind the backs of houses, crossed a street
Of blinding windscreens, smelt the fish-dock; thence
The river's level drifting breadth began,
Where sky and Lincolnshire and water meet.

All afternoon, through the tall[3] heat that slept
For miles inland,
A slow and stopping curve southwards we kept.
Wide farms went by, short-shadowed[4] cattle, and
Canals with floatings of industrial froth;
A hothouse flashed uniquely[5]: hedges dipped[6]
And rose: and now and then a smell of grass
Displaced the reek of buttoned carriage-cloth
Until the next town, new and nondescript[7],
Approached with acres of dismantled cars.

At first, I didn't notice what a noise
The weddings made
Each station that we stopped at: sun destroys
The interest of what's happening in the shade,
And down the long cool platforms whoops and skirls
I took for porters larking[8] with the mails,
And went on reading. Once we started, though,
We passed them, grinning and pomaded, girls
In parodies of fashion, heels and veils,
All posed[9] irresolutely, watching us go,

As if out on the end of an event
Waving goodbye
To something that survived it. Struck, I leant
More promptly out next time, more curiously,
And saw it all again in different terms:
The fathers with broad belts under their suits
And seamy foreheads; mothers loud and fat;
An uncle shouting smut; and then the perms[10],
The nylon gloves and jewellery-substitutes,
The lemons, mauves, and olive-ochres that

Marked off[11] the girls unreally[12] from the rest.
Yes, from cafés
And banquet-halls up yards, and bunting-dressed
Coach-party annexes, the wedding-days
Were coming to an end. All down the line
Fresh couples climbed aboard: the rest stood round;
The last confetti and advice were thrown,
And, as we moved, each face seemed to define
Just what it saw departing: children frowned
At something dull; fathers had never known

Success so huge and wholly farcical[13];
The women shared
The secret like a happy funeral[14];
While girls, gripping their handbags tighter, stared
At a religious wounding. Free[15] at last,
And loaded with the sum of all they saw,
We hurried towards London, shuffling gouts of steam.
Now fields were building-plots, and poplars cast
Long shadows[16] over major roads, and for
Some fifty minutes, that in time would seem

Just long enough to settle hats[17] and say
I nearly died,
A dozen marriages got under way.
They watched the landscape, sitting side by side
—An Odeon went past, a cooling tower,
And someone running up to bowl[18]—and none
Thought of the others they would never meet
Or how their lives would all contain this hour.
I thought of London spread out in the sun,
Its postal districts packed like squares of wheat:

There we were aimed. And as we raced across
Bright knots of rail
Past standing Pullmans[19], walls of blackened moss
Came close, and it was nearly done, this frail
Travelling coincidence; and what it held
stood ready to be loosed with all the power
That being changed can give. We slowed again,
And as the tightened brakes took hold, there swelled
A sense of falling, like an arrow-shower
Sent out of sight, somewhere becoming rain.

Notes

1. The poem is written in eight 10-line stanzas of iambic pentameter rhyming ababcdecde with the exception of the second line iambic dimeter. Whitsun (also Whitsunday, Whit Sunday or Whit) is the Christian festival of Pentecost in the UK, held on the 7th Sunday after Easter, which commemorates the descent of the Holy Spirit upon Christ's followers. In English tradition, Whitsun has long been a day of feasting and merrymaking.
2. pull out: depart.
3. tall: hard to believe.

4. short-shadowed: referring to the time in the early afternoon. Cf. "Long shadows" in Line 59.
5. uniquely: unusually.
6. dipped: lowered.
7. nondescript: lacking distinctive qualities.
8. larking: having a merry time.
9. posed: assumed a certain pose.
10. perms: permanent waves.
11. Marked off: distinguished.
12. unreally: imaginarily.
13. farcical: ridiculous.
14. a happy funeral: an oxymoron, it's a happy beginning of a new life, but it's also an end of the past life.
15. Free: referring to leaving the station.
16. Long shadows: implying the time in the late afternoon.
17. to settle hats: part of the western wedding ceremony meaning "to settle down".
18. running up to bowl: moving swiftly and smoothly.
19. Pullmans: Pullman car or coach.

诗歌赏析

拉金是第二次世界大战以后的优秀诗人，与牛津大学的同学金斯莱·艾米斯和约翰·韦恩一起被称为运动诗派诗人。他们结束了20世纪20年代开始于英国诗坛的现代主义的统治。《降灵节婚礼》是拉金的著名诗篇，讲述了他在某个圣灵降临节乘火车前往伦敦的一次旅行。这首诗由8个十行诗节组成，押abab cdecde韵，形式工整，层次分明。诗人用写实的手法描述了他所看到的铁路沿线的英国状况以及一个个婚礼场景。

在前两节中，诗人首先用一连串的数字交代了本诗的场景——某个降灵节下午一点二十，诗人坐着空了四分之三座位的火车开始了自己的旅程。接着诗人用三个all的重复和排比句式说明自己迫不及待、如释重负、终于离开的心情（第5、6行）。然后，诗人用一系列具体的意象描述了窗外的风景：田庄、牛群、运河、温室、围篱等。正当诗人沉湎于路边的自然风光时，车站上喧嚷的婚礼仪式引起了诗人的注意。

第 3 到 6 节描写了婚礼的细节及婚礼上各色人等的表现。姑娘们穿着时髦，叔伯言语粗俗，父亲们一本正经，母亲们大声嚷嚷，一派热热闹闹、喜庆的景象。然而，对于这么喜庆的婚礼，乘客们的反应却各不相同——孩子们觉得乏味，父亲们第一次意识到婚礼原来像是场闹剧，妇女们视之为欢乐的葬礼，姑娘们将之看成虔诚的伤害。随后，诗人的视线随着列车的运行，离开了站台和婚礼，转向目的地——伦敦。诗人的笔调也由联想转为现实。

在最后一节中，诗人把婚礼说成是“与这次脆弱的旅行碰巧相合的诱人事件”，并点明两者的共同特点——变化，从而揭示了本诗的主旨——变化的重要性。生活的力量来自变化。离开一个地方到另一个地方的旅程意味着变化。婚礼预示着变化——新郎、新娘要和过去的生活告别，迎接一种新生活。贯穿整首诗的旅程和旅程中看到的婚礼因为“变化”紧紧联系在一起。诗的末尾几行（第 77—80 行）被赋予了丰富的象征意义。列车刹车带来的不平衡感象征着变化给生活带来的动荡，雨水就是变化的结果，它能促使农作物生长，意味着新生。也许这就是圣灵降临节的意义所在。

另外，诗人还使用多重的形式和音韵手段加深主题，如用句子的长短不齐表示诗人在列车上看到了铁路沿线散乱的景象和零乱的生活片断；用连续的长音和双元音烘托“长长的凉爽的月台上发出的喊声和风笛声”（第 25 行）；用回旋不断的头韵和跨行、跨节现象表明诗人在呼啸而过的列车上看到的一个个变化着的婚礼场景等。

For Study and Discussion

1. Study the sound effect of this poem.
2. What's the poet's attitude toward these marriages? How do you find that?
3. How do you understand this phrase “all the power/That being changed can give”? What's the function of change in life as shown in this poem?
4. Some critics say there are some Christian hints in this poem, can you find them?

参考译文

降灵节婚礼

那个降灵节，我迟迟未走：
直到大概

一点二十分，那阳光明媚的周六
空着四分之三座位的火车才离开，
窗户全拉下，坐垫都烫人，一切存在感
刹那间消失。我们驰过
房屋背后，穿过满是耀眼的挡风
玻璃的街道，闻到鱼坞的气味；从那边
平缓流淌的河水开始变得宽阔，
天空、林肯郡与河水中那里汇拢。

整个下午，穿过内陆数英里
那沉睡的热流，
沿着一条滞缓的曲线向南行驶。
闪过了广阔的田庄，短影子的牛群，还有
运河，河上面工业的废渣浮起；
一个少有的温室闪过；围篱升沉
起伏；不时地有一阵青草的
气味取代了扣起的车厢帘布的臭气
直到下一座无法形容的新城，
迎面是数英亩拆卸的废汽车。

开头，我没注意在停留的每座车站上
那些婚礼仪式
发出怎样的喧嚣吵嚷。太阳
破坏了对树荫下发生的事情的兴致，
长长的凉爽的月台上发出的喊声和风笛声
我以为是搬运工吆呼着搬运邮件，
于是继续看书。不过我们一离站台，
就经过那些抹着发油的笑着的姑娘们
她们衣着时髦，高跟鞋、面纱俱全，
摆着不确定的姿势，望着我们走开，

仿佛是在一个事件结束时
挥手向后来
留存的东西告别。我被此吸引，下次
就更好奇地迅速斜身向着窗外，

从不同的角度再把这一切瞻视；
父亲们穿着外套，宽皮带系在腰间，
额头上布满皱纹；胖母亲们大声嚷嚷；
一个叔伯说着脏话；电烫的发式，
尼龙手套，仿制的珠宝璀璨，
柠檬，紫红，赭褐，色彩鲜亮

把姑娘们同其他人梦幻般地分隔。
是的，从数码外的咖啡厅
和宴会厅，以及一群群挂满彩旗的
车拉的活动房子来看，那婚日的喜庆
即将结束。沿着这一条铁路
新的伴侣们上车：其余的人站在周围；
抛出最后的五彩纸屑和忠告，
当我们开动时，每一张脸都似乎
在确定离去的是什么：孩子们皱着眉头
看着乏味的东西；父亲们从不知道

这样巨大的成功，又全然像闹剧；
妇女们分享这
犹如欢乐葬礼一般的秘密；
而姑娘们，更握紧手提包，瞪视着
一种虔诚的伤害。终于离开了站台，
载负着他们所看见的一切，
我们匆匆驶向伦敦，蒸汽在阵阵地喷吐。
这时的田野是建筑工地，白杨树投下来
长影子在大路上，大约
五十分钟光景，但时间却仿佛

很长，长得足以脱下礼帽，足以说
我几乎死去，
几十个婚礼仍在进行着。
他们看着美景，一对对并肩坐齐
——过去了一个音乐堂，一座高塔凉爽，
有人在迅速跑上去——谁也没有

去想那些他们将不再会遇见的人们
或他们的生活将怎样包含这一时光。
我想到伦敦铺展的阳光下头，
它紧凑的邮区，犹如麦田的方形：

那里是我们的目的地。我们疾驶过
节节闪亮的轨道
经过站立的普尔门车，布满黑青苔的
墙壁临近，与这次脆弱的旅行碰巧
相合的诱人事件快结束了；它已
准备好以"变化"能够给予的全部力量
释放出它所凝聚的一切。我们又减缓
速度，止住了紧扣的车闸，随后涌起
一种下落感，如同阵雨的箭矢那样
射到视程之外，在某地变成了雨水绵绵。

（胡家峦　译）

31. Ted Hughes

Ted Hughes（特德·休斯，1930－1998），poet，dramatist，critic，and short story writer，stands apart from the poets who came to maturity in the 1950s. He was born in Mytholmroyd，the son of a carpenter，and raised in Mexborough，a coal-mining town in Yorkshire. The harsh landscape of the northern England moors had a strong influence on Hughes' poetry. He was educated at Cambridge University. He has made his living mainly as a teacher and writer. He married the American poet Sylvia Plath in 1956，who committed suicide in London in 1963. In 1957 they moved to the US where Hughes taught English and creative writing at the University of Massachusetts，Amherst. They returned to England in 1959. He received all the major literary awards in Europe，but not the Nobel Prize. He also received the Order of Merit. Hughes died of cancer on

October 28, 1998.

His first volume *The Hawk in the Rain* (1957) made him famous. This was followed by *Lupercal* (1960), *Wodwo* (1967), and several other books of children's verse. These works proved him to be one of the most important postwar poets. In his early works Hughes questioned man's function in the universal scheme. Looking at the dark aspects of nature, he has stressed the ferocious and demonic rather than the idyllic and beautiful. Within the cruelty and violence of nature, Hughes looks for an understanding of human life and its mysterious bonds with nature. He has been named a "survivor-poet" by the critic A Alvarez because he parallels human beings with lower animals, creatures that will do anything to ensure survival. Hughes stated that poems, like animals, are each one "an assembly of living parts, moved by a single spirit."

He also produced *Crow* (1970), *Season Songs* (1976) and *Moortown* (1979) and other volumes of poetry. About his preference of poetic form, Hughes stated in *Poetry in the Making* (1970), that there is no ideal form of poetry or writing. He wrote free verse as well as highly structured forms and rhyme schemes. He gradually abandoned traditional forms and stated that the "very sound of metre calls up the ghosts of the past and it is difficult to sing one's own tune against the choir". Although he wrote for young adults a wide variety of finely illustrated poems, plays and prose, he did not soften his themes of life and death with sentimentality.

Hawk Roosting[1]

On the surface this poem describes the actions and inner thoughts of a roosting hawk. Acturally it exposes the arrogance, cruelty and tyranny of human beings, especially of the tyrants. The "falsifying dream" that the hawk rejects is the romantic view that animals are not malicious or cruel.

I sit in the top of the wood, my eyes closed.
Inaction, no falsifying dream[2]

Between my hooked head and hooked feet:
Or in sleep rehearse perfect kills and eat.

The convenience of the high trees!
The air's buoyancy and the sun's ray
Are of advantage to me;
And the earth's face upward for my inspection.

My feet are locked upon the rough bark.
It took the whole of Creation
To produce my foot, my each feather:
Now I hold Creation in my foot

Or fly up, and revolve it all slowly—
I kill where I please because it is all mine.
There is no sophistry[3] in my body:
My manners are tearing off heads—

The allotment of death.
For the one path of my flight is direct
Through the bones of the living.
No arguments assert my right:

The sun is behind me.
Nothing has changed since I began.
My eye has permitted no change.
I am going to keep things like this.

Notes

1. It is written in six quatrains of combined iambic and anapestic feet with no regular rhymes.

2. no falsifying dream: It is true; it is not a dream.
3. sophistry: plausible but fallacious argumentation.

诗歌赏析

休斯擅长描写掠夺性动物，有人因此称他为暴力诗人。《鹰》是休斯的动物诗中具有代表性的一首。本诗采用第一人称的手法表现鹰的内心独白，实际上却暗示出人类在第二次世界大战中互相屠杀的残忍本性。

第一节描写鹰的栖息状态。鹰栖息在高高的树枝上，闭目养神，一动不动，看似娴静安详，但内心却在演练“完美的搏杀和吞食”。静与动、外表与内心产生强烈的反差。第二节描写鹰高高在上、悠然自得的心情。他站在高高的树上，大地仰着脸任由他查看，大气的浮力和太阳的光线都为他所用。第三节中，鹰把自己的位置推到了极致。他把创造了自己的爪子和每根羽毛的造物主及其创造的一切攥在了爪中。万物都在他的掌控之中。第四节和第五节展示了鹰的残暴本性。他的行为就是分配死亡，他的权力无需论证。最后一节塑造了鹰专横跋扈的王者气质。他把太阳甩在身后，不允许世界改变。

这首诗生动刻画了鹰——自然中不可一世的王者形象。这种骄傲蛮横、藐视一切的态势活像一个不可一世的暴君。休斯用理智的笔调刻画了很多生动的动物形象，揭露出弱肉强食、残暴无情的自然法则。但是自然界的法则同样适用于人类世界。休斯参加过第二次世界大战，见证了战争的残酷和人性的异化，这首诗就是对现实的影射。

For Study and Discussion

1. To what kind of human being is the hawk compared?
2. What does the hawk reveal about its own nature? What is the motive for its cruelty?
3. The hawk is roosting; the scene is a peaceful one. How does this detail point out the contrast between the appearance and reality of nature?
4. What view of nature emerges in the poem? Why does what the poet suggests should be our attitude toward the natural world?
5. What's the relationship between the hawk in the poem and God, the Creator?

参考译文

栖息着的鹰

我坐在树的顶端，把眼睛闭上。
一动也不动，在我弯弯的脑袋
和弯弯的脚爪间没有弄虚作假的梦，
也不在睡眠中排演完美的捕杀或吃什么。

高高的树真够方便的！
空气的畅通，太阳的光芒
都对我有利；
地球的脸朝上，任我察看。

我的双脚钉在粗粝的树皮上。
真得用整个造化之力
才能生我这只脚、我的每根羽毛：
如今我的脚控制着天地

或者飞上去，慢悠悠地旋转它——
我高兴时就捕杀，因为一切都是我的。
我躯体里并无奥秘：
我的举止就是把别个的脑袋撕下来——

分配死亡。
因为我飞翔的一条路线是直接
穿过生物的骨骼。
我的权力无须论证：

太阳就在我背后。
我开始以来，什么也不曾改变。
我的眼睛不允许改变。
我打算让世界这样子下去。

（袁可嘉　译）

32. Seamus Heaney

Seamus Heaney（谢默斯·希尼，1939— ）was regarded by critics as the greatest Irish poet since Yeats. He was born on April 13, 1939 in Mossbawn, Northern Ireland. He was first educated at a local primary school and then at Queen's College (1957—1962) in Belfast where he took a position as a lecturer in English in 1963. In 1970—1971 he was a guest lecturer at the University of California, Berkeley. He moved from Belfast to the Irish Republic in 1972, ultimately settling in Dublin. In 1975 Heaney began teaching at Carysfort College in Dublin. In 1981 he gave up his post at Carysfort to become a visiting professor at Harvard. He held the chair of Professor of Poetry at Oxford from 1989 to 1994.

He had his first book *Eleven Poems* published in 1965 for The Queen's University Festival. In his early works, such as *Death of a Naturalist* (1966) and *Door into the Dark* (1969), Heaney is a lyrical nature poet, writing with limpid simplicity about the disappearing world of unspoiled rural Ireland. In 1972, he published *Wintering Out*. In 1979 he published *Field Work*, and in 1980 *Selected Poems* and *Preoccupations*, a collection of Prose. *Station Island* (1984), a sequence of poems, was followed by *The Haw Lantern* (1987), which contains a brilliant sonnet sequence memorializing his mother, and Heaney's latest collection, *Seeing Things* (1991), containing many poems for his father. Heaney also wrote three volumes of criticism. He is also a skillful translator. His works in this genre include the medieval Irish *Sweeney Astray* (1984), *Sophocles's Philoctetes* (tr. as *The Cure at Troy*, 1990) and *Antigone* (tr. as *The Burial at Thebes*, 2004), the highly acclaimed *Beowulf* (2000).

His work often deals with "the local"—that is, his surroundings and everything inclusive of them. Inevitably this means Ireland, and particularly Northern Ireland. Hints of sectarian violence, which began just as his writing career did, can be found in many of his poems, even works that on the surface appear to deal with something else. Despite his many travels, much of his work appears to be set in rural Derry, the county of his childhood. Like the troubles themselves, Heaney's work is deeply associated with the lessons of history, sometimes even prehistory. Many of his works concern his own family history and focus on characters in his own family. They can be read as elegies for those family members. He has acknowledged this trend.

In his life, he won many different kinds of awards. But the highest is that he was awarded the Nobel Prize in Literature in 1995. Extremely evocative yet clear and direct, balanced between the personal and the topical, Heaney's carefully crafted poetry has been praised for its powerful imagery, meaningful content, musical phrasing, and compelling rhythms. Today, he is undoubtedly the most popular poet writing in English today. His books sell by the tens of thousands, and hundreds of "Heaneyboppers" attend his readings.

Digging[1]

This poem is taken from *Death of a Natuaralist* (1966). It is the typical work Heaney associated with his family traditions: digging. He purposely contrasts their tool, the spade, with his, the pen. By this instrument he can raise their labour into art, in the process ennobling them.

Between my finger and my thumb
The squat[2] pen rests; snug[3] as a gun.

Under my window, a clean rasping[4] sound
When the spade sinks into gravelly[5] ground:
My father, digging. I look down

Till his straining rump[6] among the flowerbeds
Bends low, comes up twenty years away
Stooping in rhythm through potato drills[7]
Where he was digging.

The coarse boot nestled on the lug, the shaft

Against the inside knee was levered[8] firmly.
He rooted out tall tops[9], buried the bright edge[10] deep
To scatter new potatoes that we picked
Loving their cool hardness in our hands.

By God, the old man could handle a spade.
Just like his old man[11].

My grandfather cut more turf[12] in a day
Than any other man on Toner's[13] bog[14].
Once I carried him milk in a bottle
Corked sloppily[15] with paper. He straightened up
To drink it, then fell to[16] right away
Nicking and slicing neatly[17], heaving sods
Over his shoulder, going down and down
For the good turf. Digging.

The cold smell of potato mould[18], the squelch and slap
Of soggy[19] peat, the curt[20] cuts of an edge
Through living roots awaken in my head.
But I've no spade to follow men like them.

Between my finger and my thumb
The squat pen rests.
I'll dig with it.

1966

Notes

1. It is written in eight stanzas with irregular lengths and rhymes.
2. squat: crouch, sit on one's heels.
3. snug: warm.
4. rasping: irritable from scraping sound.
5. gravelly: full of gravel.

6. rump：(humorous) a person's buttocks.
7. drills：small furrows in which seeds are sown.
8. levered：raised，lifted.
9. tops：the upper surface of the soil.
10. edge：the edge of the spade.
11. his old man：i. e. my grandfather.
12. turf：slabs of peat that，when dried，are a common domestic fuel in Ireland.
13. Toner：a place name in Northern Ireland.
14. bog：wet land with acid，peaty soil.
15. Corked sloppily：stoppered loosely. cork：soft stopper of a bottle.
16. fell to：began to (work).
17. Nicking and slicing neatly：cutting short and dividing smartly.
18. mould：loose earth.
19. soggy：soaking.
20. curt：short.

诗歌赏析

在20世纪60年代崛起的北爱尔兰诗人中，希尼是最受人瞩目的一位。他的诗具有鲜明的地方色彩和民族背景，《挖掘》是希尼的成名作。在这首诗中，希尼描写了他在爱尔兰度过的难以忘怀的童年时光和对那片故土的热爱。他精确描写了父亲和祖父的辛勤劳作，表达了自己对他们的敬畏之情。《挖掘》一诗主要的力量来自对比和对抗：一方面是他的祖辈和父辈用铁铲对抗土地；一方面是他自己用笔来对抗占统治和主流地位的英国文学（或意识形态）。

在诗中，他通过“笔”和“铁铲”的鲜明类比，即诗人的祖父用“铁铲”挖掘泥炭，父亲挖掘白薯，诗人用“笔”挖掘爱尔兰的传统文化，揭示了三者之间的关系——从某种意义上来说，祖父和父亲的铁铲就是诗人手中的笔，祖父挖的泥炭和父亲挖的白薯就是爱尔兰的历史与文化。“挖掘”是这首诗的中心意象。希尼怀着农家子弟对故土和父老乡亲的无限眷恋之情，深沉而热情地赞颂挖泥炭的祖父和挖白薯的父亲。

欣赏这首诗还要注意它的时态变化。前三节先使用一般现在时，描写诗人看到父亲正在干活的场景，然后诗人用一般过去时对祖父和父亲的过去进行了回顾。后两节又回到一般现在时，写诗人自己的工作。最后一行用将来时结尾，强调作者的决心——他要接续先人的传统，用手中“那支粗壮的笔”去挖掘祖先留下的历史文化，去挖掘父辈的传统、他的血缘、他的根以及成年后的自我。

For Study and Discussion

1. How do you interpret the word “digging”?
2. How do you understand the comparison “snug as a gun”?
3. What's the relationship between his digging with a pen and his grandfather and father's digging with a spade?

参考译文

挖　掘

在我的手指和大拇指之间
一支结实的笔躺着；舒适得像把枪。

在我窗下，一个清晰粗粝的声响
当铁锹铲进了沙土地：
我的父亲在挖土。我望下去

看到花坛中他绷紧的臀部
弯下去，抬起来二十寒暑
在土豆畦里有节奏地屈伸
他在那里挖土。

劣质的靴子紧踩在铁锹上，长柄
贴在膝盖内侧坚实地撬动。
他把表面的厚土掀起，把发亮的铁锹插下去
翻起四散的新薯，我们捡在手中
爱着他们冰冷的坚硬。

说实话，这老头儿用铁锹的方式
就跟他的老头子一样。

我爷爷在托纳的沼泽地一天
挖出的泥炭比任何人都多。

我曾经给他送去一瓶牛奶
用纸松松地塞住瓶口。他直起腰
喝完，又马上开始
麻利地截短、切片，把泥片
扬过肩膀，挖呀挖
为找好泥炭。挖土。

白薯地的冷气，湿透的泥炭地的
嘎吱、啪嗒声，铁锹铲进新鲜白薯根
的短脆声响在我脑海中苏醒。
但我没有铁锹像他们那样去干。

在我的手指和大拇指之间
那支结实的笔躺着，
我要用它去挖掘。

（申玉革 译）

Part Three American Poetry

1. Anne Bradstreet

Anne Bradstreet（安妮·达德利·布拉德斯特里特，1612－1672）was the first noteworthy woman writer in the early period of the American literary history. She was born in Northampton, England in 1612 into a noble but very religious Puritanical family. She was well educated and married to Simon Bradstreet when she was sixteen. Two years later in 1630 the whole family migrated to the Massachusetts Bay Company and settled down there. Anne's father later became the governor of the colony, and her husband, the judge. But Anne remained a housewife. She kept writing poems while taking care of 8 children, and dealing with other household duties. Life for early settlers was harsh and hard. However, Anne managed to spare time for reading classical works and poetry writing, mainly on the theme of domestic life in the new world.

In 1647 Anne Bradstreet's brother-in-law, Rev. John Woodbridge, brought some of her poems to England and had them published in 1650 under the title of *The Tenth Muse Lately Sprung up in America*, without her knowledge. Most of them are merely imitative works based on the poetic conventions of the time. The collection was soon well received in Britain, and was also agreeable to the taste of the American readers. It has always been regarded as one of the earliest publications by a settler of the New World. Anne Bradstreet died on September 16, 1672 in North Andover, Massachusetts at the age of 60. Six years later in 1678, the second edition of her poetry was published in revised and expanded form in the New Continent, entitled *Several Poems Compiled with Great Variety of Wit and Learning, Full of Delight*.

Anne Bradstreet wrote in a traditional way to record the colonial experience, to express her appreciation of private life, and to meditate over the Puritan doctrines. She was imperfect; however, she won a position in literary history for her genuine inspiration and force of character, as well as for the rarity as the first woman poet of the country. Many of her poems are personal about domestic and religious themes. Her talent to capture the colonial experience in poetry established her place as one of America's most outstanding early writers.

To My Dear and Loving Husband[1]

This is a love poem, simple and rhythmical. The poet sings high praise of the true love between her husband and her, which she values more than anything else in the world. Their love is so firm that it could conquer time and go beyond life and death. Her husband's love is so passionate that she could find no way to repay. Thus she hopes God will reward his love in many ways and make it everlasting after their death. This poem was unique in subject matter and expression at that time.

If ever two were one, then surely we.[2]
If ever man were loved by wife, then thee;
If ever wife was happy in a man,
Compare with me, ye women, if you can.[3]
I prize thy love more than whole mines of gold
Or all the riches that the East[4] doth hold.
My love is such that rivers cannot quench,[5]
Nor ought[6] but love from thee, give recompense[7].
Thy love is such I can no way repay[8],
The heavens reward thee manifold[9], I pray.
Then while we live, in love let's so persevere
That when we live no more[10], we may live ever.

1678

Notes

1. This poem was written between 1641—1643 but was not published until

1678, when the second edition of *The Tenth Muse Lately Sprung up in America appeared in the* New *Continent*. It is written in one single 12-line stanza of heroic couplets, that is, rhymed pairs of iambic pentameter.

2. If ever two were one, then surely we: if ever two people were one, then they must be you and I.
3. If ever wife was happy in a man, /Compare with me, ye women, if you can: if ever there had been a wife who was as happy as in love with her husband, it were surely me. No women can be compared with me. ye: you.
4. the East: Asia, a place of numerous wealth in the eyes of the Europeans at that time.
5. My love is such that rivers cannot quench: here the poet's strong love for her husband is compared to a big fire that even the water of rivers cannot put it out. quench: put out, extinguish. Cf. Shakespeare's Sonnet 154: "Love's fire heats water, water cools not love."
6. ought: (archaic) anything.
7. recompense: compensation.
8. repay: reward.
9. manifold: a great deal, in many ways.
10. live no more: die. The last two lines mean let us persist in our love so much when we are alive that even we die, our love will be everlasting and we will live in our love forever.

诗歌赏析

作为美国殖民时期的第一位诗人，布拉德斯特里特的诗歌充满了时代特征，反映了拓荒时期美国人民的生活。她的诗深受英国诗歌的影响，格律工整，用细腻的笔触勾勒出对家庭、婚姻、爱情的看法。《致我亲爱的丈夫》是其中的代表作。

本诗开篇用首语重复的方法（Anaphora）接连使用了三个用“如果”引导的排比句形容了诗人深厚的夫妻感情。第一行诗把一对爱人比作一个人，形容两人水乳交融的亲密关系。17 世纪的玄学派诗人邓恩在他的《告别词：莫伤悲》也表达过同样的思想“我们俩的灵魂溶成了一片，尽管我走了，却不会破裂”。接着诗人把爱人比作世间唯一被妻子深爱的丈夫，把自己形容成与丈夫情深意笃的妻子，幸福无可比拟。

接着诗人分别使用比喻和新奇的意象来形容两人的爱情，将精神财富与物质财富进行对比。在诗人眼中，丈夫的爱比金矿还富有，比美国东部所有的财富还宝贵。殖民主义初期，广大的清教徒来到美国，靠掘金寻找自己的财富。而美国东部是他们在美洲大陆最初的落脚点。将爱情视为无价之宝是爱情诗中常用的比喻手法，但是女诗人使用了美国本土的意象，产生了新奇的效果。接着诗人用两个排比对两人的爱分别进行了描摹。自己的爱浓烈如火，所有河水都无法浇灭。世间万物无可比拟，只有丈夫的爱才能报偿。在清教时期的美国，对一个女诗人来说，这样的比喻无疑是大胆的。而丈夫对妻子爱之深，情之切是妻子无以为报的，只能祈求上天能给予回报。诗人将世俗的爱与神圣的爱联系在一起。

诗人在诗歌最后引入了清教徒来世的概念："只要我们活着，咱们就一爱到底，当我们辞世，我们也永远不分离。"在那些艰难的岁月里，两人爱情的坚守是一份强大的精神力量。诗人坚信坚贞的爱情拥有与时间抗衡的力量。最后一行用似非而是的手法，表达了肉体死亡而精神永生的基督教思想。生与死、爱情与永恒在这首诗中得到统一。

本诗由双偶句写成，即抑扬格五音步诗行，两两押韵。诗歌形式也很好地表达了合二为一的诗歌主题。

For Study and Discussion

1. Note that each of the first three lines begins with "If". What is the effect of this repetition? Does it undermine the certainty that other lines seem to express?
2. Whom is this poem addressed to? If just her husband, why does she address "ye women" here? Is she speaking to both? Or is this a private poem, probably not meant for publication?
3. Note that the word "Recompense" does not fit the rhyme scheme. What effect does this deviation have?
4. How do you understand the paradox in the last line "when we live no more, we may live ever"?

参考译文

致我亲爱的丈夫

如果有两人若一，那肯定是你和我。
如果有男人被妻子钟爱，那就是你；
如果有女人因男人而幸福，
女人们，你们跟我比。
我珍视你的爱情胜过整座整座的金矿，
胜过东方拥有的所有财富和宝藏。
我的爱是火，河水都不能把它扑灭。
也只有你的爱才能对它进行回报。
你的爱，我无论如何也难以报偿；
愿苍天成倍成倍地把你奖赏。
只要我们活着，咱们就一爱到底，
当我们辞世，我们也永远不分离。

（李正栓　译）

2. William Cullen Bryant

William Cullen Bryant（威廉·卡伦·布莱恩特，1794—1878）was born on a farm at Cummington, Massachusetts. Bryant was trained in Greek and Latin as a child and was taught a harsh Calvinism. Bryant began to write his first verses at the age of 7. When he was fourteen, he published his first verse, *The Embargo*（1808）. Bryant entered Williams College in 1810, but left a year later because of the financial problem. At 16, when his fellows were enjoying themselves in sports and games, Bryant was already a mature young man, meditating over the problems of life and death, which resulted in his greatest poem, "Thanatopsis" (Greek, meaning "view of death"), which was later published in the *North American Review* in 1817. In 1820, the year his father died, he became a justice of the peace in Berkshire County to support his family. The next year, he published his volume of poetry, *Poems*. Encouraged by the success of this book, Bryant moved to New York City to begin a new life, first as an editor of the *New York Review and Atheneum Magazine*, then a member of the New York *Evening Post*, where he worked for nearly fifty years. He traveled a lot in the United States and the Continent, and his travels were recorded in his *Letters of a Traveller* (1850). The 1876 publication of his collected *Poems* crowned his career. He died 2 years later in New York.

Bryant is famous as the first American lyric poet of distinction. He glorified the morning of the American national literature with several volumes of his brilliant poetry, which enriched the treasure house of American poetry and established himself as one of the noteworthy writers in literary history. He took American landscape as the source of his poetic inspiration and thus made American subjects worthy of celebration. Besides, Bryant contributed greatly to the development of American newspaper. He has also been remembered as the first American translator of Homer's *Iliad* and *Odyssey*.

Bryant was sometimes called "the American Wordsworth". However, his poetic works, especially "Thanatopsis," either by theme or by style, with an austere and carefully controlled melancholy, suggested a strong resemblance to the works of the "Graveyard School". In "Thanatopsis", Bryant developed a view of death which represents a sharp break from the Puritan attitude toward man's final destiny. His description of the American landscape and the close observation of natural objects are quite original.

Technically, Bryant's theme and subject were rather conventional. Most of his poems were written in blank verse. Nature was the chief theme of Bryant's poetry. Besides, religion, concern for humanitarian reforms and national morality were persistent themes. As a poet, Bryant wrote of his own experience in nature and society, opposed to the conventional insipid generalization about nature. The best of his poems provided an excellent example of truthful experience, precise expression and disciplined imagination.

When most of his contemporary poets, with the exception of Freneau, wrote after the fashion of the late 18th century English poets, Bryant's verse represented the most solid and refreshing work that had so far been produced by an indigenous American author. Here lies the significance of Bryant and his poetry.

To a Waterfowl[1]

This is a lyric of religious meditation. It records Bryant's experience of seeing a solitary water bird flying in the sky, at the close of a day of self-doubt and despair, and his sense of a divine power guiding and protecting everything in nature. The clarity of the central image and the simplicity of the moral analogy have always been admired, even by those who dislike "preaching" in poetry.

Whither[2], 'midst[3] falling dew,
While glow the heavens with the last steps of day,[4]
Far, through their rosy depths[5], dost thou pursue
Thy solitary way?

Vainly the fowler's eye
Might mark thy distant flight to do thee wrong,[6]
As, darkly painted on the crimson sky,
Thy figure floats along.

Seek'st thou[7] the plashy[8] brink
Of weedy lake, or marge of river wide[9],
Or where the rocking billows[10] rise and sink
On the chafed ocean side[11]?

There is a Power whose care
Teaches thy way along that pathless coast[12], —
The desert[13] and illimitable[14] air, —
Lone wandering, but not lost[15].

All day thy wings have fann'd[16]

At that far height, the cold thin atmosphere[17]:
Yet stoop[18] not, weary[19], to the welcome land,
Though the dark night is near.

And soon that toil shall end[20],
Soon shalt thou find a summer home, and rest,
And scream among thy fellows; reeds shall bend
Soon o'er thy sheltered nest.

Thou'rt gone,[21] the abyss of heaven
Hath swallowed up thy form[22]; yet, on my heart
Deeply hath sunk the lesson thou hast given,
And shall not soon depart.[23]

He[24], who, from zone to zone,
Guides through the boundless sky thy certain flight,
In the long way that I must tread alone,
Will lead my steps aright.[25]

1815 1821

Notes

1. This poem, called by Mathew Arnold "The most perfect brief poem in the language," was composed by Bryant after a walk from Cummington to Plainfield, Massachusetts, in December 1815. It was first published in the *North American Review* for March 18, 1818 and collected in *Poems* of 1821. It is written in eight quatrains with the first and fourth lines iambic trimeter, the second and third lines iambic pentameter. The rhyme scheme is abab. Waterfowl: bird that swims and lives near or on water, especially one of the types that are hunted for sport.
2. Whither: (archaic) to what place.
3. 'midst: amidst.
4. While glow the heavens with the last steps of day: while the heavens glow with the last steps of day. the heavens: the sky. with the last steps of day:

at the close of day.

5. their rosy depths: the far, distant reach of the rosy sky. their: the heavens'.
6. Vainly the fowler's eye/Might mark thy distant flight to do thee wrong: the hunter might see you fly in the distance but couldn't do you harm, because you are too far away to shoot. fowler's: hunter's. mark: see. to do thee wrong: to hurt or kill you.
7. Seek'st thou: do you seek?
8. plashy: marshy, swampy.
9. marge of river wide: edge of the wide river. marge: (archaic) edge, margin.
10. billows: large waves.
11. On the chafed ocean side: on the shore of the roaring ocean. chafed: irritated.
12. There is a Power whose care/Teaches thy way along that pathless coast: Somewhere in heaven there is a powerful hand (the God) that takes care of you and teaches you the direction of flight. It is the theme of the poem. Power: God. Teaches: guides, directs.
13. desert: barren, desolate.
14. illimitable: limitless.
15. Lone wandering, but not lost: (With the help of the God) though you are wandering all alone, you will not lose your way.
16. All day thy wings have fann'd: your wings have been fluttering for a whole day.
17. At that far height, the cold thin atmosphere: at that great height and in the very cold air.
18. stoop: descend rapidly from a high flight.
19. weary: though weary.
20. that toil shall end: the weary flying ought to come to an end.
21. Thou'rt gone: you are gone.
22. the abyss of heaven/Hath swallowed up thy form: your figure has disappeared in the boundless sky. abyss: the profound depth. form: figure.
23. And shall not soon depart: and (the lesson you taught me) will remain in my heart for a long time. depart: go away.

24. He: referring to God, same as "Power" in Line 13.
25. In the long way that I must tread alone, / Will lead my steps aright: in my lifetime, (God who guides the bird) will lead me to the right way as well. the long way: the life time of a person.

诗歌赏析

布莱恩特是美国19世纪的著名诗人。他的诗歌多记录自然的美景和诗人个人的生活随想，语言简单，富含哲理。《致水鸟》是其中的名篇。英国诗人、评论家马修·阿诺德认为，这首诗是"英语中最完美的短诗"。该诗音律和谐，结构严谨。全诗共八节，每节四行，其中第一行和第四行为抑扬格三音步，中间两行为抑扬格五音步，押 abab 韵。每节诗中间两个诗行长，第一和第四个诗行短，形似鸟的翅膀。整首诗可以分为三部分。第一部分由前两节组成，描写水鸟的飞行。第三至六节构成第二部分，描写诗人由水鸟引发的思考。最后两节为第三部分，诗人由水鸟联想到自身。

前两节诗描写了孤鸟在晚霞中飞翔的场景。落日、晚霞、孤鸟，与我国唐代诗人王勃《滕王阁序》中的名句"落霞与孤鹜齐飞"有异曲同工之妙。诗人不禁向水鸟发问：太阳即将走完一天的行程，而你的路途还很遥远，你迎着晚霞，孤独一身，究竟要往何处飞行？

第三节诗人猜想了水鸟的归处：湖畔、河滩或海滨，总之是有水的地方。这节诗承上启下，既回答了第一节中提出的"飞往何方"的问题，又为下一节诗中描述水鸟的明确目标作了铺垫。

第四、五节说明水鸟不倦的飞翔源自神意的指引。水鸟虽然只身孤飞，却有着明确的目标；它振翅远飞，不畏孤独，不惧路遥，因为它有神意的指引，决不会迷途。世俗与神圣联系在一起。

第六节中诗人想到水鸟的旅程即将结束。其中 soon 一词出现了三次，旨在强调水鸟很快就会苦尽甘来，找到休憩的家园，享受亲情和友谊。这既是诗人对于劳累的水鸟的抚慰，也是对人生旅途上长途跋涉的自己的勉励。

最后两节诗人从对水鸟的沉思引到自身。诗人认为自己也将会像水鸟那样，受到神意的指引，走上人生的正路，于是心中的迷茫、凄凉和困惑，便烟消云散，一扫而光。全诗暗示诗人获得了精神再生，反映了诗人的基督教信念。

For Study and Discussion

1. What power guides the waterfowl to its destination? How does it do so?
2. What does "the lesson" in Line 27 refer to?
3. Is this a mere poem of nature? Why or why not?
4. Choose one stanza that you like best and learn it by heart.

参考译文

致水鸟

露珠正在滴落，
白昼将退，天际遍洒柔辉，
天上玫瑰红一抹，
你要往何处孤独远飞？

猎鸟者也许已注意到
你振翅远飞却无法伤害你，
红霞满天，神秘轻罩，
看着你飘一般飞去。

你要寻觅杂草丛生
泥泞的湖滨、宽广河流的岸沿？
还是要寻觅波涛汹涌
海浪冲激的洋边？

有一种神力关心着你，
教你如何沿无路的海滨飞翔，
在沙漠和无以匹拟的长空里，——
你虽然独往却不迷失方向。

一整天，你拍翅飞翔，
忍受那高处寒冷稀薄的空气，
你已疲惫不堪，黑夜已临降，
可你却不肯屈栖欢迎你的大地。

这辛苦即将告一段落，

你很快会找到爱巢去歇息，
在同伴间欢鸣不已；你筑的巢窝
很快会让芦苇弯腰俯视。

你走啦。深邃的无际
已吞没了你的形象；但在我心里
已留下一个深深的教益，
它将永存我心底。

谁教你跨区飞翔，
指引你飞越无垠长空，
也会在我必须独自跋涉的征途上
指引我正确的航程。

（李正栓　译）

3. Henry Wadsworth Longfellow

Henry Wadsworth Longfellow（亨利·沃兹沃思·朗费罗，1807—1882）belongs to the "School-room Poets" or "New England Poets" or "Fireside Poets", which include Holmes, Lowell and Whittier. They began writing during the time of Emerson. Their visions, however, were neither strictly transcendental nor difficult and bleak. They did not form an organized group, but history has linked them for what they had in common. The "School-room Poets" were often concerned with ordinary American people and values. Their poems were inspiring and easy to read; they made the reading of poetry immensely popular. The name of "School-room Poets" or "Fireside Poets" suggests their honored place in American schools and homes during the 1800s. But they were likely conservative and imitative, all spokesmen for the culture of Europe. However, their contribution to the development of American poetry deserves appreciative recognition.

Longfellow was born into a well-to-do family on February 27, 1807 in Portland, Maine. He studied at Bowdoin College with fellow students

Nathaniel Hawthorne and Franklin Pierce, the 14th president of the United States (1853—1857). After his graduation in 1825, Longfellow spent three years in Europe studying the culture and languages of Italy, Spain, and Germany. In 1836, Longfellow became Smith professor of French and Spanish at Harvard, where he taught for 18 years and resigned in 1854. The next year he published his best-known narrative poem, "The Song of Hiawatha", the first American epic in blank verse that was based on American Indian legends. It proved to be an immediate success. Longfellow was the first American poet to write narrative poems.

His other major works include: *Voices of the Night* (1839), his first book of poetry, which contains "Hymn to the Night" and "A Psalm of Life"; *Ballads and Other Poems* (1841), containing such favorites as "The Village Blacksmith"; *Evangeline* (1847), a narrative poem of the former French colony of Acadia and *Christus: A Mystery* (1872), a trilogy dealing with Christianity from its beginnings. But in his later time, he turned to religious and reflective poetry, and to translation. From 1864 to 1867, most of his time was spent in the translating of *The Divine Comedy* by Dante (1265—1321). His last collection of poems appeared in 1882, the year of his death.

Longfellow was one of the most serious and most popular writers of his age. His poems were regarded as the summit of the literary work of the 19th century, which were influential to most of his contemporary writers. Actually he was so welcomed in England that 2 years after his death, his bust was placed in the Poet's Corner in Westminster Abbey and he was the first American poet to receive such an honor. But his reputation diminished soon after his death and was replaced by Whitman in the 20th century.

Longfellow's style and subjects were conventional, especially in comparison with those of Whitman or more modern writers. Usually he wrote about American subjects, but always in European styles. His poetry strongly embodied the optimistic sentiment and the love of a good lesson that characterized the didacticism. His great contribution to the exploitation of new forms, which was based on his extensive acquaintance with the major poetic techniques of the western world, achieved him fame as the master of the sonnet, reflective lyric and as one of the most versatile and sensitive craftsman among American literary figures.

A Psalm of Life[1]

This is one of Longfellow's most popular didactic poems, which stresses the value of human life. In the poem, the world is compared to the battlefield, and men, mere fighters. Since art is endless and time is limited, so as the human life, one should be brave to face any destiny and take actions. The idea is common, the words are simple, yet with parallelism and rhythmical language, the poet makes a stereotyped preaching both inspiring and powerful.

"Life that shall send
A challenge to its end,
And when it comes, say, 'Welcome, friend.[2]"

What the Heart of the Young Man Said to the Psalmist

I

Tell me not,[3] in mournful numbers[4],
Life is but an empty dream!
For the soul is dead that slumbers[5]
And things are not what they seem[6].

II

Life is real—Life is earnest[7]—
And the grave is not its goal:
Dust thou art, to dust returnest,[8]
Was not spoken of the soul.

III

Not enjoyment, and not sorrow,
Is our destin'd end or way[9];
But to *act*[10], that each to-morrow
Find us farther than to-day[11].

Ⅳ

Art is long, and time is fleeting,[12]
And our hearts, though stout and brave,
Still, like muffled drums, are beating
Funeral marches to the grave.[13]

Ⅴ

In the world's broad field of battle,
In the bivouac[14] of life,
Be not like dumb, driven cattle!
Be a hero in the strife!

Ⅵ

Trust no Future, howe'er[15] pleasant!
Let the dead Past bury its dead![16]
Act—act in the glorious Present!
Heart within, and God o'er head!

Ⅶ

Lives of great men all remind us
We can make *our* lives sublime,
And, departing[17], leave behind us
Footsteps[18] on the sands of time[19].

Ⅷ

Footsteps, that, perhaps another,
Sailing o'er[20] life's solemn main[21],
A forlorn[22] and shipwreck'd[23] brother,
Seeing, shall take heart[24] again.

Ⅸ

Let us then be up and doing[25],

With a heart for any fate;[26]
Still achieving, still pursuing,[27]
Learn to labor and to wait.[28]

1838, 1839

Notes

1. This poem was collected in *Voices of the Night* (1839). It is written in nine quatrains of alternately rhymed trochaic tetrameters. Psalm: a song or poem in praise of God.
2. These lines are adapted from "Wishes to His Supposed Mistress" by the English Metaphysical poet Richard Crashaw (1613—1649).
3. Tell me not: do not tell me.
4. mournful numbers: sorrowful words. numbers: poetic meters, rhythms.
5. the soul is dead that slumbers: the soul that slumbers is dead. slumbers: sleeps.
6. things are not what they seem: the truth of a matter may be quite different from what it appears to be.
7. earnest: serious.
8. Dust thou art, to dust returnest: dust you are, to dust (you shall) return. Cf. Genesis 3. 19: "You are dust, and to dust you shall return."
9. destin'd end or way: destined end or way, aim of life.
10. *act*: take action.
11. that each to-morrow/Find us farther than to-day: (so) that each tomorrow (we) find us go farther than today.
12. Art is long, and time is fleeting: Art is endless, but time flies quickly. It is adapted from *The Aphorisms of Hippocrates* by Hippocrates (460? B. C. —375? B. C.), a famous Greek physician.
13. And our hearts .../ Funeral marches to the grave: here the poet shows the idea that life is short and human is mortal. Cf. Thomas Gray's "Elegy Written in the Country Churchyard": "The boast of heraldry, the pomp of power, /And all that beauty, all that wealth e'er gave, /Awaits alike the inevitable hour. / The paths of glory lead but to the grave." muffled:

covered. Funeral marches: slow music for a funeral.

14. bivouac: soldiers' camp without a tent.

15. howe'er: however.

16. Let the dead Past bury its dead: don't depend on the glory of the past. the dead Past: the past that is dead. its dead: the person that died in the past.

17. departing: (when) departing, euphemism for death.

18. Footsteps: symbolizing the trace of human life.

19. the sands of time: Cf. Robert Burns' "A Red, Red Rose": "I will luve thee still, my dear, / While the sands o' life shall run."

20. o'er: over.

21. main: (poetic) sea.

22. forlorn: lonely.

23. shipwreck'd: shipwrecked.

24. take heart: cheer up.

25. be up and doing: be brave and active.

26. With a heart for any fate: with a heart ready to accept any fate.

27. Still achieving, still pursuing: always achieving (one's aims), always pursuing (one's new goals).

28. Learn to labor and to wait: learn to work hard and be patient to bide one's time. Cf. John Milton's "On His Blindness": "Thousands at his bidding speed/And post o'er land and ocean without rest: /They also serve who only stand and wait."

诗歌赏析

抒情短诗《生命礼赞》写于1838年，是朗费罗的第一部诗集《夜籁》中的一首名诗。据钱锺书先生考证，《生命礼赞》是英语诗歌中最早译成汉语的一首。这是一首抒发人生感受的浪漫主义抒情诗。全诗一气呵成，主题鲜明，感情强烈，为世人传诵。他在诗中抒发了对生活的热爱和憧憬，勉励人们在人生道路上要积极进取，不懈努力，等待机遇，争取成功。这首诗结构严谨，语言平易，韵律优美，深受读者青睐。

1. 韵律优美。全诗共九节，以四行诗的形式写成，韵脚为abab，即隔行押韵。其中韵脚又有变化，奇数行用阴韵(feminine rhyme)，偶数行用阳韵(masculine rhyme)。前者委婉平和，后者短促有力，二者的交叉运用使全诗充满了律动感，优美动听。诗的格律基本上是扬抑格四音步，即每个诗行按一重一轻为一组分四个音步。这种高昂的曲调，使全诗显得铿锵有力，具有强烈的艺术感染力。朗读这首诗，可以感受到诗人传递出的坚定自信的生活态度。

2. 结构严谨。《生命礼赞》是一首短小精悍、结构严谨的励志诗。虽篇幅短小，但内容丰富，条理清晰，层次感强。全篇分四个部分探讨了诗人眼里的人生。第一、二节回答了什么是人生。诗人告诉我们，人生不是梦幻一场，人生是真，不能虚度。第三至六节探讨了应该如何度过人生。诗人以积极入世的态度和铿锵有力的调子，歌颂了人生的价值，强调了一个行动的人生，这也是本篇的主旨。第七、八节强调了人生的价值和意义。只有实干的人生才能使你万世流芳。这也呼应了第二节中人死去的仅仅是肉体，而不是精神。灵魂会因为你人生的辉煌而不朽。最后一节是对全诗的总结和升华。诗人号召人们要行动起来，勇于面对一切挑战，要"学会苦干，还要学会等待"，以求人生最大的幸福和成功。

3. 语言平易。《生命礼赞》的副标题为"青年人的心对歌者说的话"，作者用口语体的形式，以通俗易懂的语言，反映了普通平凡的主题。这首诗简朴生动，乐观向上，受到国内外读者的赞扬。

这首诗之所以长盛不衰，还在于诗人对各种修辞手法的熟练运用。现举例分析如下：

1. 头韵和腹韵。如第 1 行："Tell me not, in mournful numbers"；第 3 行："For the soul is dead that slumbers"；第 4 行："And things are not what they seem"；第 6 行："And the grave is not its goal"；第 8 行："Was not spoken of the soul"；第 17 行："In the world's broad field of battle"，这些诗句中都使用了头韵。此外，诗歌中还有多处腹韵的例子，如第 15 行中的"muffled drums"；第 22 行："Let the dead past bury its dead"；第 25 行："Lives of great men all remind us"；第 26 行："We make our lives sublime"；第 32 行中的"take heart again."等诗人多次使用了腹韵，使诗行间不仅意义相连，声音也如余音绕梁，回旋不断。

2. 比喻。诗人在第 5 节中使用隐喻的手法，把世界比作战场，把人生比作临时的营站，劝人们要做英雄好汉，打好人生这场仗；同时告诫人们不要像任人驱使的哑畜，在人生的道路上漫无目的，这显然又是个明喻。同样的用法还有第 4 节中的明喻"我们的心……/依然像蒙住的鼓"以及第 7 节中时间的沙滩和第 8 节中人生的航行等暗喻。诗人以随手拈来的比喻将一首流于说教的诗歌装点得形象生动，妙趣横生。

3. 典故。如诗歌的第 7 行“Dust thou art, to dust returnest.”引自《旧约·创世记》第 3 章第 19 节:“For dust thou art, and into dust shalt thou be turned again.”这是上帝将亚当和夏娃逐出伊甸园时所说的话:“你本是尘土,必归于尘土。”意为“人生必死”。第 4 节中“我们的心……敲打着葬礼的鼓点走向坟墓”与博蒙特和弗莱切的《幽默的中尉》(1619 年)第 3 幕第 5 场中的“人生不过是走向坟墓的进行曲(Our lives are but our marches to the grave.)”如出一辙。而第 13 行“Art is long, and time is fleeting.”(学艺需日久,时光飞如箭。)出自古希腊希波克拉底的《格言集》第一章:“The life so short, the craft so long to learn.”(生命如此短促,学艺却如此久长)。这句格言诗同时也是一个精妙的对偶。诗人通过鲜明的对比,告诫人们人生苦短,须珍惜光阴,多干实事。

4. 排比。诗人在诗行中多次使用了简洁有力的排比,增强了气势和渲染力。如第 5 行:“life is real! Life is earnest!”;第 9 行:“not enjoyment, and not sorrow”;第 17 行与第 18 行:“In the world's broad field of battle, /In the bivouac of life.”;第 35 行:“Still achieving, still pursuing.”;最后一行:“Learn to labor and to wait.”合起来就是“人生即真,不能虚度!(人生)不是享乐,也不是忧伤;在世界辽阔的战场,在人生临时的营站,成就总是有但永处追求中,学会苦干还要学会等待。”这岂不正是诗人讴歌的时代精神写照和作者的立意所在吗?

这首诗语言浅显易懂,富有情韵,充满了乐观向上的精神。它与美国开拓时期的时代气息和民族精神相呼应,成为美国人民开拓精神在文学中留下的鲜明印记。朗费罗写《生命礼赞》时,社会上流行的是靡靡之音,这首诗是对颓废思想的反击,显示了年轻人奋发的精神和乐观的情绪,是一剂治疗精神萎靡的良药。诗中那催人奋发的精神、恰如其分的修辞、余音绕梁的韵律至今仍吸引着广大读者。

For Study and Discussion

1. What is the speaker's attitude towards life? Is he optimistic or pessimistic?
2. What is the purpose of life as shown in this poem?
3. What is the implication of “act” in the third stanza?
4. Appreciate the sound effect of the poem.
5. What figures of speech are used in this poem? Please give some examples.
6. Choose two stanzas that you like best and learn them by heart.

参考译文

生命礼赞

"生命挑战其目的，
这事发生时，就说：'朋友，欢迎。'"

这是那年轻人的心
对赞美诗作者说的话。

Ⅰ

不要用哀婉的诗句对我说：
人生只是梦幻一场！——
因为昏睡的灵魂不再有生活，
而事物也不是表面的模样。

Ⅱ

人生即真，不能虚度！
坟墓并非人生追求的目标；
你来自尘土，归于尘土，
这并非对灵魂的写照。

Ⅲ

我们命运的终点或道路，
不是享乐，也不是忧伤；
只是行动，并且每一个今天
发现我们比前一个今天都有进展。

Ⅳ

学艺须日久，时光飞如箭。
我们的心尽管坚强又勇敢，
依然像蒙住的鼓
敲打着葬礼的鼓点走向坟墓。

Ⅴ

在世界辽阔的战场，
在人生临时的营站，
不要像无言无语任人驱使的牛羊！

要在奋斗中作个英雄好汉！

Ⅵ

别指望未来，不管它多么光明！
让死的过去把死的事物埋葬！
行动吧，在活生生的现实中行动！
赤心胸中存，上帝在天堂！

Ⅶ

伟人的生平把我们提醒：
我们能使生命崇高无限，
即使辞世去也留身后美名，
在时间的沙滩上留下脚印串串。

Ⅷ

或许另有人会看到这脚印，
他在人生肃穆的航行中
偶遭不幸：船沉后只剩孤独一人，
见这脚印便又有希望重生。

Ⅸ

那么就让我们起来行动，
准备一个应对一切命运的胸怀，
成就总是有但永处追求中，
学会苦干还要学会等待。

（李正栓　译）

The Tide Rises, the Tide Falls[1]

This is one of Longfellow's popular lyrics. It not only describes the grandeur of sea and the happy life of habitants near the seas, but conveys the poet's deep thoughts of time and human life. It is about a traveler's journey to the seaside town in a day, which represents the human's life journey. The recurrence of sound, structure and line arrangement stress the idea of "The tide rises, the tide falls", that is, the perpetuity of nature, which is contrasted with the transience of life in the poem.

The tide rises, the tide falls,

The twilight[2] darkens, the curlew[3] calls;
Along the sea-sands damp[4] and brown
The traveller hastens[5] toward the town,
And the tide rises, the tide falls.

Darkness settles on roofs and walls,
But the sea, the sea in the darkness calls[6];
The little waves, with their soft, white hands,
Efface[7] the footprints[8] in the sands,
And the tide rises, the tide falls.

The morning breaks; the steeds[9] in their stalls
Stamp and neigh[10], as the hostler calls;
The day returns, but nevermore
Returns the traveller to the shore[11],
The tide rises, the tide falls.

Notes

1. This poem was written in 1879, published in 1880. It is written in three 5-line stanzas of iambic tetrameter with slight variations rhyming aabba.
2. twilight: dusk, nightfall.
3. curlew: a kind of brownish, long-legged shore birds with long, slender, down-curved bills.
4. damp: wet.
5. hastens: speeds up, hurries.
6. the sea in the darkness calls: the sea calls in the darkness.
7. Efface: wipe out.
8. the footprints: Cf. Longfellow's "A Psalm of Life": "And, departing, leave behind us/Footsteps on the sands of time."
9. steeds: (poetic) horses.
10. neigh: make loud sounds.
11. but nevermore/Returns the traveller to the shore: but the traveler nevermore returns to the shore.

For Study and Discussion

1. What is the implication of "The tide rises, the tide falls"?
2. What is the effect of the refrain?
3. What is the symbolic meaning of the footprints in the sands?
4. Why could not the traveler return to the shore?
5. What is the effect of the juxtaposition of "the tide" and "the traveler" in the poem?

参考译文

潮起潮又落

潮起潮又落，
黄昏渐黑，鹬鸟鸣叫；
沿着潮湿褐色的海滩
那旅人急匆匆往城镇赶，
潮起潮又落。

夜色往墙壁和房顶上降落，
但大海仍在黑暗中轰鸣；
微波用柔软白细的手
抹去沙滩上的脚印。
潮起潮又落。

东方已破晓，
厩里马儿踢又鸣，马夫在喊叫；
白昼复旧，那旅人却永远
不能回到海岸。
潮起潮又落。

（李正栓　译）

4. Edgar Allan Poe

Edgar Allan Poe（埃德加·爱伦·坡，1809—1849）was born on January 19，1809 in Boston，Massachusetts. He was the son of two wandering players. Poe was orphaned at the age of 2. He was then adopted by John Allan，a rich tobacco merchant in Richmond，Virginia. Poe attended the University of Virginia at seventeen，only to drop out a year later due to immense gambling debts. After a bitter quarrel between the father and son，Poe ran away from home in 1827 to Boston. He was sent to West Point in 1830，but was dismissed 8 months later for disobedience and failure in his duties. After that Poe took up residence in Baltimore and made a living by writing or editing some magazines or journals. In 1836，Poe married his cousin Virginia，who was only 13 at that time. Virginia's death in 1847，after 5 years of sickness，gave him a heavy blow，which drove him to heavy drinking occasionally. He died 2 years later，in mysterious circumstances，in October，1849.

Poe's poetry，which is very small in proportion to his total work，truthfully embodies his conviction that the function of poetry is not to educate or to summarize and interpret earthly experience，but to create a mood in which the soul soars toward supernal beauty. Some of his poems have a narrative basis，but it is often difficult for the readers to find in it a complete plot. The reasons for this lie in that Poe believes that "that intense and pure elevation of soul" should be "the poetic principle"，thus poetry must concern itself only with "supernal beauty"，not with the narration of the story，nor even with the beauty of particular things. Poe defines poetry as the rhythmical creation of beauty. He repeatedly explains that only in music can man come closest to attaining what he calls "supernal beauty". The lyrics such as "The Raven" and "Annabel Lee" best exemplify his poetic principles. His major poetic works include：*Poems*（1831），which contains both "To Helen" and "Israfel"，and *The Raven and Other Poems*（1845）.

Poe was the first American writer who formulized the technique of the short story, in pursuit of the totality of effect through compression, immediacy and finality. Poe also invented the genre of the detective story and developed a new fiction of psychological analysis. Poe has thus often been considered as the father of the modern short story. *Tales of the Grotesque and Arabesque*, a collection of stories, was published in 1839.

As a critic, Poe was the first responsible American literary critic who wrote critical essays in American magazines to say much of American writing then was terrible. Poe was right, but he was bitterly attacked by most of his contemporaries on account of his ingenuity. He wrote two important critical works: "The Philosophy of Composition" (1846) and "The Poetic Principle" (1850).

Edgar Allan Poe achieved so great a literary success during his lifetime that Tennyson considered him the greatest American genius. One century and a half after his death, he still stands among the most popular of American writers.

To Helen[1]

This poem is one of Poe's most famous lyrics. It depicts an ideal woman image—Helen, who is remote, untouchable, yet appealing. The beauty that Poe worships is a "supernal beauty", a heavenly and unearthly beauty that elevates the soul. This poem best exemplifies his poetic principle. Helen is a beautiful woman in Greek myth, whose beauty is classic and holy as shown in the poem. The archaic words, images of and allusion to the Greek myth all reinforce an ancient atmosphere of the poem. It may well convey Poe's admiration toward a Helen-like woman in his life. The musical beauty of the poem also serves its meaning.

Helen, thy beauty is to me
Like those Nicean[2] barks[3] of yore[4],
That gently, o'er a perfumed sea,
The weary, way-worn wanderer bore
To his own native shore[5].

On desperate seas long wont to roam[6],
Thy hyacinth hair[7], thy classic face,
Thy Naiad airs[8] have brought me home
To the glory that was Greece,
And the grandeur that was Rome.

Lo![9] in yon[10] brilliant[11] window-niche
How statue-like I see thee stand,
The agate lamp within thy hand!
Ah, Psyche[12], from the regions which
Are Holy-Land[13]!
1831, 1845

Notes

1. This poem was inspired by the beauty of Mrs. Jane Stith Stanard, the mother of a schoolmate of Poe, in Richmond, Virginia. She died when Poe was fifteen. Poe described the poem as "lines written, in my passionate boyhood, to the first, purely ideal love of my soul." It is written in three 5-line stanzas of iambic tetrameter with slight variations. The rhyme scheme of each stanza is ababb, ababa, and abbab respectively. Hellen: the beautiful daughter of Zeus in Greek Myth. Her abduction by Paris was the cause of the Trojan War and the source of *Iliad* of Homer.
2. Nicean: referring to the ancient city of Nicea (or Nicaea) in Turkey.
3. barks: (poetic) barques, sailships.
4. yore: (archaic) long ago.
5. That gently, o'er a perfumed sea, / The weary, way-worn wanderer bore/ To his own native shore: that gently bore the weary, way-worn wanderer o'er a perfumed sea to his own native shore. a perfumed sea: referring to Aegean sea. The weary, way-worn wanderer: the tired traveler on a long journey. It alludes to Odysseus, a prominent Greek leader in the Trojan War in Greek mythology and the hero in *Odyssey* by Homer, who ended the ten years' Trojan War and spent another ten years getting back home. bore: carried.

6. On desperate seas long wont to roam: long wont to roam on desperate seas. This phrase modifies "me" in Line 8. wont to: accustomed to. desperate seas: despairing seas. It is a transferred epithet, since it is the wanderers roaming on the seas who are desperate, not the seas.
7. hyacinth hair: curly hair. Cf. Poe's description of the Marchesa Aphrodite di Mentoni in his short story, "The Assignation": "Her hair, not as yet more than half loosened for the night from its ball-room array, clustered, amid a shower of diamonds, round and round her classical head, in curls like those of the young hyacinth." Hyacinth is a flowering plant, whose name, according to Greek mythology, came from Hyacinthus who was a beautiful boy, loved and killed by Apollo by mistake. When he died, Apollo made a flower, the hyacinth, from his spilled blood.
8. Naiad airs: nymph-like manners. Naiad: nymph in the water in Greek mythology.
9. Lo: look.
10. yon: (archaic) yonder, over there.
11. brilliant: delicate.
12. Psyche: goddess of the soul in Greek mythology, who was the lover of Cupid, and a woman so beautiful that the goddess Venus was jealous of her.
13. Holy-Land: the Kingdom of Israel, especially Jerusalem in a number of religions, including Judaism, Christianity, and Islam. Here it refers to Greece and Rome.

诗歌赏析

《致海伦》是爱伦·坡抒情诗的代表作之一。这首诗构思巧妙，音韵和谐，展示了爱伦·坡精湛的诗艺技巧。全诗仅三节，每节五行，描写了海伦——一个理想的美女形象。海伦是爱伦·坡诗歌中"超美"的象征。她的美卓尔不凡，她的美遥不可及，她的美神圣不可侵犯。诗人用古词、希腊神话中的人物形象——奥德修斯、雅辛托斯、海仙女和赛琪以及古老的押韵形式头韵等营造了这首诗古老、悠远的氛围。

第一节诗中，诗人将海伦比作一艘载着疲惫的旅人穿洋过海抵达家乡的纳尼亚古船，表达了海伦之美带给诗人的温暖与宁静。另外，诗人形容疲惫的旅人时，接连使用鲜明的头韵，恰如其分地表现了精疲力竭的流浪者所经历的漫长旅程的单调、乏味和其无奈、疲惫的精神状态。这个旅人形象无疑来自于希腊神话中的勇士奥德修斯。他结束了长达十年的特洛伊战争，又带领战士们花费十年时间才回到家乡。而这首诗的中心意象海伦，就是希腊神话中引起特洛伊战争的美女。这两个典故的使用非常经典，大大丰富了诗歌的内涵。

第二节诗塑造了海伦的古典美。在绝望的大海上长久流浪的旅人看到海伦风信子般的卷发、典雅的脸庞、海仙女的风姿，就像回到了家乡，回到了“古希腊的荣耀和古罗马的庄严”。风信子花的名字来自于希腊神话中阿波罗所钟爱的美少年雅辛托斯，后被阿波罗误杀。阿波罗为纪念他，使其血泊中长出了风信子花。如果说希腊神话中的美少年和海仙女两个隐喻突出了海伦的绰约风姿，典雅的脸庞和古希腊罗马的辉煌则直接塑造了海伦的古典美。

最后一节描写了海伦的神圣美。诗人首先把她比作壁龛里的佛像，手擎玛瑙神灯那不朽的标志。然后又把她比作希腊神话里的心灵女神赛琪，来自“天国的圣地”。Holy-Land 指耶路撒冷或巴勒斯坦一带基督教的圣地，此处用来形容海伦在诗人心中至高无上的地位。海伦的美亘古不变，是诗人灵魂的导引。

除了用意象、比喻和典故来形容海伦的美，这首诗还以其音乐美而著称。该诗格律工整，用传统的抑扬格四音步写成，三节诗的韵式分别为 ababb，ababa 和 abbab，规整又富有变化，诗行间头韵和腹韵此起彼伏。丰富的音韵手段促成了该诗超强的音乐性，并与海伦这一理想的美女形象达到了完美契合，实现了听觉和视觉的高度统一。这首诗堪称音乐与思想结合的典范。

For Study and Discussion

1. What is the implication of “Helen” in the poem?
2. Find the allusion used in the first stanza. What is its function?
3. Poe uses many figures of speech to reinforce his theme. Find examples of metaphor, simile, alliteration and assonance, etc. and explain how they reinforce the theme.
4. Can you perceive the “supernal beauty” in this poem?
5. What do you think is the striking feature of this poem?

参考译文

致海伦

海伦，对于我，你的美
正像古时纳尼亚帆船，
载着疲惫的旅人
悠悠漂过芳香的海域，
驶向他故乡的海岸。

在长久习于汹涌的海面，
你那卷发及典雅的脸，
你海仙女的风姿使我熟记
古希腊的荣耀、
古罗马的庄严。

瞧！我见你玉立亭亭，
在光彩的壁龛里，
如玉雕神女，
手里还握着玛瑙神灯！
呵，你是赛琪，来自天国的圣地。

（李正栓　译）

Annabel Lee[1]

This poem discusses the death of a beautiful woman, which is a popular subject matter in many of Poe's poems. It is written in memory of Poe's dead wife Virginia Clemm who died in 1847. This poem is also famous for its musical beauty. First, The repetition of long vowel [iː] reinforces the melancholy tone of the poem. Second, the frequent use of anapestic feet produces a slow and solemn cadence, which is suited to the occasion. The irregular lengths of lines go in harmony with the ups and downs of the sea waves and the poet's mental state.

It was many and many a year ago,

In a kingdom by the sea
That a maiden there lived whom you may know
By the name of ANNABEL LEE;
And this maiden she lived with no other thought
Than to love and be loved by me.

I was a child and *she* was a child,
In this kingdom by the sea;
But we loved with a love that was more than love—
I and my ANNABEL LEE—
With a love that the winged seraphs of heaven[2]
Coveted[3] her and me.

And this was the reason that, long ago,
In this kingdom by the sea,
A wind blew out of a cloud, chilling
My beautiful ANNABEL LEE;
So that her highborn kinsmen[4] came
And bore her away from me,
To shut her up in a sepulchre
In this kingdom by the sea.

The angels, not half so happy in heaven,
Went envying her and me—
Yes! —that was the reason (as all men know,
In this kingdom by the sea)
That the wind came out of the cloud by night,
Chilling and killing my ANNABEL LEE.

But our love it was[5] stronger by far than the love
Of those who were older than we—
Of many far wiser than we—
And neither the angels in heaven above,

Nor the demons down under the sea,
Can ever dissever[6] my soul from the soul
Of the beautiful ANNABEL LEE:

For the moon never beams, without bringing me dreams[7]
Of the beautiful ANNABEL LEE;
And the stars never rise, but I see the bright eyes[8]
Of the beautiful ANNABEL LEE:
And so, all the night tide[9], I lie down by the side
Of my darling—my darling—my life and my bride,
In her sepulchre there by the sea—
In her tomb by the sounding sea.

1849

Notes

1. This poem is written in six stanzas of six, seven or eight lines with combined iambic and anapestic meters. It was published in October, 1849 shortly after Poe's death.
2. the winged seraphs of heaven: angels of the highest rank in heaven which have three pairs of wings.
3. Coveted: envied.
4. highborn kinsmen: relatives of noble birth, here referring to the angels.
5. out love it was: our love was.
6. dissever: separate.
7. the moon never beams, without bringing me dreams: the double negation here reinforces his missing of ANNABEL LEE.
8. the stars never rise, but I see the bright eyes: every time the stars rise, I see the bright eyes (of Annabel Lee).
9. night tide: nighttime.

For Study and Discussion

1. What is the tone of the poem?
2. What contribute to the remote atmosphere of the poem?

3. This poem is famous for its sound effect. Find examples of devices used to produce the sound effect, such as alliteration, assonance and repetition.
4. Discuss the combination of sound and sense in this poem.

参考译文

安娜贝尔·李

很多很多年以前，
海边一个王国里，
君知住着一少女，
名叫安娜贝尔·李；
她在世上无杂念，
唯知与我相爱怜。

我们两人皆孩童，
住在海边王国里；
相爱程度比爱浓，
我和安娜贝尔·李；
天上六翼众天使，
垂涎我和我的李。

正是因为我们爱，
就在海边王国里，
云中吹出寒风来，
冻死我的漂亮妻；
于是高贵亲属来，
从我手中掠她去，
墓穴把她关起来，
就在海边王国里。

天上天使并不悦，
开始妒忌她和我——
的确此因人人解，
（就在海边这王国。）
寒风乘夜云端起，

冻杀我的安娜·李。

但是我们爱更浓，
胜比我们年长者——
胜比几许智多星——
天上众多神天使，
海里无数怪妖精，
妄想拆散灵与魂！
我们生死不分离！

因为月辉带我梦，
梦见漂亮安娜·李；
除非见她明亮眸，
否则星辰难升起；
所以长夜邀我睡，
伴我生命伴新娘，
就在海边墓穴内，
滔滔海边她墓内。

（李正栓　译）

The Raven[1]

This poem is Poe's most popular poem. It narrates a sad story of a young man, the speaker, who lost his love. It is famous for its musical beauty. The sound effect created by the rhymes, alliteration and assonance best expresses its content. The raven is the central image of the poem, which is popularly believed as a bird of ill omen. It helps build the supernatural atmosphere of the poem. And the only word "Nevermore" uttered by the raven repeatedly reinforces the melancholy tone of the poem.

Once upon a midnight dreary[2], while I pondered[3], weak and weary,
Over many a quaint and curious[4] volume of[5] forgotten lore[6],
While I nodded, nearly napping, suddenly there came a tapping,
As of some one gently rapping, rapping at my chamber door.
" 'Tis some visitor," I muttered[7], "tapping at my chamber door—

Only this, and nothing more."

Ah, distinctly I remember it was in the bleak December,
And each separate dying ember wrought its ghost upon the floor.[8]
Eagerly I wished the morrow[9]; —vainly I had tried to borrow
From my books surcease[10] of sorrow—sorrow for the lost Lenore[11]—
For the rare and radiant maiden[12] whom the angels name Lenore—
Nameless here for evermore.

And the silken[13] sad uncertain rustling of each purple curtain
Thrilled me—filled me with fantastic terrors never felt before;
So that now, to still the beating of my heart, I stood repeating
" 'Tis some visitor entreating[14] entrance at my chamber door—
Some late visitor entreating entrance at my chamber door; —
This it is, and nothing more."

Presently my soul grew stronger; hesitating then no longer,
"Sir," said I, "or Madam, truly your forgiveness I implore[15];
But the fact is I was napping, and so gently you came rapping,
And so faintly you came tapping, tapping at my chamber door,
That I scarce[16] was sure I heard you" —here I opened wide the door; —
Darkness there, and nothing more.

Deep into that darkness peering[17], long I stood there wondering, fearing,
Doubting, dreaming dreams no mortal ever dared to dream before;
But the silence was unbroken, and the darkness gave no token,
And the only word there spoken was the whispered word, "Lenore!"
This *I* whispered, and an echo murmured back the word, "Lenore!"
Merely this and nothing more.

Then into the chamber turning[18], all my soul within me burning,
Soon I heard again a tapping somewhat louder than before.

"Surely," said I, "surely that is something at my window lattice;
Let me see, then, what thereat[19] is, and this mystery explore[20]—
Let my heart be still a moment and this mystery explore; —
'Tis the wind, and nothing more!"

Open here I flung the shutter, when, with many a flirt and flutter,
In there stepped a stately[21] raven of the saintly days of yore[22];
Not the least obeisance[23] made he; not an instant stopped or stayed he;
But, with mien[24] of lord or lady, perched[25] above my chamber door—
Perched upon a bust[26] of Pallas[27] just above my chamber door—
Perched, and sat, and nothing more.

Then this ebony[28] bird beguiling[29] my sad fancy into smiling,
By the grave and stern decorum[30] of the countenance it wore,
"Though thy crest be shorn and shaven, thou," I said, "art sure no craven[31],
Ghastly grim and ancient raven wandering from the Nightly shore—
Tell me what thy lordly name is on the Night's Plutonian[32] shore!"
Quoth[33] the raven, "Nevermore."

Much I marvelled this ungainly[34] fowl to hear discourse so plainly,[35]
Though its answer little meaning—little relevancy bore;
For we cannot help agreeing that no sublunary[36] being,
Ever yet was blessed with seeing bird above his chamber door—
Bird or beast upon the sculptured bust above his chamber door,
With such name as "Nevermore."

But the raven, sitting lonely on the placid bust, spoke only
That one word, as if his soul in that one word he did outpour.[37]
Nothing farther then he uttered—not a feather then he fluttered—
Till I scarcely more than muttered, "Other friends have flown before—
On the morrow[38] *he* will leave me, as my hopes have flown before[39]."
Quoth the raven, "Nevermore."

Wondering at the stillness broken by reply so aptly spoken,
"Doubtless," said I, "what it utters is its only stock and store[40],
Caught[41] from some unhappy master whom unmerciful Disaster
Followed fast and followed faster—so, when Hope he would adjure[42]
Stern Despair[43] returned, instead of the sweet Hope he dared adjure—
That sad answer, "Nevermore!"

But the raven still beguiling all my sad soul into smiling,
Straight I wheeled a cushioned seat in front of bird, and bust, and door;
Then, upon the velvet sinking, I betook myself to linking[44]
Fancy unto fancy, thinking what this ominous[45] bird of yore—
What this grim, ungainly, ghastly, gaunt, and ominous bird of yore
Meant in croaking "Nevermore."

This I sat engaged in guessing, but no syllable expressing[46]
To the fowl whose fiery eyes now burned into my bosom's core;
This and more I sat divining[47], with my head at ease reclining
On the cushion's velvet lining that the lamplight gloated o'er,[48]
But whose velvet violet lining with the lamplight gloating o'er,
She shall press, ah, nevermore!

Then, methought[49], the air grew denser, perfumed from an unseen censer
Swung by angels whose faint foot-falls tinkled on the tufted[50] floor.
"Wretch[51]," I cried, "thy God hath lent thee—by these angels he hath sent thee
Respite[52]—respite and Nepenthe[53] from thy memories of Lenore!
Let me quaff[54] this kind Nepenthe and forget this lost Lenore!"
Quoth the raven, "Nevermore."

"Prophet!" said I, "thing of evil!—prophet still, if bird or devil!—
Whether Tempter[55] sent, or whether tempest tossed thee here ashore,
Desolate, yet all undaunted, on this desert land enchanted—
On this home by Horror haunted—tell me truly, I implore—

Is there—is there balm in Gilead[56]?—tell me—tell me, I implore!"
Quoth the raven, "Nevermore."

"Prophet!" said I, "thing of evil! —prophet still, if bird or devil!
By that Heaven that bends above us—by that God we both adore—
Tell this soul with sorrow laden[57] if, within the distant Aidenn[58],
It shall clasp a sainted maiden whom the angels name Lenore—
Clasp a rare and radiant maiden whom the angels name Lenore."
Quoth the raven, "Nevermore."

"Be that word our sign of parting, bird or fiend!" I shrieked, upstarting[59]—
"Get thee back into the tempest and the Night's Plutonian shore!
Leave no black plume as a token of that lie thy soul hath spoken!
Leave my loneliness unbroken—quit the bust above my door!
Take thy beak from out my heart, and take thy form from off my door!"
Quoth the raven, "Nevermore."

And the raven, never flitting[60], still is sitting, still is sitting
On the pallid bust of Pallas just above my chamber door;
And his eyes have all the seeming[61] of a demon that is dreaming,
And the lamp-light o'er him streaming[62] throws his shadow on the floor;
And my soul from out that shadow that lies floating on the floor
Shall be lifted—nevermore![63]
1845

Notes

1. This poem was first published in the *New York Evening Mirror* on January 29, 1945. It is written in eighteen 6-line stanzas with the first five lines of eight trochaic feet and the last line of four trochaic feet in each.
2. a midnight dreary: a dreary midnight. dreary: dull.
3. pondered: thought thoroughly and carefully.
4. quaint and curious: strange in an interesting way.
5. volume of: amount of.

6. lore: knowledge.
7. muttered: spoke indistinctly in a low voice.
8. each separate dying ember wrought its ghost upon the floor: each piece of the ash in the dying fire cast their shadows on the floor. wrought its ghost: made its shadow. ember: ash.
9. morrow: the next day.
10. surcease: (archaic) cease, stop.
11. Lenore: the speaker's lost love with the name of Lenore given by the angels.
12. the rare and radiant maiden: the uncommon and strikingly beautiful girl.
13. silken: soft and smooth like silk.
14. entreating: begging for.
15. truly your forgiveness I implore: I sincerely ask for your forgiveness.
16. scarce: scarcely.
17. Deep into that darkness peering: peering deeply into that darkness.
18. Then into the chamber turning: then turning into the chamber.
19. thereat: over there.
20. this mystery explore: let me explore this mystery.
21. stately: solemn, dignified.
22. yore: the past.
23. obeisance: reverence.
24. mien: manner.
25. perched: (of a bird) stood or rested (on a branch, etc.).
26. bust: a sculpture representing a person's head, shoulders, and upper chest.
27. Pallas: Greek goddess of wisdom, also known as Athena.
28. ebony: hard black wood of a tropical tree. Here it means as black as the wood.
29. beguiling: cheating, misleading.
30. decorum: polite behavior or appearance.
31. craven: coward.
32. Plutonian: of Pluto or the hell. Pluto is god of the dead and the ruler of the underworld in Greek mythology.
33. Quoth: said.

34. ungainly: plain-looking, ugly.
35. discourse so plainly: speak so clearly.
36. sublunary: earthly.
37. as if his soul in that one word he did outpour: as if he could express his soul only in that one word.
38. On the morrow: tomorrow.
39. as my hopes have flown before: like my hopes have gone with my lost love, Lenore.
40. what it utters is its only stock and store: "nevermore" is the only word that the raven knows.
41. Caught: learned.
42. adjure: ask for earnestly.
43. Stern Despair: the merciless Despair.
44. upon the velvet sinking, I betook myself to linking: sitting on the cushioned seat, I started to link (fancy to fancy). betook: (archaic) commit, apply.
45. ominous: of a bad sign.
46. no syllable expressing: saying nothing.
47. divining: guessing.
48. gloated o'er: gloated over; illuminated.
49. methought: it seemed to me that.
50. tufted: soft.
51. Wretch: poor fellow.
52. Respite: stop, pause.
53. Nepenthe: a drug mentioned in the *Odyssey* as a remedy for grief.
54. Guaff: drink up in one swallow.
55. Tempter: Satan, the devil.
56. is there balm in Gilead: it alludes to Jeremiah 8.22: "Is there no balm in Gilead; is there no physician there? Why then has the health of my poor people not been restored?"
57. this soul with sorrow laden: this soul laden with sorrow. laden with: full of.
58. Aidenn: one of Poe's vaguely evocative place names, suggesting Eden.

59. upstarting: crying in a high-pitched tone.
60. flitting: flying quickly.
61. seeming: appearance or look.
62. o'er him streaming: streaming over him.
63. And my soul from out that shadow that lies floating on the floor/Shall be lifted— nevermore: and my soul shall never be moved away from that shadow that lies floating on the floor.

For Study and Discussion

1. When and where does the story in the poem take place?
2. What is the speaker doing when the raven appears?
3. Is there any change of the speaker's mood in the poem?
4. What is the overall atmosphere created in the poem?
5. This poem is famous for its musical beauty. What devices are used to produce its musical beauty?

参考译文

乌 鸦

一次午夜时，我疲惫不堪困意浓，
稀奇古事挥不掉——
低头小憩时，忽闻窗外叩拍声，
好似有人轻轻把门敲——
心想必有来客访——
唯此无他响。

啊，我铭记那是在凄凉寒冬十二月；
死灰空留断魂烙。
欲把情愁付书海，
难忘佳丽魂已销——
举世无双窈窕女，安琪唤其叫勒诺——
香销玉逝无人叫。

丝帘哀怨簌簌响，

莫名恐惧心头涌；
屏息起身细思忖，
“过客欲求栖身所——
夜深探问把门敲，
唯此无他响。”

霎时心定意坚不狐疑，开口来问寻，
“先生/夫人请见谅，
意懒心倦正自烦，
叩门之音未听确，”
就此开门将客迎；
夜浓，无人影。

定足凝望，漫漫长夜心悬疑，
恰似幽梦初醒自难忘，
夜阑无声，静寂无形，
唯我低声唤勒诺，
凄然旷野映回声——
唯此无他响。

转身回屋，心有余悸难平息，
窗边又起叩击声，阵阵不绝耳。
“始知屋外不明之物在眼前，
欲将个中究竟细细探——
安神初定前去找，
唯风无他响。”

卷帘开窗，鼓翼振翅飞入一乌鸦，
神态自若如智者；
不卑不亢，快若迅雷栖我处，
风度无人肖——
飞旋落定如玉女神帕拉丝——
宜栖宜坐岿不动。

但见其神情肃穆现高贵，

顿使我悲郁情怀化笑颜，
“你貌若凡鸟而神自定，
让我想起古之神鹊黄泉落，
敢问你彼岸尊姓和大名，”
乌鹊答道“永不再会”。

其貌不扬一小鸟，吐字清晰令人奇，
纵然词不搭意难自圆，
世人罕有此经历，
有幸目睹它登门，
飞落室内神雕塑，
自唤名曰“永不再会”。

只见它静若雕像独端坐，
倾注灵魂于斯语，
唯此不言也不动——
我低声哀叹“亲朋皆逝我独留——
明日它亦弃我而去无望还。”
乌鸦即和“永不再会”。

惊闻接语称心又贴切，
始知其开口无他语，
必逢主人不幸遭磨难，
无奈常叹此一言，
长歌当哭忧愤起，
感慨“永不再会”。

而我已是悲思转笑颜，
侧身就座其栖息处，
慵倦陷沉思，
揣度这只亘古不祥鸟，
冷酷、笨拙、恐怖又憔悴，
缘何嘶叫“永不再会”。

我攒眉思忖不作响，
眼前它目光炯炯将我灼；

见我心驰神骛态依旧，
灯下安然斜靠丝绒衬，
而今物是人非，纵心念佳人，
已是永不再会。

暗炉幽香渐扑鼻，
疑为轻盈天使一路来，
“竟是我主送你到身边，
相赠忘忧物，解我心中千千结；
痛饮忘情水，换我痴情永相忘。”
却闻“永不再会”。

“无论你是鸟是魔，还是邪恶一先知，
不管你追随撒旦抑或屈从风暴，孤身一人不畏惧——
我如今身处荒原神恍惚——
在这闹鬼恐惧屋，恳切求尔语，
有否基列乳香将我医?”
却闻“永不再会”。

“无论你是鸟是魔，还是邪恶一先知，
看在我们头顶共青天，上帝同膜拜，
解我心中愁，在那远方乐土伊甸园，
我还能否相会梦中佳人名勒诺——
举世无双窈窕女，安琪唤其叫勒诺。”
却闻“永不再会”。

“闭口休再提!”我心中怒火不可遏，
“你就此踏归黄泉路!
收回满口荒唐言!
使我莫烦扰!离我门上半身像!
与你不相干，快些飞离我!”
却闻“永不再会”。

只见乌鸦丝毫未动依自若，
栖我门上如玉帕拉丝，
魔鬼神情眼中露，

幽暗身形灯光映，
心中隐痛难抚平。
永远不再会！

（周英莉 译 李正栓 校）

5. Walt Whitman

Walt Whitman（沃尔特·惠特曼，1819－1892）was one of the most important American poets of the 19th century and one of the great innovators in American literary history. He used a style that was quite new and special in his poetry, which is now called free verse—that is, poetry without a fixed beat or regular rhyme scheme. Shaping the American poetry out of the native elements of the New World, Whitman tried to write poetry describing the Native American experience.

Whitman was born on a Long Island farm, on May 31, 1819 and grew up in Brooklyn, New York. He received only 5 years of education but he read voraciously by himself. By nature, he was a man thirsty for experience. Thus, he tried a variety of jobs including an office boy, a printer's assistant on several of the newspapers around New York, a teacher in schools in the Long Island area, and an editor of a newspaper. In this way he picked up the first hand knowledge of life and people in the United States.

In 1848, Whitman began to have some of his writings published. In the same year, he traveled widely to New Orleans, Chicago, and the Western frontier. The journey by train, stagecoach, and steamboat helped to broaden his view of America, which he lovingly expressed in many of his works. Soon after, Whitman began to write in a new style—free verse, for which he became famous. Whitman published the first edition of *Leaves of Grass* in 1855, containing only 12 of his best poems. The collection was soon enlarged the next year into 32 poems. Whitman wrote over 400 poems in his life. Until his death on May 26, 1892, he collected 383 poems into his *Leaves of Grass*. Most of them are about man and nature, especially common people and ordinary Americans. The frequent topics of Whitman's poetry are songs for himself, for the labor of the common American people, for natural creation, for the independence of the country, for love and friendship, and for the memorizing of President Lincoln.

Whitman's poetry is an example of free verse at its most impressive. Free verse is poetry that has no fixed rhythm and line length and that attempts to avoid any predetermined verse structure; instead, it uses the cadences of natural speech. Although free verse had been used before Whitman notably in Italian opera and in the King James translation of the Bible it was Whitman who pioneered the form and made it acceptable in American poetry. It has since been used by Ezra Pound, T. S. Eliot, William Carlos Williams, Wallace Stevens, and other major American poets of the 20th century.

Walt Whitman holds a unique position in the history of American literature. He developed a poetic style of originality, which was devoid of conventional rhyme and meter. The great majority of his poems, with the exception of only a few poems like "O Captain! My Captain!", employs the line, instead of the conventional foot, as the stylistic unit, and depends on parallelism and other reiterative devices for its structure and cadence, resembling the technique of Hebrew poetry.

Not only the form of Whitman's free verse but also his thought of democracy have been influential in world literature, and remain the inspiring sources of the 20th century literature.

O Captain! My Captain![1]

This poem is written in memory of Abraham Lincoln who was assassinated on April 14, 1865, 5 days after the end of the American Civil War (1861—1865). It is so famous that many poets have imitated it. The poetic form effectively expresses its content. The first four lines in each stanza describe the rejoicing crowd welcoming Lincoln, while the last four depict the cruel reality that Lincoln was lying, cold and dead on the deck, in contrast to the happy scene in the first four. The stanza form is like a ship with the word "captain" at the head of each stanza. The uneven lines and the rhyme scheme of the poem reflect the ups and downs of the poet's mental state.

Captain! my Captain! Our fearful trip[2] is done,
The ship[3] has weather'd every rack[4], the prize[5] we sought is won,
The port is near, the bells I hear, the people all exulting[6],
While follow eyes the steady keel,[7] the vessel grim and daring[8];
But O heart! heart! heart!
O the bleeding drops of red,
Where on the deck my Captain lies,
Fallen cold and dead.

O Captain! my Captain! Rise up and hear the bells;
Rise up — for you the flag is flung[9] — for you the bugle trills[10],
For you bouquets and ribbon'd wreaths[11] — for you the shores a-crowding[12],
For you they call, the swaying mass[13], their eager faces turning;
Here Captain! dear father![14]
This arm beneath your head!
It is some dream[15] that on the deck,
You've fallen cold and dead.

My Captain does not answer, his lips are pale and still[16].
My father does not feel my arm, he has no pulse nor will,
The ship is anchor'd[17] safe and sound[18], its voyage closed and done,
From fearful trip the victor[19] ship comes in with object[20] won:
Exult, O shores, and ring, O bells,
But I with mournful tread,
Walk the deck my Captain lies,[21]
Fallen cold and dead.

Notes

1. This poem belongs to one of a series of poems commemorating Lincoln. It is written in the traditional iambic meters rhyming aabbcded.

2. Our fearful trip：referring to the hard course of the American Civil War.
3. The ship：referring to the America.
4. weather'd every rack：experienced all the hardships. weather'd：weathered.
5. the prize：the triumph of the war and the abolition of slavery.
6. exulting：rejoicing greatly.
7. follow eyes the steady keel：eyes follow the steady keel. keel：flatboat，here referring to the America，same as "vessel" in the same line and "ship" in Line 2.
8. grim and daring：stern and fearless.
9. flung：flying.
10. trills：blows with a tremulous note.
11. bouquets and ribbon'd wreaths：bunches of flowers and wreaths decorated with ribbons. ribbon'd：ribboned.
12. a-crowding：crowded.
13. the swaying mass：the moving crowd of people.
14. dear father：the poet compares Lincoln to the father of the country to show the close relationship between Lincoln and the American people.
15. It is some dream：I wish it were just a dream.
16. still：motionless.
17. anchor'd：anchored.
18. safe and sound：uninjured.
19. victor：victorious.
20. object：also referring to the abolition of slavery.
21. Walk the deck my Captain lies：walk（on）the deck（where）my Captain lies.

诗歌赏析

惠特曼的诗歌具有鲜明的人民性、民族性和时代特征。《啊，船长！我的船长哟！》是惠特曼为纪念林肯总统而作的系列悼亡诗中最具代表性的一首。著名诗人卡尔·桑德伯格在《林肯传》中称赞这首诗是“最奇幻、最富象征性”的一曲国殇。惠特曼擅长写自由诗，但是这首诗遵循了英语诗歌传统的格律，写得庄严、肃穆。

这首诗以其丰富的比喻义著称，船长是其中的中心比喻。惠特曼将林肯领导下的美国南北战争比喻成在船长带领下的船只历经艰难险阻的航行。其中林肯总统就是船长，率领美国这艘大船，完成了南北战争的艰苦航程，打赢了内战，取得了废除奴隶制的伟大胜利。这一系列的比喻贴切、恰当。

这首诗是英诗中形式表达内容的范例。全诗由三个八行诗节组成，其中每节诗前四行诗长，后四行诗短，诗行的排列形似一艘船的模样，而“船长”一词挺立在每节诗的第一行行首，就像船长在扬帆起航的船只上指挥若定、慷慨激昂。诗歌的形式和诗歌的内容相得益彰。

这首诗的声音效果同样服务于诗歌主题。首先，该诗的节奏前四行长而舒缓，后四行短而有力，形成鲜明的对比。前四行主要描写林肯胜利归来时人群的欢呼雀跃，后四行着重刻画林肯不幸遇难后人们的震惊、悲怆。其中第一节中“heart! heart! heart!”接连使用三个重读单音节词，一字一顿，形容人们极度的悲伤和痛心。三个感叹号触目惊心，音形意统一。其次，诗歌的韵脚统一押 aabbcded 韵。前四行是工整的双偶句，后四行仅偶行押韵。韵脚的变化象征着情绪的起伏。最后，他“倒下去，冰冷，永别”出现在每节诗的最后一行，形成诗歌的基调并在不断重复中得到加强。声音效果的冲击和视觉效果的震撼营造了这首诗非凡的艺术效果。

惠特曼虽然在这首诗中采用了传统的诗歌形式以示对林肯总统的尊重和题材的庄重，但第二节诗中他又采用了惯用的排比：“号角为您长鸣，旌旗为您高悬；/迎着您，多少花束花圈——候着您，千万人蜂拥岸边；/他们向您高呼，拥来挤去，仰起殷切的脸；”五个排比句勾勒出气势恢弘的欢迎场面，形式与内容达到了统一。除了船长的比喻，诗人进一步把林肯比为亲爱的父亲，非常贴切地表达了林肯在美国人心中的位置以及美国人民对他的崇敬之情。

For Study and Discussion

1. Point out the figure of speech that unifies the poem. Do you think it is appropriately employed in the poem?
2. Explain the four metaphors in the poem: Captain, ship, trip and prize.
3. Why does Whitman use the traditional metrical pattern in this poem instead of the free verse he loves?
4. What do you think of the form of the poem? And the relationship with its sense?

参考译文

啊，船长！我的船长哟！

啊，船长！我的船长！可怕的航程已完成；
这船历尽风险，企求的目标已达成。
港口在望，钟声响，人们在欢欣。
千万双眼睛注视着船——平稳，勇敢，坚定。
但是痛心啊！痛心！痛心！
瞧一滴滴鲜红的血！
甲板上躺着我的船长，
他倒下去，冰冷，永别。

啊！船长！我的船长！起来吧，倾听钟声；
起来吧，号角为您长鸣，旌旗为您高悬；
迎着您，多少花束花圈——候着您，千万人蜂拥岸边；
他们向您高呼，拥来挤去，仰起殷切的脸；
啊，船长！亲爱的父亲！
我的手臂托着您的头！
莫非是一场梦：在甲板上
您倒下去，冰冷，永别。

我的船长不作声，嘴唇惨白，毫不动弹；
我的父亲没感到我的手臂，没有脉搏，没有遗言；
船舶抛锚停下，平安抵达；航程终了；
历尽艰险返航，夺得胜利目标。
啊！岸上钟声齐鸣，啊！人们一片欢腾！
但是，我在甲板上，在船长身旁，
心悲切，步履沉重：
因为他倒下去，冰冷，永别。

（杨　霖　译）

I Hear America Singing[1]

This poem describes a vivid panorama of the working scene in America in the mid-19th century. It is a typical poem by Whitman, which sings high praise of the working people and the spirit of rising America at that time. The stylistic repetition of singing and the parallelism of working scenes of all sorts create the positive atmosphere of the poem.

I hear America singing, the varied carols[2] I hear,
Those of mechanics, each one singing his as it
should be blithe[3] and strong,
The carpenter singing his as he measures his plank or beam,
The mason[4] singing his as he makes ready for work, or leaves off work[5],
The boatman singing what belongs to him in his boat, the
Deckhand[6] singing on the steamboat deck,
The shoemaker singing as he sits on his bench,
The hatter singing as he stands,
The wood-cutters's song, the ploughboy's on his way in
the morning, or at noon intermission[7] or at sundown,
The delicious[8] singing of the mother, or of the young wife at
work, or of the girl sewing or washing,
Each singing what belongs to him or her and to none else,
The day what belongs to the day[9]—at night the party
of young fellows, robust[10], friendly,
Singing with open mouths their strong melodious[11] songs.

Notes

1. This poem was written in free verse in 1860.
2. varied carols: various joyful songs.
3. blithe: happy, joyous.
4. mason: worker who builds with stone.
5. leaves off work: goes off work.
6. Deckhand: a member of a ship's crew who works on deck.
7. intermission: a pause of work.
8. delicious: sweet.
9. The day what belongs to the day: the day (is singing) what belongs to

the day.

10. robust: strong and healthy.

11. melodious: tuneful.

For Study and Discussion

1. What kinds of workers does Whitman mention in the poem?
2. What is the theme of this poem?
3. What is the speaker's view on America and people there?
4. What is the keynote of the poem?

参考译文

我听见美利坚在歌唱

我听见美利坚在歌唱，听见各种颂歌在回响：
机械工在唱，每个人都心情愉快、歌声嘹亮；
木匠在唱，边唱歌边把木板和大梁来丈量；
泥瓦匠在唱，上工前后都在唱；
船夫在唱船上事，水手歌唱在汽艇甲板上；
鞋匠坐着凳子把歌唱，帽匠站在店铺里唱；
伐木工、农村青年清晨走路、中午间休、黄昏回家都在唱；
母亲在甜唱，少妇在边工作边唱，少女在边缝洗边唱；
每个人都在唱自己关心而不属于别人的事；
白天唱着白天的事，夜里身强力壮互相友好的青年人
张口大唱，歌声悦耳、雄壮嘹亮。

（李正栓　译）

6. Emily Dickinson

Emily Dickinson（艾米丽·狄金森，1830—1886）was born into a Puritan family in Amherst, Massachusetts on December 10, 1830. She received little formal education, but read widely at home. Living most of her life in her family house in Amherst, Dickinson was a shy New England recluse during her lifetime. She wrote more than 1,700 poems, but published only 7. However,

after death, she has come to be regarded as a chief poet, as great as Whitman, in the turbulent America of the late 19th century.

As one of the great poets of inwardness ever to write in English, she was no social poet. One could read through her *Collected Poems* and find almost no sense of the time in which she lived. Of course, social and historical ideas and values contributed in shaping her character, but Emily Dickinson's ultimate context is herself, the milieu of her mind.

Emily seems to be wholly original, taking the subject matter of her poetry merely from her personal experiences in order to express what she felt about love, nature, death, and immortality. She develops her own poetic form with many peculiar features, including the abundant use of dashes, irregular and often idiosyncratic punctuation and capitalization. Her mode of expression is characterized by clear-cut and delicately original imagery, precise diction, and fragmentary and enigmatic metrical pattern. These variations of her poetry are used systematically and effectively for rhetorical emphasis or musical pointing.

Dickinson's poetry is remarkable for its uncommon variety, original subtlety and unusual richness. It possesses the appeal that moves the 20th century readers and exerted a great impact upon the so-called "new poetry" of the early 20th century. Dickinson was a poet who could express feelings of deepest poignancy in terms of the true and wise saying. Her gemlike poems are all very short, but fresh and original, marked by the vigor of her images, the daring of her thought and the beauty of her expression.

Living in the 19th century, a comparatively religious era, Emily Dickinson did not belong to any organized religion. However, she wrote of God, man and nature; she probed into the spiritual unrest of man and often doubted about the existence and benevolence of God, because she felt that wild nature was her church and she was able to converse directly with God there. Dickinson died of disease on May 15, 1886. A posthumous collection of her poems was published in 1890, and many versions followed hereafter.

479 Because I couldn't stop for Death —[1]

This poem is one of Dickinson's most frequently chosen poems. It deals with the typical Christian theme — immortality and eternity. Dickinson compares human life with journey. Death here appears as a courteous coachman picking up the speaker on her journey, which actually covers different stages of life: the school for childhood, the Fields of Gazing Grain for adulthood, and the setting sun for old age. It begins with concrete, light images, but ends suddenly with the solemn destination of life — grave. The poem shows Dickinson's calm acceptance of death.

Because I could not stop for Death —
He kindly stopped for me —
The Carriage[2] held but just[3] Ourselves —
And Immortality.

We slowly drove — He knew no haste
And I had put away
My labor and my leisure too,
For His Civility[4] —

We passed the School, where Children strove
At Recess[5] — in the Ring[6] —
We passed the Fields of Gazing Grain —
We passed the Setting Sun —

Or rather—He[7] passed Us —
The Dews drew quivering and Chill —
For only Gossamer, my Gown[8] —
My Tippet — only Tulle[9] —

We paused before a House that seemed
A Swelling of the Ground[10] —

The Roof was scarcely visible —
The Cornice[11] — in the Ground —

Since then — 'tis[12] Centuries — and yet
Feels shorter than the Day
I first surmised[13] the Horses' Heads
Were toward Eternity —

1862

Notes

1. This poem was published in 1890. It is written in six quatrains usually of iambic meters.
2. The Carriage: referring to the hearse.
3. but just: only.
4. Civility: politeness, courtesy.
5. Recess: rest.
6. Ring: playground in round form.
7. He: referring to the Setting Sun.
8. For only Gossamer, my Gown: for my gown is only made of gossamer. Gossamer: soft light delicate material. Gown: a long, loose, flowing garment.
9. My Tippet — only Tulle: (for) my tippet is only made of tulle. Tippet: a covering for the shoulders. Tulle: soft fine silky net-like material, used especially for veils and dresses. Here "Gown" and "Tippet" both refer to the shroud.
10. A Swelling of the Ground: referring to the tomb.
11. Cornice: a raised line of plaster, wood, or stone at the edge of a ceiling, here referring to that of the tomb.
12. 'tis: it is.
13. surmised: worked out.

诗歌赏析

《因为我不能停下来等待死神》是狄金森被广为传诵的一首死亡诗。诗人使用了丰富的意象来传达她对死亡这一永恒主题的感悟。全诗分为三部分，第一节简要介绍了说话者乘坐死神的马车，踏上了死亡之旅。第二至五节详细叙述了死亡旅程的经过。最后一节是说话者在永恒世界对这一旅程的回望。

在第一节中，死亡这一抽象的概念被具象化。诗人使用拟人的手法，将死神比作一个文质彬彬的绅士，驾车载着诗中的主人公“我”和“永生”踏上死亡之旅，并且有“永生”作旅伴。直接点明主题——人生、死亡和永生之间的复杂联系。死神摆脱了传统诗歌中凶恶的形象，展现了诗人对死亡的态度。她不期待死亡，但死亡来临时，亦能从容面对。马车也许暗示着灵车。

第二至五节详述了死亡旅程的经过。说话人坐着死神的马车经过了孩子们嬉戏的学校操场、饱满的稻田和落日。这一行程寓指人生的三个阶段——孩童、成年和老年。最后，停留在一所房子，即坟墓前。“passed”在这一部分重复了四次，说明逝者曾经经历了漫长的人生阶段，如今已从尘世消失，跨越了生死，到达了另一个世界。露珠的阴凉暗指死亡来临前的恐惧。而薄纱长裙和绢质披肩分明就是尸衣。诗人将人生的终点——坟墓比喻成房屋，意味着诗人相信死后的生活，相信基督教的来世思想。诗人在这一部分用一系列的死亡比喻提示死亡的来临。

最后一节诗揭示了基督教的信念——肉体必死而灵魂永生。死后的世界已经超越了时间，诗人觉得此后的几百年比那一天还短暂。诗人这才意识到死亡之旅的马车，马头朝向永恒。第一节诗提出了问题，最后一节回答了问题。肉体的死亡带给人精神的永生。诗人用平静的语气诉说她的死亡之旅，从生到死，一气呵成，自然流畅，没有华美的道别，没有难堪的欲走还留。

除了结构美以外，这首诗还是一首音韵和谐的死亡赞美诗。首先，它采用狄金森诗歌传统的民谣体诗节形式，奇数行四个重读音节，偶数行三个，多为抑扬格音步，偶行押韵。格律工整，读起来抑扬顿挫，舒缓平和，丝毫感受不到生死之际的悲怆和激烈的情绪变化。诗歌的形式很好地表达了诗歌的内涵。其次，诗中连续频繁地使用头韵和腹韵，产生和谐的音韵美和意义的连续性。如第二节第一行中产生明显的腹韵，表达诗人投身死亡的坚定决心。第三行 labor 和 leisure 押头韵，喻示劳作和闲暇就是全部的人生。诗人抛开世间的一切，去投奔死亡。类似的表达还有多处，诗歌的音乐很好地传递了诗歌的主题。

诗中频繁出现的破折号同样表达了诗歌的内涵。诗人利用破折号进行有意的停顿，产生时间的延长和情绪的延伸。诗中众多的破折号展现诗人对死亡的思考，对人生的留恋以及面对死亡忐忑不安的心情。诗人还使用了诸如“停下

(stop)”、“缓慢”(slowly)、“不急”(no haste)、“暂停”(pause) 等表达了缓慢的行程和对漫长人生的回味。

这首诗立意奇巧、构思巧妙、音韵优美，不愧为英语诗歌中的经典。

For Study and Discussion

1. What is the tone of this poem?
2. Who is the speaker of the poem?
3. What is Dickinson's attitude towards death as shown in the poem?
4. What does the “House” in Stanza 5 symbolize?
5. Read the last stanza carefully. Does the speaker speak from Heaven or from the grave? What does she mean by saying the centuries seem shorter than “the Day”?
6. Dickinson frequently uses dashes and capitalized letters in her poems. What are their functions as shown in this poem?

参考译文

因为我不能停下来等待死神——

因为我不能停下来等待死神——
他却好心好意地停车来接我——
车内只有我和他——
不对，还有“永生”。

我们驱车慢行——他不慌不忙
而我呢，我不再劳作
也不再闲暇，
以报答他的礼貌——

我们经过学校，孩子们正追逐喧闹，
恰是课间——操场欢腾——
我们经过望着我们的谷田——
我们经过西下的太阳——

或可说——是太阳经过我们——
露水带来了凉意和寒颤——
因为我衣薄如纱——
我肩只披绢——

我们在一幢房子前停车，
它似是地面隆起——
房顶几乎看不见——
屋檐——在地中——

自那以后——几百年过去了——然而
却感觉比那一天还短，
那一天我猜测拉车的马
头朝向永恒而去。

（李正栓　译）

112 Success is counted sweetest[1]

This is a short lyric about success. The poem sets forth Dickinson's understanding of success — it is not the winner but the loser who knows best the true meaning of victory. Being a typical poem of Dickinson, it is simple, clear and unique.

Success is counted sweetest[2]
By those who ne'er[3] succeed.
To comprehend a nectar[4]
Requires sorest need[5].

Not one of all the purple Host[6]
Who took the Flag[7] today
Can tell the definition
So clear of Victory,

As he, defeated — dying —
On whose forbidden ear[8]

The distant strains[9] of triumph
Burst agonized and clear!
1859, 1864

Notes

1. This poem was first published in the *Brooklyn Daily Union*, April 27, 1864. It is written in three quatrains rhyming abcb.
2. Success is counted sweetest: success is considered to be the sweetest thing.
3. ne'er: never.
4. nectar: the drink of gods in Greek mythology, here referring to success.
5. sorest need: great need.
6. the purple Host: victorious army.
7. took the Flag: won the battle.
8. forbidden ear: It is a paradox — the ear that is forbidden to hear hears the music of victory clearly.
9. strains: melody, music.

For Study and Discussion

1. According to the poem, who understands success most?
2. Analyze the comparison in the second stanza.
3. How do you understand the last stanza?

参考译文

成功的滋味最甜美

从未成功的人认为,
成功的滋味最甜美。
有强烈的渴求
才能知道甘露的美味。

今天在紫色人群中
所有举旗的人
没有一个能像他如此清楚地
给胜利一个定义。

他，战败，将死，
耳朵震伤欲聋，
猛然听见胜利的呼叫，
清晰响亮却充满苦痛。

（李正栓　译）

I'm Nobody! Who are you?[1]

This is one of the shortest poems by Dickinson. The speaker in the poem is more than willing to be nobody, that is, a person of no importance. It goes counter to the traditional value of craving for being somebody — person with high social status. Besides, the speaker is not alone. She enjoys companionship, which is appreciated in not one of Dickinson's poems. In this poem, somebody is compared to a frog, croaking all day just to attract "the admiring bog". Being somebody is boring and disgusting. It is written in a colloquial style, short and persuasive.

I'm Nobody[2]! Who are you?
Are you — Nobody — too?
Then there's a pair of us!
Don't tell! They'd advertise[3] — you know!

How dreary — to be — Somebody[4]!
How public — like a Frog —
To tell one's name — the livelong June[5] —
To an admiring Bog[6]!

1861

Notes

1. This poem is written in two quatrains of iambic feet.
2. Nobody: a person of no importance.
3. advertise: make known.
4. Somebody: a person of importance.

5. the livelong June: the whole June.
6. Bog: here referring to herds of admiring people.

For Study and Discussion

1. How does the speaker in this poem feel about nobody?
2. What is the speaker's attitude toward somebody? Do you agree with the speaker?
3. Who are "They" in Line 4 and "an admiring bog" in Line 8?
4. Is there any tint of Dickinson's personal life?
5. Walt Whitman and Emily Dickinson are both important poets in the 19th century. Do they have similar attitude toward self? Give examples to support your view.

参考译文

我是个小人物

我是个小人物，你是谁？
你——也是——小人物？
那么我们是一对？
不要声张！你知道，他们总爱张扬。

做个名人多无聊！
像只青蛙——多招摇——
对着向它示慕的泥塘
整个六月都在自我大肆宣扬！

（唐　秀　译）

Wild Nights — Wild Nights![1]

This is an ardent poem with ambiguous meanings. Some say it is about unrestrained sexual passion. Some say it is the portrayal of a religious experience. The divergent interpretations of the poem always appeal to the readers. It is full of symbols, with the central image of the sea for passion. As for Dickinson, men and women in love have no need for compass or chart, which is the symbol of control and reason. To most readers, the calmness before death and the alienation from nature are natural for Dickinson, while the intensity of passion as shown in this poem seems abrupt.

Wild nights — Wild nights!
Were I with thee[2]
Wild nights should be
Our luxury!

Futile — the winds —
To a Heart in port —
Done with[3] the Compass —
Done with the Chart!

Rowing in Eden —
Ah — the Sea!
Might I[4] but moor[5] — tonight —
In thee!

1861

Notes

1. Dickinson's poems usually had no titles. Often the first sentence of a poem is taken as its title. This poem is the case. It is written in three quatrains with the even lines rhymed.
2. Were I with thee: if I were with you. It is an assumption. It is in the subjunctive mood.
3. Done with: no longer use.
4. Might I: if I might. It is another assumption. It is also in the subjunctive mood.
5. moor: anchor.

For Study and Discussion

1. What do "Wild Nights" symbolize? And the Sea? And the boat?
2. What does "Our luxury" in Line 4 refer to?

3. What does "port" in Line 6 refer to?
4. What is the theme of the poem? Religious experience? Or passion of love?
5. What figures of speech are used in this poem?

参考译文

暴风雨夜——暴风雨夜!

暴风雨夜——暴风雨夜!
我若与您同在,
这样的夜
应是一种奢侈。

风啊,你无能为力——
因为心已在港口回避
罗盘已不起作用——
海图也不必再用!

泛舟游于伊甸园——
啊,大海!
但愿今夜——我能——
停泊在你的胸怀!

(李正栓 译)

448 I died for Beauty — but was scarce[1]

This poem discusses the relationship between beauty and truth in a typical way of Dickinson. Through the conversation between the one who dies for beauty and the one for truth between tombs, Dickinson creates an atmosphere that is both comforting and horrifying, grotesque and appealing. The word "themself" is invented by Dickinson to express her aesthetic idea that beauty and truth are one, same as John Keats' famous saying: "Beauty is truth, truth beauty." The solemn subject is displayed in a light manner. At last, martyrdom and friendship, idealism and fame are all covered by death.

I died for Beauty — but was scarce

Adjusted in the Tomb[2]
When One who died for Truth, was lain
In an adjoining Room[3] —

He questioned softly "Why I failed[4]?"
"For Beauty", I replied —
"And I — for Truth — Themself[5] are One —
We Bretheren[6], are", he said —

And so, as Kinsmen met a Night[7] —
We talked between the Rooms —
Until the Moss had reached our lips —
And covered up — Our names —[8]

1862

Notes

1. It is written in three quatrains of alternate iambic tetrameter and trimeter lines rhyming abcb.
2. was scarce/Adjusted in the Tomb: just got used to the tomb. scarce: scarcely.
3. an adjoining Room: the next tomb.
4. Why I failed: why I died. Here "I" refers to the speaker.
5. Themself: it is misspelled but reasonable, showing the identity of "beauty" and "truth".
6. Bretheren: brothers.
7. a Night: at night.
8. And covered up — Our names —: and (the moss) covered up our names (on the tombstone), that is, we were completely forgotten.

For Study and Discussion

1. Is this a simple poem of death?
2. What is Dickinson's view of afterlife as shown in this poem? And death?
3. How do you understand the last two lines of the poem?

4. What does "our names" stand for?

参考译文

我为美而死

我为美而死，但还不怎么
适应坟墓里的生活，
这时一位为真理而死的人
被安放在隔壁墓室里。

他柔声问我我为什么失败而亡；
"为了美"，我回答说，
"我为了真理——美和真是一样，
我们俩是兄弟"，他说。

就这样，像近亲在夜里相遇，
我们隔墙而谈，
直到青苔把我们的嘴封闭，
将我们的名字埋掩。

（李正栓 译）

591 I heard a Fly buzz — when I died —[1]

This is one of Dickinson's poems on death, which retrospects the scene when she was dying. The image of "a Fly" is appealing and ambiguous, which appears at the beginning and buzzes through the poem. The speaker is calmly waiting for the coming of death. When the Death comes to guide the dead to Heaven, a fly appears and buzzes annoyingly. Being the only sign of life, it comes between the speaker and the king, life and death, triviality and solemnness. The speaker is talking of her death in a light manner.

I heard a Fly buzz[2] — when I died —
The Stillness in the Room
Was like the Stillness in the Air —
Between the Heaves[3] of Storm —

The Eyes around — had wrung them dry[4] —
And Breaths were gathering firm
For that last Onset[5] — when the King[6]
Be witnessed — in the Room —

I willed[7] my Keepsakes[8] — Signed[9] away
What portion of me be
Assignable — and then it was
There interposed[10] a Fly —

With Blue — uncertain — stumbling Buzz —
Between the light — and me —
And then the Windows failed — and then
I could not see to see —

1863

Notes

1. This poem is written in ballad stanza — a quatrain in alternate four and three iambic feet with the even lines rhymed.
2. buzz: make a humming sound.
3. Heaves: rises.
4. The Eyes around — had wrung them dry: the eyes of people standing around the speaker's deathbed were dry of tears.
5. Onset: attack.
6. the King: the God of death.
7. willed: granted in a legal will, bequeathed.
8. Keepsakes: mementoes, something that she left behind.
9. Signed: affixed one's signature.
10. interposed: came between.

For Study and Discussion

1. Why is the poem written in the past tense?
2. What is the effect of the fly being the only sign of life in the poem?

3. What does "the light" refer to in the last stanza?
4. What are the denotation and connotation of "the Windows" in the last stanza?
5. Discuss the meanings of the two "see" in the last line of the poem?
6. What is the sound effect of the poem?

参考译文

我死时——听到一只苍蝇嗡嗡叫——

我死时——听到一只苍蝇嗡嗡叫——
室内的寂静
像空气窒息了——
像风暴的间停——

周围的眼睛——已把眼泪哭干——
呼吸正在恢复平静
为了那最后的一击——有人看见，
死神——就在房中——

我立遗嘱——把我的纪念品分掉——
在想我的哪一部分
可以分赠——这时一只苍蝇嗡叫
打扰了我的事情——

嗡叫凄惨——声音飘忽，逐渐微弱——
回响在光——和我——之间——
随后，心的窗户关闭——在后来——
再也看不见先前所见——

（李正栓　译）

7. Robert Frost

Robert Frost（罗伯特·弗罗斯特，1874—1963）was born on March 26，1874 in San Francisco，of a New England family. When he was ten，his family

returned to New England where Frost grew up. Later he attended Dartmouth College and Harvard University without taking a degree.

Frost began his writing of poems very early. But after school, he had to run a farm to support his family for many years. In 1912, he sailed for England, together with his wife, 5 children and a full case of manuscripts of his poems. The year after his arrival in England, Frost's first book of poetry, *A Boy's Will* (1913) was published. After the publication of his second volume of poems, *North of Boston* (1914), Frost returned to New England and began his career as an influential poet of America. Upon his arrival, Frost was most surprised to find a warm welcome from American people and publishers.

He is a prolific writer. His volumes of poetry, except the two published in England, include *Mountain Interval* (1916); *New Hampshire* (1923), which won Frost the first of his four Pulitzer Prizes; *West-Running Brook* (1928); *Collected Poems* (1930), which won him the second Pulitzer Prize; *A Further Range* (1936), which won the third Pulitzer Prize; *A Witness Tree* (1942), which brought him the fourth Pulitzer Prize.

Frost is the best-known and most readily welcome of the New England poets. What he did was to root his poetry in New England and to reach the plane of universal meaning. Unlike most of his contemporaries in the early 20th century, Frost did not break with the older poetic tradition, nor did he make many experiments with form. Instead, Frost learned from tradition and made the colloquial New England speech into the poetic expression.

He is also famous for his deceptive simplicity. The profound ideas are often delivered under the disguise of plain language and simple form, for what Frost did is to take symbols from the limited human world and the pastoral landscape to refer to the great space beyond the rustic scenes. He wrote about the daily life of ordinary people — small rural events including fence mending and apple picking. Many of his poems are fragrant with natural beauty as well as moral implications. Poetry, he believed, was, above all, metaphor.

Along with Ezra Pound, T. S. Eliot, and Wallace Stevens, Frost is now firmly regarded as one of the undisputed masters of modern American poetry. During his life time, he won almost all the great honors a poet can receive in this world, except the Nobel Prize. In 1961, when he was 87, he was honored to read one of his poems, "The Gift Outright", at the inauguration of President John F. Kennedy. Frost received the Bollingen Prize just before his death on January 29, 1963 at the age of 88.

Stopping by Woods on a Snowy Evening[1]

This poem is one of the most quietly moving of Frost's lyrics. It is a typical work of Frost with the feature of deceptive simplicity. It seems to be a vivid description of a simple, common picture in nature. But it is deeply meditative with far-reaching meanings to the homely cadence of natural speech. The beautiful wood scene in snow makes a deep appeal to the speaker who finally resists it. It uses its superb craftsmanship to come to a climax of responsibility: the promises to be kept, the obligation to be fulfilled. Few poems have said so much within so little. The repetition of the last two lines reinforces the speaker's determination to carry on his life journey and fulfill his "promises", that is, his social duty and responsibilities.

Whose woods[2] these are I think I know.
His house is in the village, though;
He will not see me stopping here
To watch his woods fill up with snow.

My little horse must think it queer[3]
To stop without a farmhouse near
Between the woods and frozen lake
The darkest evening of the year[4].

He gives his harness bells a shake[5]
To ask if there is some mistake.
The only other sound's the sweep

Of easy wind[6] and downy flake[7].

The woods are lovely, dark, and deep,
But I have promises[8] to keep,
And miles to go before I sleep[9].
And miles to go before I sleep.

1923

Notes

1. The poem is chosen from *New Hampshire* (1923). It is written in four quatrains of iambic tetrameter with the interlocking enclosed rhyme of aaba bbcb ccdc dddd.
2. woods: In American literature, woods often imply nature, mystery, prospect, and inspiration, like Brazil in British literature.
3. queer: strange, odd.
4. The darkest evening of the year: It was written on December 22, the shortest day of the year. It may also refer to the mental state of the speaker.
5. He gives his harness bells a shake: he shakes his head to make a sound. harness bells: bells hung by a harness on a horse.
6. easy wind: breeze, light wind.
7. downy flake: soft and fluffy piece of snow.
8. promises: referring to his social duty and responsibilities.
9. sleep: referring to the final rest — death.

诗歌赏析

罗伯特·弗罗斯特是20世纪美国最负盛名的诗人，曾四次荣获普利策文学奖，被尊称为没有桂冠的桂冠诗人。骗人的简单是其诗歌的显著特点。这首诗语言平易，形式简单，看似一幅美丽的山水画，实则自然诗背后孕育着深厚的人生哲理。它表现了生活中两种互相抗衡的力量——大自然中的神秘力量的召唤以及行路人肩负的社会责任。主题依然是选择。

作者以叙事的体裁，用第一人称的方法写到“我”“过客”，在雪夜林边犹豫不决，不知该如何选择自己的行程。该诗充满了丰富的象征意味。行路人、小马分别代表“我”的两面，理性的我和感性的我，树林的主人和他所在的村落代表人类世界，而树林就是大自然的象征。诗人将时间划到一年中最黑的一个夜晚既点明了写作时间，也说出了行路人当时的心境。黑暗、雪花和睡眠都可以指代死亡。最后一行的重复表达了行路人的抉择和决心。人生的责任和义务抵住了死亡的诱惑。路漫漫其修远兮，诗人将不畏艰难，努力求索。

这首诗是声音表达内容的典范。首先，巧妙的韵式表达了诗歌主题。全诗共四节，每节四行，每行抑扬格四音步，前三节连环押韵，其中最后一节为通韵。这种环环相扣的押韵格式使全诗形成紧密结合的整体。前三节提出问题，最后的通韵喻示着问题的解决。其次，用头韵加深诗歌的意旨。第三节 sound 和 sweep 头韵，加强风吹树林的瑟瑟声响和雪花飘落的簌簌声。dark and deep 头韵加重树林幽深、神秘不可知的意味。另外，最后一节四行诗共 27 个词，其中有 15 个词含有长元音和双元音，产生深沉、舒缓、悠远的氛围。

弗罗斯特常说，一首诗应“始于欢乐，终于智慧”。这首诗韵律优美，蕴意丰富，是弗罗斯特诗歌艺术的代表作。

For Study and Discussion

1. Why does the speaker stop by the woods?
2. What tone does the last stanza present?
3. What does “sleep” imply?
4. How do the rhyme scheme and the sound effect serve the development of the poem?
5. What do you think of the didactic function of poetry? What about this poem?
6. Who is the owner of the woods? Are the poet and the owner of the woods good friends? Or are they hostile to each other? Why? If the owner of the woods is of no significance, why does the poet mention that he knows him?

参考译文

雪夜停林边

这是谁家的树林我想我知道，
尽管他家住在村子里；
他看不见我在这儿停驻并观瞧
他的林中雪栖树枝落满地。

我那匹小马肯定认为很古怪，
在这一年中最灰暗的黄昏，
湖面冰封，近无人家，林木雪盖，
停在这儿是什么原因？

它摇动缰铃，似乎在问：
你停在这里，有没有搞错？
此外别无任何的声音，
只有清风徐来，雪花飘落。

树林幽深，景色迷人，
不过，我有约要赴，
须走路程遥远才能投宿，
须走路程遥远才能投宿。

（李正栓　译）

Mending Wall[1]

This poem is about mending wall, the ritual springtime work in New England on the surface. But it has many connotations. It may reveal Frost's concern about human relationship. It may also refer to the conflict between the old and new. Frost always makes use of the commonplace things to convey deep meaning. This poem is the best example.

Something there is that doesn't love a wall,
That sends the frozen-ground-swell[2] under it,
And spills the upper boulders in the sun[3],
And makes gaps even two can pass abreast[4].
The work of hunters is another thing[5]:
I have come after them and made repair
Where they have left not one stone on a stone,
But they would have the rabbit out of hiding,
To please the yelping[6] dogs. The gaps I mean,
No one has seen them made or heard them made,

But at spring mending-time[7] we find them there.
I let my neighbor know beyond the hill;
And on a day we meet to walk the line[8]
And set the wall between us once again.
We keep the wall between us as we go.
To each the boulders that have fallen to each[9].
And some are loaves and some so nearly balls
We have to use a spell[10] to make them balance:
"Stay where you are until our backs are turned!"
We wear our fingers rough with handling them.
Oh, just another kind of outdoor game,
One on a side. It comes to little more:
There where it is we do not need the wall:
He is all pine and I am apple orchard.[11]
My apple trees will never get across
And eat the cones under his pines, I tell him.
He only says, "Good fences make good neighbors."[12]
Spring is the mischief in me,[13] and I wonder
If I could put a notion in his head:
"Why do they make good neighbors? Isn't it
Where there are cows? But here there are no cows.
Before I built a wall I'd ask to know
What I was walling in or walling out[14],
And to whom I was like[15] to give offense.
Something there is that doesn't love a wall,
That wants it down." I could say "Elves"[16] to him,
But it's not elves exactly, and I'd rather
He said it for himself. I see him there
Bringing a stone grasped firmly by the top
In each hand, like an old-stone savage[17] armed.
He moves in darkness as it seems to me,
Not of woods only and the shade of trees.
He will not go behind his father's saying,

And he likes having thought of it so well
He says again, "Good fences make good neighbors."

1914

Notes

1. The poem is chosen from *North of Boston* (1914). It is written in blank verse.
2. the frozen-ground-swell: in winter, the frozen earth expands and the ground under the wall protrudes.
3. spills the upper boulders in the sun: makes the bigger stones on the top of the wall that are exposed in the sun fall down from the wall. boulder: large piece of rock.
4. gaps even two can pass abreast: the gaps are so wide that even two men can go through it side by side. abreast: side by side.
5. another thing: another reason.
6. yelping: barking.
7. spring mending-time: it is a custom to mend the wall in spring in New England.
8. walk the line: walk along the boundary.
9. To each the boulders that have fallen to each: I pick up the rocks that have fallen on my side (of the wall) and my neighbor does so on his side.
10. spell: magic power.
11. He is all pine and I am apple orchard: I grow apples on my side of the wall and my neighbor grows pine on his side.
12. Good fences make good neighbors: it is a famous saying by the famous French philosopher Rousseau (1712—1778).
13. Spring is the mischief in me: spring is the season that inclines me to make fun of my neighbor.
14. walling in or walling out: shutting in or shutting out.
15. like: (informal) likely.
16. Elves: fairies.
17. an old-stone savage: an uncivilized man of the Old Stone Age.

For Study and Discussion

1. What does the wall symbolize in the poem?
2. What does "Something" refer to in the first line?
3. What is the speaker's attitude toward mending the wall? What is his neighbor's? What are their differences?
4. What is the effect of the simile "like an old-stone savage armed" in Line 40?
5. How does the form of the poem help express its content?
6. How do you understand and translate the sentence "Good fences make good neighbors"?

参考译文

补 墙

人们天性不喜欢墙，
它使得墙脚下的冻地膨胀，
把墙头圆石在阳光下鼓起，
使墙裂了缝，二人并肩都可以走过去。
猎人行猎时又是另一番糟蹋：
我总是跟在他们后面去修补，
他们宁可把石头掀得乱七八糟
也要把兔子从隐处赶出来，
以讨好那群狂吠的狗。这墙上的缝
怎么出现的，谁也没看见，谁也没听见，
到了春季整修时，我们才发现。
我通知了住在山那边的邻居，
约好日子巡查地界，
在两家之间再把墙重新砌起。
我们走着，中间隔着一堵墙。
落在各边的石头，由各自去料理。
有些像长面包，有些几乎圆得像球，
费了半天劲才把它们放稳当：
"老实待在那里，等我们转过身!"

我们搬弄石头，把手磨出了茧。
哦！这不过又是一种户外游戏，
一人站在一边。比游戏没强多少。
在这地方，我们根本不需要墙：
他种的是松树，我种的是苹果树。
我的苹果树永远也不会越过去
吃掉他松树下的松球，我对他说。
他只是说："篱笆牢，邻居好。"
春天在我心里作祟，我在想
能不能让他明白一点：
"为什么说'篱笆牢，邻居好'？是否指的是
有牛的人家？可是我们又都没有牛啊。"
我在筑墙之前先要弄个明白，
把什么圈进来，把什么圈在外，
并且我可能得罪的是些什么人家。
人们天性不喜欢墙，
盼着墙倒塌。我可以对他说这是"爱恶作剧的孩子"，
但严格说也不是爱恶作剧的孩子。我希望
他自己能明白。我看见他在那里
搬一块石头，两手紧抓着石头的上端，
像一个旧石器时代野蛮人手执武器。
我觉得他好像走在黑暗里，
这黑暗不仅是来自深林与树荫。
他不肯探究他父亲传给他的格言，
他很满意自己一直都没有忘记，
于是再说一遍，"篱笆牢，邻居好。"

（魏慧哲　李正栓　译）

The Road Not Taken[1]

This poem is one of Frost's best representative works. It describes the speaker's life choices in retrospect. He chose the one "less traveled by" from two similarly appealing roads, which makes all the difference in his later life. Actually, each one has to face choices in his or her life. You cannot eat the cake and have it. Simple and rhythmical, this poem is easy to read as most of Frost's poems. But it never lacks profound meanings after meditation.

Two roads[2] diverged[3] in a yellow wood,
And sorry I could not travel both
And be one traveler[4], long I stood
And looked down one as far as I could
To where it bent[5] in the undergrowth[6];

Then took the other, as just as fair,[7]
And having perhaps the better claim[8],
Because it was grassy and wanted wear[9];
Though as for that[10], the passing there
Had worn them really about the same,

And both that morning equally lay
In leaves no step had trodden black.
Oh, I kept the first for another day!
Yet knowing how way leads on to way,
I doubted if I should ever come back.

I shall be telling this with a sigh
Somewhere ages and ages hence:
Two roads diverged in a wood, and I—
I took the one less traveled by,
And that has made all the difference.

1916

Notes

1. Written in 1915, this poem was published as the first poem of *Mountain Interval* in 1916. It is written in four 5-line stanzas of four feet in iambic or anapestic meters rhyming abaab.
2. roads: implying the choices in human life.

3. diverged: separated.
4. traveler: implying one who is traveling in his long life journey.
5. bent: turned.
6. undergrowth: shrubs growing beneath the trees.
7. as just as fair: both proper and lovely.
8. claim: basis, reasons.
9. wanted wear: was not quite worn, same as "less traveled by" in Line 19. wanted: lacked.
10. as for that: as far as that is concerned. that: referring to "it was grassy and wanted wear."

For Study and Discussion

1. Who is the speaker in the poem?
2. What do the two roads imply in this poem? What does the choice of "take the one less trodden by" imply in the poet's life?
3. Why does the speaker sigh many years later? Does he regret his choice?
4. Robert Frost is good at using "the old-fashioned way to be new". So, what is new in this poem?

参考译文

一条未走的路

两条路岔开在黄叶秋林，
遗憾我不可能同时都走，
遗憾我只是孤身一人，
我伫立远眺想看到路遥终尽，
只见那路拐进矮树林里头。

于是我选了另一条，同样不错，
或许我更有理由选择它，
因为这路上长满了野草未经踩磨；
尽管这条路经人走过
与第一条路同样足迹乱杂。

那天早晨，两条路同时摆在我面前，
树叶里还没有脚印被踩黑；
第一条留待日后再去选！
但又知道，路尽路始紧接连，
我怀疑我是否还能再回归。

很久很久以后在某处，
我会叹息着把这事情讲：
两条路岔开在一林，我未踟躇——
选择了一条人们较少走的路，
而这选择竟决定了人间与天上。

（李正栓 译）

8. Carl Sandburg

Carl Sandburg (卡尔·桑德伯格，1878－1967) was born into a poor family of Swedish immigrants in Galesburg, Illinois on January 6, 1878. Carl was the second of 7 children. He left school when he was 13 and began to take on odd jobs in the southeastern states, including being a milkman, porter, brickmaker, dish-washer, carpenter, salesman and newspaper reporter. Carl enlisted in the army and participated in the Spanish-American War in 1898 as a war correspondent for the Galesburg *Evening Mail* in Puerto Rico for 8 months. Afterwards Sandburg settled down in his hometown and attended Lombard College, where he studied diligently, made a serious beginning with his writing, and earned his living as a call fireman. However, Sandburg disappeared from college a few weeks before the graduation ceremony, and very eagerly began his career as a roving reporter until 1908, when he secured a position as political organizer for the Social Democrats in Wisconsin. Feeling uninterested in politics, Sandburg gave up that position 2 years later and returned to his trade as a journalist. In 1913, Sandburg moved to Chicago on an editorial engagement. There he settled down and the history of his illustrious poems started.

In 1914, Sandburg published his first poem "Chicago", in *Poetry*, a magazine of verse. The work soon aroused dispute among the critics: some showed admiration for the passions it expressed, the straightforward style it used, and the contempt it implied for old conventions; some others bitterly denounced the work just for its vulgar language and insolent tone. He established his reputation with *Chicago Poems* (1916), and then *Cornhuskers* (1918). Soon after the publication of these volumes Sandburg wrote *Smoke and Steel* (1920), his first prolonged attempt to find beauty in modern industrialism. With these three volumes, Sandburg became known for his free verse poems celebrating industrial and agricultural America, American geography and landscape, and the American common people.

As a poet, Sandburg was an active member of the imagist group in the early part of the century: either "Fog" or "Lost—" is illustrated with vivid images. However, most critics considered Sandburg to be a close follower of Whitman. Imitating and experimenting, Sandburg reached the maturity. Having succeeded with his optimistic spirit and freedom in dealing with rhythm, Sandburg was also able to take advantage of Emily Dickinson's epigrammatic style. What's more important, he insisted on innovation in American poetry, not only by invention of new ways of expression, but also by shifting the subject matter form traditional rural landscapes to modern industrial city life. In addition, Sandburg tried to keep up with time in praising modern mechanical culture and adopting colloquial diction into versification.

His later works include those which appeared thereafter: *Good Morning America* (1928); *The People, Yes* (1936); *Abraham Lincoln: The War Years* (1939), for which he was awarded the first Pulitzer Prize; *Complete Poems* (1950), which won him the second Pulitzer Prize; and *Honey and Salt* (1963). Carl Sandburg died in 1967.

Fog[1]

This poem depicts a vivid fog scene in Chicago, an important city and harbor in America in the early 20th century. Short and simple, it is a typical poem of Imagism, with "cat" as the central image. The poet compares the immaterial, lifeless fog to a material, living cat. Through the description of the cat's movement, from the static to the dynamic, from the near to the distant, it may also reflect the alienated relationship between the country and the city, nature and man or the modern industrial civilization.

The fog comes
on little cat feet.[2]

It sits looking
over harbor and city
on silent haunches[3]
and then moves on.

1916

Notes

1. This poem is chosen from *Chicago Poems* (1916). It is written in free verse.
2. The fog comes / on little cat feet: the fog is compared to a cat whose movement is similar to that of the fog. Cf. T. S. Eliot's "The Love Song of J. Alfred Prufrock", Lines 15—22.
3. sits… on silent haunches: to squat silently. haunches: an animal's loin and leg together.

诗歌赏析

卡尔·桑德伯格是美国芝加哥诗派的代表，惠特曼风格的继承人。他写的意象诗也很经典。《雾》就是其中的一首。它描写了20世纪初美国重要的工业城市和港口城市芝加哥的雾景。

这是一首典型的意象派小诗，仅有区区六行二十一个单词。它将雾以猫的形象来描写，开头两句用猫的爪子来模拟雾的悄然而至。第三到五句是猫"蹲着"的特写。它蹲在高处，静静地俯瞰这个港口城市。最后，猫悄然离去。雾的运动恰似猫的匍行，它的消逝也如猫一样，来无影，去无踪。猫像一个猎奇者，探头探脑，好奇地观望着城市的发展和工业的进步。猫的行动由远及近，又渐行渐远，像电影中蒙太奇的镜头，飘忽不定。用"迈"、

“坐”、“蹲”、“行”几个动词将猫的行为刻画得栩栩如生，由动到静，再由静到动，构成一幅连续的画面。诗人用猫的行为来展示雾的特性，亦静亦动，赋予雾以生命。

这首简短的意象诗给人带来无限遐想。从雾到猫，由无形到有形，从静态到动态的描摹，从乡村到城市的转移，这一比拟展现出多重的变化。20世纪初，美国经济发展迅速，现代工业文明对自然界和人类生活影响巨大。动态的雾和静态的港口城市之间形成对比。猫的行为更像是一种试探，从乡间到城市，观察工业化城市的发展和喧嚣。猫的远去意味着疏离。这首小诗表达了当时的普通民众对这一时代巨变观望的态度。

桑德伯格曾说过：“简单的诗是为简单的人民而写。”这首诗意象简单，语言平易，蕴无穷之意于言外，堪称美国意象诗中的经典之作。

For Study and Discussion

1. What does the fog stand for?
2. In what way is the fog similar to a cat?
3. What features of the fog are revealed by the verbs in the poem?
4. What does the come-and-go of the fog want to tell us?
5. Explain the transitions in the poem.
6. Have you often seen fogs or haze? What casued them?
7. Learn this poem by heart and imitate it to write a short poem of your own.

参考译文

雾

雾来了
迈着碎小猫步。

它坐下来张望
港口与城市
悄悄地蹲息
之后又继续前行。

（李正栓　译）

Chicago[1]

This is the best-known of Sandburg's early poems. It vividly describes the common labor and people in Chicago. Its language is common and simple, but its craftsmanship is impressive. The poet uses personification, parallel constructions and other devices to glorify the optimistic and aggressive spirit of Chicago. The images of the working people, the present participles, and the frequent use of verbs best exemplify the mobility and vitality of Chicago.

Hog Butcher for the World,
Tool Maker, Stacker of Wheat,
Player with railroads and the Nation's Freight Handler;
Stormy, husky[2], brawling,
City of the big shoulders[3]:

They tell me you are wicked and I believed them, for I have seen
your painted women[4] under the gas lamps luring the farm boys.
And they tell me you are crooked and I answer: Yes, it is true I
have seen the gunman kill and go free to kill again.
And they tell me you are brutal and my reply is: On the faces of
women and children I have seen the marks of wanton hunger[5].
And having answered so I turn once more to those who sneer at
this my city[6], and I give them back the sneer and say to them:
Come and show me another city with lifted head singing so
proud to be alive and coarse and strong and cunning.
Flinging magnetic curses[7] amid[8] the toil of piling job on job, here
is a tall bold slugger set vivid against the little soft cities;
Fierce as a dog with tongue lapping for action, cunning as a
savage pitted against[9] the wilderness,
Bareheaded,
Shoveling,
Wrecking,[10]
Planning,

Building, breaking, rebuilding,
Under the smoke, dust all over his mouth, laughing with white teeth,
Under the terrible burden of destiny laughing as a young man laughs,
Laughing even as an ignorant fighter laughs who has never lost a battle,
Bragging and laughing that under his wrist is the pulse, and under his ribs the heart of the people,
Laughing!
Laughing the stormy, husky, brawling laughter of Youth, half-naked, sweating, proud to be Hog Butcher, Tool Maker, Stacker of Wheat, Player with Railroads and Freight Handler to the Nation.

1914, 1916

Notes

1. It is written in free verse. Chicago is the second largest city in America, the hub in the Midwest for trains, trucks, ships and planes and is famous for its developed butcher, iron and steel company. And Chicago has one of America's busiest ports. It connects the Great Lakes to the Atlantic Ocean.
2. husky: (slang) strong.
3. City of the big shoulders: it has become the slogan of Chicago to describe the aggressive feature of this industrial city.
4. painted women: prostitutes with too much make-up on their faces.
5. wanton hunger: referring to the suffering of the common people in the hard times of the Great Depression.
6. this my city: this city of mine. It is grammatically wrong but well chosen, which best expresses the pride of being a Chicagoan.
7. magnetic curses: attractive curses.
8. amid: among.
9. pitted against: struggling against.
10. Wrecking: destroying.

For Study and Discussion

1. What is the key note of this poem?

2. What impression of Chicago have you got after reading the poem?
3. What attitude toward industrialization is reflected in this poem?
4. The word "laugh" is repeated eight times in variant forms in the last six lines. What is the effect of this repetition?
5. How is the rhythm of colloquial speech used in this poem?

参考译文

芝加哥

向全世界供肉的屠夫，
粮食储藏者，工具制造商，
铁路玩弄者，国家运输王；
你脾气暴怒，声音嘶哑，喧哗不止，
是个膀大肩阔的城市。

有人说你邪恶，我相信，
因为我见过你城内浓妆艳抹的妇女
站在汽灯下引诱农家小伙子。
有人说你畸形，我就说：
是的，是真的！我见过有人持枪杀人，
逍遥法外又杀人！
有人说你残暴，我的回答是：
在城内妇女和儿童的脸上
我能读出极端饥饿的痕迹。
答完这些问题，我又一次转问那些
蔑视我们城市的人，我对他们
回报以蔑视，并且告诉他们：
来，给我展示另外一个城市，哪一城能昂首挺胸
富有活力地傲唱，唱得粗犷，
可爱又响亮？
在粗重的体力劳动中夹杂的极富魅力的咒骂，
这是一个勇敢的大个子拳击手
与娇小的城市形成鲜明的对照；

凶猛得像狗伸舌要行动，
机灵得像野兽面对荒野要谋生，
光着头，
挥着锹，
拆旧物，
想新景，
建了拆，拆了建，
在烟雾之下，满嘴泥土，大笑露齿
露着白白的牙齿，
在命运重压下，大笑
像个青年人那样大笑，
笑得像一个从未战败过的
斗士天真地大笑，
又是夸口又是大笑，说他腕下
跳动着脉搏，在他肋下是人们的心脏，
他大笑！
笑得粗犷、嘶哑、响亮，那是青年人的
大笑，半裸着身子，大汗淋漓，自豪地担当屠夫、
工具制造商、粮食储藏者、
铁路玩弄者、国家运输王。

（李正栓　韩志华　译）

The Harbor[1]

Short and powerful, this is another of Sandburg's poems about Chicago. Sandburg describes the scenes he saw as he walked through the Chicago streets. The central feature of the poem is contrast. There are two contrasted groups of images: the gloomy images (huddles, ugly walls, hunger-deep eyes, shadows, hunger-hands) in the city and the bright images (a blue burst of lake, lake waves, a spray-flung curve of shore, a fluttering storm of gulls, wheeling free) in the harbor. The crowded picture in the city is contrasted to the serene scene of the shore. It shows Sandburg's concern about the industrialization of the city.

Passing through huddled[2] and ugly walls
By doorways where women
Looked from their hunger-deep eyes[3],
Haunted with shadows of hunger-hands,
Out from the huddled and ugly walls,
I came sudden, at the city's edge[4],
On a blue burst of lake,
Long lake waves breaking under the sun
On a spray-flung curve of shore;
And a fluttering storm of gulls,
Masses of great gray wings
And flying white bellies
Veering and wheeling free[5] in the open.

Notes

1. This poem was published in 1916. It is a typical free verse containing only one stanza of thirteen lines with irregular lengths and rhythms.
2. huddled: crowded.
3. their hunger-deep eyes: deep-sunken eyes of the poor women, referring to the poverty-stricken condition of the poor people.
4. I came sudden, at the city's edge: it is the dividing line of the poem. Before this, there are lines describing the dark side of the city; after this, there are lines displaying the beauty of nature. sudden: suddenly.
5. wheeling free: gliding with freedom. The seagulls are enjoying the freedom.

For Study and Discussion

1. What does "The Harbor" symbolize?
2. What is the differences of Chicago in this poem and in "Chicago"?
3. How does the poet use contrast to convey his idea in this poem?

参考译文

港 口

穿过拥挤的人群和丑陋的城墙，
门廊里妇女们饥饿深陷的眼睛

带着饥饿魔掌的阴影
向行人张望。
离开拥挤的人群和丑陋的城墙，
突然间发现我已到了城市的边沿。
在蓝色的湖里
湖水波涌在阳光下闪现，
沿着那浪花飞溅的湖弯。
一群飞起的海鸥，
一片硕大的灰色翅膀，
飞翔中的白色肚皮
在空中一会儿变向一会儿滑翔。

（李正栓　译）

9. Wallace Stevens

Wallace Stevens（华莱士·斯蒂文斯，1879－1955）was born in Reading, Pennsylvania, on October 2, 1879. After three years at Harvard from 1897 to 1900, he went to New York University Law School, on his father's advice. After graduation, he was admitted to the U.S. Bar in 1904. In 1916, after practicing law for many years, he was engaged by the Hartford Accident and Indemnity Insurance Company and worked as an executive until 1955, the year of his retirement and his death.

Stevens began his writing of poems at Harvard. During his years in New York, he became acquainted with a number of young writers in Greenwich Village, including the poets William Carlos Williams, Marianne Moore, and E. E. Cummings. Though he wanted to be a successful lawyer, he never gave up writing poems. His first book of poems, *Harmonium*, was published in 1923. After it, more and more poems poured out over the next 20 years, including *Ideas of Order* (1935), *Owl's Clover* (1936), *The Man with the Blue Guitar* (1937), *Parts of a World* (1942), *The Auroras of Autumn*

(1950), a collection of essays on poetry, *The Necessary Angel: Essays on Reality and the Imagination* (1951), and *The Collected Poems of Wallace Stevens* (1954).

In his lifetime, Stevens was well-known first as a lawyer, then as a successful businessman and an outstanding poet. As a poet, he had a strong passion for perfecting what he wrote. Having been regarded as a poet of the imagist group, Stevens was good at applying metaphors and symbols. As with all the other imagists, he experimented a lot with styles, sound, and rhymes.

Actually Stevens made great efforts to bridge the world of reality with the world of imagination. More than any other modern poet, Stevens was concerned with the transformative power of imagination. He was interested in the relationship of chaos and order, the reconciliation of reality and imagination. He insisted that an artist should observe reality and create reality out of his imagination, and that the order and faith we have lost in modern society can be recreated in artistic work through imagination.

Most of Stevens' important poems were composed during the time of the Great Depression and the two World Wars. Yet he showed little concern with the sufferings and frustrations of the time, for he believed that, as a poet, what he should and could do is not to heal or reform society, but help his people to become more happily aware of the beauty and pleasure, excitement and meaning in the sordidness of reality.

His first book of poems, *Harmonium* exhibited the influence of the English Romanticts and the French symbolists, an inclination to aesthetic philosophy, and a wholly original style and sensibility: exotic, whimsical, infused with the light and color of an Impressionist painting.

Anecdote of the Jar[1]

This poem is a symbolic poem with the jar as the central image, which symbolizes art. It discusses the relationship between art and nature. The jar stands in contrast to the wilderness, which represents nature. In the poem, the jar has the power of making things change from their wildness and roughness to order and discipline.

I placed a jar[2] in Tennessee[3],
And round it was[4], upon a hill.
It made the slovenly[5] wilderness
Surround that hill.

The wilderness rose up to it,
And sprawled[6] around, no longer wild[7].
The jar was round upon the ground
And tall and of a port in air[8].

It took dominion[9] everywhere.
The jar was gray and bare[10].
It did not give of[11] bird or bush,
Like nothing else in Tennessee.

1923

Notes

1. This poem was chosen from his first book of poems, *Harmonium* (1923). It is written in three quatrains of iambic tetrameter lines with no regular rhymes.
2. a jar: a wide-mouthed pot, here standing for art.
3. Tennessee: a state in the middle south of America. The eastern part of the state is covered by wilderness, and the area of forests in this state is nearly equal to half of the whole area. Here it symbolizes nature.
4. And round it was: and it was round.
5. slovenly: not neat, untidy.
6. sprawled: spread out.
7. no longer wild: it has two meanings of "tame" and "orderly".

8. of a port in air：solemn in manner. port：pose. air：look，manner.
9. dominion：control.
10. bare：with no decoration.
11. give of：produce.

诗歌赏析

《坛子的轶事》选自华莱士·斯蒂文斯的第一部诗集《簧风琴》。这首诗以冷静的笔触，从具体的意象入手，探讨了艺术和自然的关系。一只放在山巅之上的坛子是其中的中心意象。该诗由三个抑扬格四音步的四行诗节组成，无固定的韵脚。这种张弛有度、节制有序又不死板的诗歌形式与诗歌的内容相得益彰。

第一节交代了人物、事件和地点。说话者将一只圆坛放在了田纳西州的山巅，它使得周围凌乱的荒野向着山丘凝聚。一只普通的坛子俨然有了统领万物的力量。人们可能将一只坛子放在桌子上，院子里，但不大可能放在一座山上。于是坛子便具有了象征意味。田纳西州位于美国中南部，它的东部大部分被荒野覆盖，面积的一半都是森林。因此，田纳西州代表大自然。坛子是手工艺品，是艺术的产物，在此象征人类文明或艺术。

第二节中坛子和周围环境形成一种对比。诗中的坛子像君临万方的君主，具有神秘的力量。它的出现改变了荒野的无序。坛子具备改变周围事物的能力，它使荒野不再荒芜，使野蛮回归秩序、文明。坛子与荒野的对立象征着艺术和自然的对立。

最后一节侧重坛子和荒野的关系。虽然荒野向坛子臣服，但是"空空的"坛子不能繁衍生命，没有生命力。这说明艺术虽然超越自然，但是离不开自然。艺术和自然是相互依托、密不可分的关系。

For Study and Discussion

1. What is the relationship between the jar and the wilderness as shown in this poem?
2. Why does the poet choose Tennessee to place the jar?
3. What does the word "dominion" imply in the last stanza?
4. What is your understanding of the last two lines in this poem?

参考译文

坛子的轶事

我把一只坛子放在田纳西，
它是圆的，置在山巅。
它使凌乱的荒野
围着山峰排列。

于是荒野向坛子涌起，
匍匐在四周，再不荒莽。
坛子圆圆地置在地上
高高屹立，巍峨庄严。

它君临着四面八方，
坛是灰色的，未施彩妆。
它无法产生鸟或树林，
不像田纳西别的事物。

（赵毅衡　译）

10. William Carlos Williams

William Carlos Williams (1883－1963，威廉·卡洛斯·威廉斯) was born in Rutherford, New Jersey, a town near the city of Paterson, on September 17, 1883. He studied medicine at the University of Pennsylvania, where he came into contact with two masters of imagism: Ezra Pound and Hilda Doolittle, whose imagist ideals had a tremendous impact on Williams' early poetic works. Williams, whose fame as a poet paralleled that of Ezra Pound and T. S. Eliot, was a physician factually all his adult life. Williams derived from his practice of medicine the knowledge of people that inspired the best of his poems. With a special knowledge of humanity and a diagnostic reserve towards the frailty or strength of mankind, he soon distinguished himself as a poet who was able to illustrate a probing and clinical realism by seeking beauty and truth in plain reality.

Williams published his first volume of poetry, *Poems*, in 1909. It was very poorly accepted by the public. The collection was followed up by a lot of others. Among them, the most popular are *The Tempers* (1913), *Kora in Hell* (1920), *Sour Grapes* (1921), *Spring and All* (1923), which contained his most famous poem, "The Red Wheelbarrow", *Complete Collected Poems* (1938), *The Desert Music* (1954), *Journey to Love* (1955), *Pictures from Brueghel* (1962), and *Paterson*, a great epic of five volumes, published in 1946, 1948, 1949, 1951, and 1958. He won the National Book Award in 1950, the Bollingen Prize in 1953, and the Pulitzer Prize in 1962. Williams died on March 4, 1963 at the age of 79 at his home in Rutherford.

Williams has always been known as an experimenter, an innovator, and a revolutionary figure in American poetry. Like Ezra Pound, Williams had been experimenting to give up the conventional and metaphysical interest, and to seek signs of permanence in the local and concrete by applying the natural American idiom and the variable rhythms and vocabulary, by concerning himself with the ordinary, the commonplace, and the specific American atmosphere. For Williams, the essence of poetry lies in "no ideas but in things". He aimed at reproducing immediate experience. His poems are always simple, direct, and apparently formless. "There is no optimistic blindness in Williams," wrote Randall Jarrell, "though there is a fresh gaiety, a stubborn or invincible joyousness."

The Red Wheelbarrow[1]

This is a famous representative of Imagist poetry. It precisely depicts a beautiful scene in a farmyard of a red wheelbarrow beside the white chickens after a rain. One can see the close relation between the poetry of Imagism and painting in this poem. The juxtaposition of different objects of different colors is quite fresh, full of visual beauty. It is like an ordinary prose sentence broken up in a peculiar way. The line arrangement of long and short pattern in each stanza imitates the zigzag course in which a red wheelbarrow went in the yard.

The poem begins with "so much depends ...", but what depends, the poet doesn't mention. Maybe the act of experiencing the object is the very significance of this poem.

So much depends
upon

a red wheel
barrow

glazed[2] with rain
water

beside the white
chickens.

1923

Notes

1. This poem was published in *Spring and All* in 1923. It is written in four couplets. In each couplet, there are two stressed syllables in the first line and one in the second.
2. glazed: varnished, glossed.

诗歌赏析

《红色手推车》是意象派诗歌的经典，也是威廉·卡洛斯·威廉斯的代表作之一。它选自诗集《春天及一切》。作者用十几个字将一幅日常生活画面生动地展现在读者眼前——雨后的园子里一个红色的手推车在前行，一群可爱的白色小鸡在旁边跑来跳去。

这是一首视觉诗。整首诗只有一句话，被分成四节八行，诗行的长短交错展示出手推车的运动曲线。全诗多跨行现象，其中 wheelbarrow 和 rainwater 两个单词被分开，读起来很拗口，好像听到了手推车运动时颠簸的声响。视觉、听觉和触觉意象堆积在一起，形成一个鲜明的感官印象。

威廉斯说过，"没有概念，除了在事物中"。这首诗仅凭手推车、雨水和小鸡等几个简单的意象勾勒出一幅生动、美丽的画面，无任何深层意义的解读。诗歌以“这么多全靠”起首，却始终没有交代到底什么全靠，给读者一个开放的想象空间。

For Study and Discussion

1. This poem is a pattern poem. How does its pattern help express its meaning?
2. Pay attention to the images used in this poem. What is the effect of these images?
3. What “depends upon” the things mentioned in the poem?
4. How does this poem resemble a haiku? How is it different?

参考译文

红色手推车

几多沉重
压在

一辆红色
手推车上

推车上雨水
闪亮

停放在几只白色
小鸡旁

（李正栓　译）

11. Ezra Pound

Ezra Pound（埃兹拉·庞德，1885—1972）was born in Hailey，Idaho on October 30，1885 and brought up in Wyancote，Pennsylvania，where his father was an assayer to the United States Mint. He graduated from Hamilton College，Clinton，N. Y. in 1905，and the next year he received a master's

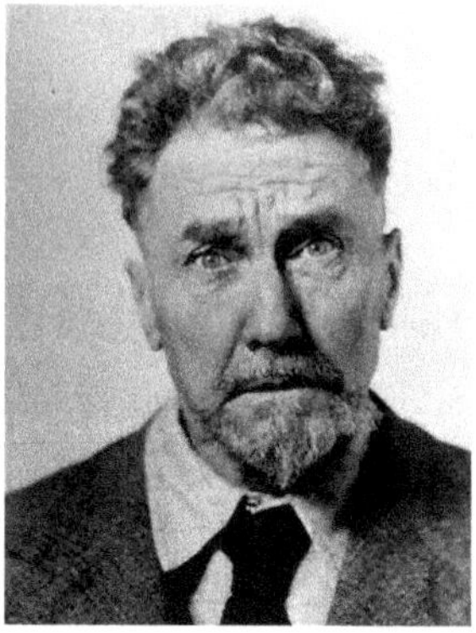

degree in the University of Pennsylvania. He became a professor of language at the age of 22. However, after 4 months of teaching, Pound left the United States for Europe in 1908, first to Venice, and then settled in London from 1908 to 1920, where he associated with many writers, including William Butler Yeats, for whom he worked as a secretary, and T. S. Eliot, whose *The Waste Land* he drastically edited and improved. Pound's first book of poetry, *A Lume Spento*, was published in Venice in 1908. From then on Pound began to lecture on romantic literature, published several volumes of verse and criticism, and translated medieval Italian poetry. What's more important, he spearheaded the new school of poetry known as the Imagist Movement.

The Imagist Movement refers to a trend of literature, especially in poetry writing, in England and the United States, which flourished from 1909 to 1917. The imagists approved the use of free verse, direct common speech, new rhythms, absolute freedom in choice of subject matter, and the evocation of precise imagery in hard, clear poetic works. They cultivated concision and directness, building their short poems around single images; they also preferred loose cadences to traditional regular rhythms. In 1914, the first anthology of imagist poems was edited by Pound, entitled *Des Imagistes*, including the works of 10 outstanding imagist poets, such as William Carlos Williams, H. D. (Hilda Doolittle), Amy Lowell and Ezra Pound.

During his lifetime, Pound produced many volumes of works, including *Personae* (1910), *Homage to Sextus Propertius* (1934), *Make It New* (1934), *The ABC of Reading* (1934), *The Pisan Cantos* (1948), which won him the Bollingen Prize, *Literary Essays* (1954), *The Cantos* (1972). Among them, *The Cantos* is the most outstanding, on which Pound spent over 50 years from 1915 to 1969. The book culminates Pound's writing and has become an important landmark of modern poetry. It is a long work consisting of 117 chapters, with neither a central theme, nor a complete plot. It is not composed in any systematic order, either. Pound also translated the poems of Li Po (701— 762). Though the translation was not good enough in terms of faithfulness, his translation and creation of images from Chinese poetry helped a lot in the forming of imagism in the United States.

Ezra Pound was one of the most influential American poets who decisively affected the course of the 20th century American literature. He is regarded as the father of modern American poetry. Impatient with the fetters of English traditional poetics, he led the experiment in revolutionizing poetry. It is he who put forward the slogan "make it new" that is illustrative of modernism. It is he who first discovered T. S. Eliot and blue-penciled the latter's famous poem, *The Waste Land*. It is he who helped William Butler Yeats, James Joyce, D. H. Lawrence, and William Carlos Williams in their literary careers. And he survived them all, writing continually right up to his death. He died in Venice as a recluse on November 1, 1972.

In a Station of the Metro[1]

This poem records a transient scene in a station of the metro, which left permanent impression in Pound's mind. It is the most representative work of imagist poetry in both England and America, which perfectly shows the principles of imagism. The whole poem, containing only two lines with two juxtaposed images, has not any words for explanation or ornaments. Yet with "a wet, black bough" to symbolize the station and "petals" to symbolize the beautiful faces of the crowd in the station, the poem brings the readers unlimited imaginations and meanings. If readers are shocked by its concentration in the first sight, they are also by its beauty after deep reading.

The apparition of these faces[2] in the crowd;
Petals on a wet, black bough.

1913, 1916

Notes

1. This poem was published in 1913. Pound has left a record of how he came to write the poem:

"I got out of a metro train at La Concorde, and saw suddenly a beautiful face, and then another beautiful woman, and I tried all that day to find words for what this had meant to me, and I could not find any words that seemed to me worthy, or as lovely as that sudden emotion." And that evening, as I went home, along the rue Raynouard, I was still trying and I found, suddenly, the expression. I do not mean that I found words, but there came an equation … not in speech, but in little splotches of colour. It was just that—a "pattern," or hardly a pattern, if by "pattern" you mean something with a "repeat" in it. But it was a word, the beginning, for me, of a language in colour …

That evening in the rue Raynouard, I realized quite vividly that if I were a painter, or if I had, often, that kind of emotion, or even if I had the energy to get paints and brushes and keep at it, I might found a new school of painting, of "non-representative" painting, a painting that would speak only by arrangements in colour.

… That is to say, my experience in Paris should have gone into paint … The point of Imagism is that it does not use images as ornaments. The image is itself the speech … The "one-image poem" is a form of super-position, that is to say, it is one idea set on top of another. I found it useful in getting out of the impasse in which I had been left by my metro emotion. I wrote a 30-line poem, and destroyed it because it was what we call work "of second intensity". Six months later I made a poem half that length; a year later I made the following hokku-like sentence: … the Metro: referring to the Paris subway.

2. The apparition of these faces: their ghost-like faces.

诗歌赏析

埃兹拉·庞德是美国著名诗人、评论家、意象派诗歌的创始人。《在地铁站口》是意象派诗歌的经典之作，它充分体现了意象主义的创作原则——主观与客观相结合，理智与情感相结合，即庞德所推崇的"一瞬间思想和感情的复合体"。

有一次，庞德从巴黎的一处地铁站走出，突然看到黑压压的人群中有几个美丽的面孔忽明忽暗，若隐若现。这一瞬间的美感给他留下了深刻的印象。为了记录下这转瞬即逝的景象及其带来的情感愉悦，庞德曾经数易其稿。最初，他写下了一首 30 行的诗歌，半年后修改为 15 行，一年后，压缩成了这首日本俳句般的意象派诗歌名作。在短短两行诗中，庞德通过意象的叠加，将地铁站口行人的脸与湿漉漉枝头的花瓣联系起来，产生了如诗如画的美感。

除了意象的叠加，比喻的叠加也是这首诗的突出特点。第一行诗将地铁站口行人的面孔比作幽灵，突出神秘感。第二行又将这些面孔比作“黑色潮湿枝头上的一片片花瓣”。黑色潮湿枝头是理性的客观场景描摹，花瓣是感性的主观审美体验。一个指代地铁站的阴暗，一个突出行人面孔的美艳。

诗是无形画，画是有形诗。通过短短两行诗，庞德将诗与画紧密联系在一起。

For Study and Discussion

1. Why is the title important to the poem?
2. What are the features of this poem? Which impress you the most?
3. What figure of speech is used in this poem?
4. What does the word “apparition” suggest?
5. What two images are juxtaposed in this poem? What is the effect of the juxtaposition?
6. Learn from Ezra Pound and write a poem like this.

参考译文

在地铁站口

（本诗是诗人在巴黎地铁车站
对他所看到的人群面孔进行的描写。）

人群中幽灵般的一张张面孔；
黑色潮湿枝头上的一片片花瓣。

（李正栓　译）

A Pact[1]

This poem conveys Pound's relationship with Whitman, and his change of attitudes towards Whitman from detestation to admiration. It also shows his positive attitude toward poetic innovation and exploitation. Whitman is a great figure that cannot be omitted in American poetry. Pound compares Whitman to a “pig-headed father”, and himself a “grown child”; he admits that Whitman is his sap and root, but he is not satisfied with the pure imitation of the great man. He would like to push the American poetry into a new age. It is written in a colloquial style, which is a common feature of Whitman's poetry, not that of imagism.

I make a pact with you, Walt Whitman—
I have detested[2] you long enough.
I come to you as a grown child
Who has had a pig-headed father[3];
I am old enough now to make friends.
It was you that broke the new wood[4],
Now is a time for carving[5].
We have one sap and one root—
Let there be commerce[6] between us.

1913, 1916

Notes

1. This poem was published in 1913. It is written in a single 9-line stanza with the cadence of natural speech.
2. detested: hated.
3. a pig-headed father: here referring to Whitman. pig-headed: stupid.
4. broke the new wood: cut down the new trees, here implying Whitman's innovation of poetry.
5. carving: sculpting, here suggesting the further exploration of poetry writing by Pound.
6. commerce: communication, exchange of views and ideas.

For Study and Discussion

1. What is the "pact" about?
2. Why does Pound compare himself to a grown child of a pig-headed father?
3. What is Pound's view on Whitman?
4. What is the tone of the poem?

5. Compare Pound's poems with those of Whitman. Are they really as described in this poem?

参考译文

合 约

沃尔特·惠特曼，我与你有约在先——
我以前一直把你讨厌。
我现在向你走近，
因为长大的孩子已离开愚蠢的父亲；
我已长大成人，能交友择朋。
是你砍下了新木，
现在已适合雕刻。
我们合一种树汁，合一条根，
我们有同种汁液同样根须——
愿你我之间存有流通和交易。

（李正栓 译）

12. T. S. Eliot

Thomas Stearns Eliot（T. S. 艾略特，1888－1965）is considered as the leader among writers in English during the first half of the 20th century. Not only was he a great poet, a great critic, a fine playwright, who had a far-reaching influence on others, but he sought to become the conscience of his generation, deliberately fitting himself for his role. He described himself in a celebrated phrase as a "classicist in literature, royalist in politics, and Anglo-Catholic in religion".

Eliot was born in St. Louis, Missouri on September 26, 1888, in the family of a rich merchant from New England and educated at Harvard, the

Sorbonne in Paris and Oxford in England. In 1914 Eliot moved to England, where he worked first as a teacher, then as a bank clerk, and in 1925 he became the director of a London publishing house, a position which he held until the end of his life. In 1927, Eliot became a British citizen and a member of the Church of England.

In September, 1914, Eliot met Ezra Pound, to whom he read "The Love Song of J. Alfred Prufrock". Pound immediately recognized its merit. Under Pound's encouragement, Eliot had his first notable poem published in 1915. What Eliot achieved was an exact expression for the spiritual disease of the 20th century. Eliot's classic expression of the temper of his age is *The Waste Land* (1922), a poem which, despite its extreme difficulty, brought him immediate fame. *The Hallow Men*, published 2 years later, is almost as powerful an expression of an age of doubt that longs in despair for belief. His poem *Ash Wednesday* was written in 1930. Nine years later he wrote the first *Four Quartets* (1943). Eliot is also noteworthy for his essays on literature. His critical works include *Tradition and Individual Talent* (1917), *The Metaphysical Poets* (1921), and *The Function of Criticism* (1923), which made him the founder of New Criticism.

In the latter part of his life, Eliot turned more and more to playwriting and to the writing of essays and books discussing social and religious themes. It was his aim to revitalize poetic drama, to write plays that would seem perfectly natural to audiences although the characters were speaking poetry. One of his modern plays, *The Cocktail Party* (1949), had a long run in both London and New York, but his earlier play, *Murder in the Cathedral* (1935), is closest to traditional poetic drama. Eliot won the Nobel Prize for Literature in 1948. He died on January 4, 1965 in London.

At first, Eliot, like Pound, attempted to produce "pure imagery" with no added meaning or symbolism. Then he began adding one image to another in such a way that his attitude and mood became clear. In his best works, the image, his own philosophy and the music of words are all harmoniously blended. Eliot mingled grand images with commonplace ones; he combined trivial and tawdry images with traditional poetic subjects. Eliot rarely made his meaning explicit. The internal logic of his poems is carried out by swiftly accumulating images, suggestions and echoes, depending for their interpretation upon the imagination of the reader.

Eliot belongs to the so-called Waste Land Painters, which include such writers as F. Scott Fitzgerald, Ernest Hemingway and William Faulkner. With their writings, all of them paint the postwar western world as a wasteland, lifeless and hopeless. In Eliot's poetry, modern civilized society turns into a waste deathly land due to ethical degradation and disillusionment with dreams.

The Love Song of J. Alfred Prufrock[1]

"The Love Song of J. Alfred Prufrock" was one of the earliest poems to earn fame for T. S. Eliot. In this poem, Eliot partly follows the aim of the Imagists to precisely use visual images and avoid all looseness of expression and sentiment, and partly tries to use more or less of the "stream-of-consciousness" technique to convey the spontaneity of the ideas and feelings welling up his mind. So there is no sequence of events, nor passage of time. In spite of its title, the poem is not a love song in a strict sense of the term. It deals with the thoughts of the central figure Prufrock intermixed with random descriptions of his environment. It is actually the confession of Prufrock, a middle-aged man and a romantic aesthete who is bored with his ineffectual life and is faced with despair because he wishes but is unable to break away from his meaningless existence. In this sense, the poem is a mild satire on the decadence and futility of life in the upper classes in bourgeois society. It is difficult to understand due to its frequent use of allusions, farfetched imagery and unusual metaphors.

S'io credessi che mia risposta fosse
a persona che mai tornasse al mondo,
questa fiamma staria senza piu scosse.
Ma per cio che giammai di questo fondo
non torno vivo alcun, s'I' odo il vero,
senza tema d'infamia ti rispondo.[2]

Let us go then, you and I,[3]

When the evening is spread out against the sky
Like a patient etherised[4] upon a table[5];
Let us go, through certain half-deserted streets,
The muttering retreats
Of restless nights in one-night cheap hotels
And sawdust restaurants[6] with oyster-shells:
Streets that follow like a tedious argument
Of insidious intent[7]
To lead you to an overwhelming question …
Oh, do not ask, "What is it?"
Let us go and make our visit.

In the room the women come and go
Talking of Michelangelo[8].

The yellow fog that rubs its back upon the windowpanes,
The yellow smoke that rubs its muzzle on the windowpanes.
Licked its tongue into the corners of the evening,

Lingered upon the pools that stand in drains,
Let fall upon its back the soot that falls from chimneys,
Slipped by the terrace, made a sudden leap,
And seeing that it was a soft October night,
Curled once about the house, and fell asleep.

And indeed there will be time[9]
For the yellow smoke that slides along the street
Rubbing its back upon the windowpanes;
There will be time, there will be time
To prepare a face[10] to meet the faces that you meet;
There will be time to murder and create,
And time for all the works and days of hands[11]
That lift and drop a question on your plate;

Time for you and time for me,
And time yet for a hundred indecisions,
And for a hundred visions and revisions,
Before the taking of a toast and tea.[12]

In the room the women come and go
Talking of Michelangelo.

And indeed there will be time
To wonder, "Do I dare?" and, "Do I dare?"
Time to turn back and descend the stair,
With a bald spot in the middle of my hair—[13]
(They[14] will say: "How his[15] hair is growing thin!")
My morning coat, my collar mounting firmly to the chin,
My necktie rich and modest[16], but asserted[17] by a simple pin—
(They will say: "But how his arms and legs are thin!")
Do I dare
Disturb the universe?[18]
In a minute there is time
For decisions and revisions which a minute will reverse.

For I have known them all already, known them all—
Have known the evenings, mornings, afternoons,
I have measured out my life with coffee spoons;
I know the voices dying with a dying fall[19]
Beneath the music from a farther room.
So how should I presume?[20]

And I have known the eyes already, known them all—
The eyes that fix you in a formulated phrase,[21]
And when I am formulated[22], sprawling on a pin,[23]
When I am pinned and wriggling on the wall,
Then how should I begin

To spit out all the butt-ends of my days and ways?[24]
And how should I presume?
And I have known the arms already, known them all—
Arms that are braceleted and white and bare
(But in the lamplight, downed[25] with light brown hair!)
Is it perfume from a dress
That makes me so digress?[26]
Arms that lie along a table, or wrap about a shawl.
And should I then presume?
And how should I begin?
…
Shall I say, I have gone at dusk through narrow streets
And watched the smoke that rises from the pipes
Of lonely men in shirt-sleeves, leaning out of windows? …

I should have been a pair of ragged claws[27]
Scuttling[28] across the floors of silent seas.
…
And the afternoon, the evening, sleeps so peacefully!
Smoothed by long fingers,
Asleep … tired … or it malingers[29],
Stretched on the floor, here beside you and me.
Should I, after tea and cakes and ices,[30]
Have the strength to force the moment to its crisis?
But though I have wept and fasted, wept and prayed,[31]
Though I have seen my head (grown slightly bald) brought in upon a platter,
I am no prophet[32]—and here's no great-matter;
I have seen the moment of my greatness flicker,
And I have seen the eternal Footman[33] hold my coat, and snicker,
And in short, I was afraid.

And would it have been worth it, after all,
After the cups, the marmalade, the tea,
Among the porcelain, among some talk of you and me,
Would it have been worth while,
To have bitten off the matter with a smile,[34]
To have squeezed the universe into a ball
To roll it towards some overwhelming question,[35]
To say: "I am Lazarus[36], come from the dead,
Come back to tell you all, I shall tell you all" —
If one, settling a pillow by her head,
Should say: "That is not what I meant at all.
That is not it, at all."

And would it have been worth it, after all,
Would it have been worth while,
After the sunsets and the dooryards and the sprinkled streets,
After the novels, after the teacups, after the skirts that trail along the floor —
And this, and so much more? —
It is impossible to say just what I mean!
But as if a magic lantern threw the nerves in patterns on a screen:
Would it have been worth while
If one, settling a pillow or throwing off a shawl,
And turning toward the window, should say:
"That is not it at all,
That is not what I meant, at all."
...
No! I am not Prince Hamlet, nor was meant to be;[37]
Am an attendant lord,[38] one that will do.
To swell a progress,[39] start a scene or two,
Advise the prince; no doubt, an easy tool,
Deferential[40], glad to be of use,

Politic[41], cautious, and meticulous[42];
Full of high sentence[43], but a bit obtuse[44];
At times, indeed, almost ridiculous—
Almost, at times, the Fool[45].

I grow old … I grow old …
I shall wear the bottoms of my trousers rolled.[46]

Shall I part my hair behind?[47] Do I dare to eat a peach?
I shall wear white flannel trousers, and walk upon the beach.
I have heard the mermaids singing,[48] each to each.

I do not think that they will sing to me.

I have seen them riding seaward on the waves
Combing the white hair of the waves blown back
When the wind blows the water white and black.

We have lingered in the chambers of the sea
By sea-girls wreathed with seaweed red and brown
Till human voices wake us, and we drown.[49]

1915, 1917

Notes

1. Composed at Harvard in 1910 and published in 1915, the poem is a sort of dramatic monologue in lines of varying lengths and occasional rimes. J. Alfred Prufrock: obviously a fictitious name whose confession of his life makes up the poem.
2. The epigraph is taken from Dante's *Inferno*, 27. 61—66. The passage may be rendered into English as follows: "If I thought my answer were given to anyone who could ever return to the world, this flame would stand still without further movement. But since no one has ever returned alive from this depth, if what I hear is true, I will answer you without fear of infamy."

The speaker of these lines is Guido da Montefeltro, who is placed in the eighth circle of hell for giving evil counsel to a pope and wrapped in a flame, confessing to Dante. This quotation suggests that the poem that follows is likewise a confession and that the speaker assumes the reader to be in the same hell that he himself is in.

3. you and I: here the "I" is the speaker, but who is the "you" is not mentioned in the poem. Maybe it is a friend of Prufrock or just a companion whom Prufrock is addressing. Maybe "you and I" refer to the two aspects of one person, in which "you" represents the objective aspect while "I" represents the subjective half.
4. etherised: anesthetized with ether. The simile of an etherised patient conveys the stillness of the evening.
5. upon a table: upon an operation table.
6. sawdust restaurants: cheap restaurants that used to spread sawdust on the floor to soak up spilled beer, etc.
7. insidious intent: treacherous purpose.
8. Michelangelo: Buonarroti Michelangelo (1475 — 1564), a great Italian sculptor, painter and poet of the Renaissance.
9. there will be time: here and in the subsequent uses of the word " time", the author is making an allusion to Ecclesiastes 3. 1—8: "For everything there is a season, and a time for every matter under heaven: a time to be born, and a time to die; … time to kill, and a time to heal; … a time to keep silence and a time to speak; a time to love, and a time to hate; a time for war, and a time for peace. " It may also allude to Andrew Marvell's "To His Coy Mistress": "Had we but world enough and time. "
10. To prepare a face: to do one's facial make up.
11. all the works and days of hands: it is in allusion to "Works and Days", a didactic poem concerning rural labor, written by the early Greek poet Hesiod (8th century B. C.). Here Eliot ironically contrasts the healthy rural labor of a pastoral life with the empty social gestures in modern urban life.
12. the taking of a toast and tea: Here "the taking of a toast and tea" brings the speaker back from his wandering thoughts given above to his trivial

realities of life.

13. Time to turn back and descend the stair/With a bald spot in the middle of my hair —: Here again the speaker comes down to earth, so to speak.
14. They: referring to the women the speaker is familiar with.
15. his: referring to the speaker's.
16. rich and modest: colorful but not showy, showing refined taste.
17. asserted: fixed.
18. Disturb the universe: obviously an ironical overstatement.
19. a dying fall: a sinking of tone. Cf. Shakespeare's *Twelfth Night*, 1. 1. 4: "If music be the food of love, play on… That strain again! It had a dying fall."
20. presume: to venture to do something.
21. The eyes that fix you in a formulated phrase: the eyes that make a stereotyped estimate of you. Here Prufrock is afraid of the prejudiced judgment that the women would pass on him.
22. And when I am formulated: when I am estimated with a specific phrase.
23. sprawling on a pin: fixed with limbs stretching under a pin in the manner of insects that are made into specimens.
24. To spit out all the butt-ends of my days and ways: to utter vehemently all the deeply-embedded thoughts reflecting my life and ways of living. Prufrock feels his life has been consumed and wasted.
25. downed: full of fine soft hair.
26. digress: turn aside from the main topic in speech or writing.
27. a pair of ragged claws: a pair of ragged claws (of a crab). Here the poet means that it would be better to be a crab in the depth of the ocean that involves no moral decisions and revisions. It alludes to Hamlet's mocking of Polonius in Shakespeare's *Hamlet*, 2. 2. 203—204: "For yourself, sir, shall grow old as I am, if like a crab you could go backward."
28. Scuttling: running or moving in a hurried way.
29. malingers: pretends to be sick.
30. ices: icecreams.
31. I have wept and fasted, wept and prayed: Prufrock wants to woo with religious rituals. Cf. 2 Samuel 1. 12: "They mourned and wept, and fasted

until evening ..."

32. Though I have seen my head ... brought in/upon a platter, /I am no prophet: it is in allusion to Matthew 14. 3—11 and Mark 6. 17—29 in the New Testament in which Salome asked for the head of John the Baptist to be brought in on a platter as a reward for her dance before King Herod. The speaker here suggests that he has visualized himself to be a great man ready for the sacrifice of his life (like John the Baptist), but then he realizes that he is not a prophet, so he needs not be afraid of having to make the sacrifice of a prophet like John the Baptist (see the words following: "and here's no great matter").
33. the eternal Footman: Death.
34. To have bitten off the matter with a smile: to 解决这件事情 in a light manner.
35. To have squeezed the universe into a ball/To roll it towards some overwhelming question: Cf. Andrew Marvell's "To His Coy Mistress": "Let us roll all our strength and all/Our Sweetness up into one ball, /And tear our pleasures with rough strife/Thorough the iron gates of life." some overwhelming question: some question of great importance.
36. Lazarus: the sick man brought back from death by Jesus (See John 11. 1—44 in the New Testament; see also Luke 16. 19—31).
37. I am not Prince Hamlet, nor was meant to be: Here the speaker suggests that he is not and cannot hope to be a great man like Hamlet.
38. attendant lord: here Prufrock suggests he may be an "attendant lord" like old Polonius in *Hamlet*, the king's adviser, a mere auxiliary character.
39. To swell a progress: Here he thinks of himself as a minor actor participating in a progress in a play. a progress: a ceremonial royal journey in Elizabethan Age.
40. Deferential: respectful.
41. Politic: prudent.
42. meticulous: showing great precision and care.
43. Full of high sentence: expressing worthy sentiments.
44. obtuse: lacking quickness of perception or intellect, stupid.
45. the Fool: a character in Elizabethan drama, who is given the permission not

only to do the clowning but also to quibble with his superiors.

46. I shall wear the bottoms of my trousers rolled: presumably here Prufrock wants to adopt the new fashion of the time.

47. Shall I part my hair behind: here the speaker is referring to a daring new hair style at that time. He seems to contemplate a series of daring gestures in defiance of advanced age.

48. I have heard the mermaids singing: Cf. John Donne's "Song": "Teach me to hear mermaids singing." to hear the mermaids singing is something that is considered impossible. The speaker refers to something seductive as well as fatal.

49. Till human voices wake us, and we drown: Here the speaker suggests that he is brought back to reality from his wandering thoughts and visions, but he would rather be drown in the sea. And we drown: and we (are) drown (in the sea). "We" refers to "you and I", that is, the physical "I" and spiritual "I".

诗歌赏析

T. S. 艾略特是20世纪上半叶美国诗坛的巨匠。他不仅是一位著名的诗人，而且还是一位杰出的批评家以及英美现代主义文学的奠基人。他推崇法国后象征派和英国17世纪玄学派的诗风。《阿尔弗莱德·普罗夫洛克的情歌》是艾略特的早期代表作。诗中的主人公普罗夫洛克是一个中年谢顶的知识分子。他穿过伦敦破败的街区，去向一位女子求婚，又害怕被拒绝。当他终于如约到达了目的地，嘈杂的人声打断了他的冥想，诗歌就此结束。这首长诗反映了主人公矛盾、彷徨的心路历程。艾略特在这首诗中使用传统的戏剧独白形式，通过全新的技巧，即意识流、独特新奇的意象和复杂多变的典故，描绘了一个现代知识分子的心理活动，实际上影射了当时社会的精神瘫痪。

从表面上看，这首诗中有两个人物，说话者"我"和听话者"你"，但是"你"的身份从来没有标明，而是一直伴随着"我"，走过大街小巷，见证了"我"，即普罗夫洛克的内心挣扎，直到最后他们一起"溺水而终"。实际上，"我"和"你"可以说代表了故事叙述者普罗夫洛克的两面——"我"代表感性的、思考的和现实的"我"，"你"代表理性的、行动的以及理想的"我"。理想的"我"，见证了现实的"我"的生活是多么琐屑、乏味。最终，理想破灭了，"我们一起溺水而终"。《阿尔弗莱德·普罗夫洛克的情歌》是自我的博弈，精神和肉体的搏杀。这首诗记录了现代社会中迷失了的自我对身份的追寻，是现代人分裂人格的再现。

艾略特用一系列新奇独特的意象把现代人的苦闷、彷徨、碌碌无为表现得淋漓尽致。如诗歌开篇将黄昏比作“手术台上麻醉过的病人”，用来描述现代社会瘫痪的精神现状。主人公“用咖啡勺把生命分配”，说明现代知识分子无所事事、百无聊赖的生活状态。“钉在别针上，在墙上痛苦扭动”的昆虫标本形象寓指现代人的无能——别人对自己的评价已经“程式化”，自己的生活也一成不变。

这首诗还以其复杂的典故著称。比如普罗夫洛克意识到自己生来不是英雄，不会像哈姆雷特做出什么丰功伟绩，不能像马维尔诗中的恋人那样勇敢地冲破生活的铁门去追求自己的幸福，也不能像先知约翰一样为了信仰献出自己的生命。诗人先后引用了圣经故事、莎士比亚剧中的人物形象和英国 17 世纪玄学派诗人马维尔《致羞涩的姑娘》中的诗句来反衬自身的琐屑与渺小。复杂多变的典故彰显了作者渊博的学识，对典籍的驾驭能力，这极大地丰富了诗歌的内容，提高了作品的艺术展现力。

这首诗的另外一个鲜明特点是反讽的运用。首先，诗的名字和内容构成反讽。诗歌的题目是“情歌”，但实际上只是就主人公是否敢于向一位女士示爱或求婚的一场“冗长的争论”，最终证明了主人公的爱无能。其次，但丁的题词的严肃性和诗歌内容的轻佻形成反讽。诸如此类的反讽不胜枚举，诗人用恢弘的气势，严肃的口吻揭示了现代社会空洞、乏味的精神实质。

最后一句“直到人声把我们唤醒，于是我们溺水而终”采用了 17 世纪玄学派诗歌惯用的似非而是的修辞手法。对说话者而言，醒来意味着死亡。在冥想中，还能有一番作为，清醒后只能过着碌碌无为、无聊透顶、行尸走肉般的日子，虽生犹死。所以说话者宁愿在幻想中死去，也不愿意面对现实。

For Study and Discussion

1. What is the function of the quotation from Dante's *Inferno* that immediately follows the title of the poem?
2. Find out the allusions in this poem and explain them.
3. What is the tone of this poem?
4. Please give some examples to show the vivid images in this poem. How do they help describe the environment and the character of Prufrock?

参考译文

阿尔弗莱德·普罗夫洛克的情歌

如果我认为我的答案是为
为一个要重返世界的人而作，
那么这火焰将不再熠熠生辉，

如果我听到的是真的
真的没有一个人能活着从这个深渊逃离
那我就回答他们，不惧任何邪恶！

那么，咱们走吧，我和你，
黄昏正在伸展倚天际，
像手术台上麻醉过的病人；
咱们走吧，穿过一些半荒废的街道，
街旁临时过夜的简易旅馆里
女人们唠叨个
不眠之夜，
街旁小饭庄，满地都是锯屑和牡蛎壳：
这些街道像很冗长的争论，
用心险恶，
引导问出难以抵抗的问题……
哦，别问："那是什么？"
咱们走吧，看看去再说。

房间里，女人们来往穿梭，
谈论米开朗基罗。

黄色的雾霭在窗棂上蹭背，
黄色的烟也在窗棂上蹭鼻和嘴。
用舌头舔着夜的各个角落，
在阴沟里小水潭流连延拖，
让烟囱里飞落的烟灰落在自己的背上，
烟灰从台阶上滑落，突然一跃，

见是一个柔和的十月夜晚
绕房子飞转一圈便入睡乡。

肯定会有足够的时间
让黄色烟雾沿街道滑行
并在窗棂上蹭背：
会有足够的时间，会有足够的时间
准备一副去见别人面孔的面容；
会有足够的时间去谋杀和创造，
会有足够的时间让那些在你的餐桌上
提问和休问的人们干活、过节；
你有你的时间，我有我的时间，
有时间犹豫上百次，
有时间上百次地看了又看，
之后才饮酒与喝茶。
房间里，女人们来往穿梭，
还谈论着米开朗基罗。

肯定会有足够的时间
反复问，“我敢吗？我真敢？”
会有时间转身下楼离去，
头顶中央秃头一片——
(她们会说，“瞧他头发多么少！”)
我的早礼服，我的领子紧顶着下巴，
我的领带贵重得体，但只简单地别着一个别针——
(但她们会说，“瞧他胳膊腿儿多细！”)
我敢吗？
一分钟就足够
犹豫不决、考虑再三、反复修正。

因为她们的一切我都知道，我都知道——
熟悉这黄昏、早晨和下午，
我用咖啡勺把生命分配；
我知道那些声音渐消，远处那房间
的音乐也在消减。

所以我怎么敢猜测？

还有，那些眼睛我早就知道，早就知道——
那些你说一句礼貌话就盯视你的眼睛，
当我语言规矩，趺趴在一根别针上，
当我扎在别针上，当在墙上痛苦扭动，
我怎么能开始
把我的生活与方式和盘托出、吐个干净？
就这样，我怎样去猜测？

还有，那些胳膊我早就知道，我早就知道——
那些胳膊戴着手镯，白皙，赤裸，
(但是在灯下，显出棕黄色软毛!)
是衣裙上的香水味？
引诱我如此离题？
那些放在桌子上或者裹着披肩的胳膊。
那么，我应当去猜测？
我该怎么去猜测？

……

我是否可以说我在黄昏时分走遍了大街小巷，
观看了穿着衬衫、身子探出窗外的孤独男人
的烟斗里冒出的烟？

我真该变成一对粗糙的蟹爪
急匆匆地在寂静的海底爬动。

这下午，这夜晚，睡得多安详！
让修长的手指抚慰，
入睡……疲倦……或装病，
平躺在地板上，就在这儿，在你我身边。
喝过茶，吃过糕点和冰淇淋，我会
有力量逼这一瞬间到一个极端？
但是尽管我哭过，斋戒过，哭过，又祈祷过，
尽管我看见了我的头（有点秃顶）被放在盘中，
但我并非先知——这也无关紧要；

我看到我伟大的那一刻扑朔迷离，
我还看到我那永恒的仆人拿着我的衣服窃笑，
简之，我害怕。

那么，到底值不值得
在喝过酒、吃过果酱、喝过茶后，
在杯盘之间，在你我对谈之间，
到底值不值得
微笑着把这事情咬掉，
把宇宙挤成一个小球，
把它滚动挤出那个重要的问题，
说，“我是拉洒路，从阴界复活，
我回来告诉你们大家，告诉你们一切”——
如果有人在她头边放个枕头
并说，“我根本不是那个意思，
不是那意思，根本不是。”

那么，到底值不值得
值不值得如此下功夫，
日落后，庭院中，洒过水的街道，
小说读毕，茶水喝完，多少扫地而过的长裙——
就这些，还有更多的吗？
要想说出我想说的，不可能！
但好像一盏魔灯把神经
在屏幕上组成一种模式，
这值不值得？
如果有人放下一个枕头，或甩掉一个披肩，
转身朝向窗户，竟然说：
“根本就不是，
我不是这意思，根本就不是。”
……

不！我不是哈姆雷特王子，也不想是；
我是一个侍臣，一个可以
国王出巡时位于其列，捧一两次场，

给王子出点主意的人；毫无疑问，是个好用的工具而已，
是个配角，有人用就高兴，
讲究策略，为人小心，处事谨慎，
满腹韬略却略显愚钝，
有时还近乎荒谬，
有时就是白痴。

我老喽……我老喽……
我要穿裤腿脚往上卷翻的裤子。

我要不要把我的头发在脑后分开？我敢吃桃子吗？
我要穿白色法兰绒裤子，在海滩上漫步。
我曾听到美人鱼歌唱，它们为彼此歌唱。

我认为它们不会为我歌唱。

我看见它们乘风破浪向海里奔去，
海风把水吹成黑白两色，
它们梳理被吹回的海浪的白发。

我们在海底的闺房流连，
海姑娘头戴红棕色海草做成的花环，
直到人声把我们唤醒，于是我们溺水而终。

（李正栓　韩志华　译）

13. E. E. Cummings

Edward Estlin Cummings（E. E. 肯明斯，1894—1962），popularly known as E. E. Cummings，was born in Cambridge，Massachusetts on October 14，1894. His father was a Congregational minister and professor at Harvard. In 1911 Cummings attended Harvard and graduated in 1916 with a master's degree. The next year，Cummings was recruited by the Red Cross for World War I and was sent to France. But he was soon imprisoned in a French detention camp for three months under suspicion of treason. This experience provided the raw material for his first literary success, *The Enormous Room* (1922).

After the war, Cummings went to Paris to study painting, with all the fascination for such post-impressionist and Cubist painters as Cezanne and Picasso. He managed to establish a life as a painter as well as a poet. His genius in art, harmoniously combined with his talent in language, freed him from the bondage of conventional style and distinguished him as one of the most outstanding poets of the 20th century. On his return to New York in 1924, he found himself a celebrity, both for *The Enormous Room*, a work of prose and for *Tulips and Chimneys* (1923), his first collection of poems. His other works include: & (1923), *is* 5 (1926), *Viva* (1931), *No Thanks* (1935), 50 *Poems* (1940), and 95 *Poems* (1958). He won the Bollingen Prize in 1957. Cummings died of a stroke on September 3, 1962, at the age of 67 in North Conway, New Hampshire.

Cummings was a poet who defined independently his own universe by expressing conventional ideas through modern techniques. He was famous for the experiments he executed. His poems are characterized by unusual capitalization and punctuation, intentional misspellings, and breaking phrases by cadence to the advantage of the melody. What's more, as a professional painter, he was much concerned with the typographical order of words. Sometimes Cummings would arrange the letters of a word or lengthen the space between letters or words, all for the same aim to convey the vividness of life and present the power of rhythm. Science, industry, and machines are often the object of condemnation in his works, while love for nature, children, normal family life, and artistic work are the frequent themes of his poems.

l (a)

This poem was published in 95 *Poems* (1958). It is a pattern poem in which the form of the poem expresses its content. The poem consists of the word "loneliness" outside and "a leaf falls" inside the parentheses. It is typographically arranged as the movement of a leaf falling down, which arouses the feeling of loneliness. That is the right emotion that the poet wants to convey.

l (a
le
af
fa

ll
s)
one
l

iness

诗歌赏析

E. E. 肯明斯是20世纪最具创新意识的诗人，以其独特的诗风著称，也因之饱受诟病。怪异的排版格式、随意的单词拼写、非常规的语法都是他用来表达诗歌内容的有力形式。这首诗是他1958年出版的诗集《诗歌95首》中的第一首。它通过拆解词汇，分行排版印刷的形式对一片翩然落地的树叶的轨迹进行描摹，揭示了现代人的精神孤独。

画家兼诗人的身份使肯明斯善于调动各种各样的视觉元素来达到意想不到的艺术效果。这首诗是他的视觉诗（visual poem）中的佳作。全诗由四个单词，二十个字母组成。但是，诗人摆脱了传统诗歌的遣词造句模式，把a leaf falls和loneliness四个单词拆解成九行，借助于括号，巧妙地联系在一起。

诗人巧用空间感和排版技巧产生视觉效果，使诗节和诗行长短不齐，断断续续，宛如一片叶子飘然落地的过程，孤独感应运而生。其次，这首诗采用偏离常规的断词和断句方法，除最后一行五个字母外，其他各行最多三个字母，形成长长的一竖，就像一个大大的1字，突出孤零零的感觉。另外，这首诗没有大写字符，小写字母l就像数字1一样。尤其是最后三行，分别由one，l和iness组成，突出个体在现代社会中的主体意识。而保持自我，张扬个性正是肯明斯一直推崇的诗学主张。

北宋著名画家郭熙在他的山水画论集《林泉高致》中精辟地阐明了诗与画之间的内在联系——诗是无形画，画是有形诗。诗人、画家肯明斯的这一名作绝佳地演绎了这一思想。

For Study and Discussion

1. Discuss the connection between what is inside and what is outside the parentheses in this poem.
2. How does the shape of the poem contribute to its theme?
3. Is there any Chinese poetic form that is similar to the visual poetry as written by Cummings?

参考译文

一　　　　孤

独　　　　　　片

独

孤　　　　　　树

飘　　　　叶

落

（韩志华　译　李正栓　校）

in Just—[1]

This poem displays the innocent happiness of the children in spring. Cummings makes good use of the line arrangement and typegraphical to express its meaning. The image of the little lame balloonman alludes to Pan in Greek myth, which reinforces the pastoral bliss. The space left on the page and the invented compounds in the poem create a vivid scene of children playing and laughing in spring.

in Just—
spring[2] when the world is mud—
luscious[3] the little
lame balloonman

whistles far and wee[4]

and eddieandbill[5] come
running from marbles and
piracies[6] and it's
spring

when the world is puddle-wonderful[7]

the queer
old balloonman whistles
far and wee
and bettyandisbel[8] come dancing

from hop-scotch and jump-rope[9] and

it's
spring
and
the

goat-footed

balloonMan whistles
far
and
wee

1920, 1923

Notes

1. This poem was published in *Tulips and Chimneys* in 1923.
2. in Just—/spring: just in spring.
3. mud—/luscious: full of luscious mud. luscious: sweet.
4. wee: very small.
5. eddieandbill: two boys' names, Eddie and Bill.

6. marbles and/piracies：two children's games often played by boys.
7. puddle-wonderful：full of wonderful puddles. puddle：a small water pit.
8. bettyandisbel：two girls' names，Betty and Isbel.
9. hop-scotch and jump-rope：two children's games often played by girls.

For Study and Discussion

1. Why is the balloonman "goat-footed"? How does this mythological allusion enrich the meaning of the poem?
2. The poet spells the children's names Eddie and Bill，and Betty and Isbel as "eddieandbill" and "bettyandisbel". What is the effect of this spelling?
3. Why does the speaker describe the world of spring as "mud-luscious" and "puddle-wonderful"?
4. What is the effect of the use of space on the page?

参考译文

正　好

正好在——
春天，当大地散发泥香——
味道甘美，那个跛脚的
卖气球的小老头
从远处 吹着口哨 哨音微弱，
艾迪和比尔跑过来
本来丢石子和
抓海盗，原来
春天到了。

当大地冰雪消融，一展魅力，

那个卖气球的
古怪的老头吹着哨子
从远处走来 哨音微弱，
贝蒂和伊莎贝尔跳着过来

她们正在跳房子，跳绳子，
原来是
春天到了，
还有，
　　那
　　　　山羊脚的
卖气球的人 吹着哨子
来自远处
还有
哨音微弱。

（李正栓　韩志华　译）

14. Langston Hughes

Langston Hughes（兰斯顿·休斯，1902－1967）was born in Joplin, Missouri, spending most of his youth in the American Midwest. In 1921, Hughes attended Columbia University and published his first poem *The Negro Speaks of Rivers*. Hughes left the university one year later for Africa and Europe, first as a sailor, then as a cook. In 1925, his talent for poetry was recognized by Vachel Lindsay（1879－1931）, a famous poet at that time, in Washington, D. C. hotel, where Hughes worked as a busboy. Under the encouragement of Lindsay, Hughes had his first book of poetry, *The Wearing Blues*, published in 1926. In the next year, another book, *Fine Clothes to the Jew*, was published.

Hughes was the first writer who brought the stories of Black people in the Harlem area into American literature and initiated a new movement in Black literature known as the "Harlem Renaissance" of the 1920s. Hughes became the spokesman of Black writers and known as "Poet Laureate of Harlem." From a very young age, Hughes has been proud of the music, history, and legend of black culture. As a Black lyric poet, Hughes took great advantage of the jazz and the blues rhythms of the black music. His poems were characterized by short lines and simple stanza patterns, but with strong rhythms of jazz and strict rhyme schemes derived from blues songs. In addition, he developed subjects from Black life and racial themes. In his poems readers of the 1920s were satisfied to find primitivism combined with classical technique.

Hughes was the first prominent Black writer in American literary history. He was a talented writer. He tried nearly every literary form and style: poetry, fiction, drama, and essays for newspapers. Hughes was also a prolific writer. He contributed to the treasure house of literature over 60 books, out of them 12 are collections of poems. Except the two mentioned, Hughes' major works include *Dear Lovely Death* (1931), *The Negro Mother* (1931), *Dream Keeper* (1932), *The New Song* (1938), *Shakespeare in Harlem* (1942), and *Ask Your Mama* (1961). Langston Hughes died of cancer in May 22, 1967, in New York.

The Negro Speaks of Rivers[1]

This is Hughes' first major poem. From the Euphrates in Asia, the Congo and the Nile in Africa to the Mississippi in America, Hughes retrospects the history of African Americans with the clue of rivers. "I" represents all Black Americans. Written in free verse, it follows a loose cadence to imitate the natural rhythm of the river flow. It arouses pride in the African heritage of the Black people in America.

I've known rivers:
I've known rivers ancient as the world and older than the
flow of human blood in human veins.

My soul has grown deep like the rivers.

I bathed in the Euphrates[2] when dawns were young.
I built my hut near the Congo[3] and it lulled[4] me to sleep.
I looked upon the Nile[5] and raised the pyramids above it.

I heard the singing of the Mississippi[6] when Abe Lincoln[7]
went down to New Orleans[8], and I've seen its[9]
muddy bosom turn all golden in the sunset

I've known rivers:
Ancient, dusky[10] rivers.

My soul has grown deep like the rivers.

1921, 1926

Notes

1. This poem was published in *The Crisis* in 1921. Langston Hughes wrote this poem on a train to Mexico in 1920 at the age of 17. When the train crossed the Mississippi River, inspired by the scene, Hughes finished this poem on an envelope. It was dedicated to W. E. B. Du Bois (1868—1963), a black American writer and civil rights leader.
2. the Euphrates: a river of southwest Asia flowing about 2,735 km from central Turkey through Syria and into Iraq, a major source of the ancient civilization in Mesopotamia.
3. the Congo: a big river of equatorial Africa, about 4,380 km long, flowing generally north and west through Congo to the Atlantic Ocean, considered as the origin of the Black culture.
4. lulled: caused to sleep or to calm.
5. the Nile: the longest river in the world, flowing about 6,677 km through eastern Africa from its most remote sources in Burundi to a delta on the Mediterranean Sea in northeast Egypt, the home of the ancient Egyptian civilization.
6. Mississippi: the longest river in the North American Continent, flowing from its northern source in Minnesota to the Gulf of Mexico, the symbol of the American civilization.
7. Abe Lincoln: Abraham Lincoln (1809—1865), the 16 th American president who played a leading role in the American Civil War and the anti-slavery movement.

8. New Orleans: the largest city in southeastern Louisiana, straddling the Mississippi River. As a major port, New Orleans played a leading role in the Atlantic slave trade and had the largest slave market in the first half of the 19th century.
9. its: the Mississippi's.
10. dusky: dark, shadowy.

诗歌赏析

兰斯顿·休斯是美国著名的黑人作家，20世纪70年代哈莱姆文艺复兴的杰出代表，被誉为“哈莱姆桂冠诗人”。他的诗歌反映了美国黑人的生活，诉说了黑人民族的苦难，表达了他们对自由、平等的追求和渴望。《黑人说河》是休斯的代表作。该诗以一个美国黑人的口吻，借助代表美国黑人发展历程的河流，讴歌了一曲雄浑壮丽的民族发展史。这首诗由五节十三行组成，诗行长短不一，诗节行数也不固定，就像不羁的河流。

诗人开篇就把河流和人类的血脉联系在一起:“我了解河：/ 我了解那像世界一样古老的河，/ 那比人类血脉里流淌的血液还古老的河。”

诗中的“我”晨起在幼发拉底河沐浴，黄昏在刚果河搭建小屋，河水催他入眠，他在尼罗河边建起了金字塔。当美国总统顺流而下，前往奥尔良，他听到了密西西比河在歌唱，看到泥泞的河水在落日的映照下变成金黄。“我”追溯了美国黑人从亚洲的幼发拉底河，非洲的刚果河和尼罗河，到美国的密西西比河的历史足迹和发展变迁。从这个意义上说，“我”就是整个黑人民族的代言人。这些河流是人类文明和黑人文化的摇篮，代表着美国黑人苦难、艰辛的发展史。

这首诗充满了历史沧桑和民族自豪感。诗人利用美国黑人发展史上重要的地点和人物，追古溯今，对美国黑人的历史进行回顾，并对未来寄予美好期望。这是一个活力四射的民族，他参与了各个历史时期人类古老文明的建设，也经历了美国废奴运动前后的沧桑巨变。新奥尔良在19世纪上半叶曾经是美国的黑奴交易中心。新奥尔良之行促使林肯下决心废除奴隶制。“我”看到密西西比河“泥泞的胸膛在落日里金光闪耀”，喻示着美国总统林肯率领美国人民赢得内战的胜利，废除奴隶制的史实。

回顾了黑人的发展史后，诗人再次重申“我了解河：/ 那古老，朦胧的河。”其中，dusky起双关的作用。它既指美国黑人黑色的肌肤，也寓指美国黑人经历的苦难。

除象征外，重复也是这首诗的鲜明特征。河流在这首诗中重复六次，具有丰富的象征意义。雄浑浩瀚的大河象征美国黑人宽广的胸怀和黑人文化的博大精深，是美国黑人的精神象征。“我的灵魂已变得像河一样深沉”这行诗单独成节，并两次重复，强调美国黑人的灵魂已经和孕育着美国黑人文化和人类古老文明的河流紧密结合在一起。

For Study and Discussion

1. What is the tone of the poem?
2. What is the symbolic meaning of “rivers” in the poem?
3. Who is the “I” that is speaking in the poem? In what respects does the poet define the identity of an entire people?
4. What is the effect of the simile in the last line?
5. What’s the function of the title of the poem?

参考译文

黑人说河

我了解河：
我了解那像世界一样古老的河，
那比人类血脉里流淌的血液还古老的河。

我的灵魂已变得像河一样深沉。

我在曙色微现时分畅游于幼发拉底河中。
我搭小屋在刚果河畔，河水诱我沉沉入梦。
我远望尼罗河水，视野中金字塔高于尼罗河。
我听到密西西比河在歌唱，伴着亚伯·林肯
顺流而下到新奥尔良，我看到
她泥泞的胸膛在落日里金光闪耀。

我了解河：
那古老，朦胧的河。

我的灵魂已变得像河一样深沉。

（李海云　译　李正栓　校）

15. Elizabeth Bishop

Elizabeth Bishop (伊丽莎白·毕晓普, 1911—1979) was born in Worcester, Massachusetts. Her father died when she was only eight months old and her mother was permanently institutionalized because of mental breakdown when she was only five. She was raised in Nova Scotia, Canada and Boston, Massachusetts. She earned a bachelor's degree from Vassar College in 1934. In the same year she met the poet Marianne Moore, whose poetry of closely observed detail greatly influenced her.

Independently wealthy, from 1935 to 1937 she spent time traveling to France, Spain, North Africa, Ireland, and Italy and then settled in Key West, Florida for 4 years. She once traveled to Brazil, which was so appealing to her that she stayed there for more than 16 years. Her poetry, including her first book of verse, *North and South* (1946) and *Questions of Travel* (1965), is filled with descriptions of her travels and the scenery which surrounded her,

Unlike her contemporary and good friend Robert Lowell, who wrote in the "confessional" style, Bishop avoids explicit accounts of her personal life in her poetry, and focuses instead with great subtlety on her impressions of the physical world. She often functioned as an impersonal observer capable of detachment and understanding at the same time. She used subtle rhythms, unlikely rhymes, and the impressionist's technique of implication and suggestion. She had a painter's eye for surfaces and appearances, yet her portrayals of the stark landscapes of the matter-of-fact world frequently evolved into dreamlike sequences, contrasting the commonsense world of everyday reality and the world of impressions and the imagination. Her images are precise and true to life, and they reflect her own sharp wit and moral sense. When she wrote about her early life, she resisted sentimentality and self-pity, but looked at the events of her own life with the same unflinching gaze she turned on the landscapes which so consistently compelled her.

For years Elizabeth Bishop was considered a "poet's poet". She received the Pulitzer Prize for the combined volume *North & South and A Cold Spring* (1955) and the National Book Award for *The Complete Poems* (1969). She was awarded the Fellowship of The Academy of American Poets in 1964 and served as a Chancellor from 1966 to 1979. Her last book, *Geography* Ⅲ, appeared in 1976. She died in Cambridge, Massachusetts, in 1979, and her stature as a major poet continues to grow through the high regard of the poets and critics who have followed her.

The Fish[1]

This poem is one of Bishop's most famous poems. It is written in objective mood as her other works will do. Bishop's poetry never fails to provide the cold reality as it is. It gives a true-to-life description of a caught fish, big, old and ugly, covered with scratches. The turn happens in the end of the poem when the oil spillage of the boat makes a rainbow and the speaker, overwhelmed by the dignity of the fish, releases it. It is simple in structure, but profound in moral implications.

I caught a tremendous fish
and held him beside the boat
half out of water, with my hook
fast in a corner of his mouth.
He didn't fight.
He hadn't fought at all.
He hung a grunting[2] weight,
battered and venerable[3]
and homely[4]. Here and there
his brown skin hung in strips
like ancient wallpaper,
and its pattern of darker brown
was like wallpaper:
shapes like full-blown roses
stained and lost through age.
He was speckled with barnacles[5],

fine rosettes of lime[6],
and infested
with tiny white sea-lice,
and underneath two or three
rags of green weed hung down.
While his gills were breathing in
the terrible oxygen
— the frightening gills,
fresh and crisp with blood,
that can cut so badly —
I thought of the coarse white flesh
packed in like feathers,
the big bones and the little bones,
the dramatic reds and blacks
of his shiny entrails,
and the pink swim-bladder
like a big peony.
I looked into his eyes
which were far larger than mine
but shallower, and yellowed,
the irises backed and packed
with tarnished tinfoil
seen through the lenses
of old scratched isinglass[7].
They shifted a little, but not
to return my stare.
— It was more like the tipping
of an object toward the light.
I admired his sullen[8] face,
the mechanism of his jaw,
and then I saw
that from his lower lip
— if you could call it a lip —

grim, wet, and weaponlike,
hung five old pieces of fish-line,
or four and a wire leader
with the swivel still attached,
with all their five big hooks
grown firmly in his mouth.
A green line, frayed at the end
where he broke it, two heavier lines,
and a fine black thread
still crimped from the strain and snap
when it broke and he got away.
Like medals with their ribbons
frayed and wavering,
a five-haired beard of wisdom
trailing from his aching jaw.
I stared and stared
and victory filled up
the little rented boat,
from the pool of bilge[9]
where oil had spread a rainbow[10]
around the rusted engine
to the bailer rusted orange,
the sun-cracked thwarts,
the oarlocks on their strings,
the gunnels—until everything
was rainbow, rainbow, rainbow!
And I let the fish go.

1946

Notes

1. It is written in free verse in a long single stanza of seventy-six lines.
2. grunting: uttering a deep guttural sound.
3. battered and venerable: worn and respectable.
4. homely: plainly looking, ugly.

5. barnacles: small shellfish that attaches itself to objects under water, here implying the old age of the fish.
6. lime: referring to the alkaline substance that naturally occurs on an old fish.
7. isinglass: 云母.
8. sullen: silent, bad-tempered and gloomy.
9. bilge: the dirty water that gathers at the bottom of the boat near the engine, usually mixed with oil from the engine.
10. rainbow: it alludes to Genesis 9.8-17, in which rainbow is a sign of the covenant that God established with Noah — there shall never be a flood to destroy the earth and all flesh.

诗歌赏析

伊丽莎白·毕晓普是20世纪美国最重要、最有影响力的女诗人之一。她一生中囊括了普利策奖和国家图书奖在内的几乎所有美国的重要文化奖项，被称为“诗人中的诗人”。毕晓普的诗歌以敏锐的洞察力和瑰丽的想象著称，注重细节描写。《鱼》是其代表作之一。这首诗构思严谨，音律和谐，展示了诗人高超的诗艺。

首先，诗人用一系列第一人称的排比句贯穿了全诗，从我抓住，我想到，我看到，到我敬仰，我看啊看，最终我放走了他。随着“我”的动作变化，这首诗经历了从客观到主观，从外在到内心的发展过程。从捉鱼到放鱼，这首诗结局突兀又顺理成章。鱼用他的历史荣耀赢得了生的机会，渔民通过内心的救赎对生命有了新的感悟，这无疑是个双赢的结局。

其次，内在的韵律使这首诗成为一个密不可分的整体。这首诗虽然是一首自由体诗歌，没有固定的韵式，但是它有口语化的自然节奏，伴随头韵和腹韵的频繁使用，最后以双偶句结束。外松内紧、张弛有度形成了该诗独特的音乐美。最后的双偶句喻示着一个圆满的结局。

另外，彩虹虽然出现在诗歌的末尾，却是本诗的中心意象，起统领全诗的作用。大鱼皮肤的褐，花纹的深褐，海虱和鱼肉的白，海草的绿，鱼内脏的红与黑，鱼鳔的粉红，鱼眼的昏黄，绿色及黑色渔线的绿与黑，这些五彩斑斓的颜色最后汇集成彩虹，昭示了这首诗的道德寓意。在基督教中，彩虹是上帝与地上一切生灵的立约符号。看到了彩虹，渔民就像得到了神的旨意。于是，“我放他走了。”在彩虹面前，鱼和人便具有了共性，代表世上一切的生命，都受到上帝的眷顾，都值得尊敬。诗歌的最后，鱼获得了重生，渔民得到了心灵的救赎。这种短篇小说中常见的顿悟使这首诗产生了寓言般的奇幻效果。

比喻在这首诗中广泛应用，诗人通过八个明喻生动勾勒出这条大鱼的形象。他褐色的皮肤像经年的壁纸，有着玫瑰般的深褐色花纹，白白的鱼肉像填充的羽毛，粉红的鱼鳔像一朵大大的牡丹花，五根陈旧的渔线像武器一般，钓钩像勋章挂在他的嘴上。但这首诗的中心比喻是诗人将一条伤痕累累的大鱼，刻画成一个身经百战、历经沧桑、英勇顽强的战士形象，鱼嘴上的五个鱼钩就是战士的勋章，让人肃然起敬。这场渔人和鱼的斗争孕育着人与自然的关系，联系到成败、荣辱、是非观念等人生种种，总之，这首诗充满了道德寓意。

For Study and Discussion

1. What is the poet's attitude toward the fish?
2. Why does the speaker let the fish go at the end of the poem?
3. What is the symbolic meaning of "rainbow" in this poem?
4. The poet used many images to describe the fish. What aspect of the fish is reflected in each image?

参考译文

鱼

我抓住了一条巨大的鱼
把他放在了船边
一半露出水面，我的鱼钩
紧紧勾住他的嘴角。
他没有挣扎。
他自始至终没有挣扎。
他拖着笨重的身躯，
憔悴不堪、肃穆庄严、
相貌普通。这里那里，
他棕色的皮肤一条条垂下
像古老的壁纸。
上面深棕色的花纹
也像壁纸一样：
图案像绽放的玫瑰，
污渍斑斑，在岁月里褪了颜色。

他的身上星星点点布满了藤壶
和石灰质的玫瑰花饰，
还寄生着
白白的小海虱，
身子下面挂着两三根
绿色海草的残片。
他的鱼鳃在拼命地
呼吸着氧气
——那吓人的鱼鳃，
新鲜、血腥，
能锋利地切割——
我想到了他那粗劣的白肉
像羽毛一样堆积，
大大小小的骨头，
亮泽的内脏那
鲜活的红和黑，
还有粉红的鱼鳔
像一朵硕大的牡丹。
我盯着他的眼睛
它比我的眼睛大得多
但是更浅、昏黄
虹膜深陷，像是裹着
失去光泽的锡纸，
又好比隔了一层古老磨损的云母镜片。
它们转动了一下，但没有
和我对视。
——更像一个物体对
光线的反应。
我欣赏这张阴沉的面孔，
这呆板的下颌，
接着我看到
他的下唇上
（如果能把它叫做嘴唇）

可怕、潮湿、武器一般，
挂着五根陈旧的渔线
或者四根，外加一根金属导线
依旧和一个线轴相连，
那五个巨大的钓钩
结实地长在他的嘴里。
一根绿线，被他挣断那头
已经磨损，两根更粗的线
和一根细细的黑线
依旧卷曲着，那是他逃脱的时候
线因绷紧而折断的痕迹。
就像奖杯上的丝带
磨损、摇摆，
五根须的智慧
从他痛苦的下颌垂下来。
我注视着，注视着，
胜利充满了
这只小小的租船。
船底的油污
扩散成一道彩虹，
围绕着锈迹斑斑的引擎
和生锈发黄的泥浆泵，
太阳晒裂的横梁，
悬挂的桨托，
船舷——直到一切都是
彩虹、彩虹、彩虹！
我放他走了。

（申玉革　译）

16. Randall Jarrell

Randall Jarrell（兰德尔·贾雷尔，1914—1965）was born in Nashville,

Tennessee, but spent most of his childhood in California. From Vanderbilt University he earned the bachelor's degree as a major of psychology and a master's degree as an English major. He studied there with John Crowe Ransom, the New Critic and Fugitive poet. Later his mentor would be, for a short time, another Vanderbilt graduate, Allen Tate. These poet critics were associated with the Fugitive group of writers that had come together in Nashville in the 1920s. But Jarrell showed little interest in Fugitive or "Southern" political and cultural ideas. From 1937 to 1939 he taught at Kenyon College, where he met John Crowe Ransom and Robert Lowell, and then at the University of Texas and Sarah Lawrence College.

Jarrell wrote 6 volumes of poetry. His first book of poems, *Blood for a Stranger*, was published in 1942, the same year he enlisted in the Army Air Corps. He soon left the Air Corps for the army and worked as a control tower operator, an experience which provided much material for his poetry. Jarrell's reputation as a poet was established in 1945, while he was still serving in the army, with the publication of his second book, *Little Friend, Little Friend*, which bitterly and dramatically displays the intense fears and moral struggles of young soldiers. Another volume of war poems, *Losses*, appeared in 1948. His collection *The Woman at the Washington Zoo* (1960) displays his concern about women's dreams, loneliness, and disappointments.

Jarrell is also highly regarded as a peerless literary essayist, and was considered the most astute (and most feared) poetry critic of his generation. His books of essays include *The Third Book of Criticism* (1969) and *Kipling, Auden & Co.* (1980). Following the war, Jarrell accepted a teaching position at the Woman's College of the University of North Carolina, Greensboro, and remained there, except for occasional absences to teach elsewhere, until his death. Randall Jarrell was struck down by a car and died at the age of 51 in 1965. His *Complete Poems* was published posthumously in 1969.

The Death of the Ball Turret Gunner[1]

This is a poem that arose out of the poet's service as a control tower operator in World War II. The calm account of the soldier's story turns out to be a sharp exposure of the cruelty of the war and its destructive power toward human nature. The soldier in a ball turret is in comparison with a baby in a mother's womb. It is quite sarcastic.

From my mother's sleep I fell into the State[2],
And I hunched in its belly[3] till my wet fur froze[4].
Six miles from earth, loosed from its dream of life,
I woke to black flak[5] and the nightmare fighters.
When I died they washed me out of the turret with a hose[6].

1945

Notes

1. This poem consists of only one single 5-line stanza with five stressed syllables in each line. Ball Turret: (on a ship, an aircraft, a fort or a tank) low flat steel structure (often revolving), inhabited by the guns and the gunner, usually a short and small man, here referring to that on a bomber.
2. State: it is a pun, referring to the current situation of the gunner or the country.
3. belly: it is also pun, referring to mother's belly or the belly of the bomber, that is, the turret.
4. my wet fur froze: the low temperature in the high sky made his flight fur suit frozen.
5. flak: (=flack) gunfire.
6. hose: steam hose.

诗歌赏析

兰德尔·贾雷尔以战争诗著称。《旋转炮塔炮手之死》取自贾雷尔第二次世界大战期间在空军服役的真实经历，揭露了战争的残酷及对人性的摧残。诗歌用短短五行描述了年轻炮手的一生，意象密集，转换迅速。蜷缩在炮塔中的士兵被比作母亲子宫里的胎儿，炮手的皮衣就像是胎儿身上的绒毛。他在对生命的向往中，被敌人的炮火惊醒，却要面对死亡的现实。他死后被水管冲出，就像胎儿经历了流产术。生与死，母体的温暖与战争的严酷形成鲜明的对比。其中，State 是双关，既指炮手不幸降临到这个国家即美国，又指年轻炮手生逢乱世，应征入伍的状况。最后一行诗人用低调陈述的手法，用冷静的笔触描写了炮手之死，凸显战争的残酷以及对人性的摧残。尤其是诗人刻意使用舒缓的抑抑扬格形式描写旋转炮手的突然死亡，加大了诗歌的讽刺效果。

For Study and Discussion

1. What is the tone of the poem?
2. Who is the speaker of the poem? What is his attitude toward war? Toward his death? Toward other men?
3. In the poem, the gunner in the turret is compared to a baby in a mother's belly. How are they similar to each other? How are they different?
4. How do you understand the last line? Is it a mere description of the gunner's death?

参考译文

旋转炮塔炮手之死

从母亲的睡眠中，我落入这个状态，
蜷缩在她的腹部，直到潮湿的绒毛冻结，
离地六英里，脱离了世间生活的梦幻，
我醒来，发现炮火的黑烟和噩梦般的战斗机。
我死了，他们用蒸汽管把我从炮塔里冲出。

（胡家峦　译）

17. Robert Lowell

Robert Lowell（罗伯特·洛威尔，1917—1977），was born into one of Boston's oldest and most prominent families (related through his father to the poets James Russell Lowell and Amy Lowell) on March 1，1917. He attended Harvard in 1935，but a year later，he transferred to Kenyon College in Ohio，

where he studied poetry under the distinguished poet John Crowe Ransom (1888 — 1974) and received a bachelor's degree in 1940. He took graduate courses at Louisiana State University where he studied with Robert Penn Warren and Cleanth Brooks.

In 1944 his first volume of poems, *Land of Unlikeness*, was published and he was well accepted as one of the important poets of the time. Two years later, another volume of poems, *Lord Weary's Castle*, appeared which brought him a Pulitzer Prize and secured his position as a leading poet of the new generation. Most of his early poems were concerned with his conversion to Catholicism and exposed the dark side of American society. Poems of this period were scrupulously created with ironies, symbols and obscurity.

Lowell suffered from frequent mental breakdowns for which he was repeatedly hospitalized. In the mid-fifties he began to write more directly from personal experience, and to loosen his adherence to social affairs. With the publication of his masterpiece, *Life Studies* (1959), Lowell became more inclined for intense self-examination and revelation, which marked the beginning of a new school of "confessional poets". The subjects were tended more and more towards the description of internal world of human beings.

In his last years he turned more radically to political activities. In protest over America's foreign policy he refused to attend a White House Fine Arts Festival in 1956, and in 1967 he was arrested for participating in a Pentagon March to protest against the Vietnam War. Themes of this period also shifted from trivial private affairs to social problems, the deterioration of social morality, and to the spiritual sufferings of modern people. His later works include *For the Union Dead* (1964), *History* (1973), and *Day by Day*, which was published shortly before his death in 1977. He died a sudden death from a heart attack at the age of 60.

Skunk Hour[1]

For Elizabeth Bishop

This poem is one of Robert Lowell's most frequently anthologized poems and a famous example of Confessional poetry. Lowell wrote it as a response to Bishop's "The Armadillo". In the poem, the speaker is mentally ill and haunts here and there in a coastal town in Maine. As the subjects drift from one to another, all the speaker observes is loneliness and depression. It exposes the mental crisis that modern people suffered from.

Nautilus Island's hermit[2]
heiress still lives through winter in her Spartan cottage[3];
her sheep still graze above the sea.
Her son's a bishop. Her farmer
is first selectman in our village;
she's in her dotage.

Thirsting for
the hierarchic privacy
of Queen Victoria's century,
she buys up all
the eyesores facing her shore,
and lets them fall.

The season's ill—
we've lost our summer millionaire,
who seemed to leap from an L. L. Bean[4]
catalogue. His nine-knot yawl
was auctioned off to lobstermen.
A red fox stain covers Blue Hill[5].

And now our fairy[6]
decorator brightens his shop for fall;

his fishnet's filled with orange cork,
orange, his cobbler's bench and awl;
there is no money in his work,
he'd rather marry.

One dark night,
my Tudor Ford climbed the hill's skull[7];
I watched for love-cars[8]. Lights turned down,
they lay together, hull to hull[9],
where the graveyard shelves on the town....
My mind's not right.

A car radio bleats,
"Love, O careless Love ....[10]" I hear
my ill-spirit[11] sob in each blood cell,
as if my hand were at its throat ....
I myself am hell;[12]
nobody's here—

only skunks, that search
in the moonlight for a bite to eat.
They march on their soles up Main Street[13]:
white stripes, moonstruck[14] eyes' red fire
under the chalk-dry and spar spire
of the Trinitarian Church.

I stand on top
of our back steps and breathe the rich air[15]—
a mother skunk with her column of kittens[16] swills[17] the garbage pail[18].

She jabs her wedge-head in a cup
of sour cream, drops her ostrich tail,
and will not scare.

1959

Notes

1. This poem was published in Lowell's most famous work *Life Studies* (1959). It is written in eight 6-line stanzas with no regular rhymes but particular rhyme scheme in each stanza.
2. Nautilus Island's hermit: the poem is set in Castine, Maine, where Lowell had a summer house.
3. Spartan cottage: here referring to the simple living condition.
4. L. L. Bean: A mail-order house in Maine, which mainly deals with sporting and camping goods.
5. Blue Hill: a sea town in Maine, close to Lowell's residence.
6. fairy: (derogatory) a gay.
7. the hill's skull: referring to the hilltop.
8. love-cars: cars with lovers in them.
9. hull to hull: next to each other.
10. Love, O careless Love.... : lyrics of a popular song, "Careless Love".
11. my ill-spirit: my spirit that is ill. See Line 30: "My mind's not right."
12. I myself am hell: Cf. John Milton's *Paradise Lost* 4.75: "Which way I fly is Hell, myself am Hell."
13. Main Street: implying Maine, the setting of the poem.
14. moonstruck: frenetic.
15. the rich air: the strong smell of the skunk.
16. her column of kittens: the baby skunks.
17. swill: gulp.
18. garbage pail: dustbin.

诗歌赏析

罗伯特·洛威尔开创了美国自白派诗歌。他的诗注重个人经验和自我剖析，《臭鼬的时光》是其诗集《生活研究》的压轴作，表现了洛威尔作品中自白派诗歌的艺术特点。这首诗是献给当时的另一位自白派女诗人伊丽莎白·毕晓普的。毕晓普曾写诗《犰狳》献给洛威尔。诗中展现了个人精神的痛苦、狂乱与恍惚。

前四节诗分别描述了当地的三个人物，揭露了当地人的精神世界的堕落与绝望。一个是行将就木、脾气古怪的女继承人，一个是自杀的百万富翁，一个是同性恋的装饰商。三个人物都是毫无生机、衰败的象征。第五节转入对基督教地狱的描绘。在一个漆黑之夜，说话者驱车上山，发现山上停着一辆辆汽车，情人在里面幽会。爱情本来是精神力量的象征，可是在他看来这些幽会汽车像一座座坟茔。说话人觉得自己不对劲，说明这只是说话人的幻觉。第六节说话人已经分不清是现实还是幻觉，精神还是物质，他已经和地狱融为一体："我就是地狱。"第七、八节中，臭鼬成了现实的主人，在街上大摇大摆地走。臭鼬是说话者幻想中的地狱的唯一陪伴者。这一意象让人深思。实际上，臭鼬也是说话人现实世界的见证者。臭鼬是连接诗中物质世界和精神世界的桥梁。一老一少两只臭鼬在空无一人的街道觅食的形象让人在冷漠绝望中感受到一丝温暖。而人类虽然在现代社会中面临种种危机，同样需要相互温暖，在夹缝中求生存。

诗人通过一个精神病人的视角，用冷静的笔触，描写了当时社会的异化现象——人们乖张、变态的心理，怪诞、颓废的色彩，动物一样的嚣张行径。在诗人看来，这样的世界就是活脱脱的人间地狱。这首诗的诗行参差不齐，有的冗长拖沓，有的简短快捷，像是顺着一个精神病人信马由缰的思路在游走。

For Study and Discussion

1. What is the function of the skunks in this poem?
2. How do the color, animal imagery and diction suggest the speaker's state of mind?
3. What does the term "lover-cars" imply?
4. What does the speaker compare himself to in Stanza 6? What is the effect of this comparison?
5. Explain how Lowell transforms a Maine coastal village into a hellish landscape.

参考译文

臭鼬的时辰

（给伊丽莎白·毕晓普）

隐居在鹦鹉螺岛的
女继承人仍一冬天住在斯巴达式的村舍里，

她的羊群仍在海边牧放。
她的儿子是个主教。她的佃户
是我们村里的首席议员；
她已年老昏聩。

向往
维多利亚女王时代的
等级森严的幽居，
她买下对岸
所有碍眼的房子，
任其破败颓废。

这季节不好——
我们失去了夏天的百万富翁，
他好像是从一家邮购商店上
跳下来的。他的时速九里的小艇
已拍卖给捞龙虾的渔民，
蓝山沾满了红狐般的血迹。

我们那位搞同性恋的
装饰商正为秋市装潢着他的店铺；
他的渔网上挂满了橘坠，
橘子，还有鞋匠的板凳和锥子；
这买卖不赚钱，
不如快结婚。

一个漆黑的夜晚，
我驾着都铎福特牌汽车爬上山顶；
看见情人幽会汽车。车灯熄灭了，
一辆辆并排躺在一起，
在那里，垒垒坟茔排列在城市上空……
我的脑子不对头。

一辆汽车里的收音机在嚎叫，
“爱情，啊荒唐的爱情……”我听见
我的恶魔在每个血球中啜泣，

仿佛我用手在掐他的喉咙……
我自己就是地狱，
这里空无一人——

只有臭鼬
在月光下觅食。
它们大摇大摆地走在大街上：
它们身上有白纹，狂乱的眼睛血红似火，
在三一教堂
白垩般干燥的晶石尖塔下。

我站在
后门楼梯口，闻到强烈的气味——
一只母臭鼬带着一帮鼬仔在泔脚桶里啃食。
她把尖脑袋扎进一只
酸乳酪杯子，像鸵鸟似的拖着尾巴，
什么也不怕。

（顾子欣　译）

18. Allen Ginsberg

Allen Ginsberg（艾伦·金斯堡，1926—1997）was born in Newark，New Jersey on June 3，1926 into a Russian Jewish immigrant's family. His father was a high school teacher and a poet，while his mother was an atheist. Ginsberg encountered the poet William Carlos Williams in Paterson when he received his high school education there. With the encouragement of Williams，Allen Ginsberg began his career of poetry writing. In 1948，he graduated from Columbia University，where he began close friendships with William S. Burroughs（1914—1997），Jack Kerouac（1922—1969）and Neal Cassady（1926—1968）. They later became the leading figures of the Beat movement，from whom he received formative influence on his poetry writing.

In the early 1950s, he moved to San Francisco and joined his old friend Jack Kerouac, who was already the leading figure of the Beat Generation. In 1956, Ginsberg published his volume of poems: *Howl and Other Poems*, which established him as a major "Beat" poet. Ginsberg's position as a prominent poet was secure. Afterwards, Ginsberg worked diligently and more collections of poems appeared. His major works include *Empty Mirror* (1960), *The Change* (1963), *Reality Sandwiches* (1963), *Planet News* (1968), *The Fall of America* (1972), which won him the National Book Award, *Iron Horse* (1972), *Mind Breaths* (1978), *Poems All over the Place* (1978), and *Straight Hearts' Delight* (1980), *Collected Poems*, 1947—1980 (1984).

Ginsberg traveled widely in Europe, Asia and South America. He was a sincere advocate of Zen Buddhism but, at the same time, a drug addict and a homosexual. Ginsberg involved himself in the civil rights campaign, war resistance, and attacks on the CIA. He carried on an active social schedule until his death on April 5, 1997 in New York City.

Influenced chiefly by Walt Whitman and William Blake, Ginsberg strove to write prophetically with language sacred and profane in freer lines than Whitman's. He prefers the usage of common words and varieties of long lines following the speech and breathing patterns. In his long sentences he was able to, quite fluently, record the psychological experiences of a person, and present the images of the mind. In his poems, some certain words are repeated over and over to induce an atmosphere of mystery. Sometimes, his language was rather obscene. His free verse and his intensity of expression proved himself to be the most conspicuous "Sidewalk bard of America."

from Howl[1]

For Carl Solomon[2]

The following excerpt is taken from Part I, Lines 1-50 of "Howl", Allen Ginsberg's best-known poem. Reversing Whitman's celebration of the people, Ginsberg laments the degeneration and alienation of the postwar Americans in 1950s whom his novelist friend Kerouac named the "Beat Generation". This poem is full of descriptions of absurd and crazy behaviors, such as drug hallucinations, homosexuality, and rage against a repressive, war-mad America. Ginsberg has said that each line of the poem should be read in a single breath. He also uses many run-on lines to show the insanity of the "best minds". Ginsburg uses long lines of the speech pattern in his poem to show his anger and his concern for the fates of the individuals and the country.

I

I saw the best minds[3] of my generation destroyed by madness, starving
Hysterical[4] naked,
dragging themselves through the negro streets at dawn looking for an angry
fix[5], angelheaded hipsters[6] burning for[7] the ancient heavenly connection
to the starry dynamo[8] in the machinery of night,
who poverty and tatters[9] and hollow-eyed and high[10] sat up smoking in the
supernatural darkness of cold-water flats floating across the tops of
cities contemplating jazz,
who bared their brains to Heaven under the El[11] and saw Mohammedan[12]
angels staggering on tenement[13] roofs illuminated,
who passed through universities with radiant cool eyes hallucinating
Arkansas[14] and Blake-light[15] tragedy among the scholars of war,
who were expelled from the academies for crazy & publishing obscene odes
on the windows of the skull,[16]
who cowered in unshaven rooms in underwear, burning their money in
wastebaskets and listening to the Terror through the wall,
who got busted in their pubic beards[17] returning through Laredo with a belt
of marijuana[18] for New York,
who ate fire in paint hotels or drank turpentine in Paradise Alley[19], death, or
purgatoried their torsos[20] night after night
with dreams, and drugs, with waking nightmares, alcohol and cock[21] and
endless balls[22],
incomparable blind streets of shuddering cloud and lightning in the mid
leaping toward poles of Canada & Paterson[23], illuminating all the
motionless world of Time between,
Peyote[24] solidities of halls, backyard green tree cemetery dawns, wine

drunkenness over the rooftops, storefront boroughs of teahead joyride[25] neon blinking traffic light, sun and moon and tree vibrations in the roaring winter dusks of Brooklyn[26], ashcan rantings[27] and kind king light of mind[28],
who chained themselves to subways for the endless ride from Battery[29] to holy Bronx[30] on benzedrine[31] until the noise of wheels and children brought them down shuddering mouth-wracked and battered bleak of brain all drained of brilliance in the drear light of Zoo[32],
who sank all night in submarine light of Bickford's[33] floated out and sat through the stale beer afternoon in desolate Fugazzi's[34], listening to the crack of doom on the hydrogen jukebox,
who talked continuously seventy hours from park to pad[35] to bar to Bellevue[36] to museum to the Brooklyn Bridge,
a lost battalion of[37] platonic conversationalists jumping down the stoops off fire escapes off windowsills off Empire State[38] out of the moon,
yacketayakking[39] creaming vomiting[40] whispering facts and memories and anecdotes and eyeball kicks and shocks of hospitals and jails and wars,
whole intellects disgorged in total recall for seven days and nights with brilliant eyes, meat for the Synagogue[41] cast on the pavement,
who vanished into nowhere Zen[42] New Jersey[43] leaving a trail of ambiguous picture postcards of Atlantic City[44] Hall,
suffering Eastern sweats[45] and Tangerian bone-grindings and migraines of China under junk-withdrawal[46] in Newark[47]'s bleak furnished room,
who wandered around and around at midnight in the railroad yard wondering where to go, and went, leaving no broken hearts,
who lit cigarettes in boxcars boxcars boxcars racketing through snow toward lonesome farms in grandfather night,
who studied Plotinus Poe St. John of the Cross[48] telepathy and bop kaballah[49] because the cosmos instinctively vibrated at their feet in Kansas.
who loned it through the streets of Idaho[50] seeking visionary indian angels who were visionary indian angels,

who thought they were only mad when Baltimore[51] gleamed in supernatural ecstasy,
who jumped in limousines with the Chinaman of Oklahoma[52] on the impulse of winter midnight streetlight smalltown rain,
who lounged hungry and lonesome through Houston[53] seeking jazz or sex or soup[54], and followed the brilliant Spaniard to converse about America and Eternity, a hopeless task, and so took ship to Africa,
who disappeared into the volcanoes of Mexico leaving behind nothing but the shadow of dungarees and the lava and ash of poetry scattered in fireplace Chicago,
who reappeared on the West Coast investigating the FBI in beards and shorts with big pacifist eyes sexy in their dark skin, passing out incomprehensible leaflets,
who burned cigarette holes in their arms protesting the narcotic tobacco[55] haze of Capitalism,
who distributed Supercommunist pamphlets in Union Square[56] weeping and undressing while the sirens[57] of Los Alamos[58] wailed them down, and wailed down Wall[59], and the Staten Island[60] ferry[61] also wailed,
who broke down crying in white gymnasiums naked and trembling before the machinery of other skeletons,
who bit detectives in the neck and shrieked with delight in policecars for committing no crime but their own wild cooking pederasty and intoxication,
who howled on their knees in the subway and were dragged off the roof waving genitals and manuscripts,
who let themselves be fucked in the ass by saintly motorcyclists, and screamed with joy,
who blew and were blown by those human seraphim[62], the sailors, caresses of Atlantic and Caribbean love,
who balled in the morning in the evenings in rosegardens and the grass of public parks and cemeteries scattering their semen freely to whomever come who may,
who hiccupped endlessly trying to giggle but wound up with[63] a sob behind a

partition in a Turkish Bath when the blonde & naked angel came to
pierce them with a sword,
who lost their loveboys to the three old shrews of fate[64] the one eyed shrew
of the heterosexual dollar the one eyed shrew that winks out of the
womb and the one eyed shrew that does nothing but sit on her ass and
snip the intellectual golden threads of the craftsman's loom,
who copulated ecstatic and insatiate with a bottle of beer a sweetheart a
package of cigarettes a candle and fell off the bed, and continued
along the floor and down the hall and ended fainting on the wall with
a vision of ultimate cunt and come eluding the last gyzym of
consciousness,
who sweetened the snatches of a million girls trembling in the sunset, and
were red eyed in the morning but prepared to sweeten the snatch of
the sunrise, flashing buttocks[65] under barns and naked in the lake,
who went out whoring through Colorado in myriad stolen nightcars, N. C.[66],
secret hero of these poems, cocksman and Adonis of Denver — joy to
the memory of his innumerable lays of girls in empty lots & diner
backyards, moviehouses' rickety rows, on mountaintops in caves or
with gaunt waitresses in familiar roadside lonely petticoat upliftings &
especially secret gas station solipsisms of johns, & hometown alleys
too,
who faded out in vast sordid movies, were shifted in dreams, woke on a
sudden Manhattan, and picked themselves up out of basements hungover
with heartless Tokay[67] and horrors of Third Avenue iron
dreams & stumbled to unemployment offices,
who walked all night with their shoes full of blood on the snowbank docks
waiting for a door in the East River to open to a room full of steamheat
and opium,
who created great suicidal dramas on the apartment cliff-banks of the
Hudson under the wartime blue floodlight of the moon & their heads
shall be crowned with laurel in oblivion,
who ate the lamb stew of the imagination or digested the crab at the muddy

bottom of the rivers of Bowery[68],
who wept at the romance of the streets with their pushcarts full of onions and bad music,
who sat in boxes breathing in the darkness under the bridge, and rose up to build harpsichords in their lofts,
who coughed on the sixth floor of Harlem crowned with flame under the tubercular sky surrounded by orange crates of theology,

San Francisco, 1955-56 1956

Notes

1. This poem was published in *Howl and Other Poems* in 1956. Written in free verse, it is a classic work of the "Beat Generation" in 1950s.
2. Carl Solomon: a friend and fellow psychiatric patient in the Columbia Psychiatric Institute in 1949 when Ginsberg was forced to stay there for eight months to avoid imprisonment for a drug charge, to whom Ginsberg dedicated this poem.
3. best minds: the elite, the outstanding persons, here referring to the Beats, including Jack Kerouac, William Burroughs, Neal Cassady, in addition to Carl Soloman and the poet.
4. Hysterical: frenzied, of uncontrollable emotion.
5. fix: (slang) an intravenous injection of a narcotic.
6. hipsters: a word first appeared after WW II in America, referring to a group of people characterized by belief in existentialism, or drug, or addiction in jazz, against the traditional opinions. The beats can be considered as hipsters.
7. burning for: longing for.
8. dynamo: a generator.
9. tatters: wearing ragged clothes.
10. high: high (on drugs).
11. the El: the elevated railway in New York City.
12. Mohammedan: an English term for a Muslim, commonly used in Western Literature until the mid-20th century.

13. tenement: a rundown apartment house barely meeting minimal standard, usually for tenancy use.
14. Arkansas: a state in the southern United States with a large rural population.
15. Blake-light: referring to Ginsberg's vision of the English poet William Blake (1757—1827).
16. who were expelled from the academies for crazy & publishing obscene odes/ on the windows of the skull: referring to Ginsberg's experience of being expelled from Columbia University for writing an obscenity on his windowpane.
17. who got busted in their pubic beards: who got arrested in their long beards. The long beards were the mark of the hipsters in the 1950s. busted: (slang) arrested.
18. marijuana: drug made of the cannabis plant. They tried to smuggle marijuana from Mexico to New York through the border at Laredo, Texas, but was arrested.
19. Paradise Alley: a slum courtyard on the New York's East Village; setting of Kerouac's novel *The Subterraneans* (1958).
20. purgatoried their torsos: made their bodies suffer temporarily. purgatory: (usu. Purgatory) place or condition in Roman Catholicism, in which the souls of the dead are purified by suffering in preparation for Heaven. In the metaphorical meaning, it refers to a temporary condition of torment or suffering. torsos: human body except the head and limbs.
21. cock: (slang) the penis.
22. balls: the testicles.
23. Paterson: a city in New Jersey, where Ginsberg grew up.
24. Peyote: a plant that can make people have visions, often used to make psychedelic drug.
25. joyride: a drive for fun.
26. Brooklyn: the most populous of New York City's five boroughs, on western Long Island, with approximately 2.5 million residents, and the second-largest in area.
27. rantings: speaking loudly, violently or theatrically.

28. kind king light/of mind: referring to the beats. Jack Kerouac nicknamed himself "Kind King Mind" in his poem "Mexico City Blues".
29. Battery: a park at the southern tip of Manhattan Island at the upper end of New York Bay in southeast New York.
30. Bronx: a borough in New York City, end of a New York subway.
31. benzedrine: a brand of amphetamine.
32. Zoo: referring to the Bronx Zoo, the northern terminus of a New York subway.
33. Bickford's: an all-night cafeteria in New York City where Ginsberg worked in his college years and the Beats often came.
34. Fugazzi's: a bar in Greenwich Village frequented by the Beats in the 1950s and 1960s.
35. pad: (slang) place where somebody lives.
36. Bellevue: a famous mental hospital in New York.
37. a lost battalion of: a large number of.
38. Empire State: another name for the New York State.
39. yacketayakking: (slang) talking continuously.
40. vomiting: pouring out (more words).
41. Synagogue: (Judaism) a building in which Jewish people worship or study their religion.
42. Zen: Zen Buddhism, which was popular among the Beats.
43. New Jersey: a state in the Northeastern and Middle Atlantic regions of the United States.
44. Atlantic City: a city in Atlantic County, New Jersey, and an internationally renowned resort city for gambling, conventions and leisure. It is located on the coast of the Atlantic Ocean.
45. sweats: an anxious, fretful condition.
46. junk-withdrawal: a painful condition caused by suddenly stopping drug use.
47. Newark: the largest city in New Jersey, where Ginsberg was born.
48. Plotinus Poe St. John of the Cross: referring to Plotinus (205—270), a Roman philosopher, Edgar Allan Poe (1809—1849), an American writer and St. John of the Cross (1542—1591), a Spanish mystic.
49. kaballah: (=cabala) mystical interpretation of Hebrew scriptures.

50. Idaho: a state of the northwest United States.
51. Baltimore: a city of northern Maryland, a busy port.
52. Oklahoma: a state of the south-central United States.
53. Houston: the largest city in Texas, located in southeast Texas northwest of Galveston.
54. soup: (slang) nitroglycerine.
55. narcotic tobacco: an addictive drug that can relieves pain.
56. Union Square: a gathering place for radical speakers in New York in the 1930s, once the gathering place of smuggling drugs.
57. sirens: referring to the police sirens, that is, hooters that make long loud sounds as a signal of warning.
58. Los Alamos: a center in New Mexico for the development of the atomic bomb.
59. Wall: Wall Street. It also alludes to the Wailing Wall, a place of public lamentation in Jerusalem.
60. Staten Island: a district in New York City.
61. ferry: ferryboat.
62. seraphim: plural form for seraph, a celestial being having three pairs of wings, which is of the highest rank of angels in the Bible.
63. wound up with: end up with.
64. the three old shrews of fate: an allusion to the Three Fates, mythological goddesses who decided when a person's life would end by cutting a thread.
65. buttocks: ass.
66. N. C.: Neal Cassady (1926—1968), friend of Ginsberg, also a major figure of the Beat Generation.
67. Tokay: a naturally sweet wine made in Hungary.
68. Bowery: Southern extension of Third Avenue in New York City, traditional haunt of alcoholics and a slum at that time.

诗歌赏析

艾伦·金斯堡是美国当代诗坛的杰出人物和“垮掉派”的代表诗人。他秉承惠特曼豪迈奔放的诗风，而在神秘性上深受布莱克影响。《嚎叫》被称为“五十年代的荒原”。《嚎叫》由三部分及后面的《脚注》组成，本文选自第一部分。它以愤怒的嚎叫、奔放的气势、不羁的语言对传统进行反击，表达了对现实的不满。

诗人开篇就大声疾呼“我看到这一代才子俊杰毁于疯狂”，他们吸毒、酗酒、纵欲、狂欢，搞同性恋，生活穷困、精神苦闷，用吸毒后的幻觉麻痹自己。这些离经叛道、惊世骇俗的行为是对当时美国压抑的社会的反抗和控诉。

金斯堡采用比惠特曼更自由的自由诗形式，重复使用以“who”开头的惠特曼式的平行结构，突出“垮掉一代”疯狂的自暴自弃的思想和生活方式。通俗粗鄙的语言、朗诵的节奏和一气呵成的散文式长句子，宣泄了当时美国青年那种激烈、衰败、愤世嫉俗的情绪。诗歌的形式与内容相得益彰，难怪1955年金斯堡因在旧金山的一次朗诵会上朗诵这首诗而一举成名。

这首诗不避冗言秽语，内容颓废，但一定程度上反映了当时的社会现实，阅读时需加以注意。

For Study and Discussion

1. What attitude toward American society is shown in this poem?
2. What do you think of the absurd behaviors described in the poem?
3. Comment on the stylistic features of the poem. How does they serve the theme of the poem?
4. What do you know about the Beat Generation?

参考译文

嚎　叫

致卡尔—所罗门

我看到这一代才子俊杰毁于疯狂，
他们饥饿，歇斯底里，一丝不挂，
黎明时分挣扎着穿过黑人街巷，
四下觅寻一针痛快的海洛因。
一群长着天使般头颅的嬉皮士们渴望在黑夜机械中
和那星光灿烂的发电机沟通，那种古老美妙的关系；
他们穷困潦倒，衣衫褴褛，眼窝深陷，
坐在只有冷水的公寓那超乎寻常的黑暗中吸毒，

昏昏沉沉，飘过城市上空，冥想着爵士乐；
他们在高架铁道下向上天袒露一切，
看见回教的天使在灯火通明的屋顶上踉跄蹒跚；
他们穿过大学校园，眼睛明亮目光却冰冷，
幻觉中恍惚身在军事学家间看到阿肯色和布莱克式的悲剧，
他们被逐出校园，因为错乱疯狂，
还有在学校掌权人物的窗口发表猥亵的颂歌；
他们蜷缩在简陋混乱的房间，只套着短裤，
在废纸篓里烧着纸币，还听着隔墙恐怖的声音；
他们经过拉雷多返回纽约时被逮捕，
赤裸着身体，腰间捆着大麻叶；
他们在涂脂抹粉的旅馆里吞火或在天堂小巷中饮松节油，寻死，
或者夜夜让躯体惨遭炼狱般的蹂躏，
用梦幻、毒品、醒着的梦魇、酒精，
还有那荒淫无度和纵欲狂欢；
战栗的乌云是无可比拟的死路，
心中的闪电却在加拿大和帕特森两地间跳跃奔驰，
将这两极间静止的时光世界通通照亮，
充斥着毒品的门厅，院后绿树墓地的黎明，
屋顶上烂醉如泥，吸毒后驱车风驰电掣于闹市，
看见红绿灯如霓虹般闪烁，布鲁克林咆哮的冬日黄昏中，
但见太阳和月亮，还有那树木摇撼，
垃圾箱轰鸣，那些友善的精英们，他们将自己囚禁在地铁中吸毒，
没完没了地进行着巴特里到布朗克斯间的旅行，直到
车轮的噪音和孩子的喧闹将他们震醒，哆嗦着，
嘴唇开裂，在动物园的惨淡灯光中，
他们大脑的光辉已消失殆尽，憔悴而凄凉；
他们通宵沉浸于比克福德自助餐馆的水下灯光中，
飘游而出，然后又在冷清的福加西酒吧消磨一个下午，
喝着跑了气的啤酒，听着氢气点唱机播放世界末日的来临；
他们一连七十个小时无休止地说，说，说，
从公园到住所到酒吧到贝勒维医院到博物馆到布鲁克林大桥；
一群迷惘的柏拉图式的空谈家跳下台阶，

从防火梯，从窗台，从帝国大厦，
逃开月亮；
喋喋不休地闲扯着那些要放低了声说的
让人尖叫、令人作呕的事实、往事、轶闻、眼珠被踢、
医院休克、牢房和战争等事情。
所有的才智沉浸于回想，
七天七夜，目光炯炯，然后把它抛出，
恰如将犹太会堂的祭肉扔在路边；
他们消失在新泽西的禅宗里，留下
一堆印有大西洋市政厅照片含混不清的明信片；
在纽瓦克带家具的阴冷房间里吸毒，
忍受着海洛因消退后的痛苦，东方的大汗淋漓，
丹吉尔的骨头研磨，还有中国式的偏头痛；
他们深更半夜在铁路调车场流浪、徘徊，
不知何去何从，但最终还是去了，没有心碎神伤；
他们在货车厢里，车厢里燃起一支又一支香烟，
一路喧嚣穿过雪场在祖父般的黑夜驶向寂寥的农场；
他们研读普罗提诺、爱仑·坡和圣约翰的心灵感应，
用爵士乐来解读犹太教的神秘哲学，因为
在堪萨斯宇宙本能地在他们脚下颤抖；
他们穿行在爱达荷的街上，形影相吊，搜寻着
幻觉中的印第安天使，那些本来就虚幻的印第安天使
他们觉得巴尔的摩沉浸于极度狂喜中，
他们只是疯了；
他们在冬季小镇街灯闪烁的雨夜，一时冲动，
跳上大轿车，与俄克拉荷马的华人同行，
他们在休斯敦游荡，饥肠辘辘，形单影只，
寻找着爵士乐、性和汤，
追随那位非凡的西班牙人谈论美国和永恒，
无望了却心愿，只好远渡非洲；
他们消失在墨西哥的火山中，没有留下什么，
只有粗布工装的影子、熔岩，还有
芝加哥壁炉中散落诗稿的灰烬；

他们又在西海岸现身，对联邦调查局进行探查，
蓄着胡须，穿着短裤，睁着大眼睛，皮肤黝黑而性感，
这群和平主义者们，散发着莫测高深的传单；
他们用烟蒂在胳膊上烧出千疮百孔，
抗议资本主义那麻醉害人的烟草阴霾；
他们在联合广场散发超级什么主义的小册子，
流着眼泪，脱光衣服，而这时
洛斯阿拉莫斯的警笛在尖叫，声音穿过华尔街，让他们安静，
斯塔登岛的渡船也在尖叫；
他们在苍白单调的体育馆里失声痛哭，
在别的骷髅机械前赤身裸体，颤抖不已；
他们咬侦探的脖子，在警车里高兴地尖叫，
因为他们没犯什么罪，仅仅是自己放荡地鸡奸和醉酒中毒而已；
他们跪在地铁里嚎叫，从车顶被拖下，
挥舞着手稿，抖动着生殖器；
他们任由圣洁的摩托车手与之从后边做爱，
还快活地高声尖叫；
他们口交，同时也被那些人类的六翼天使和水手玩弄，
那来自大西洋和加勒比海爱的抚摸和拥抱；
他们纵情寻欢，不分清晨或夜晚，
在玫瑰园，在公园与墓园的草地上，
可以与任何人做爱，不管来者何人；
他们不停地打嗝想要傻笑取乐可结果却是
在土耳其浴室的隔墙后哽咽抽泣，
此刻那金发碧眼的赤裸天使赶来要拿剑刺穿他们；
他们将自己的爱侣输给了三个命运的老悍妇，
她们都是独眼，一个是异性恋，爱的是美元，
一个爬出子宫，还眨着眼睛，
一个无所事事就坐在那儿剪着
工匠织机上的智慧金线；
他们纵情交欢，没完没了，攥着一瓶啤酒，拥着一个情人，
外加一包香烟，还有一支蜡烛，跌落于床下，
便在地板上继续，一直到客厅，最后虚弱地瘫靠在墙上，

朦胧中最后阴门的幻影在眼前浮现，
闪躲着意识最后的高潮；
他们花言巧语诱骗数以百万在落日中颤抖的姑娘，
清晨，眼睛布满血丝，他们却准备要抓住日出的美好时刻，
还有那谷仓下面闪动的屁股和湖水中的赤身裸体；
他们趁着夜色在科罗拉多放浪寻欢于无数偷来的汽车中，尼尔·卡塞迪，
那位暗藏于这些诗篇中的英雄，丹佛的雄鸡和阿东尼——回想起他令人欣喜，
他征服过的姑娘数不胜数，他们随便在哪儿都可以做爱，
无人的停车场、宴会后院、影院破烂的座椅、山顶洞穴，
抑或独在熟悉的路旁撩起憔悴女招待的衬裙，尤其是
在僻静加油站的单人洗手间里，连家乡的小巷也不放过；
他们渐渐隐没在偌大肮脏的影院里，在梦中被赶走，
突然惊醒于曼哈顿，挣扎着走出地下室，余醉未消，浑身不适，
那是无情的托克葡萄酒和第三大道铁般噩梦的结果，
然后跌跌撞撞地赶往失业救济所；
他们整夜徘徊在白雪堆积的码头，鞋里尽是殷红的血，
期待着东河有一道门朝他们敞开，通向
满是蒸汽热和鸦片的房间；
他们以战争年代泛光灯那般的幽蓝月色为背景，
用哈德逊河陡峭河岸的公寓楼顶做舞台，上演伟大的自杀悲剧，
其头颅将戴上彻底被忘却的桂冠；
他们咀嚼着幻想中的炖羊肉，要么
在包沃里泥泞肮脏的河底将螃蟹消化掉；
他们为街头的浪漫传奇呜咽，陪伴身边的是
他们的手推车，装满了洋葱和粗俗音乐；
他们坐在桥下的箱子里，在黑暗中喘息着，
然后起身爬上阁楼去造大键竖琴；
他们在火焰般通亮的哈莱姆区的六层楼上咳嗽，
糟糕的天气犹如生了结核病，天空被神学的橘箱团团围住。

（李海云　译　李正栓　校）

19. Anne Sexton

Anne Gray Harvey Sexton (安·塞克斯顿, 1928—1974) was born in Newton, Massachusetts on November 9, 1928. She attended Garland Junior College for one year and married Alfred Muller Sexton Ⅱ at the age of 19. She enrolled in a modeling course at the Hart Agency and lived in San Francisco and Baltimore. After her second daughter was born in 1955, she began to suffer from frequent mental breakdowns and was repeatedly sent to the hospital for help. Encouraged by her doctor, she began writing poetry that she had developed in high school. In the fall of 1957 she enrolled in a poetry workshop at the Boston Center for Adult Education and later she studied poetry with Robert Lowell at Boston University with fellow student Sylvia Plath. In her introduction to Anne Sexton's *Complete Poems*, the poet Maxine Kumin, who enrolled with Sexton in the 1957 workshop and became Sexton's close friend, describes her belief that it was the writing of poetry that gave Sexton something to work towards and develop and thus enabled her to endure life for as long as she did. Published in 1960, Sexton's first book of poems, *To Bedlam and Part Way Back*, established her status as one of the first confessional poets. She won the Pulitzer Prize for poetry in 1967 for *Live or Die* (1966) and an American Academy of Arts and Letters traveling fellowship. In 1974 at the age of 46, despite a successful writing career, she lost her battle with mental illness and committed suicide. That same year, she had published *The Death Notebooks*. *The Awful Rowing toward God*, a posthumous volume, appeared in 1975.

Like Robert Lowell, Sylvia Plath, W. D. Snodgrass (who exerted a great influence on her work), and other "confessional" poets, Sexton offers readers an intimate view of the emotional anguish that characterized her life. She made the experience of being a woman a central issue in her poetry. Though she endured criticism for bringing subjects such as menstruation, abortion, and drug addiction into her work, her skill as a poet transcended the controversy over her subject matter.

The Truth the Dead Know[1]

For My Mother, Born March 1902, Died March 1959 and My Father, Born February 1900, Died June 1959

This poem is a representative work of the Confessional poets. It reflects the poet's meditation on death. It is famous for the shocking images and odd notion of death.

Gone[2], I say and walk from church,
refusing the stiff[3] procession to the grave,
letting the dead ride alone in the hearse.
It is June. I am tired of being brave.

We[4] drive to the Cape. I cultivate
myself where the sun gutters[5] from the sky,
where the sea swings in like an iron gate
and we touch[6]. In another country people die.

My darling, the wind falls in like stones
from the whitehearted water and when we touch
we enter touch entirely. No one's alone.
Men kill[7] for this, or for as much[8].

And what of the dead? They lie without shoes
in their stone boats. They are more like stone
than the sea would be if it stopped. They refuse
to be blessed, throat, eye and knucklebone.

1962

Notes

1. This poem is written in four quatrains of combined iambic and anapestic

tetrameter lines.
2. Gone：euphemism for death.
3. stiff：rigid.
4. We：referring to the poetess' parents and her.
5. gutters：flows.
6. touch：(of a ship) stop.
7. kill：be killed，die.
8. for as much：for the same reason like that.

诗歌赏析

安·塞克斯顿是美国著名自白派女诗人。她的诗歌以深刻的自我剖析著称。她的诗艺早已得到肯定，但是她的诗歌内容却备受争议，其中包括自杀倾向、吸毒、精神错乱和乱伦等。她生前饱受精神病困扰，诗歌是她与疾病抗争的工具和精神支撑。《死者知道的真理》是塞克斯顿为1959年相继去世的父母而创作的，记录了诗人对死亡的冥想。

在这首四节的短诗中，死亡意象贯穿始终。第一节中诗人用委婉语“去了”(gone) 点出亲人的离世。她拒绝让死板的送葬队伍跟去坟墓，而宁愿让死者坐着柩车独自前往，给人造成虽死犹生的假象。“我厌倦了坚强”点出生者的自杀倾向。在第二节中生者已经和死者聚到一处，共同驱车去海角。那里阳光流淌、大海摇摆，他们靠岸了。人们在另一个世界死亡，而他们好像已经摆脱了生死的羁绊。第三节暗示一旦靠岸，生者和死者便再也不会分开，没有人会感到孤单。人们大抵因此不再惧怕死亡。如果说前三节是生者对死的感悟，最后一节直接描述死者对死亡的感悟。死者的身体比死寂的大海更像石头。正如第一节中生者拒绝世俗的葬礼队伍为死者送行，死者也拒绝神的护佑。这是一个冷冰冰、孤单、绝望的世界。大海像铁门，风像石头，水像毫无知觉的白心脏。僵硬、死板，这些意象都是死亡的象征。

For Study and Discussion

1. There are three “touches” in the poem. Are they the same? Why?
2. What's the attitude towards death as shown in the poem?
3. What do you think of the images in this poem?

参考译文

死者知道的真理

致我的母亲（生于1902年3月，卒于1959年3月）
和我的父亲（生于1900年2月，卒于1959年6月）

去了，我喃喃地从教堂走出，
拒绝刻板的送殡队伍跟去坟场，
宁愿让死者坐着灵车独自前往。
那是六月。我厌倦了坚强。

我们驱车去海角。我修身养性。
那里，太阳从天际流淌，
那里，大海像铁门摇摆，
我们抛锚。另一个国度人们死亡。

亲爱的，风像石头一样
从白色的漩涡中落下，当我们停泊
我们已经深入接触。没有人孤单。
人们为此而死，或大致一样。

死了会怎样？他们赤足
躺在石棺里。他们比寂静的大海
更像石头。他们的喉咙、眼睛
和关节骨拒绝神佑。

（申玉革　译）

20. Sylvia Plath

Sylvia Plath（西尔维亚·普拉斯，1932－1963）was born in Boston, Massachusetts. She has a German father and an Austrian mother whose attitudes and personalities were restlessly exposed in her writing. In 1940, when Sylvia was 8 years old, her father died, whose authoritarian attitudes and death drastically defined her relationships and her poems — most notably in her

elegiac and infamous poem, "Daddy." She began to write poetry at an early age and published her poems in regional magazines and newspapers. Her first national publication was in the Christian Science Monitor in 1950, just after graduating from high school.

In 1950, Plath attended Smith College. She was an exceptional student, and despite a deep depression she went through in 1953 and a subsequent suicide attempt, she managed to graduate with top honors in 1955. Later she studied at Cambridge University in England on a Fulbright Scholarship, where she met and married the English poet, Ted Hughes, in 1956.

Plath returned to Massachusetts in 1957, and began studying with Robert Lowell. Her first collection of poems, *Colossus*, was published in 1960 in England, and 2 years later in the United States. She returned to England where she gave birth to Freida and Nicholas Hughes, in 1960 and 1962, respectively. In 1962, Ted Hughes left Plath for another woman. That winter, in a deep depression, Plath wrote most of the poems that would comprise her most famous book, *Ariel* (1965). In 1963, Plath published a semi-autobiographical novel, *The Bell Jar*, under the pseudonym Victoria Lucas. Then, on February 11, 1963, Plath committed suicide in England.

Plath's poetry is often associated with the Confessional movement. Compared to poets such as her teacher, Robert Lowell, and fellow student Anne Sexton, her work is singled out for the intense coupling of its violent or disturbed imagery and its playful use of alliteration and rhyme.

Although only *Colossus* was published while she was alive, Plath was a prolific poet, and in addition to *Ariel*, Hughes published three other volumes of her work posthumously, including *Crossing the Water* (1971), *Winter Trees* (1972), and *The Collected Poems* (1981), which won her the 1982 Pulitzer Prize.

Daddy[1]

This is one of the masterpieces of confessional poetry, in which Plath records her complex feeling toward her father — hatred combined with love. Many startling images help create a vivid image of the poet's father.

You do not do, you do not do
Any more, black shoe
In which I have lived like a foot
For thirty years, poor and white,
Barely daring to breathe or Achoo[2].

Daddy, I have had to kill you.
You died before I had time ——
Marble-heavy, a bag full of God,
Ghastly statue with one gray toe[3]
Big as a Frisco[4] seal[5]

And a head in the freakish Atlantic
Where it pours bean green over blue
In the waters off beautiful Nauset[6].
I used to pray to recover you.
Ach, du.[7]

In the German tongue, in the Polish town[8]
Scraped flat by the roller
Of wars, wars, wars.
But the name of the town is common.
My Polack[9] friend

Says there are a dozen or two.
So I never could tell where you
Put your foot, your root,
I never could talk to you.
The tongue stuck in my jaw.

It stuck in a barb wire snare.
Ich[10], ich, ich, ich,
I could hardly speak.
I thought every German was you.
And the language obscene

An engine, an engine
Chuffing me off like a Jew.
A Jew to Dachau, Auschwitz, Belsen[11].
I began to talk like a Jew.
I think I may well be a Jew.

The snows of the Tyrol[12], the clear beer of Vienna
Are not very pure or true.
With my gypsy ancestress and my weird luck
And my Taroc pack and my Taroc[13] pack
I may be a bit of a Jew.

I have always been scared of *you*,
With your Luftwaffe[14], your gobbledygoo[15].
And your neat mustache
And your Aryan[16] eye, bright blue.
Panzer[17]-man, panzer-man, O You ——

Not God but a swastika[18]
So black no sky could squeak through.
Every woman adores a Fascist,
The boot in the face, the brute
Brute heart of a brute like you.

You stand at the blackboard[19], daddy,
In the picture I have of you,
A cleft in your chin instead of your foot

But no less a devil for that, no not
And less the black man who

Bit my pretty red heart in two.
I was ten when they buried you.
At twenty I tried to die
And get back, back, back to you.
I thought even the bones would do.

But they pulled me out of the sack,
And they stuck me together with glue.
And then I knew what to do.
I made a model of you,
A man in black with a Meinkampf[20] look

And a love of the rack and the screw.
And I said I do, I do.
So daddy, I'm finally through.
The black telephone's off at the root,
The voices just can't worm through.

If I've killed one man, I've killed two——
The vampire who said he was you
And drank my blood for a year,
Seven years, if you want to know.
Daddy, you can lie back now.

There's a stake in your fat black heart
And the villagers never liked you.
They are dancing and stamping on you.
They always *knew* it was you.
Daddy, daddy, you bastard, I'm through.

1962　　　　1966

Notes

1. This poem is written in sixteen 5-line stanzas of combined iambic and anapestic trimester and tetrameter lines with no regular rhymes.
2. Achoo: sound made by sneezing, here meaning "to sneeze".
3. one gray toe: Plath's father's toe turned black from gangrene, a complication of diabetes.
4. Frisco: San Francisco.
5. seal: a large sea animal.
6. Nauset: a beach in Massachusetts.
7. Ach, du: (German) Ah, you.
8. in the Polish town: Plath's father, though of German origin, was born in Grabow, Poland.
9. Polack: (German) Polish.
10. Ich: (German) I.
11. Dachau, Auschwitz, Belsen: all Nazi concentration camps in Germany or Poland.
12. Tyrol: the Austrian Alps.
13. Taroc: Tarot fortune-telling cards.
14. Luftwaffe: Nazi air force.
15. gobbledygoo: (=gobbledegook) mere formalities, nonsense.
16. Aryan: a Caucasian gentile, the Nazi ideal race.
17. Panzer: (German) armored.
18. swastika: a cross symbol served as a Nazi emblem.
19. You stand at the blackboard: Plath's father had been a professor of biology at Boston University.
20. Meinkampf: Hitler's political autobiography, *My Battle*, here standing for Hitler.

诗歌赏析

西尔维亚·普拉斯和安·塞克斯顿、罗伯特·洛威尔一起并称为美国自白派诗人。她的诗作关注女性的内心体验和女性自我意识的觉醒。《爸爸》诉说了普拉斯对父亲爱恨交加的复杂情结，是一首经典的自白诗。普拉斯的父亲是一个纳粹分子，母亲有犹太血统。普拉斯八岁的时候，她的父亲离世。年幼的普拉斯曾经视父亲为上帝，可是父亲的德国血统和过早辞世给普拉斯留下了挥之不去的阴影。这首诗共十六节，每节五行，口语体的语言，行文流畅，一气呵成。

该诗前三节表达了诗人对父亲的复杂情感。诗歌开篇将父亲比作鞋子，预示父亲的角色对诗人而言，既是保护者也是破坏者。三十年来她一直生活在父亲的阴影里。第二节中父亲既像神，又像可怖的雕像。尽管对父亲又敬又怕，诗人依然依恋自己的父亲。在第三节中她表达了想让父亲复活的愿望。

接下来普拉斯控诉了父亲的德国血统给自己带来的耻辱以及纳粹分子的暴行。她将父亲比作魔鬼，讲述父亲的早逝给她的心灵造成的伤害。可是，这样的父亲她依然愿意为她去死。她曾经为他自杀一次，可是被救活了。诗歌的最后“我完了”显然是一个双关，说明诗人终于结束了对父亲的控诉，同时她的生命也已完结。而现实中的普拉斯也是以自杀的方式结束了自己的生命。

普拉斯将父亲的个人经历引入到诗中，给人强烈的写实感。如普拉斯的父亲死于糖尿病导致的坏疽，一个脚趾烂掉了。她父亲是德国血统，在波兰出生，有曾在空军服役的背景以及当过大学教授的经历等。这首诗虽然以《爸爸》为名，表现的却不仅仅是父女之间的复杂感情，也代表着纳粹分子对犹太民族的迫害，同时也是女性对男权社会的控诉。

For Study and Discussion

1. Analyze the image of the father described in this poem.
2. What do you think of the relationship between the father and the daughter?
3. Why does the speaker compare herself as a foot living in black shoe?
4. What does “a man in black” refer to? Why does the poet give him “a Meinkampf look”?
5. How do you understand the last sentence “I am through”?

参考译文

爸　爸

你不要做，你再也不要
做黑色的鞋子了，
我像一只脚，在里面待了

三十年，苍白、可怜，
只敢呼吸和打喷嚏。

爸爸，我本想杀了你。
可是没等动手你已死掉——
大理石般重，一只充满神祇的袋子，
可怖的雕像，有着一只灰色脚趾
大如旧金山海豹！

头在无常的大西洋
它喷涌着豆绿色的海水卷过
美丽的诺赛特港蓝色的波面。
我过去常常祈祷你复活。
啊，你。

说德国话，长在波兰的
已被战争，战争，战争
的压路机碾平的小镇
但是小镇的名字很普通。
我的波兰老朋友们

说这样的镇子有一二十个。
所以我从来不知道你
在哪里落足、根在何处，
我从来不能和你交谈。
舌头卡在我的下巴里。

它卡在勒除器的倒钩里。
我，我，我，我，
我几乎不能说话。
我觉得每个德国人都是你。
我认为德语下流。

一个引擎，一个引擎
噗噗地把我像犹太人一样吹走。
一个去达豪、奥斯威辛、贝尔森的犹太人。
我开始像犹太人一样说话。

我想我也可以做个犹太人。

蒂罗尔的雪，维也纳的清啤
实际上没那么纯洁和正宗。
就凭我的吉卜赛女祖先和我怪异的运气
以及我的塔罗克纸牌啊我的塔罗克纸牌
我也许有点犹太人血统。

我一直都很害怕您，
害怕您的空军，您的高谈阔论，
您整洁的胡髭和
雅利安人的蓝眼睛，亮晶晶
装甲兵啊装甲兵，您——

不是上帝，而是一个卍字徽章
黑得连天空都无法穿越。
每个女人都爱慕法西斯党人，
那踢在脸上的靴子，那畜生般的
粗暴的、粗暴的心，像你一样。

我有你一张照片，爸爸——
你站在黑板前，
下巴上有一条裂缝，而不是脚上，
但是没有影响你像魔鬼一样的形象，
比那个黑衣人也不差半分，

他把我鲜红娇弱的心脏劈成两半。
我十岁那年，他们埋葬了你。
二十岁那年，我试着用死亡，
回到，回到，回到你身边。
我想即便变成白骨也无妨。

但是他们把我从袋子里拖出来，
用胶水把我粘在一起。
于是我知道该做什么了。
我做了一个你的模型，

一个穿着黑衣，带着希特勒的神气

一个绞刑架和螺丝钉的拥泵。
然后我说我做到了，我做到了。
就这样，爸爸，我终于完了。
黑色电话机彻底坏了，
声音压根穿不过去。

如果说我杀死了一个人，我已经杀死了俩——
那个自称是你的吸血鬼
吸食了我的血一年，
不，已经七年了，如果你想知道。
爸爸，你现在可以安息了。

你肥大的黑心里有根木桩，
村里人从来没有喜欢过你。
他们在你身上跳舞、踩踩。
他们一直都知道那是你。
爸爸，爸爸，你个杂种，我完了。

（申玉革　译）

Mirror[1]

In this poem, the mirror is personified. It reflects everything truthfully without disguise. It also witnesses the woman getting old day by day.

I am silver and exact. I have no preconceptions[2].
Whatever I see, I swallow immediately.
Just as it is, unmisted by love or dislike
I am not cruel, only truthful—
The eye of a little god, four-cornered.
Most of the time I meditate on the opposite wall.
It is pink, with speckles[3]. I have looked at it so long
I think it is a part of my heart. But it flickers.
Faces and darkness separate us over and over.

Now I am a lake. A woman bends over me.
Searching my reaches for what she really is.
Then she turns to those liars, the candles or the moon.
I see her back, and reflect it faithfully
She rewards me with tears and an agitation of hands.
I am important to her. She comes and goes.
Each morning it is her fact that replaces the darkness.
In me she has drowned a young girl, and in me an old woman
Rises toward her day after day, like a terrible fish.

Notes

1. Written in 1961, this poem was published in *Crossing the Water* in 1971.
2. preconceptions: belief or opinion formed in advance.
3. speckles: small marks or spots.

For Study and Discussion

1. What does the mirror reflect?
2. What is the effect of personification in this poem?
3. In what sense is a mirror similar to a lake?
4. What relationship does the first stanza have with the second stanza?
5. How is the simile used in the final line of the poem?

参考译文

镜　子

我银亮、精准。我从不先入为主。
不管看到什么，我都立刻吞掉。
原封不动，不会被好恶蒙蔽。
我并不残酷，只是真实——
我有小神的眼力，我四四方方。
大多数时间我在思量对面墙壁。
它粉红、斑驳。我注视它良久
已经将它视为心的一隅。但是它忽隐忽现。

脸庞和黑暗将我们一次次分离。

现在的我是一汪湖水。一个女人俯下身来，
探寻她到底是个怎样的人。
然后她转向那些谎话连篇者，蜡烛或月亮。
我看到她的背影，将它忠实地映照。
她用眼泪回赠，还有手的焦虑。
我于她重要。她来来去去。
每个清晨她的出现驱走了黑暗。
在我这里，她埋葬了一个少女；在我这里，
一个老妇一天天向她走去，像条骇人的鱼。

（申玉革 译）

Bibliography

1. 常耀信.《美国文学简史》. 天津：南开大学出版社，1990
2. 常耀信.《英国文学简史》. 天津：南开大学出版社，2006
3. 陈才宇主编.《英美诗歌名篇选读》. 杭州：浙江大学出版社，2007
4. 陈嘉.《英国文学史》1—4 册. 北京：商务印书馆，1981
5. 陈嘉编.《英国文学作品选读》1—4 册. 北京：商务印书馆，1981
6. 董素华编著.《英语名诗欣赏》. 延吉：延边人民出版社，2003
7. 辜正坤主编.《英文名篇鉴赏金库·诗歌卷》. 天津：天津人民出版社，2000
8. 郭群英，毛卓亮主编.《英国文学教程》. 石家庄：河北教育出版社，1998
9. 何功杰主编.《英美名诗品读》. 上海：上海交通大学出版社，2002
10. 侯维瑞主编.《英国文学通史》. 上海：上海外语教育出版社，1999
11. 胡家峦编著.《英国名诗详注》. 北京：外语教学与研究出版社，2003
12. 胡家峦编著.《英美诗歌名篇详注》. 北京：中国人民大学出版社，2008
13. 胡开杰编著.《诗艺：美国现当代诗歌赏析》. 上海：复旦大学出版社，2005
14. 胡全生，林玉珍，胡开宝，索宇环编著.《20 世纪英美文学选读——后现代主义卷》. 上海：上海交通大学出版社，2003
15. 胡全生，林玉珍，胡开宝，索宇环编著.《20 世纪英美文学选读——现代主义卷》. 上海：上海交通大学出版社，2003
16. 胡荫桐，刘树森主编.《美国文学教程》. 天津：南开大学出版社，1995
17. 黄家修主编.《英美诗歌鉴赏》. 武汉：武汉大学出版社，2009
18. 黄源深，周立人编著.《外国文学欣赏与批评》. 上海：上海外语教育出版社，2003
19. 黄宗英编著.《英美诗歌名篇选读》. 北京：高等教育出版社，2007
20. 姜涛主编.《美国诗歌赏析》. 北京：新华出版社，2006
21. 李赋宁，何其莘主编.《英国中古时期文学史》. 北京：外语教学与研究出版社，2006
22. 李赋宁.《英国文学论述文集》. 北京：外语教学与研究出版社，1997
23. 李正栓，白凤欣编著.《英语诗歌教程：诗歌要素与诗歌种类》. 北京：高等教育出版社，2008
24. 李正栓，陈岩.《美国诗歌研究》. 北京：北京大学出版社，2007

25. 李正栓，郭群英主编.《新编英国文学教程》. 石家庄：河北教育出版社，2006
26. 李正栓，吴晓梅编著.《英美诗歌教程》. 北京：清华大学出版社，2004
27. 李正栓.《英国文艺复兴时期诗歌研究》. 保定：河北大学出版社，2006
28. 刘炳善，罗益民编.《英国文学选读》. 郑州：河南人民出版社，2006
29. 刘炳善编著.《英国文学简史：新增订本》. 郑州：河南人民出版社，2007
30. 刘守兰编著.《英美名诗解读》. 上海：上海外语教育出版社，2003
31. 陆如刚编著.《英语诗歌欣赏》. 北京：外语教学与研究出版社，2007
32. 罗选民主编.《英美文学赏析教程》. 北京：清华大学出版社，2002
33. 罗益民编著.《莎士比亚十四行诗名篇详注》. 北京：中国人民大学出版社，2010
34. 蒲度戎，彭晓华主编.《英美诗歌选读》. 重庆：重庆大学出版社，2000
35. 钱青主编.《英国19世纪文学史》. 北京：外语教学与研究出版社，2006
36. 陶洁主编.《美国诗歌选读》. 北京：北京大学出版社，2008
37. 王守仁，方杰.《英国文学简史》. 上海：上海外语教育出版社，2006
38. 王守仁，何宁.《20世纪英国文学史》. 北京：北京大学出版社，2006
39. 王守仁主编.《英国文学选读》. 北京：高等教育出版社，2001
40. 王佐良，何其莘.《英国文艺复兴时期文学史》. 北京：外语教学与研究出版社，1996
41. 王佐良，李赋宁等主编.《英国文学名篇选注》. 北京：商务印书馆，1999
42. 王佐良，周珏良主编.《英国二十世纪文学史》. 北京：外语教学与研究出版社，1994
43. 王佐良主编.《英国诗选》. 上海：上海译文出版社，1993
44. 吴定柏编著.《美国文学欣赏》. 上海：上海外语教育出版社，2002
45. 吴景荣，刘意青主编.《英国十八世纪文学史》. 北京：外语教学与研究出版社，2000
46. 吴伟仁编.《美国文学史及选读》. 北京：外语教学与研究出版社，1990
47. 杨金才，于建华主编.《英美诗歌：作品与评论》. 上海：上海外语教育出版社，2008
48. 杨仁敬.《20世纪美国文学史》. 青岛：青岛出版社，1999
49. 袁洪庚，卢雨菁，杜丽丽编.《英诗及诗学文选》. 北京：北京大学出版社，2008
50. 袁若娟主编.《美国现代诗歌精选评析》. 开封：河南大学出版社，2006
51. 张剑，赵冬，王文丽编著.《英美诗歌选读》. 北京：外语教学与研究出

版社，2008
52. 张致祥主编.《西方引语宝典》. 北京：商务印书馆，2001
53. [英] 德拉布尔编.《牛津英国文学词典》(第 6 版). 北京：外语教学与研究出版社，2005
54. [英]柯恩斯(Corns，T. N.)编.《英国诗歌：从多恩到马维尔》. 上海：上海外语教育出版社，2001
55. [美]罗扎基斯，杨惠中主编.《怎样赏析诗歌》. 上海：上海译文出版社，2005
56. [美]尼古拉斯 . H. 纳尔逊.《英国经典诗歌阅读与欣赏——从多恩到彭斯》. 中国人民大学出版社，2009
57. [美]沃伦(Warren，R. P.).《理解诗歌》(第 4 版). 北京：外语教学与研究出版社，2004
58. Barbara A. Mowat，Paul Werstine. ed.，*Shakespeare's Sonnets*，NY：Washington Square Press，2004
59. Nina Baym，General Editor，*The Norton Anthology of American Literature*，7th edition，New York：W. W. Norton & Company，2007.
60. Stephen Greenblatt，General Editor，M. H. Abrams，founding editor emeritus. *The Norton Anthology of English Literature*，8th edition，New York：W. W. Norton & Company，2006.